Law Relating to

RAGGING

It's a crime....Don't risk it !!!

"India's 1st Comprehensive Legal Text on Ragging."

"*The daring publisher, Universal Law Publishing Company, among the foremost in the law publishing field and progressive in venturing to bring out rare legal literature of* avant garde *character has rightly enriched the* corpus juris *of India*"

Justice V R Krishna Iyer
Random Reflections, page 14

Law Relating to

RAGGING

It's a crime....Don't risk it !!!

Naman Mohnot

Foreword by

Justice Ashok Mathur
Former Judge, Supreme Court of India
Founder Chairperson, Armed Forces Tribunal (Retd.)

Mr. Ram Jethmalani
Former Law Minister, Government of India, Member of Parliament,
Rajya Sabha & Senior Advocate, Supreme Court of India

Introduction by

Dr. Justice Arijit Pasayat
Former Judge, Supreme Court of India
Former Chairman, Competition Appellate Tribunal

Universal
Law Publishing Co. Pvt. Ltd.
NEW DELHI - INDIA

2014 Edition

ISBN: 978-93-5035-470-4

Published by

Universal
Law Publishing Co. Pvt. Ltd.
NEW DELHI - INDIA

A-58, G.T. Karnal Road Industrial Area,
(Near Azadpur Metro Station), Delhi-110033
Tel. : 011-47082254, 27458529, 27215334 Fax : 011-27458529
e-mail: unilaw@vsnl.com

- Showroom : C-27, Connaught Place, New Delhi-110001
- Sales : sales@unilawbooks.com
- Editorial : edit@unilawbooks.com
- Website : **www.unilawbooks.com**

Join us on Facebook
www.facebook.com/unilawbooks

Recommended citation: Naman Mohnot, *Law Relating to Ragging – It's a crime....Don't risk it !!!* (New Delhi: Universal Law Publishing Co. Pvt. Ltd., 2014).

Computer Typeset at Aesthetic and *Printed* at Mudrak, Delhi.

In Unforgettable memory of
Dadaji and Dadiji

And

Specially dedicated to my living God...
Papa and Mummy, without whom
this day would not have been possible

CONTRIBUTORS

Tarun Agarwal

Harish Choudhary

Shubham Gupta

Justice A.K. Mathur
Former Judge, Supreme Court of India
Chairperson

Armed Forces Tribunal
Principal Bench
West Block-8, Section-1,
R.K. Puram, New Delhi-110066
Tel.: 011-26105363

सत्यमेव जयते

3rd July, 2013

Foreword

Today, ragging has become deeply rooted in the Indian educational set up. Gradually this is taking shape of black hole for the temples of education, thus ragging is the imminent danger which the educational institutions are facing currently. It is unfortunate that this serious issue lacks wide-ranging study.

For, that this book is the first book of its own kind on Ragging, which encompasses each and every aspect of ragging *viz.*, definition, psychological aspect, legal aspect, judicial trend, alarming statistics, role of different machineries etc.

The book is not limited to these points, but goes beyond it and gives the steps to be followed after being ragged. Thus, this is the first benefit oriented book which provides social steps, legal steps and other steps after being ragged.

Further, the do's and don'ts of parents, educational institutions, students etc., have been discussed. There is elaborate discussion on law on ragging which in its conclusion shows the dire need of Central Legislation on ragging in the country.

Every page of the book, therefore, is crammed full of useful hints and tips so that you can profit from them. This book will help in bringing the awareness in the society. I wish all the success of ideas of author compiled in it. The time has come to be part of this revolution and replace our ill thoughts with righteous thoughts.

Justice Ashok Kumar Mathur
Chairman, 7th Central Pay Commission
Former Judge, Supreme Court of India
Founder Chairperson (Retd.), Armed Forces Tribunal

RAM JETHMALANI
Member of Parliament
(Rajya Sabha)
Senior Advocate
Supreme Court of India
Professor Emeritus
Symbiosis College of Law, Pune

सत्यमेव जयते

Res.-Cum-Office:
2, Akbar Road,
New Delhi-110011 (INDIA)
Tel.: 23794651, 23792287
Fax: 23795095

Foreword

It is sad that evil of ragging has to form the subject of a whole book of about 310 pages. The young Naman Mohnot deserves congratulations for producing the first authoritative book on the law relating to this evil practice. It is an attack on independence of weaker mortals, usually vulgar in motivation and serving no decent public purpose or even worthwhile private interest. I heartily recommend the book to all responsible citizens particularly those who are teaching the young.

I wish Naman the best of luck in life.

Ram Jethmalani.

RAM JETHMALANI

29-05-2014

OFF.: 29, JOLLY MAKER CHAMBERS-2, NARIMAN POINT, MUMBAI-400021 (INDIA)
TEL.: 22820550, 22028470 FAX: 22875829
RES.: 41, ADVENT, 12-A, GENL. BHONSALE MARG, MUMBAI-400021 (INDIA) TEL.: 22024990
RES.: 11, GERAS GREENS VILLE, KHARDI NAGAR ROAD, PUNE-411014 TEL.: 32940732

Introduction by Dr. Arijit Pasayat

The students at comparatively young ages enter educational institutions. Their first steps there should be on petals of love, warmth and not on fears of unwelcome behaviour, apprehension of physical, emotional or mental torture/ injury. They should have the assurance that the menace of ragging would not be the first to encounter them.

Ragging is rationalized and justified as a way of "Introduction or getting familiar" with the freshers at the starting of an academic session of any educational institution.

In a very positive aspect, "Ragging" could not be considered as an abridgement between the seniors and the freshers, whereas "Introduction" could be considered as genesis of relationship between the two.

When any student is admitted in a particular institution he/she has to face certain problems and one of them which affects the most is staying away from home and especially away from the dear ones. Because of these problems, the freshers expect some one to look after them, with whom they can have homely environment as they were enjoying at their respective homes. But nowadays the seniors have crossed the barriers, by which they have changed the meaning of "Introduction" into "Ragging".

"Seniors" under the garb of "Introduction" have started ragging the freshers and due to which, in recent years, it has become the talk of the day that the freshers who have faced severe ragging are leaving the educational institutions and some have attempted to commit suicide and even some have committed it.

In modern era, "Ragging" has become to be known only as synonym of "teasing", "terror", "harassment", "cruelty", "fear" and "physical and mental torture".

By perusal of records and survey, it has come to be accepted that "Ragging" is a systematized form of Human Rights' abuse as embodied under the Constitution of India as well as other Constitutions of the World.

Over the years in all over the world and especially in South Asia, the practice of "Ragging" has come to be meant as an extreme "harassment", "terror" and even "physical and mental torture" of freshers.

Ragging is a set of undisciplined activities undertaken by the seniors to break the ice with the juniors, who have been suddenly thrown into a totally new environment. The contention of seniors behind all such activities is simply to bring the freshers down to earth, because in their opinion the freshers do not respect the seniors and by doing all such inhuman activities under the garb of "Introduction", the seniors rag the freshers so that the freshers may respect them and be under their control. But this act cannot be reasonable and just. The act by the seniors is a "fist of steel against ice" and likewise by doing so, they shatter the ambition, aim and object of freshers and they become aloof in this practical world.

To prohibit "Ragging", this Court has given a series of guidelines to the educational institutions whether being Central, State or Private Institute. [See: *Vishva Jagriti Mission* v. *Central Government*, (AIR 2001 SC 2793)].

Ragging in essence is a human rights' abuse. Ragging can be in various forms. It can be physical abuse or mental harassment. In present times shocking incidents of ragging have come to the notice. Sometimes violence is used. The student is physically tortured or psychologically terrorized. All human beings should be free to claim, as a matter of right in the society in which they live, for life of dignity but when it is intentionally or recklessly damaged or departed then the person's human right is abused; in that sense ragging is the best example of human rights' abuse.

Everyman's Encyclopaedia (1938 Edition, Vol. II) and Random House Dictionary of the English Language (1967 Edition) have references about ragging. The synonyms of ragging as racking, ducking, teasing, etc., are mentioned in detail in these reference books. In England the credit/discredit goes to Duke of Exeter to introduce the practice of ragging. Racking was another form of ragging in which a special instrument called 'rack' was used to torture the victim. Gradually it mixed up with the term of ragging. Egyptians, Romans and Greeks were also not lagging behind. Some form or the other of ragging was found in their societies.

Ragging is not a new phenomenon. It existed even in older times. It was part of civilised societies. In ancient seats of learning, *e.g.*, Berytus and Athens ragging was prevalent. In army schools of England ragging existed as a tradition. Later on this tradition took its root in medical and engineering colleges. In English society ragging took the form of freshers being paraded on street which caused much annoyance not only to freshers but even to general public especially girls.

Ragging is a form of systematic and sustained physical, mental and sexual abuse of fresh students at the college/university/any other educational institution at the hands of senior students of the same institution and sometimes even by outsiders. Although some form of ragging is present in every educational institution but serious abuses of human rights take place generally in medical and engineering colleges and Armed Forces. The form and effect of ragging differ from institution to institution. It creates a sense of fear in the minds of first year students and they become apprehensive of unforeseen incidents which later come true and culminates in actual form of action.

Ragging is "display of noisy, disorderly conduct and great high spirits considered by perpetrators (raggers) as excellent fun and by many outsiders as a bloody nuisance".

Another meaning of ragging is "to question vigorously and jocularly, horseplay or assail roughly and noisily".

Yet another definition of ragging refers to popular Spanish game of "Bull-Fight", wherein Bull is shown red 'rag' and a person shouts which infuriates the Bull in fighting.

As noted above "Ragging" means display of noisy, disorderly conduct or doing any act which causes or is likely to cause physical or psychological harm or raise apprehension or fear or shame or embarrassment to a student in any educational institution and includes,

(a) teasing, abusing of, playing practical jokes on, or causing hurt to, such students; or

(b) asking the student to do any act or perform something which such student will not, in the ordinary course, willingly do.

"Ragging" means doing an act which causes or is likely to cause insult or annoyance or fear or apprehension or threat or intimidation or outraging of modesty or injury to a student.

"Ragging" means causing, inducing, compelling or forcing a student, whether by way of a practical joke or otherwise, to do any act which detracts from human dignity or violates his person or exposes him to ridicule or to forbear from doing any lawful act, by intimidating, wrongfully restraining, wrongfully confining, or injuring him or by using criminal force to him or by holding out to him any threat of such intimidation, wrongful restraint, wrongful confinement, injury or the use of criminal force.

The word "ragging" colloquially means to tease or play practical jokes on someone, specially on students who are the fresh entrants in the schools, colleges, Universities or any other educational institutions. In the beginning, it was a way of introduction of the first year students in the institutions which gradually has become not only serious problem but also a social stigma. While in the age of a child in cradle, it was a harmless practice by senior students over their juniors. Regarding the origin or initiative steps of the ragging, it can be traced back to the Seventh or Eighth Century A.D.

In 1828-1845, in United States' Colleges and Universities Campus, several student-organizations called 'fraternities' popped up. Freshers to these fraternities were known as pledges. In its rudimentary form, it as called 'hazing' which was merely ritual to test the courage of the pledge.

In ancient Greece, freshers to the sporting communities were subjected to humiliation and teasing to inculcate team spirit. After the passage of time this type of activities were adopted by Armed Forces in which new entrants have to pass out by obeying the seniors in off-duty time. As has been said above, in the age of child in cradle, the ragging was a harmless practice rather permissible in the society but it had taken shape of brutality, humiliation and harassment after the First World-War. In fact the technique, style or forms which the soldiers participating in the War had learnt and faced in army atmosphere, were brought by them, when they re-entered in the colleges after returning from the War. Actually these forms were devised to highlight the importance of the team.

Gradually these techniques and forms passed on those persons who did not know the real meaning of the technical word 'hazing' or 'ragging'. Now the ragging has acquired a new heinous meaning which indicates any disorderly conduct whether by words spoken or written or by an act which has the effect of teasing, treating or handling with rudeness any other student, indulging in rowdy or undisciplined activities which cause or is likely to cause annoyance, hardship or psychological harm or to raise fear or apprehension thereof in a fresher or a junior student or asking the student to do any act or perform something which such student will not do in the ordinary course and which has the effect of causing or generating a sense of shame or embarrassment so as to adversely affect the physique or psyche of a fresher or a junior student.

A rare and strange case of ragging is as follows -Pyotr Ilyich Tchaikousky was a renowned composer of Russia. It was reported in 1893 that he died due to cholera and cholera was caused due to drinking of contaminated water. This was a blatant lie. However, this lie prevailed for about a century. The truth was revealed by, Alexandra Orlova, the biographer of the composer and that too when the composer died and the biographer migrated to America. The biographer revealed that the Russian composer was a homosexual during his education period and this fact became known to college authorities and they decided to punish the composer and was likely to be expelled. The news of proposed punishment leaked to his old classmates and they thought that if the composer is punished it will bring a bad name to the institution. Therefore, the composer was summoned before eight former classmates in the "Court of Honour" and was asked to end his own life to "preserve the good name of the school". The composer ended his life by consuming poison brought by one of the Judges and story of death by cholera was concocted.

These aspects were highlighted by the Hon'ble Supreme Court in *University of Kerala* v. *Council of Principals of Colleges in Kerala,* (Civil Appeal No. 887 of 2009) order dated 11th February, 2009.

When I wrote the order, I had nurtured a pious hope that the menace of ragging would be reduced, particularly after the subsequent order on 8-5-2009. But subsequent events belied those hopes. Though the number of cases involving ragging has been reduced, yet the unfortunate instances of ragging still continue. The efforts to root out the menace should be by a combined effort of the authorities of the Educational Institutions, Parents and Students community as a whole.

I am happy that the author has taken great pains to bring out this book. His efforts are praiseworthy since he has taken a giant leap to highlight the horrors of the monstrous menace. My blessings to him.

Dr. Justice Arijit Pasayat

Judge Supreme Court (Retd.)

Former Chairman, Competition Appellate Tribunal

Message

Ragging is uniquely an Indian phenomenon. It does not exist any where else except in India and in a few of her neighboring countries. Several decades ago it was harmless fun, meant to break ice between students but over the years this *'harmless pet'* has undergone metamorphosis into a *'deadly beast'* that has taken the lives of many and permanently injured many more, physically and psychologically. The national help line that was setup soon after Aman's death in June 2009 has recorded nearly 2500 cases of ragging in the past 5 years. And we believe that these numbers are only a tip of the ice berg. There is much more happening that is not reported. In the past 5 years 30 members of parliament, cutting across the party lines, asked ragging related questions in both Houses of the parliament. It is an indicator of the high level of anxiety that exists in our society on ragging.

Despite the anxiety and obvious ill effects of ragging there are many who do not agree that ragging should be eradicated. They believe, of course incorrectly, that it enhances the personality of those who are shy. Many say it improves bonding between students and so on. Many narrate their own experiences of 20 or 30 years ago and conclude that we are making too much of nothing. They are wrong. They do not realize that what starts as harmless fun can soon turn into a platform for a perverted mind to operate upon. Such minds are always on the look out for opportunities and ragging provides a brilliant cover much like a sick husband who beats his wife in the night and puts the blame on alcohol the following day. Alcohol is just an excuse. This man is sick. He derives pleasure from inflicting pain on others and he knows that his wife is an easy prey because she is a prisoner of her own false beliefs. She is ready to suffer pain, humiliation and abuse because she believes in keeping the matters of home within the boundaries of her home. Perpetrators of ragging are mentally sick who like the drunk husband use ragging as an excuse to satisfy their sadistic pleasures. Victims of ragging, on the other hand, are like those wives who believe that matters within the family must remain within the family. They would rather commit suicide than stand up to their husbands. Many students who commit suicide due to ragging are sexually abused. They would rather take their lives than live with the shame of the act.

No doubt, ragging is a foreign phenomenon but it has flourished in India because India is the land of Dhronacharya. We justify the cruel demand by Dhronacharya of asking Eklavya for his thumb as his right as a teacher. We do not condemn Eklavya but glorify him for his sacrifice. The irony is that Dhronacharya did not even know that Eklavya was his student and Eklavya had learnt nothing from Dhronacharya. It is deeply embedded in our culture to respect and obey our teachers, elders and parents. We have taught our youngsters to be like Arjun who killed his own teacher, the same Dronacharya, for Dronacharya had made an unjust demand on Arjun. We have to learn to distinguish between the ones who deserve obedience and the ones who don't. For a very long time we have given undue importance to seniority on the false pretence that seniors are wiser and talented. It has damaged the psychology of our society. As a nation we suffer from *'Seniority Syndrome'*.

The solution to the problem of ragging, of course, lies in making new laws, putting preventive measures in place and punishing the perpetrators but most importantly it lies in educating the victims of their rights. We have to get rid of age old beliefs like *'Pati* is always the *Parmeshwar''*; a grand father is always the wisest person in the house and a senior is always better than a junior. We have to understand that while tolerance is a virtue, unconditional obedience is stupidity and suffering injustice is a sin.

Following the tragic death of Aman Satya Kachroo, 5 years ago, a Trust in his name, has spearheaded the movement for eradication of ragging across the nation. The trust designed the National Ragging Prevention Programme and now works in close cooperation with the Union Ministry of Human Resources to manage and monitor the programme. I am pleased to report to you that while ragging has not completely disappeared it is on its way out. I am pleasantly surprised to note that awareness has spread faster than we had expected. The credit, of course, goes to the media. Public were crying for change. Aman's death provided the tipping point. News papers, Radio and Television editors rose to the occasion and gave ragging the amount of time and space that it deserved. The results are visible. There is no doubt that we still have a long way to go but we have gone over the cliff. My only disappointment is that many college authorities are still in denial. Winning the trust of students is not on the agenda of many college Principals. Punishment is still the preferred solution. Ragging is still considered a peripheral matter by many Principals. They still give highest preference to getting good marks in Physics/History. Despite these problems I wish to say with confidence and humility that it will not be very long before India will become a ragging free nation.

The Trust has also started work on designing a prevention program for bullying in schools. We believe that through a programme of regulation and education we should be able to reduce bullying in schools. We believe reduction and elimination of bullying in schools will have a huge impact on how we behave in our day-to-day lives. We have seen how children of Delhi Schools were able to convince their parents not to burn fire crackers during Diwali. Similarly, we hope that children in the future will stop their parents from engaging in violence publicly in the streets or in the privacy of their homes. I look forward to that day.

I am happy that Naman has taken the initiative to write this book. I am impressed by the research he has done and the manner in which he has put together the book. It is important to note that Naman is himself a student.

This book is a guide on all aspects of ragging. Let us hope that this book contributes to the movement towards eradication of the evil practice of ragging. We at Aman Movement appreciate the effort that the author and the publishers of the book have put in this project.

6 May, 2014

Raj Kachroo
Founder Trustee
Aman Satya Kachroo Trust.

Prologue

It is always a moment of pride for any Vice-Chancellor to have a student from his institution to author a book. My student Naman Mohnot has been able to achieve, what is a daunting task for the most!

I have known Naman for the past three years who without restricting himself to the four walls of the classroom has moved beyond. His interest in the field of research has led to the presentation of various papers at several international conferences, in addition to other co-curricular achievements which include, filing and arguing PIL's in the High Court and the Supreme Court, securing of bail for under trial prisoners and earning the state award from the cabinet minister of Rajasthan for doing legal aid services. He has successfully amalgamated the theory learnt from the classroom lectures and its application. This helped him to refine his advocacy skills, which is an important pre-requisite for qualifying as a successful lawyer. I was not surprised by his idea of putting his analytical talent to make a difference by exploring the important issue of ragging and bringing out a book on it. Given his methodical and dedicated approach, I was confident that he would accomplish this task.

The book covers comprehensively and elaborates on the practice of ragging, its cause-effect analysis, psychological perspective, comparative state law analysis with graphical representation, analysis of all the landmark cases of the Judiciary regarding ragging, steps to be followed if some gets ragged etc.

I am certain that, this is only the beginning and we are going to see that Naman will reach great heights in the field of law and, as well as, an author. I wish him success for all his future endeavors.

Prof. (Dr.) Ranbir Singh

New Delhi

Vice-Chancellor, National Law University, Delhi
Vice-President, SAARC Law (India) Chapter

PREFACE

"If you want something very badly, you can achieve it. It may take patience, very hard work, a real struggle & long time, but it can be done. That much faith is a pre-requisite of any undertaking artistic or otherwise."

Margo Jones

It has been my childhood dream to write a book, which would be a source of awareness for the mankind, across the borders of nation-State. I still remember the first time I expressed my dream to Mr. Anant Asthana, Delhi High Court Lawyer, who advised me to write a book on the vital issue of "Ragging", due to the lack of any proper and comprehensive work and research by anyone on the issue. This gave me the motivation and laid down the foundation of this book.

Among the many ills that plague higher education in our country and the one that dominates public concern these days is not the capitation fees or the poor quality of teaching but the evil practice of ragging, a crime that has brought infamy to our education system and has become nightmare to parents. Each year, reports of ragging showcase the intensity of this rampant practice in the educational institutions, of which some are so extreme, that the victims are reported to be the recipients of depression or worse commit suicide. Even then, no proper research has been done on the causes, the psychology behind the justification of the practice, the consequences and the solution to the problem of ragging. The reasons for its existence are not well understood despite being considered by many psychologists, anthropologists, sociologists and educationalists. People till date believe that ragging is nothing but a form of casual joke played at the beginning of the academic sessions by some seniors in the college class rooms, canteens or at the hostels to get themselves acquainted with the newly admitted students. Despite the increasing gravity and the intensity of the situation as portrayed by many reports and cases, there has been no acknowledgment of the issue by the academia. Also, the purpose of ragging is unclear, for perpetrators, its victims and for bystanders. This makes the topic of ragging especially interesting, highly ambiguous and hence very worthwhile exploring.

The main objective of this book is to provide a message that "Ragging" is a crime; hence indulging in it is a mistake. Also, to make people aware of the reality of this practice and to provide a solution, if the incidence occurs. In one line the crux of the book is that "Ragging is a crime...Don't risk it".

This book has been written not only from the perspective of the students but also from the perspective of lawyers, teachers, researchers etc. In this book I have tried my best to represent and compile every bit of information in a lucid and a systematic manner. Various topics like different dimensions of ragging, types of ragging, causes of ragging, consequences of ragging, the application of the legal procedure that incorporates the institution of college, police station, the format of RTI, the gist of all the previously decided cases by the Supreme Court and the High Courts etc., have been researched comprehensively and mentioned in the book.

My journey as an author of this book was amazing. I remember working for twenty hours straight in a day and the sleepless nights to make my dream come true. In order to achieve my target, I had to lose out on the time that could have been spent with my family and friends. Every morning used to start with a new and exciting spirit. My excitement and zeal increased considerably, when I went to Sri Lanka for conducting a research on this issue. There I had the opportunity to meet a number of people who helped me in providing a valuable insight into the subject matter of ragging in their respective country. It took two years of time to complete this endeavor; but it could have been completed in a short span of time, if I had been a full-time researcher and not a student. These two years of my life, have considerably taught me how to balance my work and the personal life, along with the inculcation of certain attributes of teamwork, confidence etc., that has helped me evolve as a person. I hope that this hard work would result in the creation of a "Ragging Free Society".

This book would not have been possible without the co-operation and active involvement of a number of friends and well-wishers, who have helped me both substantially and otherwise in achieving this target. I would like to acknowledge the generous help from several friends, teachers and colleagues, without whom the journey would have been full of difficulties and hardships.

A project as large as this requires full-fledged help of a likeminded person with a similar sense of commitment. Due to Harish's hard work and commitment, I requested him to help me in this journey and he was kind and humble enough to accept my request. With his help in preparation of excellent case summaries the work was considerably reduced. I thank him and wish that he continues to be hardworking and achieves the desired goals of his life.

"The completion of this book required people who could provide new horizons to this research work. Shubham Gupta and Tarun Agarwal proved to be two most suitable and enriched minds for the task. Being well aware of my requirements, they met them with utmost competence. They worked with complete honesty. The valuable inputs, they provided were instrumental and have proven to be of great help in the successful compilation of this book. Their brilliant research and analytical skills coupled with their hard work were major assets in the completion of this book. Their writing and drafting skills must also be appreciated. I sincerely acknowledge that without them, embarking upon this journey would have been extremely difficult for me. I am also happy to acknowledge that the title of the book was the brainchild of Tarun Agarwal."

All the above three are pursuing B.A. LL.B. (HONS.) from National Law University, Delhi.

I owe my special thanks to Mehak Kapur, student of Lady Shri Ram College who has provided prompt and deft assistance with respect to my limited command over English language. Her inputs have solved many problems which had emerged, and she helped me in bringing my dream into reality.

Without the undaunted spirit of support and perseverance of all the above four, this book would not have been completed. I hope and trust that they will continue to bestow their love and support in future too.

I shall fail in my duty, if I do not express my heartfelt gratitude for Dr. R.K. Raghavan Committee, NGOs like CURE, SAVE, SPACE & Aman Movement, GNIT College and others, whose reports and research became the source for the foundation of this book.

Throughout my endeavor Professor (Dr) Ranbir Singh, Vice Chancellor of National Law University, Delhi, was a never ending source of encouragement and without fail enquired about my progress every time he met me. I also acknowledge that the support given by Registrar, Prof. Sri Krishna Deva Rao was of great significance.

I am indebted to Mr. M.P. Singh, former Chairman of Delhi Judicial Academy & former Vice Chancellor of NUJS, Kolkata for giving their insights on the book. I am also grateful to Hon'ble Mr. Justice Sandeep Mehta, Rajasthan High Court, Mr. Colin Gonsalves, Senior Advocate of the Supreme Court and founder director of Human Rights Law Network (HRLN) for putting faith in me.

Sri Lankan Government has also obliged the author by giving its support and help in research on ragging in Sri Lanka.

I gladly recognize that Dr. (Mrs.) Priya Rai, Deputy Librarian and Mr. Akash, Assistant Librarian of NLU Delhi, had pitched in at crucial junctures and supported me from the beginning to the end and provided the moral support, for which I extend my deep gratitude to them. I am also grateful to Dr. Ruhi Paul, Associate Professor (Law) and Dr. Aparna Chandra, Assistant Professor (Law), NLU Delhi for their suggestions and inspiration.

Along with all these, I would like to acknowledge the valuable time given by Hon'ble Mr. Justice Arijit Pasayat (former Supreme Court judge and former Chairman of Competition Appellate Tribunal) who, despite his busy schedule was humble enough to write an introductory chapter for this book.

I am highly indebted to Mr. Ram Jethmalani (former Law Minister, Government of India, Member of Parliament, Rajya Sabha & Senior Advocate, Supreme Court of India) who saw the depths of my work with praise and recommended this book to the readers. I am also thankful for his guidance and motivation.

I also express my sincere gratitude to Hon'ble Mr. Justice Ashok Mathur (former SC judge, former Chairman of Armed Forces Tribunal and Chairman of 7th Pay Commission) who has been kind enough to write a foreword for this book.

I am also thankful to Mr. Sagar Joshi (Director of Law Prep. Tutorial) and my Gurus of Adarsh Vidya Mandir who have played a vital role in my learning process over the years.

I express my sincere and deep thanks to Prof. Raj Kachroo, founder trustee of Aman Satya Kachroo Trust, who has been kind enough to go through this book and write a message to this book.

I am grateful to Mr. Vineet Kumar Mathur, Assistant Solicitor General of India, Mr. Farzand Ali and Mr. Siddharth Tatiya, Lawyers, Rajasthan High Court for their directions.

I am extremely thankful to Vivek Kumar Singh, my classmate in NLU Delhi for supporting me during this phase. I also praise and give thanks to my friends Jitendra Chhajer, Jitesh Laddar, Pallavi Asari and others, who have directly or indirectly helped me in this book.

I take this opportunity to express my deep appreciation and thanks to Shri Manish Arora and Shri Hasan Imam, M/s. Universal Law Publishing Co. Pvt. Ltd. who have taken splendid, terrific and meticulous care in bringing out this book with high quality printing.

The most important are often saved for the last and I have to mention here my family, which has given me the strength and the conviction to pursue this goal. The debt one owes to the family is seldom acknowledged. This is more than a dedication than anything else to my parents for being so liberal and encouraging when everybody else was prescriptive and felt that the task was beyond my capacity.

In the end I would like to say that this is my first attempt as an author. With the limited knowledge and experience that I have, I have sincerely tried to give my readers a holistic insight into the subject. I recognize and am aware that there may be several areas in book which require modifications.

Of course, in the midst of all this tremendous help and support, all faults and errors are exclusively mine. I sincerely apologize, if I have hurt feelings of any person while making comments or observations while expressing my views in the book. Please pardon for any inadvertent inaccuracies that may have crept in, due to my inexperience. Suggestions, modifications, by the readers are welcome with an earnest gratitude.

July, 2014
New Delhi

Naman Mohnot
Roop Kalyan Group

"A Journey of a thousand miles begins with a single step......."

Where is What

Introduction – by Hon'ble Justice Arijit Pasayat

The informative introduction has laid down the foundation of this book. He has shown that how the meaning of "Formal Introduction" has changed into a menace of "Ragging". This chapter of the book compiles various definitions of ragging, from numerous sources like dictionary, State laws etc. He has tried to break all the myths which justify ragging. He has very well reflected upon the history of this heinous crime. He has mentioned about the history of raging in other countries. He has dealt with the issue, that how the idea of ragging has entered into the educational institutions from armed forces. Lastly, he has written about his feelings that even after giving a strong judgment, unfortunate instances of ragging still persist which has mellowed his hopes.

Chapter 1: 'Ragging Through Cannons of History'

The book proceeds and reflects upon the origin of the phenomena of ragging and describes how the practice of ragging emerged in different countries of the world. The major focus has been laid on India, and the Indian context of "Ragging", tracing it from the Gurukul System to the medieval period to the present context. It also discusses, that how this practice was an implant of the British education system in the country. This chapter also highlights that over the period of time the practice of ragging has taken its worse avatar; hence it is of vital relevance to dig into the causes and consequences of the phenomena.

Chapter 2: 'General Concepts'

In the chapter named 'General Concepts', various dimensions of ragging, types of ragging, most popular forms of ragging, vulnerable locations for ragging, causes of ragging, reasons of ragging, reasons for the denial of ragging, consequences of ragging and its harmful effects on various people, are elucidated. This chapter is an attempt to elucidate ragging as human right abuse. It reminds us that ragging is simply a manifestation of a form of discrimination. Lastly, by making a reference to movies, it showcases that how ragging is seen as humorous phenomena, which makes the audience forget about its negative connotation and cruelty.

Chapter 3: 'Psychology behind Ragging'

The tendency, nature and actions of the human being are driven by reasons, and in the same way there are certain reasons also which fuel and promote the practice of ragging in the various spheres of life. This chapter explains that ragging is a "vicious circle" created by the practice of ragging itself *i.e.*, the victim of the practice eventually turns into the perpetrator of the practice due to psychological reasons.

Chapter 4: 'Initiatives to Stop Ragging In India'

There have been several steps initiated by various authorities like the Judiciary, the Legislatures, NGO's and the regulatory bodies to curb the practice of ragging in the educational institutions. This chapter deals with all these measures. The landmark judgment of the Hon'ble Supreme Court along with the direction given to various authorities, formation of various committees and recommendations submitted by them, the action taken by regulatory bodies, initiation taken by Aman movement, have been discussed at length here.

Chapter 5: 'Law on Ragging'

It is quite disheartening to learn that even after 67 years of independence; the Parliament of India could not enact a Central legislation on such a crucial issue. Although some States have enacted anti-ragging legislations but still there remains some lacunae in one or the other form, in these legislations, due to which these have not been implemented successfully. This chapter depicts the analytical picture of various State anti-ragging legislations in tabular form and the lacunae of which are becoming hurdle in the successful implementation. It also deals critically with the private member Bills which were raised in the Parliament but faced their unlucky fate.

Chapter 6: 'Ragging and the Legal Provisions'

Although there has not been any Cntral legislation enacted by the Parliament to deal specially with this baneful practice, but it does not in any case imply that there is no other provision in the "law" to deal with this issue. Even though it is not clearly stated in the Indian Penal Code, but reference can be made to various offences mentioned in different sections which resemble with the practice of ragging. This chapter deals with the legal provisions which can be resorted in the case of the commission of this crime. It also suggests some changes which should be brought in the existing law.

Chapter 7: 'Ragging and Myths'

The next chapter counters the 'myths' related to the practice of ragging which internalise and justify the act of ragging and poses a hurdle in curbing this menace. These myths are accepted among the seniors, juniors, parents, teachers etc., which need to be broken in order to realise that the so-called "harmless jokes" have dangerous and serious repercussions.

Chapter 8: 'Role of Different Stakeholders'

This chapter lays out the role of different machineries associated with the practice of the Ragging and discuses about their role in the practice and prevention of this menace. These machineries include parents, seniors, teachers, government, colleges/universities, police and health professionals.

Chapter 9: 'Role of Media'

This chapter outlines the contribution of both the mediums of media *i.e.*, the print and the electronic media. It includes the newspaper clippings from the leading national newspapers and depicts the sorry state of the affairs in the educational institutions with respect to the subject of ragging.

Chapter 10: 'Role of NGO and Civil Society'

This chapter highlights the role of the NGO's and the civil society in curbing the practice of ragging. This includes detailed introduction, objectives, contribution and the achievements of various famous NGO's like CURE, SAVE, SPACE etc. It also reminds us the need of active participation of civil society in order to make a ragging free society.

Chapter 11: 'Alarming State'

This chapter is an attempt to give, as far as possible, an exhaustive critical analysis of the statistics of alarming state of incidents of ragging in tabular comparative form.

Chapter 12: 'Live Cases on Ragging'

This Chapter includes the case study of the recent cases reported in the media which show the real picture of this menace. Along with this, it also encompasses the cases of ragging discussed by the Raghavan Committee in its report. In the end the experiences and views of the celebrities are given.

Chapter 13: 'Ragging in Sri Lanka'

The book in addition to India also deals with another South Asian country i.e. Sri Lanka. As a matter of fact Sri Lanka has been ranked as the worst country in the context of ragging. The chapter is an attempt to deal with the historic profile of ragging, politicisation of ragging and major incidents of ragging in Sri Lanka. Along with this, the legal framework and directives given by the authorities regarding ragging have been discussed in detail.

Chapter 14: 'Steps to be Followed – If Ragged'

This chapter, one of the most important of all the chapters, deals with the steps, which are to be followed if someone gets ragged like Medical step, Legal steps etc. The draft of the complaint which should be given to the head of the institutions has also been given in this chapter. Also, the basic knowledge of criminal law, right from approaching to the police, the basic details of the FIR, draft copy of the FIR, to the stages of case, to the final appeal are discussed in this chapter, which would help in the understanding of the legal provisions and procedures.

Chapter 15: Do's and Don'ts

This chapter deals with the preventive strategies *i.e.*, the Do's and the Don'ts in order to avoid the situation of ragging for the freshers, guardians, seniors and colleges.

Chapter 16: 'Ways to Stop the Menace of Ragging'

In this chapter, the general corrective measures/steps have been listed out which should be taken by the college authorities, seniors, juniors, the regulatory bodies etc., to fight against and eradicate the menace of ragging.

Chapter 17: Scope of Ragging

This chapter is a breakthrough in the existing concept of ragging. It goes beyond the conventional thinking and adds new dimension to this practice. It breaks the conception that ragging happens only in educational institutions and that too only in colleges, by showing its existence in schools, workplaces, prisons also.

CASE LAWS – This part presents a comprehensive analysis of the important cases decided by the Hon'ble Supreme Court, the High Courts and the tribunals.

ANNEXURES – This part includes all the Committee Reports, Notifications issued by various authorities, International Law, Private Member Bills, State anti-ragging legislations and the affidavits which have been used as reference in this book.

CONTENTS

Chapter V
Law on Ragging 34

Chapter VI
Ragging and the Legal Provisions 49

Chapter XIII

Ragging in Sri Lanka 96

Chapter XIV

Steps to Be Followed – If Ragged 104

Conclusion 141

Case Laws

Annexure 3
State Legislations 265

Annexure 4
Bills 288

Annexure 5
International Legislation 299

Annexure 6
Affidavit 303

TABLE OF CASES

T

U

V

Chapter I
Ragging Through Cannons of History

ORIGIN OF RAGGING

Ragging is not a recent or modern phenomenon, it existed even before. Although ragging dates back to 7th or 8th century A.D. but the cases of ragging were reported as early as in the 8th century BC during the Olympics in Greece. In Greek culture, new entrants to the sport community were subjected to all kinds of humiliations and teasing to inculcate a team spirit in them.[1]

Later on, these types of activities were adopted by the armed forces in which new entrants had to obey the seniors in their non-duty hours. The basic reason behind it was that these activities were a sort of fun in their otherwise monotonous camp life.[2] Surprisingly, these incidents of ragging were never used to flash in public.

But, as the time passed, the practice of ragging entered into the educational institutions across the globe. Unfortunately, since its inception in the educational arena, ragging has undergone several modifications before morphing itself into an organized form of campus violence. Subsequently, the first ragging related death occurred in 1873 when a fresher from Cornell University (U.S.) fell into a gorge as a consequence of ragging.[3]

TRANSITIONAL PERIOD

Ragging underwent a massive transformation after World-War I. It was World-War I that injected cruelty into ragging. The main reason was that soon after World-War I, many of the war brigades were dislocated and soldiers had returned to the civilian life. Young soldiers who returned from war, re-entered the colleges and were grimly determined to use the newly learnt methods of torture in the campuses.[4] These methods were used to make the individual fail as an isolated entity and succeed as a team. This philosophy of team development

1. Rajesh Garg, Ragging: A Public Health Problem in India, Indian Journal of Medical Sciences, Vol. 63, Issue No. 6, June, 2009, p. 264.
2. Ragging: March Against A Social Menace, p. 8, available at http://www.gnit.ac.in/pdf/Anti-RaggingHandbook.pdf, last accessed on 16th February, 2014.
3. Harsh Agarwal, Evolution of Ragging, CURE Report CR2005/07-27, available at http://noragging.com/index.php/Research/Ragging-The-Phenomenon/Evolution-of-Ragging.html, last accessed on 16th February, 2014.
4. *Ibid.*

continued to be used in different fraternities. Gradually these techniques and forms were passed on to those persons who didn't know the real/technical meaning of the word 'hazing' or 'ragging' and ragging became a brutal and hazardous exercise.[5]

Gradually, in the early 20th century ragging related violence started to escalate in the western universities and soon became a tool to take revenge between the blacks and the whites.[6] In army schools of England, ragging existed as a tradition but later on this tradition took its root in medical and engineering colleges also. Ragging took the form of freshers being paraded on streets which not only caused annoyance to the freshers but also to the general public, especially girls. In brief the practice of ragging spread from the army training institutions to the arena of engineering, medical and other residential institutions.

HISTORY OF RAGGING IN VARIOUS COUNTRIES

Between the 18th-19th centuries, formation of student organization was very much in vogue in the American and European countries. During the period between 1828-1845 in Universities of U.S. several student organizations were formed. These were named after Greek letters like Alpha, Phi, Beta, Kappa, Epsilon, Delta etc., and were known as Greek Letter Organizations (GLO's) or Fraternities.[7] The new entrants to these fraternities were known as PLEDGES.[8] During this time ragging existed in its rudimentary form and was merely a ritual to test the courage of the pledges.[9] In England, the Duke of Exeter is supposed to be responsible for the beginning of the practice of ragging. France also faced problems in controlling young men. The French term *'brimade'* includes hazing, ragging, silly and dangerous jokes and forced drinking.[10] According to a report published in the New York Times in 1928, practice of *brimade* had too often gone beyond the fun making activities. During the 1920s in France, a national campaign was raged against *brimade*. The minister of public instruction and the minister of war emphasized that new boys must be welcomed cordially, fairly and kindly. Also, the ministers ordered an end to such practices in all the French schools.[11] *Brimade* was a substantial problem affecting Canadian children also, because this country had imported such customs from the British, French, American and Greeks. Similar activities like Hazing also flourished on its border.[12]

---

5. *Ibid.*
6. *Ibid.*
7. *Ibid.*
8. *Ibid.*
9. *Ibid.*
10. Ms. Jayasree Sar, Ragging: Is it a pathological or casual phenomenon of college culture? an exploratory study, unpublished M.Sc. dissertation from Dept of Psychology, Univ. of Calcutta, 2006.
11. *Ibid.*
12. *Ibid.*

HISTORY OF RAGGING IN INDIA

RAGGING IN ANCIENT INDIA

The Education System in ancient India originated with the Gurukul system. The students used to live in the house of the 'Guru' for a couple of years along with the other *Shishyas* or students, who used to come from far and different places to learn lessons from their 'Gurus' & 'Guru-Matas'. They used to stay at 'Guru-grihas' (Gurukul) irrespective of their social standing till they were declared successful by gurus in their endeavor to pursue knowledge and then were permitted to return to their homes, where they could practice and utilize the acquired knowledge.[13]

Mutual respect was strongly infused in the *Shishyas* and given the highest importance in the ancient Indian educational institutions (Gurukul). *Shishyas* were like members of the Guru's family[14] and their attitude was of complete submission. The Vocational aim of education was to bring the happiness in the lives of others. Mere intellect wasn't of worth if the person was devoid of morality, so, the education was believed to be based upon the principle that education must form and cherish the character and thus, the morality or the right behavior was regarded as the higher "Dharma".[15] Education was regarded as a means of inculcating values such as strict obedience to elders, truthfulness, honesty and temperance. All these reasons led to non-existence of ragging incidents in the educational institutions, which can be inferred from the mythological stories or the ancient documents, where there is no reference of practice of ragging. This lets us to conclude that ragging has never been a part of Indian Educational culture.

RAGGING IN MEDIEVAL INDIA

In this period, students used to come to India from different parts of the world to seek education. Education had become accessible to everyone and many famous sites of learning like Vikramshila, Taxila (Takshashila), Nalanda etc., were established all over India.[16] All these famous centers of learning were frequented by the students from across the world. Hyun Tsang, Fa-hien and Megasthenes were some of those students who had come to India to study. These students used to live for a long duration for the purpose of study. They also used to visit many other centers of learning across the nation and make vivid accounts of their stay in their travelogues.[17] But there was nowhere mention of any sort of ragging of students in educational institutions, in spite of being residential in nature, due to the fact that since ancient times itself Indian learning institutions have taught about mutual respect, peace and honour between elders and youngers or seniors and juniors.

---

13. Vedic and Post – Vedic Education, pp. 3-7, available at http://www.mu.ac.in/myweb_test/ma%20edu/History%20of%20Edu..pdf last accessed on 16th February, 2014.
14. *Ibid.*
15. *Ibid.*
16. *Supra note* 2, p. 11.
17. *Ibid.*

RAGGING IN MODERN INDIA

History has taught us that practices of the foreign culture have proven sometimes unfortunate for this nation. Ragging is another example in this list.[18] Britishers invaded India and introduced the concept of ragging in educational institutes, so it is a western evil which was seeded in our country on western lines.[19] In India, incidents of ragging came into existence with the introduction of modern education system under the British rule. Initially it started in English colleges and universities but slowly and steadily it spread to more or less in all the Indian educational institutions. [20]

Although ragging was in existence in the Army and English public schools much before the country's independence, but it became conspicuous only after independence. Ragging then only meant seniors mocking and jesting at juniors.[21] Even after independence it was not as much severe as it is now and was relatively in a much milder form because higher education was confined only to some particular civilized sections of the society. But gradually as the access to higher education increased and it became accessible to different communities, the form of ragging also changed and became a weapon to settle the animosity among students of different castes, communities, religions etc.[22]

In 80's ragging became more brutal and violent in India. In Harsh Agarwal's[23] words ragging became a measuring rod to test the grit of the seniors and many seniors who were reluctant to rag their juniors, had succumbed to the peer pressure.[24]

During the 90's period, the mushrooming of degree and diploma colleges along with acute dearth of infrastructure and lack of effective administrative control over the massive number of students in engineering, medical, technical and general streams of education gave rise to many incidents of ragging which shattered the dreams of many young students. Southern India became a hub of this brutal activity. During this period, ragging started to elucidate its horrible repercussions with the passage of time and ragging related suicides increased at a hasty rate.[25] The Mild form of ragging transformed itself into a great nightmare not only for students but also for parents and guardians, college and hostel authorities and the administration at different levels.

Unfortunately, after taking so many steps towards its prevention, it is still prevalent in its horrible form which is evident from the incidents of ragging

---

18. *Supra note* 3.
19. Ramandeep Kaur, Ragging ends in a ragged life, available at http://www.mapsofindia.com/my-india/education/ragging-ends-in-a-ragged-life, last accessed on 16th February 2014.
20. *Ibid.*
21. *Supra note* 3.
22. *Ibid.*
23. Cofounder of Coalition to Uproot Ragging from Education (CURE) which is India's first and largest non-profit organisation dedicated solely towards the elimination of ragging and promotion of more positive ways of interaction between the freshers and seniors in Indian Universities and Colleges.
24. *Supra note* 3.
25. *Ibid.*

as reported in the media, that are not only shocking and undesirable but also portray a horrific picture of the practice. It is also true that whatever is reported in the media is only the tip of the ice. Day by day the nature of torture committed on the freshers by the senior students reveals that new methods of ragging are constantly being developed which were previously unheard of.

Has this evil phenomenon reached on its zenith or is the worst yet to come? How many *Aman Kachrus*[26] would have to sacrifice their lives before our society wakes up? Nobody can give the answers, only time will answer these questions.

---

26. On 7th March, 2009 Aman Kachru, 19, a first year student of Dr. Rajendra Prasad Medical College, Tanda, Kangra, HP, India, had repeatedly complained to his parents about the brutal ragging that took place on the Medical College campus — often by completely drunk third-year students. The boy was beaten so badly that he died of brain haemorrhage.

Chapter II
General Concepts

MULTIDIMENSIONAL ASPECTS OF RAGGING

The Raghavan Committee[1] pointed out that ragging has several dimensions like psychological, social, political, economic, criminal and academic. These are:—

1. Psychological dimension – Any act or abuse by spoken words, gestures, e-mails, snail-mails, public insults that affect the mental health and self confidence of students can be described in terms of the psychological aspects of ragging. This aspect would also include deriving perverted pleasure, vicarious or sadistic thrill from actively or passively participating in the discomfiture to others etc.

2. Academic dimension - Any act that prevents, disrupts or disturbs the regular academic activity of a student should be considered within the academics related aspect of ragging. Similarly, exploiting the services of a junior student for completing the academic tasks assigned to an individual or a group of seniors is also an aspect of academics related ragging prevalent in most of the institutions, particularly in the professional institutions.

3. Economic Dimension - Any act of financial extortion or burden of forceful expenditure put on a junior student by a senior student should be considered as an economic aspect of ragging.

4. Criminal Dimension - Any act of physical abuse including all variants of it: sexual abuse, homosexual assaults, stripping, forceful obscene and lewd acts, unwelcome gestures, causing bodily harm or any other danger to health or person can be put in the category of ragging with criminal dimensions.

5. Human Rights dimension – The human rights perspective of ragging involves the injury caused to the fundamental right to human dignity through humiliation heaped on juniors by seniors; often resulting in the extreme step of suicide by the victims. In one instance, the mother of a victim committed suicide as she could not bear the ignominy of sexual assault on her son by his seniors.

6. Political dimension - The political aspect of ragging is apparent from the fact that incidents of ragging are low in those institutions which promote democratic participation of students and provide a platform to participate in

---

1. The Menace of Ragging in Educational Institutions and Measures to Curb It, Report of the Committee constituted by the Hon'ble Supreme Court of India In SLP No. 24295 of 2006, headed by R.K. Raghavan, para. 4.

governance and decision making than those institutions which do not promote democratic participation.

TYPES OF RAGGING

Ragging may vary from a formal interaction to a severe physical and mental abuse which may even lead to victim's death. It can be divided into two types:—

1. Severe Ragging

This type of ragging consists of extreme level of physical and sexual torture which is generally prevalent in college hostels rather than college campuses. Its consequences lead to serious mental trauma and psychological disorders which ultimately affect daily routine of a victim and one may find oneself in a position which can rightfully be compared with that of a slave.[2]

Examples - stripping juniors naked, involving them in sexual acts or obscenity, hurting them physically, kissing a 1000 Watt bulb, standing on hot electric heater, urinating on electric wires, standing blindfolded on railway tracks, walking atop narrow guardrails on rooftops/terrace, stabbing, throwing out of balcony, nailing and burning of body parts etc.

2. Mild Ragging

This type of ragging generally includes verbal abuse which may hurt mentally or psychologically but it does not have an element of physical or sexual torture. It is generally prevalent in college campuses rather than in hostels. It leads to embarrassment and depression in extreme cases which instills constant fear in the mind of the junior during the ragging period.[3]

Examples–asking a fresher to sing a song or demanding respect, ask to follow a particular dress code, ask to dance or solve tricky puzzles etc.

So, generally severe ragging happens in hostels rather than campuses and mild ragging happens in campuses rather than in hostels but there are some acts which might be classified as severe ragging, even though they happen in campuses, for example - forced sexual acts in public, passing urine in public or forced public masturbation etc.

MOST POPULAR FORMS OF RAGGING

1. Dress Code Ragging: It is the most common form of ragging. The juniors are asked to dress in specific manners like dressing totally in white or in black clothes, forced to wear shoes of different colours for some period of time, asked to put a lot of oil on their heads, use red ribbon on hairs or comb them in humorous style etc. This type of ragging makes the junior feel awkward.[4]

2. Formal Introduction: In the name of formal introduction, juniors are asked to introduce themselves in 'Shudh Hindi' or in their regional language

2. Varun Aggarwal, Ragging: Why at All?, available at http://noragging.com/index.php/Research/Ragging-The-Phenomenon/-Ragging-Why-at-All.html, last accessed on 16th February 2014.

3. *Ibid.*

4. Madhavi Chopra, Ragging in Educational Institutes: A Human Rights Perspective available at http://www.legalserviceindia.com/articles/ragging.htm, last accessed on 16th February, 2014.

or in a language in which they are not fluent, thus, creating embarrassing and humiliating situations for them.[5]

3. Verbal Torture: In this form of ragging seniors humiliate the juniors by making them to sing a vulgar song or use abusive language in their talk.[6] Seniors force them to answer personally/socially unacceptable questions, use slang and humiliating words about their parents and other relatives.[7] It does nothing but leads to mental trauma, uneasiness and discomfort for the juniors.

4. Physical Torture: In this form juniors are targeted with the purpose of inflicting physical injury or compromising the dignity. It includes beating and hitting of fresher with objects, asking the fresher to slap her/himself, sitting in 'cuckoo' position, drinking/eating something inedible, standing for a long duration on one foot, sweeping her/his room, standing naked in bitter cold, doing several hundreds or thousands of push ups at a stretch, running miles after miles, beating the juniors black and blue etc.[8]

5. Sexual Abuse: This is one of the most severe forms of ragging. In this form juniors are asked to do the acts which damage the sexual dignity of the junior. It includes forced sexual acts in public, including unnatural sex with person(s) of opposite or same sex, forced public masturbation, touching of private parts, asking to do sexual favours, passing of urine in public etc. There have been cases, where juniors were asked to strip before the seniors; they were even forced to run completely naked by the seniors of opposite sex.[9] Sometimes seniors even videotape the abuses, make pornographic clips and use these clips for blackmailing them on the fear of circulation through MMS.[10]

6. Playing the Fool: In this form, juniors are asked to do mimicry or to act in a silly manner. Juniors have to enact scenes from a particular movie or of particular person in order to amuse other people. It also includes asking a newcomer to sing a song, to dance or solve tricky puzzles etc. For instance in *'Main Hoon Na'* movie Shahrukh Khan was asked to sing a song for the girl who enters the gate first.

7. Hostel Ragging: Junior students who stay in the hostel are the most vulnerable to ragging. They are forced to do all the odd jobs like cleaning of the rooms, shoes, toilets of seniors, washing of their clothes, fetching them water or milk, filling their coolers, carrying their luggage, completing their assignments etc.[11] Sometimes juniors are forced to drink their own or senior's urine, to take alcohol, tobacco or illicit (addictive) drugs etc.[12]

---

5. *Ibid.*
6. *Ibid.*
7. Common Forms of Ragging, available athttp://www.no2ragging.org/raggingforms.html, last accessed on 16th February, 2014.
8. *Ibid.*
9. *Ibid.*
10. *Ibid.*
11. *Ibid.*
12. *Ibid.*

VULNERABLE LOCATIONS FOR RAGGING

Following are the common places where ragging takes place:—

1. Hostel blocks and Mess halls,
2. Canteen/Cafeteria,
3. Stadium or playground,
4. Vacant class rooms,
5. Favourite points of students in the vicinity of college,
6. Student activity centres,
7. Bus stands etc.

CAUSES OF RAGGING[13]

The main causes for indulging in ragging are:

1. An attitude of backlash: "do-unto-others what others did to you."
2. Eagerness of seniors to show off their power, authority and superiority.
3. Importance the seniors get in the initial stages of admission by helping and guiding the new comers in various things in the absence of or ineffectiveness of institutional mechanism, results in juniors getting indebted to seniors and thereby feeling compelled to do their biddings.
4. Lack of morality, erosion of values and discipline.
5. Lack of interest and involvement in such matters among majority of faculty members.
6. Liberal nature of parents in giving too much money to their children leads to increase in incidences of drinking, drug abuse etc.
7. External pressure due to powerful connections of students hinders enforcement of law and order against them.
8. Fear among victims that the head of the departments and others may pressurize them for withdrawal of complaints to save the image of college from being tarnished.

REASONS OF RAGGING[14]

1. Use of alcohol in hostels

One of the important factors perpetuating ragging is the use of alcohol in hostels. The prevalence of unhindered, non-prohibited flow of liquor in the hostels is strongly denied by the authorities but it is still a naked reality of the most of the colleges.[15] Under the influence of alcohol, the students get swayed

---

13. *Ibid.*
14. Rajesh Garg, Ragging: A Public Health Problem in India, Indian Journal of Medical Sciences, Vol. 63, Issue No. 6, June, 2009, p. 266.
15. Raheel Khursheed, Ragging claims medical student's life, authorities blamed, available at http://ibnlive.in.com/news/ragging-claims-medical-students-life-authorities-blamed/87337-3.html, last accessed on 16th February, 2014.

away by emotions and their so-called hidden chauvinism comes out and they set out on their mission to 'improve and guide' the juniors through ragging and to show them the right path, as according to them the junior students know nothing about this cruel world.

2. Lack of supervision and lack of implementation of serious anti-ragging measures by college authorities

There is a lack of supervision and implementation of anti-ragging measures by many college authorities. Whenever a case of ragging is reported, the first reaction of the authorities is to wrap up the things as early as possible as it will hamper the prestige and reputation of the institute.[16]

3. Vacant or No Posts of wardens in the hostel

The vacant or no post of wardens in the hostels is also a major reason which indirectly aids in the commission of crime. Many a times, the warden doesn't actually stay in the hostel, particularly during the night, when the ugly demon of ragging raises its head.

4. Ragging is not considered a social evil

Still, ragging is not considered as a social evil. If people come across any severe case of ragging they take it as an exception.[17] People consider ragging as simple teasing, dancing etc., and don't know the real extent of ragging in the hostels. Many a times when a ragging incident is reported, as it involves a severe punishment, generates sympathy for the senior and leads to compromise and suppression of the case.[18] Colleges even deny its acceptance to save their reputation and to avoid the possibility of strike and hooliganism by students.

REASONS FOR THE DENIAL OF EXISTENCE OF RAGGING[19]

1. Since, generally most of the people have indulged in ragging as seniors at some point in their lives; they try to defend this conduct as moral.
2. Colleges deny its existence in campuses for the sake of maintaining good reputation and also because of their inability to control it.
3. Parents (of fresher) don't know the full extent of ragging and henceforth think ragging as a little teasing for personality enhancement.
4. Macho image is associated with the act of ragging so its criticism is considered a weakness among the youth.

CONSEQUENCES OF RAGGING

The catastrophe on a victim of ragging seems to be limited to that individual and his family; but when we look deep into the skin we come to know its vast

---

16. *Ibid.*
17. Ragging in Indian Universities and Colleges, p. 15, available at http://www.noragging.com/CURE1.pdf, last accessed on 16th February, 2014.
18. *Ibid.*
19. Ragging in India, A Summary Report on Incidents, Social Perceptions and Psychological Perspectives, CURE REPORT: CR2007_05-16,May 16 2007, p. 19, available at http://www.noragging.com/analysis/CR2007_05-16_RaggingInIndiaSummary.pdf, last accessed on 16th February, 2014.

consequences on the life of others also.[20] Following are the shocking consequences of ragging:—

(A) Consequences of ragging on the victim[21]

1. A permanent scar of unpleasant memory of ragging in victim's mind may haunt him for the years to come.
2. Ragging discourages the victim from joining other institutions in future which may also hamper her/his career prospects.
3. Ragging causes grave psychological stress and trauma to the victim which results in his/her alienation from the rest of the world.
4. Students protesting against ragging are very likely to face ostracism from their seniors.
5. Instances of suicides and culpable homicides have been reported in extreme cases.

(B) Consequences of ragging on the victim's family

Plight of a victim's family especially of parents is unimaginable. Parents bear the trauma of seeing the prospective career of their child coming to an end just because of ragging.[22]

(C) Consequences of ragging on the educational institutions

Extreme cases of ragging attracts media barrage which results into loss of reputation of the educational institutions. Thus, those who indulge in ragging bring a bad name to their college, thereby hampering its reputation and goodwill in the society.[23]

(D) Consequences of ragging on the raggers

The practice of ragging does well to none. From those who are victims of ragging to those who commit or encourage it, ragging spares none. Raggers get rigorous imprisonment under law.[24] They may also get suspended, blacklisted or even permanently expelled from college. Further this might affect their career and family as well.

STRESS AS CONSEQUENCE OF RAGGING

Stress is somewhat nonspecific biological, emotional and behavioural process that occurs when physical or psychological well-being is disturbed or threatened.[25] It is believed to be caused mostly by external events. Ragging induces stress not only in the mind of ragged student but also in the minds of fellow students. Even the very thought of ragging provokes enough stress

---

20. *Supra* note 14.
21. *Suprea* note 4.
22. *Ibid.*
23. *Ibid.*
24. *Ibid.*
25. Ragging: March Against a Social Menace, p. 47, available at http://www.gnit.ac.in/pdf/Anti-RaggingHandbook.pdf, last accessed on 16th February, 2014.

among the students. Stress can result in a variety of physiological, psychological, cognitive and behavioural problems which are as follows[26]:—

1. Physiological Problems[27]

- Nausea, headaches, hypertension, asthma, rheumatoid arthritis, sleep disturbance,
- Skin disorders,
- Elevated blood pressure,
- Increased heart rate and
- Reduced immune function and thereby increase in chances of infectious diseases.

2. Psychological Problems[28]

- Anxiety is the most common reaction to stress and it affects the performance level,
- Loss of concentration and attention,
- Anger, irritability and nightmares,
- Inferiority complex,
- Feeling of insecurity arising out of financial exploitation,
- Reduced productivity,
- Negative self image, reduced self-esteem and loss of faith in oneself,
- Depression, lack of interest and behavioural changes in cognitive pattern and
- Forgetfulness, errors in judgement etc.

3. Behavioural Problems[29]

- Rise in aggressive behaviour and criminal activities,
- Alcohol, drug addiction and increase in smoking and
- Compulsive behaviour, itinerant lifestyle.

4. Other Problems[30]

- Interpersonal relationships may get disturbed,
- Prolonged stress gradually minimizes the ability to function effectively,
- Stress may generate Post Traumatic Stress Disorder (PTSD) that is the most long-drawn-out and serious of all reactions to severe stress and
- Stress may produce much stronger psychological reaction than simple anxiety.

Knowledge regarding stress and its harmful effects may teach a student not to rag his junior students. Parents may also take necessary steps to treat their

26. *Ibid*, p. 48.
27. *Ibid.*
28. *Ibid.*
29. *Ibid.*
30. *Ibid.*

ward appropriately with the help of medical practitioners and psychologists. Following are the ways through which we can cope up with the stress:—

How to cope with stress:[31]

- Confiding in trustworthy people and seeking suggestions from them,
- Curbing exaggeration and overreacting by analysing the actual intensity of stress in the situation,
- Meditating,
- Regular Exercise,
- Exercising relaxation techniques,
- Joining of stress management programmes,
- Modification of the environment as far as possible and
- Bringing positive change in personal behaviour.

RAGGING AS A FORM OF DISCRIMINATION

Ragging is simply a manifestation of a form of discrimination that we see in our society but it has always been showcased and misunderstood as a personality boosting therapy or something like a friendship catalyst because of which the discriminatory fact is hidden and has never really been identified or analysed.[32] One of the important reasons for the prevalence of ragging is the cultural rivalry that exists in India.[33] It is a harsh reality that the most explicit forms of discrimination take place during ragging which perhaps sows the seeds of discrimination and revenge in the young minds then and there itself.

Students are bullied on the basis of their origin, ethnicity, caste, race, community, accent, economic background, culture, language, region, religion etc.[34] Seniors are also divided into different groups on the similar lines. Each one uses ragging as a tool to ridicule the fresher who comes from different background. Even in the west, ragging called as hazing or bullying has been used to take out revenge between the blacks and the whites. Though one cannot call these sorts of discrimination as racist but are certainly an example of sub-racism.[35]

Therefore, everywhere in the world whether in the form of ragging, hazing or bullying the basis of this evil practice has always been sociological in nature.

RAGGING AS HUMAN RIGHTS ABUSE

A careful and an analytical analysis of this issue shows the abuse of all the principles that fortify the notion of human rights. *Firstly*, the equality principle

31. *Ibid.*
32. Discrimination and Ragging, CURE REPORT CR 2006/02-25,available athttp://www.noragging.com/analysis/CR2007_02_25_DiscriminationAndRagging.pdf, p. 2, last accessed on 16th February, 2014.
33. Conversation happened between Harsh Agarwal and Michael Britton in 2007 that began with Harsh's research report on "ragging" in colleges in India, available at http://www.humiliationstudies.org/documents/BrittonAgarwalConversationonRagging.pdf, last accessed on 16th February, 2014.
34. *Ibid.*
35. *Ibid.*

is invaded by the very act of ragging. *Secondly,* liberty of the victim student is disregarded and *thirdly,* the victim is stripped of dignity. It is indisputable that the dignity of a man is inviolable and that the right to life includes right to live with human dignity.[36]

But, still ragging is hardly perceived as a serious human right abuse in India. Even United Nations declaration on Human Rights and Dignity to which India is also a signatory, states that, "Parties to this convention shall protect the dignity and identity of all human beings and guarantee everyone, without discrimination, respect for their integrity and other rights and fundamental freedom".[37] UN has considered ragging as an issue of 'Human Rights in education', thus education laws of India should take proper note of this traditional and systemic human rights abuse in educational institutions. Now, it is high time that human rights communities in India (including governmental and non-governmental players) take adequate safeguards against ragging.[38]

RAGGING AS SHOWN IN MOVIES

In movies like Munnabhai MBBS & 3 idiots ragging has been used as a theme to make the audience laugh. Millions of people watch such movies, take pleasure and believe that ragging is all about dance and fun and forget about the cruelty of ragging. Perhaps, they try to find humour in such practices. That is why CURE, a voluntary organisation working against ragging complained to the Supreme Court, who then appointed Anti-ragging Committee about the menace being glorified in the movie '3 Idiots'. On this Harsh Agarwal said that *"the movie is glorifying it. Treating it as a subject of fun. This must end as hundreds of students across India suffer a lot due to ragging."*[39]

This act of glorifying ragging by showcasing it in a lighter way in movies does nothing but strengthens the justifications which are given by people in support of ragging. This strand reflects the lack of sensitivity with regards to the issue of ragging.

But recently, a bollywood movie 'Table No. 21' showcased the ugliness of this crime and showed the worst effects and consequences of all the pervading evils of ragging. It gives us the message that "RAGGING IS NOT A JOKE... IT'S A CRIME".

---

36. Dr. Ch. Venkateswarlu and N Satyasri, Effects of Ragging on Human Dignity-A Critique, International Journal of Multi-disciplinary Educational Research ISSN: 2277-7881, Volume1, Issue 4, Sept., 2012, p. 233.
37. Article 1 of Convention for the Protection of Human Rights and Dignity of the Human Being.
38. Anant Kumar Asthana, Eradication of Ragging: Realities and Recommendations a legal Perspective, CURE Report: CR2007/03-03, available at http://noragging.com/index.php/Research/Reports/Ragging-and-Human-Rights.html, last accessed on 16th February, 2014.
39. 3 *Idiots* glorified ragging, NGO complains to SC, Available at http://www.hindustantimes.com/News-Feed/Entertainment/3-Idiots-glorified-ragging-NGO-complains-to-SC/Article1-491999.aspx, last accessed on 16th February, 2014.

Chapter III

Psychology Behind Ragging

The concept of ragging has been a debatable issue for past many years but the psychological aspect of it, which is the root cause, has always been ignored by the policy makers. They never tried to solve the mystery that, why a ragged fresher follows the same line of attack of a senior on her/his own juniors. There are some important questions which need to be answered to solve this problem, like why at all ragging happens, why does it get mass support, why the victim herself/himself becomes the perpetrator of this heinous crime in subsequent years etc.? Answers to all these questions lie in the mystery of psychology itself.

Ragging is more of a psychological problem than anything else. The mystery of the psychology of students about ragging revolves around two major beliefs. *Firstly,* that ragging is a positive phenomenon and thus has a positive effect on the personality of the fresher and *secondly,* through this process the seniors and freshers get the chance to interact with each other. Seniors make every effort to ensure that these beliefs are well passed on to their juniors. Gradually, freshers familiarize themselves with these myths of ragging and slowly mould their thought process, which ensures the phenomenon of ragging to pass on from batch to batch.

The common psychological belief prevalent among the students is that as they were ragged so they have every right to rag their juniors too. According to the misconception among the students, ragging has become the only process which can establish communication between seniors and freshers. Further, freshers also surrender themselves with the logic that seniors who rag them will help them later through study material, notes etc.

The irony is that for the sake of bonding, such destructive methods are being wrongly justified at the cost of one's liberty, dignity and personality.

With this psychological aspect freshers are also scared that they would be singled out by the seniors in case they don't adhere to the practice of ragging. It is also commonly noted that most often the freshers who drop out of the college or commit suicide are the ones who were singled out from their batch or were ragged severely sometime in the past. It is observed that this sometimes leads to severe depression among juniors who then unwittingly decide to harm themselves.[1]

1. Ragging in India, A Summary Report on Incidents, Social Perceptions and Psychological Perspectives, CURE REPORT: CR2007_05-16, May 16, 2007, p. 17, available at http://www.noragging.com/analysis/CR2007_05-16_RaggingInIndiaSummary.pdf, last accessed on 16th February, 2014.

Surprisingly, ragging is unique in itself as this is the only phenomenon in which the victim her/himself becomes the perpetrator in a short span of just one year. One after the other, every batch adopts this tradition, thus making it a never ending chain. Therefore, ragging has always been considered a phenomenon of vicious cycle.[2] But what are the factors which ensure this legacy? What are the components of this chain? How and where does it actually get its strength from? These are some of the questions which haven't been answered, because of lack of psychological study done to understand ragging.

PSYCHOLOGICAL REASONS OF RAGGING[3]

Probably, precise psychological reasons for the continuation of this phenomenon are:—

1. Revenge: The main psychological cause of ragging is revenge. Ragged students get happiness by watching their juniors suffering in the same way as they suffered. Due to this psychology they think as they were ragged, they should also rag their juniors for their sadistic fun and pleasure.[4]

2. Sexual desires: There is a delusion in senior's mind that they can easily satisfy their sexual frustration and desires from a junior, as according to them she/he won't be able to retaliate or oppose out of the fear of damage to her/his image in the society. In this situation, seniors get full freedom unlike in the society where there is a fear of social boundaries. They also think that no one will ever come to know about the incident and they will escape clean. Homosexual desires which the person has no hope to be ever fulfilled, also find an expression in these acts.

3. Machoism: There is a general tendency in the minds of senior boys to show the masculinity in front of the general public, especially girls by subjecting the juniors to their will. Just to show physical power and to prove that they are the bosses in the college, juniors are brutally ragged by the seniors.

4. Indirect support from the society and college: Seniors feel safe somewhere in their mind while committing the crime of ragging, as they think they have indirect support from both the college and the society because ragging is seen as a traditional practice in the society which is being followed from a long time. This factor plays an important role in encouraging the students to practice ragging.

5. Ego hurt: Many seniors want others to follow what they think is right and if a junior goes opposite to that then their ego gets hurt which turn into seniors using more devilish ways of ragging to teach the fresher a lesson.

6. Anger disposal bins: Anger raised within seniors is being faced by the juniors unnecessarily and involuntarily. Seniors treat the juniors as object to

---

2. *Ibid.*
3. Varun Aggarwal, Ragging: Why at All?, available at http://noragging.com/index.php/Research/Ragging-The-Phenomenon/-Ragging-Why-at-All.html, last accessed on 16th February, 2014.
4. Rajesh Garg, Ragging: A Public Health Problem in India, Indian Journal of Medical Sciences, Vol. 63, Issue No. 6, June, 2009, p. 266.

extract relief at the time of their being in angry temper. Thus, they become just like an anger disposal bins for seniors.

7. Hegemony: Most of the seniors who practice ragging are a group of people who are tyrants. They derive their power from the fact that they are famous *'gundaas'* or a part of some union. Their unity with their own kinds encourages them to do the wrong but they are nothing but an organisation of bullies.

8. Dreams realized: Seniors take ragging as a chance to realize all their dreams and fantasies (like to see a girl with a moustache, a boy with lipstick, a person acting like a monkey etc.) under the garb of such a non-sensical tradition at the cost of someone else's emotions, feelings and principles.

9. Fun in troubling and embarrassing: Many a times juniors are told to do the things which neither bring fun to the senior, nor realize any of her/his dreams. They are just interested in troubling and embarrassing by asking one to walk up and down the building 10 times or ask sexually oriented questions in an embarrassing way etc.

These are not the end of the psychological justifications which one generally gives to oneself while committing the crime of ragging. But, hopefully after knowing that ragging is a psychological disorder, many would just hate to be identified with it and would be forced to rethink about the virtues of ragging they believe in. This might eventually lead to eradication of ragging by the simple method of thinking and application of logic. Thus, spreading awareness of this psychological aspect of ragging would surely help in prevention of ragging.

Chapter IV

Initiatives to Stop Ragging in India

Government has setup various committees and commissions from time to time to wipe out ragging from educational institutions but it is unfortunate that as usual most of the guidelines have just remained on paper and nothing fruitful seems to have been done.[1] Efforts have also been taken to eradicate the devil of ragging by various other sections of the society but to no avail. Although after the kindly intervention of the Hon'ble Court, a hope has kindled.[2]

FIRST HAMMER OF THE APEX COURT

In 1998, a Public Interest Litigation was filed by Vishwa Jagriti Mission in the Hon'ble Apex Court to curb the practice of ragging. The Apex Court vividly explained that the things had gone out of hand and it is high time to bring out the enormity of the problem. Thus the Court issued the directives to all the concerned authorities, for effective implementation of measures.[3]

UNNI COMMITTEE

In response to this public interest petition, in the year 1999, the UGC set up a four-member Committee, chaired by K.P.S. Unni of the Jawaharlal Nehru University for framing the course of action to fight the threat of ragging in Universities/Educational Institutions. The Committee's recommendations were exhaustive. It recommended the following[4]:—

- Enactment of Central and the State laws, making ragging a cognizable offence, identifying the perverse forms of ragging under such law(s), giving punishments appropriate to the cruelty of offence;
- Anti-ragging movement in respect of ban on ragging and the consequences of violation should start from the publication of advertisements for admissions. Prospectus, application forms and admission forms should contain clear message against ragging;
- An undertaking for not indulging in ragging should be made mandatory for taking admission in hostels;
- Various actions should be taken at the beginning of each academic session, like an address by head of institution to wardens, student activists, parents/guardians, police and faculty, and constituting anti-ragging

1. Gulshan Naveen, Ragging – The Red Alert, 1st Edn. 2010, p. 59.
2. *Ibid.*
3. *Ibid, p. 60.*
4. Ragging: March Against a Social Menace, pp. 24-25, available at http://www.gnit.ac.in/pdf/Anti-RaggingHandbook.pdf, last accessed on 16th February, 2014.

vigilance committees comprising some senior faculty members, students and wardens;

- Defaulting institutions should be penalized in the form of reduction in grants-in-aid or even dis-affiliation from UGC;
- Different grades of punishments ranging from suspension of offenders from institution to a fine of Rs. 25,000 and, even rigorous imprisonment up to 3 years depending on degree of severity of offence. In addition, punishments should also be given by the concerned institutional authorities and
- Positive steps and incentives to create an anti-ragging environment.

The University Grants Commission had circulated this report to all the universities on 13th January, 2000 for necessary action.

ORDER ON PIL OF VISHWA JAGRATI MISSION

The major boost to anti-ragging efforts was given by the Hon'ble Supreme Court of India by giving landmark judgment on this PIL in May, 2001. In this case, Hon'ble Court defined ragging as: '*Any disorderly conduct, whether by words spoken or written or by an act which is the effect of teasing or handling with rudeness any other student, indulging in rowdy or in-disciplined activities which causes or is likely to cause annoyance, hardship or psychological harm or to raise fear or apprehension thereof in a fresher or a junior student or asking the students to do any act or perform something which such student will not do in the ordinary course and which has the effect of causing or generating a sense of shame or embarrassment so as to adversely affect the physique or psyche of a fresher or a junior student.*' In this judgment, Hon'ble Court had issued several guidelines. Very briefly, which are:[5]

1. **Anti-ragging movements to be initiated by all the colleges and educational institutes**: Anti-ragging movements should be initiated by the institutions right from the time of advertisement for admissions. If there is any legislation governing ragging or any provision in the statutes/ordinances it should be brought to the notice of the students/parents seeking admissions. The prospectus, the forms for admission and/or any other literature issued to aspirants for admission must clearly mention that ragging is banned in the institution and any one found indulging in ragging is likely to be punished appropriately with the punishment which may include expulsion or suspension from the institution or class for a limited period or/ and fine with a public apology. The punishment may also take the shape of: (i) withholding scholarships or other benefits (ii) debarring from representation in events (iii) withholding results (iv) suspension or expulsion from hostel or mess, and the like.
2. **Undertakings to be taken from the freshers and their parents/guardians**: The application for admission/enrolment shall have a printed undertaking to be filled up and signed by the applicant to the effect that he/she is aware of the institution's approach towards ragging and the punishment

---

5. Madhavi Chopra, Ragging in Educational Institutes: A Human Rights Perspective available at http://www.legalserviceindia.com/articles/ragging.htm, last accessed on 16th February, 2014.

to which he/she shall be subjected if found guilty. A similar undertaking shall also be obtained from the parent/guardian of the applicant.

3. **Undertakings to be taken from seniors and their parents / guardians too:** The undertakings should be obtained from the students already studying in the institutions and their parents/guardians before the commencement of the next educational year/session.
4. **Notices to be issued indicating where to approach for redressal in case of ragging:** A printed leaflet detailing when and to whom one may turn for information, help and guidance for various purposes, keeping in view the needs of new entrants in the institution, along with the addresses and telephone numbers of such persons, should be given to freshers at the time of admission so that the freshers need not look up to the seniors for help in such matters.
5. **Management, principal and the teaching staff should have personal interaction with the freshers:** The Management, the Principal and the Teaching Staff should interact with the freshers and take them into confidence by apprising them of their rights as well as obligations to fight against ragging and to generate confidence in their minds that any instance of ragging to which they are subjected or which comes to their knowledge should forthwith be brought to the knowledge of concerned authorities. It would be better if the head of the institution or a person of high authority addresses collective meetings of teachers, parents and students.
6. **Proctorial Committee to be set up:** At the commencement of the academic session, the institution should constitute a Proctorial Committee consisting of senior faculty members and hostel authorities like wardens and a few responsible senior students:-
   (A) to keep a continuous watch and vigil over ragging activities so as to prevent its occurrence and recurrence,
   (B) to promptly deal with the incidents of ragging brought to its notice and summarily punish the guilty either by itself or by putting forth its findings/recommendations/suggestions before the authority competent to take decision.
7. **Ragging - prone zones to be identified and carefully guarded:** All vulnerable locations in the college such as the canteen, the playground, etc., shall be identified and specially watched.
8. **Society to be sensitized on the issue of ragging:** The local community and the students in particular must be aware of the dehumanizing effect of ragging inherent in its perversity. Posters, notice boards and signboards wherever necessary, may be used for the purpose.
9. **Failure to prevent ragging to be construed as an act of negligence:** Failure to prevent ragging should be construed as an act of negligence in maintaining discipline in the institution on the part of the management, the principal and the persons in authority of the institution. Similar responsibility shall be shared with hostel wardens/superintendents.

10. **Hostels/accommodations to be carefully guarded**: The hostels/accommodations where freshers are accommodated shall be carefully guarded, if necessary by posting security personnel with a warden/superintendent who should herself/himself reside there, and wherein the entry of seniors and outsiders shall be prohibited before and after a specified hour of night except under the permission of the person in-charge. Entry at other times may also be regulated.
11. **Migration certificates to mention whether the student ever indulged in ragging**: Migration Certificates issued by every institution should have an entry apart from that of general conduct and behaviour whether the student had participated in, and in particular, was punished for ragging.
12. **Withdrawal of financial assistance to institutes where ragging incidents are reported**: If an institution fails to curb ragging, the UGC/funding agency may consider withdrawal of financial assistance to such an institution till such time as it achieves the same.
13. **Students to first approach their colleges**: In case of any incident of ragging, the students must approach the disciplinary Committee of their respective colleges first and only if the said committee does not take cognizance of the matter or if they feel dissatisfied with its decision, they should approach the police. The objective behind this is to restore the faith in the ability of educational institutions to maintain discipline and protect the interests of their students.

It may be important to note here that the above stated guidelines are only illustrative and are not intended to come in the way of the educational institutions and authorities in devising ways and means to curb the ragging. If there are any local laws governing ragging, they should be implemented and knowledge about such laws should also be disseminated.

These directions of the Hon'ble Supreme Court were brought to the notice of all the State Governments and Universities/Institutions covered under its purview by the Central Government (Ministry of Human Resource Development). State Governments were requested to call for 'action taken reports' from institutions. Further, the government called for strict action against those indulging in ragging so that the incidents do not take place again.

UNIVERSITY OF KERALA CASE

The Hon'ble Apex Court was concerned with the shortcomings in the implementation of its judgment in the Vishwa Jagriti Mission case and felt the need for another committee to examine the measures afresh. In furtherance of this view on 27th November, 2006, in the case of *University of Kerala* v. *Council of Principals of Colleges*,[6] Hon'ble Court stated in its interim order that, *"practically very little has been done to prevent the menace of ragging in educational institution"*.[7] Thus, Court directed that a committee to be notified to give suggestions on the means of prevention of ragging in educational institutions. The Apex Court

6. AIR 2009 SC 2223.
7. *Supra note 1*, p. 67.

expected from this proposed committee to make the recommendations as to how ragging can be eliminated effectively.

RAGHAVAN COMMITTEE

As per Hon'ble Court order, Ministry of Human Resource Development (MHRD), Government of India constituted a Committee on 5th December, 2006. The terms of reference of the committee were to study various aspects of ragging, to suggest means and methods of prevention of ragging, to suggest possible action that can be taken against persons indulging in ragging and to suggest possible actions that can be taken against college/university authorities in the event of ragging.[8] It submitted its report to the Hon'ble Supreme Court in May, 2007.

The Committee pointed out that the forms of ragging listed in the report of UGC Committee (Unni Committee) have become outmoded or outdated because extremely vulgar, most inhuman and unprintable forms of ragging are being resorted to these days. It noted that ragging has now assumed perverse forms like physical assaults, wrongful confinement, use of criminal force, threats, intimidation and denial of basic human rights, also college administration is not keen to indulge in this issue and thus punishments or preventive measures have not been implemented.[9] It also recommended insertion of a special section under IPC by drawing analogy from section 498A of IPC.[10]

THE LANDMARK ORDER

The Hon. Supreme Court in this case ordered that a number of recommendations made by the Raghavan Committee should be implemented immediately. These included[11]:—

- Confidence building measures such as appointment of counsellors, arrival of senior students a week or two weeks after the Juniors have arrived; joint sensitization programmes; joint orientation programme of 'freshers' and 'seniors' to be addressed by the principal/head of the institution; organization on large scale of cultural, sports and other activities; make provisions for faculty members to dine with the hostel residents in their respective hostels etc.
- Hostels must be registered with the local police authorities and permission to start or register such hostels must necessarily be recommended by the heads of educational institutions. Local police, local administration and the institutional authorities must ensure vigil on incidents that may come within the definition of ragging.
- There must be an anti-ragging squad and anti-ragging committee in every institution and a monitoring cell on ragging at the university level that

8. *Ibid*, p. 64.
9. *Ibid*, *pp*.67-68.
10. Y.S. Rao Judge, Ragging, available at http://www.legalservicesindia.com/article/article/ragging-1168-1.html, last accessed on 16th February, 2014.
11. Available at http://www.amanmovement.org/summary_of_judgement_of_hon_supreme_court.pdf.

would coordinate with the affiliated colleges and institutions under its domain.

- Wardens must be accessible at all hours and therefore it is important that they, be available on telephone and other modes of communication. Similarly, the telephone numbers of the other important functionaries like head of institutions, faculty members, members of the anti-ragging committees, district and sub-divisional authorities and State authorities where relevant, should also be widely disseminated for the needy to get in touch or seek help in emergencies.
- The educational institutions shall ensure that each hostel has a full-time warden who resides in the hostel, or at the very least, in the close vicinity thereof.
- Brochures or booklet/leaflet distributed to each student at the beginning of each academic session for obtaining undertaking not to indulge or abet ragging, shall contain the blueprint of methods of prevention and redressal.

CENTRAL CRISIS-HOTLINE AND ANTI-RAGGING DATABASE

The Hon'ble Court had acknowledged in this case that the MHRD, in consultation with UGC, MCI, AICTE and other similar regulatory bodies was in the process of setting up a central crisis-hotline and anti-ragging database in the manner suggested by Dr. Raj Kachroo. The Hon. Court, however, added that:-

- A non-governmental agency should monitor the database which is to be immediately nominated by the Union of India to boost confidence in the public and also to provide information of compliance to the regulatory bodies and to the Raghavan Committee.
- The database shall be created out of affidavits affirmed by each student and her/his parents/guardians, which shall be stored electronically, and shall contain the details of each student.
- The database shall function as a record of ragging complaints received and the status of the action taken thereon.

Note:—In accordance with the orders, UGC (University Grants Commission), Government of India has developed a web portal *i.e.*, www.antiragging.in. The aim of this portal is to eliminate ragging in all forms from universities, deemed universities and other higher educational institutions in the country.

DIRECTIONS TO REGULATORY BODIES:

The Hon'ble Court ordered that regulations on curbing the menace of ragging, formulated by the UGC, must be adopted by all other regulatory bodies, such as AICTE, MCI, DCI, NCI etc.

ACTION AGAINST NON-ACTION:

The Hon'ble Court ordered penal consequences, departmental enquiries to be initiated against those heads of the institutions/members of the administration/ faculty members/non-teaching staff, who display an apathetic or insensitive attitude towards the complaints of ragging.

SENSITIZATION

Not only the students, but also the faculty members must be sensitized towards the ills of ragging and the prevention thereof. Non-teaching staff, which includes administrative staff, contract employees, security guards, have also to be regularly sensitized towards the evil consequences of ragging.

DIRECTIONS TO HEAD OF THE INSTITUTION:

Principal or head of the institution/department shall obtain an undertaking from every employee of the institution including teaching and non-teaching members of staff, contract labour employed in the premises either for running canteen or as watch and ward staff or for cleaning or maintenance of the buildings/lawns etc., that she/he would report promptly any case of ragging which comes to her/his notice. A provision shall be made in the service rules for issuing certificates of appreciation to such members of the staff who report ragging which will form a part of their service record.

DIRECTION TO PARENTS/GUARDIANS:

The Hon'ble Court said that it was necessary that the parents/guardians of freshers assume responsibility for promptly bringing to the notice of the head of the Institution any instance of ragging.

DIRECTIONS TO STATION HOUSE OFFICER/SUPERINTENDENT OF POLICE:

The Hon'ble Court said that the SHO/SP, within whose jurisdiction a particular college falls, shall be responsible for ensuring that no ragging takes place on the campus of the concerned college and to effectively deal with the incidents of ragging, if take place. Once a central database/crisis hotline is made operative then as soon as SHO/SP, within whose jurisdiction a particular college falls, is contacted by the crisis hotline staff, then such SHO/SP shall deal effectively with the incident and cooperate and communicate with the crisis hotline staff and/or the independent monitoring agency. This will build confidence and encourage people to report incidences of ragging without fear or delay.

FACTORS NEED TO BE FOCUSED ON TO TACKLE THIS PROBLEM:

Hon'ble Supreme Court perused the report of the Committee to suggest remedial measures to tackle with the problem of ragging in educational institutions. Hon'ble Court said, according to the Committee, the following factors need to be focused on to tackle the problem:[12]

a. Primary responsibility for curbing ragging rests with academic institutions themselves.

b. Ragging adversely impacts the standards of higher education.

c. Incentives should be available to institutions for curbing the menace and there should be disincentives for failure to do so.

d. Enrolment in academic pursuits or a campus life should not immunize any adult citizen from penal provisions of the laws of the land.

12. *Supra note 1*, p. 64.

e. Ragging needs to be perceived as a failure to inculcate human values from the schooling stage.

f. Behavioural patterns among students, particularly potential 'raggers' need to be identified.

g. Measures against ragging must deter its recurrence.

h. Concerted action is required at the level of the school, higher educational institution, district administration, university, State and Central Governments to make any curb effective.

i. Media and the Civil Society should be involved in this exercise.

FINAL ORDER:

The Apex Court stated that Raghavan Committee has made several recommendations. For the present, we feel that the following recommendations should be implemented without any further lapse of time[13]:-

1. The punishment to be meted out has to be exemplary and justifiably harsh to act as a deterrent against recurrence of such incidents.
2. Every single incident of ragging where the victim or her/his parent/guardian or the head of institution is not satisfied with the institutional arrangement for action, a First Information Report [FIR] must be filed without exception by the institutional authorities with the local police authorities. Any failure on the part of the institutional authority or negligence or deliberate delay in lodging the FIR with the local police shall be construed to be an act of culpable negligence on the part of the institutional authority. If any victim or his/her parent/guardian intends to file FIR directly with the police, that will not absolve the institutional authority from the requirement of filing the FIR.
3. Courts should make an effort to ensure that cases involving ragging are taken up on a priority basis to send the correct message that ragging is not only to be discouraged but also to be dealt with sternness.
4. In addition, Court directed that the possibility of introducing in the educational curriculum a subject relating to ragging shall be explored by the National Council of Educational Research and Training (NCERT) and the respective State Council of Educational Research and Training (SCERT). This aspect can be included in the teaching of the subjects "Human Rights".
5. In the prospectus to be issued for admission by educational institutions, it shall be clearly stipulated that in case the applicant for admission is found to have indulged in ragging in the past or if it is noticed later that she/he has indulged in ragging, admission may be refused or she/he shall be expelled from the educational institution.
6. It shall be the collective responsibility of the authorities and functionaries of the concerned institution and their role shall also be open to scrutiny for the purpose of finding out whether they have taken effective steps

13. *Ibid*, pp. 64-66.

for preventing ragging and in case of their failure, action can be taken; for example denial of any grant-in-aid or assistance from the State Governments.

7. The Central and State Governments shall launch a programme giving wide publicity to the eradication of menace of ragging and the consequences which follow in case any student is detected to have been involved in ragging.
8. Anti-ragging committees and squads shall be forthwith formed by the institutions and it shall be the job of the committee or the squad, as the case may be, to see that the Committee's recommendations, more particularly those noted above, are observed without exception and if it is noticed that there is any deviation, the same shall be forthwith brought to the notice of this Court means Apex Court.
9. The Committee constituted pursuant to the order of this Court shall continue to monitor the functioning of the anti-ragging committees and the squads to be formed. They shall also monitor the implementation of the recommendations to which reference has been made above.

Welcoming the Supreme Court's judgment, Dr. Raghavan, the former CBI director said, "finally there are signs that the recommendations to prevent ragging in colleges will be taken seriously".

UGC REGULATION ON CURBING THE MENACE OF RAGGING IN HIGHER EDUCATIONAL INSTITUTIONS, 2009

In 2009, in the wake of *Aman Kachroo's* death, University Grants Commission (UGC) passed 'UGC Regulation on Curbing the Menace of Ragging in Higher Educational Institutions, 2009' which have the force of law. According to UGC's notification,[14] ragging constitutes one or more of any of the following acts:

a. any conduct by any student or students whether by words spoken or written or by an act which has the effect of teasing, treating or handling with rudeness a fresher or any other student;
b. indulging in rowdy or undisciplined activities by any student or students which causes or is likely to cause annoyance, hardship, physical or psychological harm or to raise fear or apprehension thereof in any fresher or any other student;
c. asking any student to do any act which such student will not in the ordinary course do and which has the effect of causing or generating a sense of shame, or torment or embarrassment so as to adversely affect the physique or psyche of such fresher or any other student;
d. any act by a senior student that prevents, disrupts or disturbs the regular academic activity of any other student or a fresher;
e. Exploiting the services of a fresher or any other student for completing the academic tasks assigned to an individual or a group of students.

14. UGC Regulations on Curbing the Menace of Ragging in Higher Educational Institutions, 2009.

f. any act of financial extortion or forceful expenditure burden put on a fresher or any other student by students;

g. any act of physical abuse including all variants of it: sexual abuse, homosexual assaults, stripping, forcing obscene and lewd acts, gestures, causing bodily harm or any other danger to health of person;

h. any act or abuse by spoken words, emails, posts, public insults which would also include deriving perverted pleasure, vicarious or sadistic thrill from actively or passively participating in the discomfiture to fresher or any other student;

i. any act that affects the mental health and self-confidence of a fresher or any other student with or without an intent to derive a sadistic pleasure or showing off power, authority or superiority by a student over any fresher or any other student.

In terms of these regulations it is the mandatory responsibility of every college to curb the menace of ragging by strict pre-emptive measures like lodging freshers in a separate hostel, surprise raids especially at nights by the anti-ragging squad and submission of affidavits by all senior students. The punishable ingredients of ragging are clearly spelt out in this version. It calls for a zero-tolerance policy towards ragging. It specifies the measures to be taken by institutions before, during and after the process of admission. It says that ragging should be a cognizable offence. It also talks about incentives that can be offered to institutions complying with strict enforcement of anti-ragging measures in the form of additional financial grants and incentives for wardens who carry out their responsibilities effectively. Punishment of different types has been proposed for students who indulge in ragging, like it may be in the form of suspension, withholding scholarships or results, debarring participation outside the college, cancellation of admission, rustication, expulsion and a fine of Rs. 25,000–1,00,000 etc.[15] The main features of the regulation are:

RESPONSIBILITIES OF EDUCATIONAL INSTITUTIONS

Applicable to **ALL** higher educational institutions, imparting education beyond 12 years of schooling.

BEFORE AND DURING ADMISSION AND REGISTRATION:

1. The institution to prominently display posters detailing laws and punishment against ragging.
2. **Every public declaration, brochure of admission/instruction booklet** or the prospectus to print these regulations in full.
3. Every student and her/his parents to file an **affidavit** avowing not to indulge in ragging.
4. **Printed leaflet** to be given to every fresher detailing addresses and telephone numbers of the Anti-Ragging Helpline, Wardens, head of the institution, all members of the anti-ragging squads and committees, and relevant district and police authorities.

15. Sumit Malhotra, Ragging in medical colleges: Call for adopting a zero tolerance policy, The National Medical Journal of India VOL. 23, NO. 2 of 2010, p. 122.

AFTER ADMISSION:

1. Anti-ragging squad to ensure **vigil at odd hours** during first few months at hostels, inside institution premises as well as privately commercially managed hostels.
2. Identity of **informants** of ragging incidents to be fully protected.
3. Faculty members assigned to make **surprise visits** to hostels and to maintain a diary of her/his interaction with the freshers.
4. Freshers to be lodged, as far as may be, in a **separate hostel block.**
5. Head of the institution, at the end of each academic year, to send a letter to the parents/guardians of the students who are completing their first year in the institution informing them about these Regulations.

ANTI-RAGGING COMMITTEE and ANTI-RAGGING SQUAD

6. Anti-Ragging Committee to be nominated and headed by the Head of the institution, and consisting of representatives of **civil and police administration**, local media, Non-Governmental Organizations involved in youth activities, representatives of faculty members, representatives of parents, representatives of students belonging to the **freshers'** category etc.
7. Duty of the Anti-Ragging Committee to ensure compliance with the provisions of these Regulations.
8. Anti-Ragging Squad to be nominated by the Head of the Institution for maintaining vigil, oversight and **patrolling** functions and shall remain mobile, alert and active at all times.
9. Anti-Ragging Squad to make **surprise raids** on hostels.
10. Discreet random surveys to be conducted amongst the freshers every fortnight during the first three months.
11. Heads of institutions affiliated to a University or a constituent of the University to submit a **weekly report** on the status of compliance with Anti-Ragging measures and a monthly report on such status thereafter, to the Vice-Chancellor of the University.
12. The Vice Chancellor of each University to submit **fortnightly reports,** including those of the monitoring cell on Ragging, in case of an affiliating university, to the State Level Monitoring Cell.

COMPLAINT OF RAGGING

13. **First Information Report (FIR)** to be filed within **twenty four hours** of receipt of such information or complaint of ragging, with the police and local authorities.
14. Head of the institution to forthwith report the incident of ragging to the District Level Anti-Ragging Committee and the Nodal officer.
15. Institution shall also continue with its own enquiry and remedial action to be completed with-in seven days.

RESPONSIBILITIES OF UNIVERSITY GRANTS COMMISSION (UGC)

1. The **Commission to verify that the institutions strictly comply** with the requirement of getting the affidavits from the students and their parents/guardians as envisaged under these Regulations.
2. The Commission to make it mandatory for the institutions to incorporate in their **prospectus**, the anti-ragging directions of the Central Government or the State Level Monitoring Committee.
3. The **Commission to maintain an appropriate data base** to be created out of affidavits, and such database to also function as a record of ragging complaints received, and the status of the action taken thereon.
4. The Commission shall make available the database to a non-governmental agency.
5. The Commission to include a specific condition in the **Utilization Certificate,** in respect of any financial assistance or grants-in-aid to any institution, that the institution has complied with the anti-ragging measures.
6. The **Commission to constitute an Inter-Council Committee** to coordinate and **monitor** the anti-ragging measures in institutions across the country.
7. The Commission to institute an **Anti-Ragging Cell** within the Commission to provide secretarial support for collection of information and monitoring, and to coordinate with the State Level Monitoring Cell and University level Committees for effective implementation of anti-ragging measures

ALL INDIA COUNCIL OF TECHNICAL EDUCATION [AICTE]

The All India Council of Technical Education (AICTE), New Delhi has put up a circular on its web-site that, "ragging in educational institutions in any form is banned under law; all the AICTE approved institutions must ensure that ragging does not take place at their campuses in any form; should such a case be reported or brought to the notice of the AICTE, then the Council shall take necessary action including withdrawal of approval".[16]

MEDICAL COUNCIL OF INDIA [MCI]

Medical Council of India (MCI) has issued following guidelines to curb the menace of ragging in medical colleges:-[17]

(1) Every student for the purposes of her/his admission to Medical College shall furnish a Character Certificate from the institutions wherefrom she/he has passed his qualifying examination, which would mention the status of his/her behavioural pattern specially in terms as to whether she/he has displayed persistent violent or aggressive behaviour or any desire to harm others.

(2) The admitting medical institution shall keep intense watch upon students who have a negative entry in this regard.

---

16. *Supra note* 4, p. 28.
17. Notification by Medical Council of India, Date:21/02/2009, No. MCI-34 (1)/2009-Med./99639, available at http://medicaleducation.rajasthan.gov.in/Anti_Ragging.pdf, last accessed on 16th February, 2014.

(3) An annual undertaking signed by each student, whether fresher or senior and her/his parent(s) jointly stating that each of them have read the relevant instructions/regulations against ragging, as well as punishments, and that if the ward has been found guilty, she/he shall be proceeded against, shall be procured.

(4) Such an undertaking shall be furnished in English as well as in vernacular (mother tongue of the parent) at the beginning of each academic year by every student.

(5) An undertaking to the similar effect should be obtained every year from each student admitted to the hostel.

(6) The undertaking should be appended to the brochure containing the guidelines and other relevant instructions in regard to ragging and consequences of indulging in ragging.

(7) The compliance to the above effect shall be ensured by each of the affiliating university to which the concerned medical institution is affiliated and would be verified by the Council annually.

(8) In order to ensure the 'ragging free environment' in the campus, each institution shall compulsorily in the 'prospectus' and other admission related documents, shall depict the earlier directions of the Apex Court and/or of the Central or State Governments as applicable, so that candidates and their parents are sensitized in respect of the prohibition and consequences of ragging.

(9) Each institution should engage or seek the assistance of 'professional counselor' at the time of admissions to counsel 'freshers' in order to prepare them for the life ahead, specially for adjusting to the life in hostels.

(10) It should be ensured that there would be a clear gap of one to two weeks between the date of joining of 'freshers' and the 'seniors', ensuring that classes for the seniors shall commence later, so as to enable the 'freshers' to familiarize themselves with the campus environment and adjust to the sudden changeover from schools to higher education.

(11) It shall be mandatory for the institutions to inform the parents of senior students to send their wards only on the due date of commencement of the academic session and not earlier.

(12) All the examining Universities with which the institutions are affiliated or the deemed to be Universities shall compulsorily amend their relevant ordinances or byelaws, as the case may be, to incorporate the schedule gap of one or two weeks between the date of joining of 'freshers' and 'seniors'.

(13) Each institution shall arrange a joint 'sensitization' programme and 'counselling' of both 'freshers' and 'seniors' to be addressed by the Principal/Head of the institution and the Convener of the Anti-Ragging Committee. The inmates of the Hostel shall be addressed on this count by the Hostel Warden.

(14) Each institution shall have an Anti-Ragging Committee and Anti Ragging Squad, which shall comprise of other than senior teachers of the institution, representatives of Civil and Police administration and local media.

(15) Each institution shall constitute a 'Mentoring Cell' to oversee and involve senior students as 'Mentors' for the 'freshers'.

(16) Such a Mentoring Cell shall be constituted at the end of every academic year, where applications shall be invited from the students to join the Mentoring Cell as Mentors for the succeeding academic year.

(17) An anonymous random survey shall be conducted by each institution across the entire first year batch of students every fortnight during the first three months of the academic session in order to verify and cross-check whether the campus is genuinely ragging free or not.

(18) The methodology of such survey may be designed by the institution appropriately. However, doing so it shall be ensured that the institution does not compromise with the anonymity of the 'whistle-blowers'.

(19) The institution shall ensure that private commercially managed lodges or hostels outside campuses must be registered with the local Police Authorities and permission to start such hostel or their registration must necessarily be recommended by the Heads of the Medical Institutions.

(20) In case the victim of ragging his/her parent/guardian is not satisfied with the action taken by the Head of the Institution or by other institutional authorities, or where Head of the institution is of the opinion that the incident ought to be so reported, it shall be mandatory for the institution to file a First Information Report with the local police authorities.

(21) It must be ensured by each of the institution that the complaints or information in regard to ragging could be oral or written and even from third parties and the confidentiality thereof must be protected at all costs.

(22) Each institution shall ensure that remedial action is initiated and completed within a week of the incident itself, so that complaints do not linger and allow either interest in pursuing the matter to vane or enable the culprits to tamper evidence or influence witnesses.

MINISTRY OF HUMAN RESOURCE DEVELOPMENT [MHRD]

The Ministry of Human Resource Development in consultation with the UGC, MCI and other regulatory bodies has set up a round-the clock anti-ragging helpline (Phone: 1800-180-5522; email:helpline@antiragging.net).[18] The helpline is currently operational in 10 languages since June, 2009. A web-based anti-ragging database has also been created which would store all complaints with respect to ragging along with the action taken.[19]

AMAN ALARM: A MOVEMENT

Dr. Rajendra Kachroo, father of late *Aman Kachroo*, a 19 year old medical student at RPGMC, Tanda (HP) who was beaten to death by his seniors, initiated a civil reform movement 'Aman Movement' to eradicate ragging from its roots and to demand speedy justice for his son.[20] This movement was launched on

18. *Supra note* 19.
19. *Ibid.*
20. More information about Aman Movement, available at *http://www.amanmovement.org*.

14th March, 2009 with a candle-light protest held at Jantar Mantar, New Delhi. Under this movement Prof. Kachroo designed a 'Call Centre Concept', which is the most cost efficient and cost effective model to combat the menace of ragging without depending on the sums of money. The concept has emerged out of the recommendations of the Raghavan Committee and from the regulations of the UGC.[21] It uses modern web and database management technology for direct communication with the students, their parents and the college administration.[22] This service can be accessible from any part of the country through all modes of communications. The concept has two salient features: (i) its application; and (ii) design.[23]

With the objective to ensure prevention of ragging, the contact centre shall provide these three types of professional services to its callers on 24x7x365 basis.

(i) The first and the most important is to report cases of ragging.

(ii) The second is to help those who do not have any access to a web site to get their affidavits.

(iii) The third service is to provide information on anti-ragging laws and on anti-ragging affidavits.[24]

Achievements of the Movement[25]

1. The Movement prepared a 'Technology based Plan' for eradication of ragging and got it approved from various authorities like—

(a) The Raghavan Committee;

(b) The University Grants Commission and other regulatory bodies;

(c) A committee of three Senior Lawyers nominated by the Supreme Court including the ASG;

(d) Technical Team of EdCil (India) Ltd.;

(e) Committee of 3 senior people dealing with telecommunications, web technologies and contact centre management.

2. The Hon. Supreme Court of India made the implementation of the plan developed by the Aman Movement mandatory for execution by the Union Government. This process has been already started. The help line was inaugurated on the 20th June, 2009. Work on monitoring and related data bases is going on.

3. Media comprising TV, Radio & Newspapers have been very co-operative but sustaining their interest and persuading them to continue with the movement is no mean task. The movement plans to have a nation wide TV campaign with the help of Door Darshan.

---

21. *Supra note 1*, p. 87.
22. *Ibid*, p. 88.
23. *Ibid*.
24. *Ibid*, p. 89.
25. Available at http://amanmovement.org/archive/achievement.htm, last accessed on 16th February 2014.

4. The founder trustee of the movement met with her Excellency, Smt. Pratiba Singh Patil, former President of India, who expressed her support for the movement. This meeting resulted in her Excellency writing to all Chancellors of Universities in the Country to take a pro-active role in the matter.

5. The founder trustee of the movement met with the Hon. Prime Minister, Dr. Manmohan Singh who assured him full support of the Government of India for this worthy cause.

6. The movement launched its awareness campaign by making a short film which was shown on Home Media LCD advertising TV's in shopping malls, Cinema Halls, Call Centres etc., for 2 weeks in all metro cities across the country.

7. The movement has launched a comprehensive web site which provides information on all matters concerning ragging. The movement will keep this web site continuously updated as more information keeps on coming in.

8. The movement has started launching a campaign of declaring several colleges 'RAGGING FREE' and publicize them widely. This initiative will encourage various colleges and their authorities to take a more active role in the matter.

Note:—Some States have come forward and taken the initiative to enact anti-ragging legislations in their respective territories which are discussed in detail in the next chapter.

Chapter V

Law on Ragging

ANTI- RAGGING LEGISLATIONS (ENACTED BY STATES)

In the recent years the act of ragging has intensified to such an extent that the governments at the state level have started enacting anti – ragging legislations, but only a few states have enacted legislations to deal with the issue, despite the fact that the incidents of ragging are reported from almost all the states of India. These legislations are:–

1. The Tripura Educational Institutions (Prevention of Ragging) Act, 1990
2. Tamil Nadu Prohibition of Ragging Act, 1997
3. Andhra Pradesh Prohibition of Ragging Act, 1997
4. The Kerala Prohibition of Ragging Act, 1998
5. Maharashtra Prohibition of Ragging Act, 1999
6. The West Bengal Prohibition of Ragging in Educational Institutions Act, 2000
7. Chhattisgarh Shaikshanik Sansthaon Me Pratarna Ka Pratishodh Adhiniyam, 2001
8. The Goa Prohibition of Ragging Act, 2008
9. The Himachal Pradesh Educational Institutions (Prohibition of Ragging) Act, 2009
10. The Uttar Pradesh Prohibition of Ragging in Educational Institutions Act, 2010
11. The Jammu and Kashmir Prohibition of Ragging Act, 2011

As far as other States and the Union Territories in India are concerned, ragging is banned but only through circulars and administrative orders.[1] For better understanding of the above anti–ragging legislations, a comparative analysis has been given below:—

---

1. Karnataka has not made anti ragging legislation, but section 116 of The Karnataka Education Act, 1983 talks about penalty for ragging. It stated that:—

   Penalty for ragging.—(1) No person who is a student in an educational institution including an institution under the direct management of the University or of the Central Government shall commit ragging.

   (2) Any person who contravenes sub-section (1) shall on conviction be punished with imprisonment for a term which may extent to one year or with fine which may extend to two thousand rupees or with both.

COMPARATIVE ANALYSIS OF STATE ANTI-RAGGING LEGISLATIONS

Parameter	Tripura (1990)	Tamil Nadu (1997)	Andhra Pradesh (1997)	Kerala (1998)	Assam (1998)	Maharashtra (1999)	West Bengal (2000)
Purpose	To prevent and eradicate the menace of ragging from the Educational Institutions.	To prohibit ragging in educational institutions.	To prohibit ragging in educational institutions.	To prohibit ragging.	To prohibit ragging in educational institutions.	To prohibit ragging in educational institutions.	To prohibit ragging in educational institutions.
Definition of Ragging	Ragging will mean the following kind of offence:- Whoever, being a student in any Educational Institution, causes a fellow student to suffer physically or mentally by way of assault, intimidation, insult, tease, torment or any other form of torture commits ragging.	Display of noisy, disorderly conduct doing any act which causes or is likely to cause physical or psychological harm or raise apprehension or fear or shame or embarrassment to a student.	Doing an act which causes or is likely to cause insult or annoyance of fear or apprehension or threat or intimidation or outrage of modesty or injury to a student.	Doing of any act, by disorderly conduct, to a student of an educational institution, which causes or is likely to cause physical or psychological harm or raising apprehension or fear or shame or embarrassment to that student.	Display of noisy or disorderly conduct or doing of any act which causes or likely to cause social, physical and psychological or raise apprehension or of fear or shame or embarrassment to any student.	Doing of any act which causes or is likely to cause physical or psychological harm or raise apprehension or fear or shame or embarrassment to a student.	Doing of any act, by disorderly conduct, to a student of an educational institution, which causes or is likely to cause physical or psychological harm or raising apprehension or fear or shame or embarrassment to that student.
Scheme of Prevention	As mentioned in Statement of Object & Reasons.	Section 3 prohibits ragging.	----	Section 3 prohibits ragging.	Section 3 prohibits ragging.	Section 3 prohibits ragging.	Section 3 prohibits ragging.
Institutional Mechanism /Official	Not mentioned.	Head or Manager in case of *prima facie*.	Head or Manager in case of *prima facie*.	Head in case of *prima facie*.	Head in case of *prima facie*.	Head in case of *prima facie*.	Head or manager.
Appellate form	Not mentioned.	Not mentioned.	Not mentioned.	Not mentioned.	Commissioner or secretary to Govt. of Assam.	Not mentioned.	Committee constituted by the State Government whose decision shall be final.

	1	2	3	4	5	6	7
Penalty (a) Offender (b) Institution	(a) Imprisonment of either description for a term which may extend to four years or with fine or with both. And such student shall cease to be a student of that Institution and he shall be deemed to have been expelled from the Institution with effect from the date of his conviction. (b) Not mentioned.	(a) Imprisonment upto 2 yrs and fine upto Rs. 10,000 dismissal from the educational institution and denial of admission in any other educational institution for a period of 2 years from the date of order of such dismissal, suspension. (b) Same as in (a) for head or manager in case of default.	(a) Imprisonment upto six months or with fine upto Rs. 1000 or with both (b) Same as in (c) for head or manager in case of default.	(a) Imprisonment upto 2 yrs and fine upto Rs. 10,000 dismissal from the educational institution and denial of admission in any other educational institution for a period of 3 years from the date of order of such dismissal, suspension. (b) Same as in (a) for head or manager in case of default.	(a) Imprisonment upto 6 months or fine upto 10,000 or both; expulsion or rustication for not less than one academic session. (b) in accordance with the rule of the government for the time being in force.	(a) Imprisonment upto 2 yrs and fine upto Rs. 10,000 dismissal from the educational institution and denial of admission in any other educational institution for a period of 5 years from the date of order of such dismissal, suspension. (b) Same as in (a) for head or manager in case of default.	(a) Imprisonment upto 2 yrs and fine upto Rs. 5,000 dismissal from the educational institution and debarred from the readmission in the same institution. (b) not mentioned.
Nature of Offence	As given in the definition.	As in the definition and including teasing, abusing, playing practical jokes, causing hurt, coercion into wrongful acts.	Teasing or embarrassing or humiliation, assaults or uses criminal force or criminal intimidation, wrongful restraint, causing grievous hurt, kidnapping, abduction, rape, causing death, abetting suicide.	As in the definition and including teasing, abusing, playing practical jokes, causing hurt, coercion into wrongful acts.	Committing, participating, abetting propagating, teasing, abusing, playing practical jokes, causing hurt, coercion into wrongful acts.	As in the definition and including teasing, abusing, playing practical jokes, causing hurt, coercion into wrongful acts.	As in the definition and including teasing, abusing, playing practical jokes, causing hurt, coercion into wrongful acts.
Whether Compoundable/ Cognizable /Bailable	Cognizable and non-bailable.	Not mentioned.	Not mentioned.	Not mentioned. ↓	Compoundable, bailable.	Not mentioned.	Not mentioned.

[Although, High Court of Kerala, in 2011 in *Ahammed Manaf* v. *Sub-Inspector of Police*, had directed Public Prosecutor to bring to the notice of the government, to make appropriate amendment to the Act making the offence under section 4, a cognizable offence.]

Parameter	Chhattisgarh (2001)	Goa (2008)	Himachal Pradesh (2009)	Uttar Pradesh (2010)	Jammu & Kashmir (2011)
Purpose	To prevent ragging.	To prohibit ragging in educational institutions.	To provide for prevention of the evil practice of ragging in educational institutions.	To provide for the prohibition of ragging in educational institutions and for matters connected therewith or incidental thereto.	To prohibit ragging in educational institutions.
Definition of Ragging	Causing, inducing, compelling or forcing a student by way of a practical joke or otherwise to do any act which detracts from human dignity or violates his person or expose him to ridicule or forbear from doing any unlawful act intimidating wrongfully restraining, wrongfully confining, and injuring him, or holing out to him any threat or such intimidation, wrongful restraint, wrongful confinement, injury or the injury of use of force.	Any disorderly conduct, whether by words spoken or written or by an act which has the effect of teasing, treating or handling with rudeness any other student indulging in rowdy or indisciplined activities which causes or is likely to cause annoyance, hardship or psychological harm or to raise fear or apprehension thereof in a fresher or a junior student or asking the student to do any act or perform something which such student will not do in the ordinary course and which has the effect of causing or generating a sense of shame or embarrassment or adversely affect the physique or psyche of a fresher or a junior student	"Ragging" means any act, conduct or practice by which dominant power of senior students, former students or outsiders, is brought to bear on students freshly enrolled or students who are in any way considered junior by other students and includes individual or collective acts or practices which- (i) involve physical or psychological assault or threat or use of force or wrongful confinement or restraint; or (ii) violate the status, dignity and honour of such students; or (iii) expose students to ridicule and contempt and affect their self-esteem; or (iv) entail verbal abuse and aggression, indecent gestures and obscene behaviour	"Ragging" means asking a student to do or perform something, causing, inducing, compelling or forcing a student by way of either by words or sign or signal to do any act which detracts from human dignity or violates his person in any way or holding out to him ridicule, intimidating, wrongfully restraining, wrongfully confining and injuring him or holding out to him any threat or intimidation, wrongful restrain, wrongful confinement, injuring or the use of criminal force.	"Ragging" means any disorderly conduct, whether by words spoken or written, or by an act which has the effect of teasing, treating or handling with rudeness any other student, indulging in rowdy or undisciplined activities which causes or is likely to cause annoyance, hardship or psychological harm or to raise fear or apprehension thereof in a fresher or a junior student, or asking the student to do any act or perform something which such student will not do in the ordinary course and which has the effect of causing or generating a

	1	2	3	4	5
					sense of shame or embarrass-ment or adverse affect on the physique or psyche of a fresher, or a junior student.
Scheme of Prevention	Section 3 prohibits ragging.	Section 3 & 4 prohibit ragging.	Section 3 prohibits ragging.	Section 3 prohibits ragging.	Section 3 & 9 prohibit ragging.
Institutional Mechanism/ Official	Head in case of *prima facie* & Magistrate of the First Class.	Headed by the head of the institution and includes representatives of civil and police administration, local media, Non-Government Organizations involved in youth activities, representatives of faculty members, representatives of parents, representatives of freshers, seniors and non-teaching staff.	Every person who is the Officer-in-Charge of the educational institution or who is in the service or pay of or remune-rated by the educational institution to do any work assigned to him in connection with the maintenance of discipline therein.	Head in case of *prima facie.*	Head in case of *prima facie.*
Appellate form	Not-mentioned.	Not-mentioned.	Not-mentioned.	Divisional Commissioner (in case of College or School imparting education upto secondary level) or Vice Chancellor (in case of affiliated degree college) or Chancellor (in case of University).	Not-mentioned.

	1	2	3	4	5
Penalty (a) Offender (b) Institution	(a) Imprisonment upto 5 years or with fine which may extend to five thousand rupees or with both (b) not mentioned.	**(a) Any student so convicted shall further be removed from the roll of the educational** institution and such students shall not be admitted in any other educational institution in the State of Goa for a period of three years from the date of such conviction. The punishment may also take the shape of: (i) Withholding scholarships or other benefits; (ii) Debarring from representation in events; (iii) Withholding results; and (iv) Suspension or expulsion from College or hostel or mess, and the like. (b) If, the Head of the educational institution fails or neglects to take action in the manner specified hereinabove in sub-section (1) when a complaint of ragging is made, such person shall be deemed to have abetted the offence of ragging and shall be made personally accountable and liable for disciplinary proceedings before the authority competent to conduct such proceedings.	(a) Imprisonment for a term which may extend to three years or with fine which may extend to fifty thousand rupees or with both and such student shall be expelled otherwise on account of ragging shall not be admitted in any other educational institution for a period of three years from the date of order of such expulsion. (b) imprisonment for a term which may extend to one year or with fine which may extend to ten thousand rupees, or with both.	(a) Imprisonment of wither description of for a term which may extend to two years or with fine which may extend to ten thousand rupees or with both. And such student shall not be admitted in any educational institution for a period which may extend to five years from the date of order of debarring. (b) Not mentioned.	(a) Section 4: imprisonment for a term which may extend to two years or with fine which may extend to ten thousand rupees or with both. If the particular person committing or abetting ragging is not identified, every person participating in, or present at, such ragging activity shall be liable to punishment under the Act and collective punishment shall be resorted to so as to act as a deterrent punishment and to ensure collective pressure on the potential raggers. And shall be removed from rolls of the educational institution and shall not be admitted in any educational institution in the State for a period of three years from the date of such removal. (b) he shall

	1	2	3	4	5
					be deemed to have abetted the offence of ragging and shall, on conviction, be punished as provided for in section 4.
Nature of Offence	As given in the definition.	Directly or indirectly, commission, participates in, abetment or propagation.	As given in the definition.	As given in the definition.	As given in the definition.
Whether Compoun-dable/ Cognizable/ Bailable	Non-compoundable, Cognizable, non-bailable.	Not-mentioned.	Compoundable with the permission of the court, cognizable, non-bailable.	Not-mentioned.	Not-mentioned.

COMMON ESSENTIAL FEATURES OF STATE LEGISLATIONS

The common essential features of the aforementioned legislations are:—

1. Define ragging more or less in the similar tone.
2. Provide for setting up of Disciplinary Committees for taking immediate and effective steps against ragging.
3. Ragging is generally declared to be a cognizable and non-bailable offence. Only Assam has made it a bailable offence.
4. They provide imprisonment but it varies from State to State for example, Andhra Pradesh provides imprisonment only upto 6 months whereas J&K provides imprisonment upto 10 years. On the other hand Goa's State Legislation is silent on the provision of imprisonment.
5. The general scheme of the existing State laws casts a duty on the Head of the Institution to prohibit ragging. The Head is not to be a mute spectator and has to conduct an enquiry on the receipt of any complaint and has to take action thereon.[2]

LACUNAE IN STATE LEGISLATIONS

1. Prohibition v. Prevention

There are very few States in India that have enacted comprehensive laws with respect to ragging but even those few existing State laws are lacking in provisions intended to prevent ragging because all State laws merely seek to

2. The Menace of Ragging in Educational Institutions and Measures to Curb It, Report of the Committee constituted by the Hon'ble Supreme Court of India in SLP No. 24295 of 2006, headed by R.K. Raghavan, para 3.16.

'prohibit' ragging except Tripura, Chhattisgarh (although does not really address the concern of prevention) and Himachal Pradesh.[3]

Broadly prohibition and prevention may appear to be intended to achieve the same purpose but there is a subtle difference between both. While prevention must lead to prohibition, the reverse need not be true. Prevention implies anticipating the problem of ragging, forestalling the occurrence of it, taking precautionary measures to make it difficult if not impossible to take place. Such law helps in becoming a facilitator in enforcing the prohibition of the menace of ragging.[4] On the other hand, prohibition is just intended to authoritatively forbid or restrain the act of ragging. The subtle difference lies in the fact that while prohibition of ragging is a top-down approach where the law can be cryptic, any law on prevention is more participative with a bottom-up approach laying down the detailed mechanism of preventive measures and instrumentalities.[5] A law which is prohibitive emphasizes on the consequences of violating the prohibition and therefore builds on the procedures and instrumentalities of punishment, while a law which is preventive in comparison would provide for the procedures and instrumentalities of strengthening the prevention of the offence. For our broad purposes of weeding out the menace of ragging, any law must contain elements of both prevention and prohibition and it can be said that in the absence of any statutory provision in this regard it is easy to imagine that there is hardly any compulsion on authorities or institutions to take preventive measures.[6]

2. No Implementation

Although some of the States have made anti-ragging legislations, but even these have not been implemented properly. Raghavan Committee had analyzed 198 incidents of ragging occurred between the years 1998 and 2007, from the compilation forwarded by CURE. The purpose was to see whether enactment of State laws since 1997 had been effective in curbing the menace and incidence of ragging.[7] Tamil Nadu and Andhra Pradesh were among the first States to enact a dedicated legislation way back in 1997 to prohibit ragging. ***[Note: Here author wants to bring to the notice of readers that Raghavan Committee failed to appreciate an important fact about the Tripura anti-ragging legislation which came in year 1990 only and was indeed the first anti-ragging legislation in the country.***] But, surprisingly Andhra Pradesh happened to have the largest number of reported incidents of ragging (23) during the period which was under review. West Bengal was yet another State with its law (enacted in 2000) against ragging, where the third highest incidents of ragging (16) were reported in that period of time.[8] Maharashtra enacted a State law in the year 1999 and Kerala did so in 1998; both States had recorded 14 incidents each – the fourth highest among

3. *Ibid.*
4. *Ibid*, para 3.15.
5. *Ibid.*
6. *Ibid.*
7. *Ibid*, para 3.21.
8. *Ibid.*

all the States in the period which was under review.[9] Still, hundreds of cases of ragging are reported every year from almost all parts of the country which shows that till now these anti-ragging legislations have not been implemented properly.

So there is a need of effective implementation of existing anti-ragging legislations, and for this educational institutions and police should be reoriented to use these legislations.[10] However, the Hon'ble Supreme Court of India has warned against undue intervention of police in educational institutions and only in grave and extra-ordinary situations (sexual abuse and death etc.) police should intervene. Otherwise for general cases, these laws must make provisions for internal settlement, without allowing any role to police.[11]

3. No Delegated Legislations/ Rules

In order to be effective, statutory provisions have to be followed up with appropriate delegated legislations or rules, which empower the instrumentalities of the State or institutional authorities to enforce the laws but the Raghavan Committee did not come across with any notification of rules or regulations.[12]

PRIVATE MEMBER BILLS

Even after the seven decades of our independence from the hostility of the colonial rulers our leaders have failed to free us from the hands of bad practice of ragging and till now we do not have any Central legislation on anti-ragging. Although, some initiatives have been taken in the last decade in the Parliament in the form of private member Bills which are as follows:—

1. Prevention of Ragging in Colleges and Institutions Bill, 2005[13]

The Bill is aimed at prevention of ragging in colleges and institutions and intends to build ragging-free campuses for the matters connected therewith.[14] Ragging means display of disorderly conduct, doing of any act which causes or is likely to cause physical or psychological harm or raise apprehension or fear or shame or embarrassment to a student in any college or institution.[15]

Task Force: For the active implementation of this Bill, a task force or a special unit under the respective local police department shall be constituted at the time of admission and start of the first quarter of the academic session.[16] The task force shall comprise of both young policemen and women which shall be headed by a person not below the rank of a Police Inspector of the area in

9. *Ibid.*
10. Anant Kumar Asthana, Eradication of Ragging: Realities and Recommendations a legal Perspective, CURE Report: CR2007/03-03, available at http://noragging.com/index.php/Research/Reports/Ragging-and-Human-Rights.html, last accessed on 16th February, 2014.
11. *Ibid.*
12. *Supra note* 2, para 3.17.
13. Prevention of Ragging in Colleges and Institutions Bill 2005, Introduced in 2005 by Congress's Rajya Sabha MP Santosh Bagrodia.
14. *Ibid,* Statement of object and reasons.
15. *Ibid.,* section 2(e).
16. *Ibid,* Section 5(1).

districts/towns/small cities for State-level.[17] The task force would present the facts and figures of each ragging case and details of action taken against each case to their respective Commissioner of Police.[18] The task force shall have the following duties:[19]

(a) Intimate the managements of all the Colleges and the Institutions in their campus areas of their objectives.

(b) Ensure compliance of all the Rules made under this Act.

(c) To move around in civil clothes and whenever required, in uniforms.

(d) Ensure the safety of all the staff and students (both freshers and seniors) in and around the campus area.

(e) Maintain strict secrecy and impartiality during exercises, operations and investigations.

(f) Follow out number of surveillance exercises on campus areas.

(g) Make surprise checks in any and all Colleges and Institutions to keep a check on ragging.

(h) Make surprise checks in the hostels.

(i) To be in constant touch with the staff and consult on various ragging incidences in their respective College or Institution.

(j) Take inputs from various people including staff and freshers on any incident that comes to light.

(k) To give necessary support in terms of maintaining secrecy, moral, mental, medical, etc., to all students who have been victims of ragging.

(l) After thorough investigation, consider reports or complaints of parents of victims against any senior(s).

(m) To issue one formal warning after asserting the identity of any senior(s) either caught red handed or on a formal complaint by a junior or fresher against ragging.

(n) To intimate the management of that college about the warning of the student(s) on charges of ragging.

(o) After the warning if the same senior(s) indulge(s) in ragging or harassing, officers of the Task Force will make an arrest and inform the college of the arrest.

Critical Analysis:

1. This Bill empowers the government or its agencies such as the University Grants Commission (UGC) to penalise institutes which fail to take steps to curb ragging.

---

17. *Ibid,* Section 5 (5).
18. *Ibid,* Section 6 (1).
19. *Ibid,* Section 5 (5).

2. It empowers Central and State Governments to set-up task forces to monitor the implementation of the anti-ragging laws and take necessary action against any violation.
3. This Bill contains preventive mechanism.
4. There is no provision of punishment for guilty student.
5. This Bill does not encompass the procedure for filing a complaint.
6. No provision regarding the penalty in case the head of the institution or any other person fails to inquire into the incident of ragging.
7. No provision regarding compensation to the victim.
8. No provision of anti-ragging committee and anti-ragging squad.
9. No provision of anti-ragging helpline.

2. The Prohibition and Eradication of Ragging Bill, 2011[20]

The Bill is aimed at both, to prohibit and to eradicate ragging in colleges and educational institutions and for matters connected therewith and incidental thereto.[21] It extends to the whole of India including J&K. This Bill covers all institutions coming within the definition of a university under sub-section (*f*) of Section 2 of the University Grants Commission Act, 1956, and to all institutions deemed to be a university under Section 3 of the University Grants Commission Act, 1956, to all other higher educational institutions, or elements of such universities or institutions, including its departments, constituent units and all the premises, whether being academic, residential, playgrounds, canteen, hostel or other such premises of such universities, deemed universities and higher educational institutions, whether located within the campus or outside, and to all means of transportation of students, whether public or private, accessed by students for the pursuit of studies in such universities, deemed universities and higher educational institutions.[22]

Definition of ragging: Under this act, ragging shall be one or more of the following acts:[23]

(*i*) Any conduct by any student or students whether by words spoken or written or by an act which has the effect of teasing, treating, torturing, or handling with rudeness a fresher or any other student;

(*ii*) Indulging in rowdy or indiscipline activities by a student or students which causes or is likely to cause annoyance, hardship, physical or psychological harm or to raise fear or apprehension thereof in any fresher or any other student;

(*iii*) Asking any student to do any act which such student shall not in the ordinary course do and which has the effect of causing or generating a sense of shame, or torment or embarrassment so as to adversely affect the physique or psyche of such fresher or any other student;

20. The Prohibition and Eradication of Ragging Bill 2011, Bill No. XXVII of 2011, Introduced in Rajya Sabha on 19th August, 2011 by NCP's Rajya Sabha MP Janardhan Waghmare.
21. *Ibid*, Long title.
22. *Ibid*, section 3(1).
23. *Ibid*, Section 4.

(*iv*) Any act by a student that prevents, disrupts or disturbs the regular academic activity of any other student or a fresher;

(*v*) Exploiting the services of a fresher or any other student for completing the academic tasks assigned to an individual or a group of students;

(*vi*) Any act of financial extortion or forceful expenditure burden put on a fresher or any other student by students;

(*vii*) Any act of physical abuse including all variants of it; sexual abuse, homosexual assaults, stripping, forcing obscene and lewd acts, gestures, causing bodily harm or any other danger to health or person;

(*viii*) Any act or abuse, by use of spoken words, telephone, short-message service (SMS), e-mails, multi-media messaging service, post, public insults, pornographic material, photographs or video clips, etc., to derive perverted pleasure, vicarious or sadistic thrill from actively or passively participating in the discomfiture to fresher or any other student;

(*ix*) Any act that affects the mental health and self-confidence of a fresher or any other student with or without an intent to derive a sadistic pleasure or showing-off power, authority or superiority by a student over any fresher or any other student.

It seems that this Bill has the wider approach towards ragging. The burden of the proof as to the innocence shall be on the accused.[24] Under this Bill, Central Government has to formulate such directives for prohibition of ragging in all the colleges and educational institutions functioning under Central Government within the period of six months from the date of commencement of this Act and shall issue directives to all State Governments for prohibition of ragging in all colleges and educational institutions in their respective jurisdiction.[25]

Anti-ragging committee: Unlike previous Bill, under this Bill an anti-ragging committee is to be constituted in every educational institution headed by the senior most faculty of the institution and consisting of the representatives of civil society and police administration including at least one female representative. It would also include representation from non-governmental organisations, parents, freshers and seniors.[26] The anti-ragging committee shall receive complaints on ragging and submit a report to the head of the institution, take inputs from various people including staff and freshers on any incident of ragging and conduct necessary awareness programme to enlighten the students regarding the effects of ragging.[27]

Anti-ragging squad: There shall be an anti-ragging squad in every educational institution which shall function under the guidance of anti-ragging committee consisting of the representatives nominated by the head of the

24. *Ibid,* Section 5.
25. *Ibid,* Sections 6(1) & 6(2).
26. *Ibid,* Section 7(1).
27. *Ibid,* Section 7(3).

educational institution.[28] The anti-ragging squad shall make surprise checks in hostel and campus to keep a check on ragging, report any incident of ragging to the committee and shall be in constant touch with the staff and students and consult various incidences of ragging.[29]

Anti-ragging helpline: There shall be an anti-ragging helpline in the country which will be operative round the clock, to register complaints from students, parents, friends or anybody who is a witness to the act of ragging. The telephone numbers of the helpline and other functionaries in the district shall be published by every educational institution.[30]

Punishment: Any student convicted under this Act shall be debarred from continuing his studies in any educational institution for a period of three years.[31] Also, any person who contravenes provisions of this Act shall be punished with fine which shall not be less than rupees twenty-five thousand but which may extend to rupees one lakh or with rigorous imprisonment for a term which may extend to three years or, with both.[32]

Critical Analysis:

1. The bill has wider approach towards ragging.
2. The Bill has prohibitory as well as preventive mechanism.
3. Provision of anti-ragging committee & anti-ragging squad.
4. Provision of anti-ragging helpline.
5. There is no provision of providing compensation to the victim of ragging.
6. No provision regarding penalty in case the head of the institution or any other person fails to inquire into the incident of ragging.

3. Prohibition of Ragging and Unfair Practices in Educational Institutions and Universities Bill 2012[33]

Last but not the least in the series of private member Bills, this Bill provides for prohibition of ragging as well as unfair practices incidental to ragging in educational institutions and universities.[34] Under this Bill, the head of the institution or any other person responsible for the management of the educational institution shall, upon notice of any act of ragging, enquire the matter expeditiously.[35]

Definition of ragging: The Bill envisages wider definition of ragging. It covers an act by a student or group of students inside or outside the educational institution which causes or is likely to cause physical or psychological harm or

28. *Ibid*, Sections 8(1) & section (2).
29. *Ibid*, Section 8(3).
30. *Ibid*, Section 9(2).
31. *Ibid*, Section 10(1).
32. *Ibid*, Section 10(2).
33. Prohibition of Ragging and Unfair Practices in Educational Institutions and Universities Bill 2012, Introduced by Shri Rakesh Singh, M.P.
34. *Ibid*, long title.
35. *Ibid*, Section s 4(1).

bring embarrassment to or creates fear in another student and includes acts of teasing, abusing, causing hurt or making one to do any act or perform something which he will not willingly do in the ordinary course.[36]

Punishment: If any student is found guilty of committing or participating in or abetting the act of ragging in such enquiry, such student shall be expelled from the educational institution and shall not be admitted in any other educational institution.[37]

Appellate Authority: If the student so expelled is not satisfied by the findings of the inquiry and such findings are disputed by him, the enquiry report shall be forwarded to the Redressal Committee which is the appellate authority.[38] It shall be consisted of seven members. One of them shall be Chairperson, two judicial members, two academic members and two administrative members.[39] The primary function of the Committee is to inquire into every case of ragging transferred by the educational institutions or received directly from any aggrieved person or any other person on behalf of such person.[40] The Committee shall dispose of every complaint within a period of ninety days from the date of receipt of such complaint.[41] It shall afford an opportunity of being heard to every person or institution against whom a complaint is made.[42] After the conclusion of the inquiry, the Committee shall recommend punitive action against the erring educational institution and also recommend compensation to the victims of ragging or unfair practices by the institution concerned.[43] After completion of the inquiry, the Committee shall forward its report of enquiry to the appropriate statutory authority, which shall recommend such action against the institution.[44]

Critical Analysis:-

1. Provision of appeal to redressal committee and then to appropriate statutory authority.
2. Provision regarding compensation to the victim.
3. There is no provision regarding prevention of ragging.
4. There is no provision of imprisonment or fine in case the guilt of the student is proved.
5. No provision regarding penalty in case head of the institution or any other person fails to inquire into the incident of ragging.
6. No provision of anti-ragging committee and anti-ragging squad.
7. No provision of anti-ragging helpline.

---

36. *Ibid,* Section 2 (f).
37. *Ibid,* Section 4 (2).
38. *Ibid,* Section 4 (3).
39. *Ibid,* Section 11.
40. *Ibid,* Section 12 (1) (i).
41. *Ibid,* Section (2).
42. *Ibid,* Section (3).
43. *Ibid,* Sections (1) (iii), (1) (iv).
44. *Ibid,* Section (4).

Although, such Private Member Bills have been introduced in Parliament from time to time but to no avail. Till now no Bill has been passed on this issue. They have been either withdrawn or got lapsed.

NEED OF COMPREHENSIVE LAW[45]

Although some States have already promulgated anti-ragging law but what we need now is a comprehensive law having applicability across the whole nation enacted by the Parliament of India. In view of this following are the recommendations:—

1. A centralized comprehensive Anti-Ragging Act should be enacted.
2. (i) An amendment should be made in Indian Penal Code to include a chapter on *"Offences Related To Ragging"* wherein ragging should be made a cognizable, non-bailable, non-compoundable offence with punishment ranging from one year imprisonment to 7 years rigorous imprisonment and fine. Broadly, ragging can be categorized in following ways for which various terms of punishment should be prescribed:

    (A) Verbal: Where senior causes mental harassment, discomfort to junior by forcing her/him to answer unacceptable/personal questions, dance, sing etc., is said to rag the junior. It also includes within its ambit cyber ragging.

    Punishment: 1 year imprisonment or fine or both.

    (B) Severe Verbal Ragging: Where the mental harassment, discomfort is to such an act as forces the junior to withdraw from the college.

    Punishment: 7 year imprisonment with fine.

    (C) Physical: Any act by the senior towards the junior which inflicts bodily injury on the junior. Like beating the junior, hitting her/him with objects etc.

    Punishment: 7 year imprisonment with fine.

    (D) Sexual Ragging: where the senior asks the junior to do an act which damages sexual dignity of the junior.

    Punishment: 7 year rigorous imprisonment and fine.

    (ii) All kinds of ragging cases should be decided in a time bound manner by fast track courts, keeping in mind the student mobility and burden of syllabus completion.

    (iii) Pending the enactment and amendment in IPC, some guidelines may be made available to the institutional authorities whereby the institutions can draw some measures to check ragging. Court may also lay down guidelines within which the authorities have to function, making it more feasible for the victim to pursue her/his case under general sections in IPC.

It will do a great help if all these State legislations and Circulars are replaced by a Central Law, applicable to the whole of India.

---

45. Based on "Recommendation by the Group of Consultants", Annexure – V of Raghavan Committee.

Chapter VI

Ragging and the Legal Provisions

Students who indulge in ragging know very well that they can roam around caught free despite committing a very heinous crime. In the highly improbable event of being caught, they are suspended for some time or in the worst case, they might be expelled. These criminals with sadist tendencies go about their whole lives without any fear of punishment for which the whole society pays the price. So it is high time that these criminals are brought to justice.[1]

GENERAL FORMS OF PUNISHMENT[2]

If a senior is caught doing ragging then she/he may get one or more of the following punishments from college:—

- Her/his admission may be cancelled;
- Her/his result may be withheld;
- She/he may be debarred from representing the institution in any national or international meet, tournament, youth festival etc.;
- Suspension/expulsion from the hostel/mess;
- She/he may be banned/debarred from attending classes;
- Scholarship/fellowship/stipend/financial grant and other benefits may be withdrawn/cancelled by the university and;
- She/he may be debarred from appearing in future tests/examinations of university or other evaluation process.

PUNISHMENT PROVIDED UNDER LAW

Although there are some general forms of punishment which have been listed above but still there is a need of penal provisions because general forms of punishment cannot be the substitutes of the penal provisions of law. They are only in addition to the punishments that are handed out under the Indian Penal Code.[3] Any student of 18 years of age or above is treated as an adult for the purpose of criminal law that is why the students should not have a misconception that their "student" status at an academic institution might help them to get away without being punished. The Raghavan Committee

1. Available at http://www.competitionmaster.com/ArticleDetail.aspx?ID=2654af17-85a1-4584-8c02-18018fdf75e9, last accessed on 16th February, 2014.
2. Based on, The Menace of Ragging in Educational Institutions and Measures to Curb It, Report of the Committee constituted by the Hon'ble Supreme Court of India In SLP No. 24295 of 2006, headed by R.K. Raghavan.
3. *Ibid*, para 5.47.

had discussed following provisions of the Indian penal code which might get attracted in the case of ragging. For example -

- Whosoever abets the punishable ingredient offences of ragging attracts the provisions **(Section 107 onwards) under Chapter V;**
- Senior students conspiring to commit the offences attract the **provisions (Section 120A and 120B) of Chapter VA;**
- Incidents of ragging leading to unlawful assembly or rioting and promoting enmity *vis a vis* 'freshers' or hiring outside elements for the purpose of rioting or unlawful assembly clearly attract **Chapter VIII (Sections 141 onwards);**
- Parading 'freshers' in the nude or making them sing obscene songs or act lewdly are offences that are a public nuisance, affect decency and morals covered under **Chapter XIV;**
- Offences affecting the human body under **Chapter XVI** of the Code, varying as can be discerned from offences causing hurt, wrongful restraint, wrongful confinement, use of criminal force, assault as well as sexual offences or even unnatural offences;
- Extortion from 'freshers' or mischief by seniors committed after preparation is made for causing hurt of the 'freshers', criminal trespass by senior students, in to the wing of the hostel or rooms where entry of seniors is barred, with the intention to cause hurt or intimidate the 'freshers' would attract **Chapter XVII** dealing with offences against property;
- Criminal intimidation of juniors by the seniors during the act of ragging attracts the provisions of **Chapter XXII** of the Code and lastly,
- **Section 511 in Chapter XXIII** is attracted in all cases of attempts to commit the offences punishable with imprisonment under the Code.[4]

Before, we discuss these important sections in detail; we need to understand the legal terms used here. Thus, the terms have been explained in the following way:—

KINDS OF OFFENCES

1. Cognizable & Non-Cognizable Offences

- **Cognizable offence**[5]
    - A police officer can arrest without a warrant.
    - A police officer can investigate without the order of magistrate.
    - Example: Wrongful confinement, wrongful restraint etc.
- **Non-Cognizable offence**[6]
    - A police officer cannot arrest without a warrant.
    - A police officer cannot investigate without the order of a Magistrate.
    - Example: Criminal Intimidation etc.

4. *Ibid*, para 4.17.
5. Section 2 (c) of CrPC.
6. Section 2 (l) of CrPC.

2. Bailable & Non-Bailable Offences

- **Bailable offence**[7]
    - The arrested accused is entitled to get bail as a matter of right.
    - Example: voluntarily causing grievous hurt etc.
- **Non-Bailable offence**[8]
    - The arrested accused is not entitled to get bail as a matter of right.
    - The accused can apply to the court for bail, the court has the power to grant or refuse bail.
    - Example: murder, voluntarily causing grievous hurt by dangerous weapons or means, etc.

3. Compoundable and Non-Compoundable Offences [Section 320 of the Cr.P.C.]

- **Compoundable offence**
    - The injured party/complainant and the accused can enter into a settlement.
    - Compounding has the effect of an acquittal.
    - Example: Wrongful restraint, voluntarily causing hurt by dangerous weapons or means, etc.
- **Non-Compoundable offence**
    - No settlement can be entered into between the injured party/complainant and the accused.
    - Example: voluntarily causing grievous hurt by dangerous weapons or means etc.

4. Summons-Triable & Warrant-Triable Offences

- **Summons-Triable offence**[9]
    - Offences punishable with less than two years of imprisonment.
    - Example: Voluntarily causing hurt, etc.
- **Warrant-Triable offence**[10]
    - Offences punishable with more than two years of imprisonment.
    - Example: Voluntarily causing hurt by dangerous weapons or means, etc.

SPECIFIC SECTIONS UNDER THE INDIAN PENAL CODE (IPC)

(Extracts from the Indian Penal Code, 1860)

If a senior is caught doing ragging then she/he may attract following sections. For better understanding, these sections have been divided into three parts. These are:—

---

7. Section 2 (a) of CrPC.
8. Section 2 (a) of CrPC.
9. Section 2 (w) of CrPC.
10. Section 2 (x) of CrPC.

[A] MINOR COMPLAINTS AGAINST RAGGING:

If there is a minor complaint against ragging then following sections may get attracted:—

1. Section 294 - Obscene acts and songs —

When a person, to the annoyance of others does any obscene act in any public place, or sings, recites or utters any obscene song, ballad or words, in or near any public place then -

Punishment—Imprisonment for 3 months, or fine, or both—Cognizable—Bailable—Triable by any Magistrate—Non-compoundable.

2. Section 341- Punishment for wrongful restraint[11]-

Punishment—Simple imprisonment for 1 month, or fine of 500 rupees, or both—Cognizable—Bailable—Triable by any Magistrate—Compoundable by the person restrained or confined.

3. Section 342 - Punishment for wrongful confinement[12]—

Punishment—Imprisonment for 1 year, or fine of 1,000 rupees, or both—Cognizable—Bailable—Triable by any Magistrate—Compoundable by the person restrained or confined.

4. Section 506 - Punishment for criminal intimidation[13]—

Para I: Punishment—Imprisonment for 2 years, or fine, or both—Non-cognizable, Bailable—Triable by any Magistrate—Compoundable by the person intimidated.

Para II: Punishment—Imprisonment for 7 years, or fine, or both—Non-cognizable, Bailable—Triable by Magistrate of the first class—Non-compoundable.

---

11. Section 339 of IPC defines **"Wrongful restraint"** - A person shall be liable for wrongful restraint when he voluntarily obstructs any person so as to prevent that person from proceeding in any direction in which that person has a right to proceed.
    Illustration:
    A obstructs a path along which Z has a right to pass. *A* not believing in good faith that he has a right to stop the path. Z is thereby prevented from passing. *A* wrongfully restrains Z.
12. Section 340 of IPC defines **"Wrongful confinement"**—A person is said to have committed offence of wrongful confinement when he wrongfully restrains any person in such a manner as to prevent that person from proceedings beyond certain circumscribing limits.
    Illustrations:
    (a) *A* causes Z to go within a walled space, and locks Z in. *A* is thus prevented from proceeding in any direction beyond the circumscribing line of wall. *A* wrongfully confines Z.
    (b) *A* places men with firearms at the outlets of a building, and tells Z that they will fire at Z if Z attempts to leave the building. *A* wrongfully confines Z.
13. Section 503 of IPC defines "**Criminal intimidation**".—Whoever threatens another with any injury to his person, reputation or property, or to the person or reputation of any one in whom that person is interested, with intent to cause alarm to that person, or to cause that person to do any act which he is not legally bound to do, or to omit to do any act which that person is legally entitled to do, as the means of avoiding the execution of such threat, commits criminal intimidation.
    Explanation:
    A threat to injure the reputation of any deceased person in whom the person threatened is interested, is within this section.
    Illustration:
    A, for the purpose of inducing *B* to resist from prosecuting a civil suit, threatens to burn *B's* house. *A* is guilty of criminal intimidation.

(This is applicable if threat is to cause death or grievous hurt, or to cause destruction of any property by fire, to impute chastity of woman, or to cause an offence punishable with death or imprisonment for life, or with imprisonment for a term which may extend to seven years)

S. No.	Section	Offence	Punishment	Cognizable/ Non-Cognizable	Bailable/ Non-Bailable	Compoundable/ Non-Compoundable
1.	294	Obscene Acts and Songs	Imprisonment for 3 months or fine or both	Cognizable	Bailable	Non-Compoundable
2.	341	Punishment for Wrongful Restraint	Simple Imprisonment for 1 month or fine or both	Cognizable	Bailable	Compoundable
3.	342	Punishment for Wrongful Confinement	Imprisonment for 1 year or fine of 1,000 rupees or both	Cognizable	Bailable	Compoundable
4.	506 (Para1)	Punishment for Criminal intimidation	Imprisonment for 2 years or fine or both	Non-Cognizable	Bailable	Compoundable
5.	506 (para2)	Punishment for Criminal intimidation	Imprisonment for 7 years or fine or both	Non-Cognizable	Bailable	Non-Compoundable

[B] MAJOR COMPLAINTS AGAINST RAGGING:

If there is a major complaint against ragging then following sections may get attracted:—

1. Section 323 – Punishment for voluntarily causing hurt[14]—

When a person voluntarily causes hurt he shall be punished with imprisonment of either description for a term which may extend to one year, or with fine which may extend to one thousand rupees, or with both.

2. Section 324 – Voluntarily causing hurt by dangerous weapons or means—

Punishment—Imprisonment for 3 years, or fine, or both—Cognizable—Bailable— Triable by any Magistrate—Compoundable by the person to whom hurt is caused with the permission of the court.

3. Section 325 – Punishment for voluntarily causing grievous hurt[15]—

Punishment—Imprisonment for 7 years, and fine—Cognizable—Bailable—Triable by any Magistrate—Compoundable by the person to whom hurt is caused with the permission of the court.

14. Section 319 of IPC defines **"Hurt"**.- Whoever causes bodily pain, disease or infirmity to any person is said to cause hurt.
15. Section 320 of IPC defines **"Grievous hurt"** - The following kinds of hurt only are designated as" grievous":- Emasculation, permanent privation of the sight of either eye, permanent privation of the hearing of either ear, privation of any member or joint, destruction or permanent impairing of the powers of any member or joint, permanent dis-figuration of the head or face, fracture or dislocation of a bone or tooth, any hurt which endangers life or which causes the sufferer to be during the space of twenty days in severe bodily pain, or unable to follow his ordinary pursuits.

Contd. on next page

4. Section 326 – Voluntarily causing grievous hurt by dangerous weapons or means—

Punishment—Imprisonment for life, or imprisonment for 10 years and fine—Cognizable—Non-bailable—Triable by Magistrate of the first class—Non-compoundable.

5. Section 326A – Voluntarily causing grievous hurt by use of acid, etc.—

When a person causes permanent or partial damage or deformity to, or burns or maims or disfigures or disables, any part or parts of the body of a person or causes grievous hurt by throwing acid on or by administering acid to that person, or by using any other means with the intention of causing or with the knowledge that he is likely to cause such injury or hurt, shall be punished with imprisonment of either description for a term which shall not be less than ten years but which may extend to imprisonment for life, and with fine. Provided that such fine shall be just and reasonable to meet the medical expenses of the treatment of the victim and fine imposed under this section shall be paid to the victim.

6. Section 326B – Voluntarily throwing or attempting to throw acid—

If a person throws or attempts to throw acid on any person or attempts to administer acid to any person, or attempts to use any other means, with the intention of causing permanent or partial damage or deformity or burns or maiming or disfigurement or disability or grievous hurt to that person, shall be punished with imprisonment of either description for a term which shall not be less than five years but which may extend to seven years, and shall also be liable to fine.

7. Section 354 – Assault[16] or Criminal force[17] to woman with intent to outrage her modesty—

If a person assaults or uses criminal force to any woman, intending to outrage or knowing it to be likely that he will thereby outrage her modesty,

---

Contd. from previous page

16. Section 351 of IPC defines **"assault"**- Whoever makes any gesture, or any preparation intending or knowing it to be likely that such gesture or preparation will cause any person present to apprehend that he who makes that gesture or preparation is about to use criminal force to that person, is said to commit an assault.

    Explanation:

    Mere words do not amount to an assault. But the words which a person uses may give to his gestures or preparation such a meaning as may make those gestures or preparations amount to an assault.

    Illustrations:

    (a) *A* shakes his fist at *Z*, intending or knowing it to be likely that he may thereby cause *Z* to believe that *A* is about to strike *Z*. *A* has committed an assault.

    (b) *A* begins to unloose the muzzle of a ferocious dog, intending or knowing it to be likely that he may thereby cause *Z* to believe that he is about to cause the dog to attack *Z*. *A* has committed an assault upon *Z*.

    (c) *A* takes up a stick, saying to *Z*, "I will give you a beating". Here, though the words used by *A* could in no case amount to an assault, and though the mere gesture, unaccompanied by any other circumstances, might not amount to an assault, the gesture explained by the words may amount to an assault.

17. Section 350 of IPC defines **"Criminal force"**—Whoever intentionally uses force to any person, without that person's consent, in order to the committing of any offence, or intending by

Contd. on next page

shall be punished with imprisonment of either description for a term which shall not be less than one year but which may extend to five years, and shall also be liable to fine.

8. Section 354A – Sexual harassment and punishment for sexual harassment—

A man committing physical contact and advances involving unwelcome and explicit sexual overtures; or a demand or request for sexual favours; or showing pornography against the will of a woman; or making sexually coloured remarks, shall be guilty of the offence of sexual harassment and shall be punished with imprisonment for a term which may extend to three years, or with fine, or with both in case of first three acts or imprisonment of either description for a term which may extend to one year, or with fine, or with both in case of making sexually coloured remarks.

9. Section 354B – Assault or use of criminal force to woman with intent to disrobe—

Any man who assaults or uses criminal force to any woman or abets such act with the intention of disrobing or compelling her to be naked, shall be punished with imprisonment of either description for a term which shall not be less than three years but which may extend to seven years, and shall also be liable to fine.

10. Section 354C – Voyeurism—

Any man who watches, or captures the image of a woman engaging in a private act in circumstances where she would usually have the expectation of not being observed either by the perpetrator or by any other person at the behest of the perpetrator or disseminates such image shall be punished on first conviction with imprisonment of either description for a term which shall not be less than one year, but which may extend to three years, and shall also be liable to fine, and be punished on a second or subsequent conviction, with imprisonment of either description for a term which shall not be less than three years, but which may extend to seven years, and shall also be liable to fine.

11. Section 354D – Stalking—

1. Any man who—

    i. follows a woman and contacts, or attempts to contact such woman to foster personal interaction repeatedly despite a clear indication of disinterest by such woman; or

---

Contd. from previous page

the use of such force to cause, or knowing it to be likely that by the use of such force he will cause injury, fear or annoyance to the person to whom the force is used, is said to use criminal force to that other.

Illustration:

(a) Z is sitting in a moored boat on a river. *A* unfastens the moorings, and thus intentionally causes the boat to drift down the stream. Here *A* intentionally causes motion to Z, and he does this by disposing substances in such a manner that the motion is produced without any other action on any person's part. *A* has therefore intentionally used force to Z; and if he has done so without Z's consent, in order to the committing of any offence, or intending or knowing it to be likely that this use of force will cause injury, fear or annoyance to Z, *A* has used criminal force to Z.

ii. monitors the use by a woman of the internet, e-mail or any other form of electronic communication, commits the offence of stalking:

Provided that such conduct shall not amount to stalking if the man who pursued it proves that—

i. It was pursued for the purpose of preventing or detecting crime and the man accused of stalking had been entrusted with the responsibility of prevention and detection of crime by the State; or
ii. It was pursued under any law or to comply with any condition or requirement imposed by any person under any law; or
iii. In the particular circumstances such conduct was reasonable and justified.

2. Whoever commits the offence of stalking shall be punished on first conviction with imprisonment of either description for a term which may extend to three years, and shall also be liable to fine; and be punished on a second or subsequent conviction, with imprisonment of either description for a term which may extend to five years, and shall also be liable to fine.

12. Section 509 – Word, gesture or act intended to insult the modesty of a woman—

When a person, intending to insult the modesty of any woman, utters any word, makes any sound or gesture, or exhibits any object, intending that such word or sound shall be heard, or that gesture or object shall be seen, by such woman, or intrudes upon the privacy of such woman, shall punished with simple imprisonment for a term which may extend to three years, and also with fine.

S. No.	Section	Offence	Punishment	Cognizable/ Non-Cognizable	Bailable/ Non-Bailable	Compoundable /Non-Compoundable
1.	323	Voluntary causing hurt	Imprisonment for 1 year or fine or both	Non-Cognizable	Bailable	Compoundable
2.	324	Voluntary causing hurt by dangerous weapon or means	Imprisonment for 3 years or fine or both	Cognizable	Non-Bailable	Compoundable
3.	325	Voluntary causing grievous hurt	Imprisonment for 7 years and fine	Cognizable	Bailable	Compoundable
4.	326	Voluntary causing grievous hurt by dangerous weapon or means	Imprisonment for life or imprisonment for 10 years and fine	Cognizable	Non-Bailable	Non-Compoundable

1	2	3	4	5	6	7
5.	326A	Voluntary causing grievous hurt by use of acid etc.	Imprisonment (for not less than 10 years but which may extend to life) and fine (to be paid to victim)	Cognizable	Non-Bailable	
6.	326B	Voluntary throwing or attempting to throw acid	Imprisonment and fine (Minimum imprisonment-5 years and Maximum Imprisonment-7 Years)	Cognizable	Non-Bailable	
7.	354	Assault or use of Criminal Force to woman with intent to outrage her modesty	Imprisonment and fine (Minimum imprisonment-1 year and Maximum Imprisonment-5 Years)	Cognizable	Non-Bailable	
8.	354A	Part I — Sexual harassment and Physical conduct and advances involving unwelcome and explicit sexual overtures or a demand or request for sexual favours or showing pornography against the will of a person –	Punished with imprisonment for a term which may extend to three years or with fine or with both.	Cognizable	Bailable	
		Part II – Making sexually coloured remarks	Punished with rigorous imprisonment for a term which may extend to one year or with fine or with both.	Cognizable	Bailable	

1	2	3	4	5	6	7
9.	354B	Assault or use of criminal force to woman with intent to disrobe	Imprisonment and fine (Minimum imprisonment-3 years and Maximum Imprisonment-7 Years)	Cognizable	Non-Bailable	
10.	354C	Voyeurism	On 1st Conviction-Imprisonment and fine (Minimum imprisonment-1 years and Maximum Imprisonment - 3 Years)	Cognizable	Bailable	
			On 2nd Conviction-Imprisonment and fine (Minimum imprisonment -3 years and Maximum Imprisonment - 7 Years)	Cognizable	Non-Bailable	
11.	354D	Stalking	Imprisonment up to 3 years and with fine for first conviction	Cognizable	Bailable	
			Imprisonment up to 5 years and with fine for second or subsequent conviction	Cognizable	Non-Bailable	
12.	509	Word, gesture or act intended to insult the modesty of a woman	Simple Imprisonment which may extend to 3 years and fine	Cognizable	Bailable	Compoundable

[C] DEATH OR LOSS OF LIFE:

If the ragging incident ultimately leads to death then following sections may get attracted:—

1. Section 299 – Culpable homicide

When a person causes death by doing an act with the intention of causing death, or with the intention of causing such bodily injury as is likely to cause death, or with the knowledge that he is likely by such act to cause death, commits the offence of culpable homicide.

2. Section 300 – Murder

A person shall be liable for Culpable homicide amounting to murder, if the act by which the death is caused is done with the intention of causing death, or

Secondly.—If it is done with the intention of causing such bodily injury as the offender knows to be likely to cause the death of the person to whom the harm is caused, or—

Thirdly.—If it is done with the intention of causing bodily injury to any person and the bodily injury intended to be inflicted is sufficient in the ordinary course of nature to cause death, or—

Fourthly.—If the person committing the act knows that it is so imminently dangerous that it must, in all probability, cause death or such bodily injury as is likely to cause death, and commits such act without any excuse for incurring the risk of causing death or such injury as aforesaid.

3. Section 302 – Punishment for murder.

Whoever commits murder shall be punished with death, or imprisonment for life, and shall also be liable to fine.

4. Section 304 – Punishment for culpable homicide not amounting to murder—

Para I: Punishment—Imprisonment for life, or imprisonment for 10 years and fine—Cognizable—Non-bailable—Triable by Court of Session—Non-compoundable. If death was caused with intention]

Para II: Punishment—Imprisonment for 10 years, or fine, or both—Cognizable— Non-bailable—Triable by Court of Session—Non-compoundable. [Intention to cause death is absent but knowledge is there]

5. Section 304A - Causing death by negligence

When a person by doing any rash or negligent act not amounting to culpable homicide causes death of a person, shall be punished with imprisonment of either description for a term which may extend to two years, or with fine, or with both.

6. Section 306 – Abetment of suicide—

If any person abets other person to commit suicide, such abettor shall be punished with imprisonment of a descripted term which may extend upto ten years, and shall also be liable to pay fine.

7. Section 307 – Attempt to murder —

When a person does any act with such intention or knowledge, and under such circumstances that, if he by that act causes death, he would be guilty of murder, shall be punished with imprisonment of either description for a term which may extend to ten years, and shall also be liable to fine; and if hurt is caused to any person by such an act, the offender shall be liable either to imprisonment for life, or to such punishment as has been mentioned before.

S. No.	Section	Offence	Punishment	Cognizable/ Non-Cognizable	Bailable/ Non-Bailable	Compoundable/ Non-Compoundable
1.	300	Murder	As mentioned in Section 302	As mentioned in Section 302	As mentioned in Section 302	As mentioned in Section 302
3.	302	Murder	Death or imprisonment for life and fine	Cognizable	Non-Bailable	
4.	304	Culpable homicide not amounting to murder,				
		(i) if act by which the death is caused is done with intention	Imprisonment for life or imprisonment for 10 years and fine	Cognizable	Non-Bailable	Non-Compoundable
		(ii) if intention to cause death is absent, but knowledge is there	Imprisonment for 10 years or fine or both	Cognizable	Non-Bailable	Non-Compoundable
5.	304 A	Causing death by rash or neglegent act	Imprisonment for a term which may extend upto 2 years or fine or both	Cognizable	Bailable	
6.	306	Abetment of Suicide	Imprisonment for a term which may extend upto 10 years and fine	Cognizable	Non-Bailable	
7.	307	Attempt to murder				
		Part I – If such act causes hurt to any person	Imprisonment for life or imprisonment for 10 years and fine.	Cognizable	Non-Bailable	
		Part II – Attempt by life convict to murder, if hurt is caused	Death or imprisonment for 10 years and fine	Cognizable	Non-Bailable	

NEED FOR SPECIFIC PROVISIONS IN LAW

Considering the fact that the age of leaving the senior school is 18 years, both the freshers and the senior students are adults. From the various accounts *i.e.*, how ragging takes place, what leads to ragging, the intention of those who commit ragging, the trauma suffered by its victims, the desirability of its prevention etc., ragging, fits the description of an offence with a multiplicity of ingredients, each of which constitutes an offence punishable under the existing provisions of the Indian Penal Code and none of these offences can escape penalties on the grounds of being General *Exceptions* under Chapter IV of the Code.[18]

But still there are no specific provisions for ragging and its punishments; that is why the Raghavan Committee had suggested that there should be an amendment in the Indian Penal Code in order to provide for the offence of Ragging and punishment thereof. The Committee recommended that, rather than subjecting each incident of ragging to a different penal treatment under various sections of the Indian Penal Code, a new section should be added to the IPC, making ragging a punishable offence, same on the analogy of section 498A of IPC (which specifically talks about cruelty on women).[19] The Committee also recommended that the Indian Evidence Act should also be suitably amended on the analogy of section 113A of that Act,[20] to shift the burden of proof on those accused of ragging.[21] Although it would indeed be sad if the penal provisions of law were to be used as a matter of routine to enforce deterrence in campuses.[22]

---

18. *Supra note* 2, para 4.17.
19. *Ibid,* para 5.45.
20. *Ibid.*
21. *Ibid.*
22. *Ibid, para* 5.47.

Chapter VII
Ragging and Myths

"We don't see things as they are;
we see things as we are

— Anais Nin

There are several myths related to ragging given below on which raggers justify this cruel and inhuman practice. It is astonishing that how this practice finds so many defenders from every stream of society. When a fresher enters the college he gets hostility rather than hospitality. It ranges from singing a song for seniors to brutal sexual abuse, which leads to immeasurable suicides and murders. Yet ragging finds defenders.

1. Ragging Makes the Freshers Bold

The act of ragging is strongly justified on the ground that it makes the freshers bold. It is argued that it makes the fresher comfortable in the hostel and she/he feels free to interact with seniors thereafter. It is thought to be the solution of shyness and assumed that it helps the person to forget her/his family. This belief is nothing but the courage on the part of seniors to do wrong which can be attributed to anti-social elements like eve-teasers, bullies and even murderers.[1] One can understand that this courage is actually *'gunda-gardi'*. Tolerating wrong-doing to oneself and not breaking-down in such circumstances is not boldness, but 'learning' to accept exploitation non-resistively.[2] Thus, it is a perverted boldness/courage that seniors think of, as right. In real sense meaning of boldness is taking a stand for ones principles and truth, even if there is risk of losing everything involved.[3]

Juniors lose self confidence when confronted by seniors as they think that they are weak in front of them. In this way, the argument, that ragging makes the fresher bold is not plausible. Ragging merely encourages an individual to do socially unacceptable wrong which gives an immoral, unethical message to the society. It is to be noted that this behaviour challenges a person's fundamental freedom of choice, adds to destroying her/his individuality and plays with her/his sensitivity. There can be many other well-mannered ways to do so, like extending a warm welcome, behaving like a family, interacting in group discussions, debates, theatre, sports, social visits etc.[4]

1. Varun Aggarwal, Ragging makes us bold, available at http://noragging.com/index.php/Research/Articles/Ragging-Makes-Us-Bold.html, last accessed on 16th February, 2014.
2. *Ibid.*
3. *Ibid.*
4. *Ibid.*

Conclusively, this is one of the most formidable myths related to ragging that, it makes freshers bold and instills courage into them.[5]

2. Ragging is a Harmless Fun

It is true that ragging was originated for harmless fun and humour but now it has become a social evil in the name of verbal interaction or ice-breaking session with the freshers. Today, freshers are emotionally, sexually and physically harassed and also subjected to many other abuses. Seniors commit rape, murder etc., is this harmless? Juniors are embarrassed, traumatized and commit suicide, is this all harmless? These are the questions everyone needs to look at, and think that now ragging is no more a fun activity but an unfair and harmful tool in the hands of seniors to exploit juniors.

3. Ragging Doesn't Mean More than Doing Odd Jobs for Seniors

Generally, it is considered that ragging is not more than cleaning the senior's room or doing their other odd jobs but it is the harsh reality that ragging can even take severe form which includes stripping of all clothes, public sexual acts to the extent of sexual intercourse & sodomy, merciless beating of freshers, asking them to take drugs, making them to work 24x7 and forcing them into rules such as not removing shoes for months etc.[6]

4. Ragging Helps in Breaking the Ice Between the Seniors and the Freshers

Ragging is justified by raggers on the ground that it is the only way by which the freshers can be taught about the traditions of the institution. They also believe that it helps in facilitating their interaction and develop friendship between them, but, there are more positive ways of interaction which can develop the friendship more effectively without causing any human rights abuse.[7]

5. Ragging Generates a Feeling of Unity and Oneness

People view ragging as a way to generate feeling of unity among students. However, it is noteworthy that the causes of ragging itself are on the lines of caste, region, class etc. It is simply a manifestation of different forms of discrimination which sets up a mob mentality among the students.[8]

6. Severe Ragging is Not Prevalent Anymore

Severe ragging is still widely prevalent in most of the colleges, be it in smaller cities or the metropolitans.[9] Even after the landmark judgment of Hon'ble Supreme Court the problem is not solved, but hidden, because colleges have just geared up to keep ragging incidents under the cover to save their image.[10]

---

5. *Ibid.*
6. Rajiv Ram, Common Myths about Ragging, available at http://noragging.com/index.php/Research/Reports/Common-Myths-about-Ragging.html, last accessed on 16th February, 2014.
7. Ragging in Indian Universities and Colleges, p. 11, available at http://www.noragging.com/CURE1.pdf, last accessed on 16th February, 2014.
8. *Ibid.*
9. *Supra note*, 6.
10. *Ibid.*

7. Colleges are Pro-Active Against Ragging

Colleges are not pro-active against ragging, as it is evident from the fact that despite so many initiatives taken by Legislature, Judiciary and other regulatory bodies in this direction, there are no as such suitable guidelines placed in the colleges to curb the menace. More surprisingly, colleges even deny the incidents of ragging at the expense of fresher's trauma, and the victims themselves are blamed for starting the altercation, as it may deteriorate the reputation of the college.[11] Shockingly, punishment for ragging shifts sympathy from the victim to the perpetrator, which has made justice difficult.[12]

8. Ragging Gives a Person a Taste of Real Life and Teach How to Sustain the Difficulties

It's been argued that ragging is like a grow-up-tonic in one's challenging life,[13] but they forget, tastes of real life are enjoyed voluntarily and come through practical experiences which cannot be taught.

"You can't shakehands with clinched fist"

— Indira Gandhi

---

11. *Supra note*, 7.
12. *Ibid.*
13. Varun Aggarwal, Ragging: Why at All?, available at http://noragging.com/index.php/Research/Ragging-The-Phenomenon/-Ragging-Why-at-All.html, last accessed on 16th February, 2014.

Chapter VIII

Role of Different Stakeholders

It is generally believed that ragging is a phenomenon limited to only juniors and seniors, but there are other stakeholders also in the practice which includes college authorities, police, parents, student bodies etc. Epidemiologically speaking, the agent (senior students), host (junior students) and environment (college and society), each has a different role to play in the practice of ragging.[1] So, the role of various stakeholders has been discussed below:—

[A] ROLE OF PARENTS

1. **Encouraging the victim:** Ragging should not be treated as 'normal' and 'an accepted way of introduction' by the parents.[2] It is necessary for them to encourage the victim to share the burden of her/his pains and hardships, so that appropriate action can be taken immediately to deter such practice from happening again in the future.

2. **Discouraging the act of ragging:** Wards suspected to be involved in the crime of ragging should be instructed to discontinue and apologize to the victim, and she/he should be discouraged to do so in the future.[3]

3. **Helping the educational institutions by signing undertaking:** Parents should sign an undertaking at the time of admission that their children will not indulge in the crime of ragging.[4] This will help institutions in a way that parents will share the responsibility of preventing their children from not indulging into any type of ragging.

4. **Following up with the authorities:** Parents should be constantly in touch with the authorities as to what steps have been taken against the ragging.[5]

5. **Action against college authorities:** A genuine effort is needed from the side of the parent community. If they all form a group and oppose ragging and pressurize the college authorities, they can change the system. Thus, their job is to collectively force the college to take some steps regarding prevention of ragging.[6]

---

1. Sumit Malhotra, Ragging in medical colleges: Call for adopting a zero tolerance policy, The National Medical Journal of India VOL. 23, NO. 2 of 2010, p. 121.
2. By Meera Kaura Patel, available at http://www.no2ragging.org/parentsduties.html, last accessed on 16th February, 2014.
3. *Ibid.*
4. *Ibid.*
5. *Ibid.*
6. Varun Aggarwal and Mohit Garg, Parents, Teachers and Seniors, available at, http://noragging.com/index.php/Research/Finding-a-CURE/Parents-Teachers-and-Seniors.html, last accessed on 16th February, 2014.

6. Lodging an FIR: Parents should lodge an FIR immediately after they come to know about any incident, because the time of lodging FIR is crucial and vital.

[B] ROLE OF TEACHERS

In a country like India, where a teacher is respected and compared to God, should take the moral responsibility to prevent this menace.[7] Teachers have the magic stick in their hands and can stop this menace immediately, if they wish to. Teachers should not only be concerned with the academic excellence of the students, but should take progressive steps in their moral structuring too. They are like parents to the students living in hostels far from their homes. This puts some responsibility on them towards their well-being. Thus, indifference from their side is unacceptable.

In this direction, teachers need to take some strict steps and should not think about reputation of institution, because the name and fame of the institution is not more important than justice. Surprise visits to the hostel at odd timings by the teachers/wardens can end the ragging there and then. Proper implementation of strict rules against ragging in college by the teachers will be a boon for educational life of the student.[8]

[C] ROLE OF SENIORS

Seniors are the most important key to this problem. They can break this tradition of ragging, if they decide to end it once and for all rather than perpetuating what happened with them by inflicting the same pain and suffering on newcomers. They should take a strong resolve on this and have control over their will. They must bear in mind that everyone likes fun, but not at the expense of one's feelings, emotions and many a times health. They should treat freshers like their own brothers and sisters and should become friends with them. At the end, they HAVE THE POWER they can either use or abuse.[9]

[D] ROLE OF POLICE

Police is one of the most important part of our society because it protects and safeguards the interests of the people. It is said to be the chief law enforcement agency in a society. It is expected that in the case of ragging police will immediately take action on the report received by it and would register the crime for initiating appropriate and adequate action in the matter. Any lapse on the part of police in this regard will land them in a situation of condemnation. Registration of a crime and recording of an FIR is thus, one of the fundamental duties of the police. Also, police must co-operate with the victim and ensure the proper and transparent investigation in the case to help her/him in getting the justice.

[E] ROLE OF HEALTH PROFESSIONALS

Health professionals have distinctive responsibility of promoting the development of the community initiatives for the prevention of ragging and

7. *Ibid.*
8. *Ibid.*
9. *Ibid.*

related health problems. Physicians need to be aware of the physical and psycho-social symptoms associated with ragging so that they can screen the victims involved and provide the support needed to develop healthy relationships.[10]

[F] ROLE OF THE GOVERNMENT

The government should maintain a 'special cell' to monitor and control the unwanted barbaric incidents of ragging in educational institutions. The casual approach in this issue is the matter of concern. Government has merely declared ban on this heinous crime. Many of the State Governments are busy in paying lip service,[11] but there is need of a firm hand that would punish and curb such behaviour.[12]

[G] ROLE OF INSTITUTES/COLLEGES

Even after various initiatives and the judgments of the Hon'ble Apex Court, the practice of ragging continues unabated. The most compelling reason behind this failure has been the lack of enforcement by the institutions.[13] Generally, the colleges deny the incidents, to save the reputation. Even after a murder, the institute first tries to cover it up and then denies the responsibility.[14] Neither college authorities dare to indicate number of ragging incidents per year nor is the hostel management spontaneous enough with their information to share.[15]

Institutes must understand that ultimately, the responsibility of preventing ragging lies on them. Anti-ragging movements should be initiated by the institutions right from the time of advertisement for the admissions. Administration needs to realize that outright denial or blaming the freshers for the incidents will simply perpetuate ragging. Instead, they need to build a coalition with the students, police and the hostel wardens to actively monitor the violent acts.[16] Colleges should control brutal ragging in the hostels through spot checks by the hostel wardens because hostels provide a closed circuit environment where many of the worst cases occur. Surprise checks in the hostels at odd hours with strict punishment to the guilty poses an efficient solution to the problem.[17] There should be compulsorily an anti-ragging Committee in every institution which should meet freshers on a regular basis and encourage them to raise their

---

10. Lamb J., Pepler DJ and Craig W., Approach to bullying and victimization, Can Fam Physician 2009; 55:356-60.
11. Ragging: March Against a Social Menace, p. 1, available at http://www.gnit.ac.in/pdf/Anti-RaggingHandbook.pdf, last accessed on 16th February, 2014.
12. Conversation happened between Harsh Agarwal and Michael Britton in 2007 that began with Harsh's research report on "ragging" in colleges in India, available at http://www.humiliationstudies.org/documents/BrittonAgarwalConversationonRagging.pdf, last accessed on 16th February, 2014.
13. Rajiv Ram, Ragging: A Vision for the future, available at http://noragging.com/index.php/Research/Finding-a-CURE/-Ragging-A-Vision-for-the-future.html, last accessed on 16th February, 2014.
14. *Ibid.*
15. *Supra note 11.*
16. *Supra note 13.*
17. *Ibid.*

problems posed by the seniors. Further, the colleges should adopt and implement the guidelines issued by the Hon'ble Supreme Court, recommendations made by the Raghavan Committee and other regulatory bodies, to deal with the hurdles created by ragging.[18]

---

18. Dr. Ch. Venkateswarlu and N Satyasri, Effects of Ragging on Human Dignity-A Critique, International Journal of Multidisciplinary Educational Research ISSN: 2277-7881, Volume 1, Issue 4, September, 2012, p. 235.

Chapter IX
Role of Media

Media is an important set of communication agency in the social system. Edmund Burke of England considered the media as the fourth estate of democracy.[1] In India, media has a powerful presence because of the social responsibilities performed by it. It has been positively involved with social issues in form of print, audio visual and radio or web media. This pillar is successful and quite encouraging because of freedom of publication, plurality in media ownership, diversity in information, culture and opinion, support for the democratic political system, support for public order and security of the state, universal reach, quality of information and culture disseminated to the public, respect for human rights and avoiding harm to individuals and the society.[2]

Earlier, media did not highlight the ragging incidents in critical manner but after *Aman's* unfateful demise, it has become pro-active in this area and played a vital role in the sphere of ragging eradication.

1. Print Media

Print media is one of the oldest and basic forms of mass communication which includes newspapers, weeklies, magazines, monthlies and other forms of printed journals.[3] It creates awareness among the people regarding their rights and duties. The in-depth sight of ragging in the published writings touches the emotions of the whole nation.[4] Due to the effect of print media, people associated with practice of ragging work in an apprehension of being caught and recognized. Following newspaper clippings elucidate the role of print media in this respect:—

- **UP ranks first in ragging cases – February 5, 2014, the Times of India[5]**

  Ragging continues unabated in the educational institutions of Uttar Pradesh. Technical, polytechnic and medical institutions are worst-hit. As per government figures, UP ranks first in ragging incidents in the country.

  According to latest data of the National Anti-Ragging Helpline (1800-180-5522), 471 ragging cases were registered in UP between June, 2009 and

---

1. http://www.caluniv.ac.in/Global%20mdia%20journal/Commentaries/C%207.%20%20%20%20%20SOUMYA%20DUTTA.pdf, last accessed on 15th February, 2014.
2. *Ibid.*
3. http://download.nos.org/srsec335new/ch5.pdf,last accessed on 16th February, 2014.
4. Gulshan Naveen, Ragging – The Red Alert, 1st Edn. 2010, p. 100.
5. http://timesofindia.indiatimes.com/city/lucknow/UP-ranks-first-in-ragging-cases/articleshow/29872418.cms.

February 4, 2014. West Bengal is next with 310 complaints. After a sharp decline in the cases in 2011 to 2012, the number has gone up to 94 in 2013. In a little over month in the year, three ragging cases have already been registered in the State.

Other States with high ragging cases include Odisha (247), Madhya Pradesh (230), Maharashtra (127), Tamil Nadu (123), Rajasthan (125), Bihar (114) and Delhi (52).

Figures show boys are more vulnerable to ragging; about 90% ragging victims are boys. Since 2009, more than 8.8 lakh students (seniors and freshers) have submitted affidavits which are available on the Central Government's anti-ragging web portal.

- **Curb the Ragging Menace with an Iron Hand: CJI- December 20, 2013, The New Indian Express**

  According to Chief Justice of India P. Sathasivam, "the menace of ragging in educational institutions adversely impacts the standard of education and has to be curbed with an iron hand, and not only students but the faculty too must be sensitised towards the ills of ragging and help to prevent it. Educational institutes must show zero tolerance for ragging on their campus and non-teaching staff, which includes administrative staff, employees and security guards, should be sensitised towards the evils and consequences of ragging. The true social value of education includes personal empowerment as well as the ability to contribute to social welfare. To be successful, you must first be a good citizen".[6]

- **Ragging medicos to manage traffic as punishment – December 19, 2013, The Times of India**

  BJ Medical College has suspended three students for ragging juniors. Another 42 students who were called 'boss' by their juniors were debarred from the hostel. The five-member anti-ragging committee requested police commissioner Shivanand Jha to use them as traffic volunteers.[7]

- **HC holds 3 guilty of ragging, tells them to donate blood – December 12, 2013, The Indian Express**

  As punishment for ragging a fresher in 2002, Justice J.R. Midha of the Delhi High Court has ordered three former students of Delhi University's Ramjas College to donate one unit of blood and Rs. 15,000 to the Prime Minister's Relief Fund — being utilised towards rehabilitation of victims of the Uttarakhand floods and conduct a seven-day anti-ragging workshop to educate others about the consequences of ragging. The students had approached the Delhi High Court with a plea to quash the FIR registered against them for wrongfully restraining and causing hurt to the student while ragging him in the college hostel in 2002. In their plea, they had

---

6. http://www.newindianexpress.com/education/student/Curb-the-Ragging-Menace-With-an-Iron-Hand-CJI/2013/12/20/article1954435.ece.
7. http://articles.timesofindia.indiatimes.com/2013-12-19/ahmedabad/45376713_1_three-students-first-year-mbbs-students-inquiry-committee.

claimed that they had reached a settlement with the victim and that they would abide by any orders of the court.[8]

- **Students lead anti-ragging campaign in AP – November 25, 2013, The Times of India**

  Due to anti-ragging measures taken by students, there has been a decline in number of ragging cases in the Andhra Pradesh this year. From conducting road shows to counselling seniors and promoting the cause on social networking platforms, students have taken the lead in preventing ragging on campuses. The measures have considerably reduced the number of cases in the city.[9]

- **Now, freshers to take on ragging demon in Lucknow - October 07, 2013, The Hindustan Times**

  The fight against ragging has taken a new, innovative and bigger dimension. Now, the first year students will be inducted in the anti-ragging cell of universities and technical colleges of Lucknow. Not only this, even parents of senior students will be a part of the anti-ragging cell and will help develop fellow feeling in the hearts of senior students for their juniors, so that the freshers may enjoy their campus entry.[10]

- **College suspends student who filed ragging plaint - September 26, 2013, The Hindu**

  Filing a police complaint after allegedly being ragged by his seniors proved costly for a first year B.Com student Siddharth Kumar Singh of Dayananda Sagar College of Arts, Science and Commerce, who has now been suspended from college. The college has accused him of fighting and creating a nuisance on campus.[11]

- ***Aman Kachroo* ragging death case: All accused freed on 'good conduct' – August 22, 2013, Zee News**

  Four medical college students, who were convicted of ragging to death their junior Aman Kachroo in Himachal Pradesh four years back, have been set free on account of their 'good conduct'. The conviction of Ajay Verma, Naveen Verma, Abhinav Verma and Mukul Sharma, who were punished for ragging Aman Kachroo to death in the 2009, was upheld by the Himachal Pradesh High Court in April, 2013. All four convicts were freed after the Himachal Pradesh Government decided to write off their remaining sentence on account of their 'good conduct' and allow them to complete their medical course at a medical college in Kangra.[12]

---

8. http://archive.indianexpress.com/news/hc-holds-3-guilty-of-ragging-tells-them-to-donate-blood/1206619/.
9. http://articles.timesofindia.indiatimes.com/2013-11-25/hyderabad/44448609_1_colleges-measures-police officials.
10. http://www.hindustantimes.com/india-news/lucknow/now-freshers-to-take-on-ragging-demon-in lucknow/article1-1131947.aspx.
11. http://www.thehindu.com/news/cities/bangalore/college-suspends-student-who-filed-ragging-plaint/article5168371.ece.
12. http://zeenews.india.com/news/himachal-pradesh/aman-kachroo-ragging-death-case-all-accused-freed-on-good-conduct_870868.html.

- **Police going that extra mile to create ragging-free campuses - August 11, 2013, The Hindu**

  Coimbatore Police are taking special efforts to take the message of 'ragging-free campuses' to the doorsteps of institutions. Station House Officers and supervisory officers have been asked to hold periodical meetings with heads of institutions to ensure that not even a single incident of ragging goes unnoticed. In Coimbatore city, Inspectors have started visiting colleges and sensitizing students by talking to them about the ill-effects of ragging and the law that deals with those who indulge in ragging. They also distribute handbills.[13]

- **IIT students protest against separate hostels for freshers and seniors – July 13, 2013, The Times of India**

  IIT-Madras has, from this academic year, introduced a separate hostel for freshers. Nearly 100 students of IIT-M held a protest against the campus administration, demanding that juniors and seniors should be allowed to continue in the same hostel. While the students said the new accommodation rule denied them the opportunity to interact and bond, the management said the move was to prevent incidents of ragging.[14]

- **Seniors appointed as mentors to curb ragging – July 13, 2013, The Times of India**

  Colleges have come up with an all new way to curb ragging, if at all it exists anymore. Turning the senior-junior, love-hate relationship around, now colleges are not only promoting friendship but are also taking a step further by appointing seniors as mentors for new students.[15]

- **Most no-ragging college panels only on paper – May 12, 2013, Times of India**

  Though several colleges and universities claim to have initiated several measures to curb the menace of ragging on and off campuses, but, serious cases keep cropping up, indicating major lapses in the system.[16]

- **Sibal launches anti-ragging helpline – New Delhi, July 26, 2012, Tribune India**

  Students and parents do not have to put up with ragging anymore. The government launched an all new anti-ragging portal where anyone, even a witness of ragging, can lodge a complaint and get an identification number for the same to see it followed up to the logical end. The complaints can be lodged at helpline number 18001805522 or on web-sites www.antiragging.in and www.amanmovement.org.[17]

---

13. http://www.thehindu.com/news/cities/Coimbatore/police-going-that-extra-mile-to-create-raggingfree-campuses/article5012020.ece.
14. http://articles.timesofindia.indiatimes.com/2013-07-13/chennai/40553674_1_freshers-separate-hostel-l-s-ganesh.
15. http://articles.timesofindia.indiatimes.com/2013-07-13/people/40553441_1_college-hostels-seniors-rural-students.
16. http://timesofindia.indiatimes.com/city/mumbai/Most-no-ragging-college-panels-only-on-paper/articleshow/20010462.cms.
17. http://www.tribuneindia.com/2012/20120727/main6.htm.

- **Facebook, a ragging tool on campus – Hindustan Times Kolkata, August 02, 2011**

  Social networking has come as an ugly age in this time. What is considered as a medium of connecting people online has become a tool of intimidation.[18]

- **SC gives freshers a weapon against ragging: FIR and law – May 17, 2007, Indian Express**

  "A new section should be added to the IPC, making ragging a punishable offence on the analogy of section 498A, dealing with cruelty towards women," said a Bench headed by Hon'ble Justice Arijit Pasayat.[19]

2. Electronic Media

The reach and efficacy of electronic media as an educational medium is finding increasing relevance in the wake of information explosion and choices available to a student in recent times.[20] Powerful visuals and impressive scripts create an intense and long lasting impact in the minds of viewer. Almost every news channel has illustrated the concern with exclusive stories and programmes on ragging; [21] for example, Barkha Dutt came up with a programme "Ragging – from tradition to abuse" on 31 May, 2009 in her popular chat show 'We the People;, on July 12, 2009, Aaj Tak presented the discussion based news on ragging, etc.

Role of Social Media

Social Media being another important medium of information is the only platform which brings people together from different walks of life and provides them the opportunity to share their experiences. It is very inclusive in terms of participation and membership which helps in creating effective large scale awareness against ragging. In this modern time social media has become a fast medium to convey a message from one corner to other corner of the world. There are innumerable social media web-sites, out of which the most popular and effective are very few, like Facebook, Twitter, Youtube, Wikipedia etc. Through such social media, one may pressurize respective authorities to take appropriate action against the accused which can help the victim in getting the justice.

To conclude, these examples are just representative ones. The founder head of Aman movement, Dr. Rajendra Kachroo appreciated the role played by media and said that media kept the issue of the death of Aman and ragging alive in the minds of people.[22] Truly, the freedom of press in the country is blessing for the people.

---

18. http://www.hindustantimes.com/India-news/Kolkata/Facebook-a-ragging-tool-on-campus/Article1-728565.aspx.
19. http://www.indianexpress.com/news/sc-gives-freshers-a-weapon-against-ragging-fir—law-/31146.
20. http://tojde.anadolu.edu.tr/tojde24/pdf/article_2.pdf, last accessed on 16th February, 2014.
21. *Supra note* 4.
22. *Ibid*, p. 103.

Chapter X

Role of NGO & Civil Society

The origin of the term "Non-governmental Organization" relates back to 1950, when the United Nations (UN) coined the expression.[1] UN describes an NGO as: "any non-profit, voluntary citizens' group which is organized on a local, national or international level"[2] but there is no absolute or formal definition of it. Although, it can be generally defined as "private organizations characterized primarily by humanitarian or co-operative, rather than commercial, objectives that pursue activities to relieve suffering, promote the interests of the poor, protect the environment, provide basic social services, or undertake community Development."[3]

India is estimated to have had around 3.3 million NGOs in 2009, *i.e.*, one NGO per 400 Indians, which is many times the number of primary schools and primary health centres in India.[4] But there are very few NGO's which are working in the field of Ragging. The Raghavan Committee could not come across more than two or three NGOs engaged in creating awareness against ragging or involved in any significant manner in the movement against ragging.[5]

NGOs WORKING IN THIS FIELD

1. Vishwa Jagriti Mission

Vishwa Jagriti Mission, established on March 24, 1991, is a social and cultural organization oriented towards revival of the spiritual and cultural richness of India.[6] His divine grace Sudhanshu Ji Maharaj is the Patron-in-Chief and founder

---

Note – Information has been gathered from concerned NGO's websites and from various resources. Author would not be personally liable for it.

1. Michael Yaziji and Jonathan Doh, NGOs and Corporations: Conflict and Collaboration, pp. 4-6, available at http://assets.cambridge.org/97805218/66842/excerpt/9780521866842_excerpt.pdf, last accessed on 16th February, 2014.
2. *Ibid.*
3. Eric D. Werker and Faisal Z. Ahmed, What Do Non-Governmental Organizations Do, p. 3, available at http://www.hbs.edu/faculty/Publication%20Files/08-041.pdf, last accessed on 16th February, 2014.
4. "First official estimate: An NGO for every 400 people in India", *The Indian Express*. 7 July, 2010.
5. The Menace of Ragging in Educational Institutions and Measures to Curb It, Report of the Committee constituted by the Hon'ble Supreme Court of India In SLP No. 24295 of 2006, headed by R.K. Raghavan, para 4.03.
6. Vishwa Jagriti Mission, available at http://noragging.com/index.php/Resources/Laws/Vishwa-Jagriti-Mission.html, last accessed on 16th February, 2014.

of the mission. It is registered as a social, cultural, and religious society in Delhi, India.[7] The golden principles of service, devotion, contentment, meditation, co-operation, dedication, tolerance and sympathy are deeply rooted in the soul of the Mission. The curriculum of the Mission is inspired by the path of meditation, yoga, and devotional prayers as suggested by Swami Sadanand and Swami Muktanand.[8]

The anguish of the students forced his divine grace Sudhanshu Ji Maharaj to knock the doors of Apex Court and therefore, filed a public interest litigation under article 32 of the Constitution of India on issue of ragging in August, 1998[9] which played a crucial role in the history of ragging. Subsequently, Hon'ble Supreme Court in its order in May, 2001 passed a ruling that ragging should be banned immediately in academic and educational Institutions and declared ragging as a punishable offence.[10] The Honourable Judge Sujata Manohar had remarked that *"Ragging is not a part of our culture. Its evil influence is increasing in educational institutions. This is a matter of great sorrow and humiliation"*.[11]

2. Coalition to Uproot Ragging From Education (Cure)

CURE was started by two students, who were themselves victims of the horrible practice of ragging.[12] Their fight against the evil of ragging got shape in July, 2001 when they started a web discussion group called "The No Ragging Group" (NRG). It brought various ragging cases committed over the past years, steps taken by Government legislations, analysis etc., under one roof. According to CURE, every year, many students are severely affected by the horrible practice of ragging; out of which many turn into perpetrators of the crime in the following years and many others get deeply pained due to the existence of brutal practice.[13] CURE observes 'No Ragging Day' on October 11, since Amit Sahay, a student, committed suicide by jumping in front of a train on that day in 2005 due to ragging.[14]

Cure Principle

CURE is against the practice of non-consensual ragging in any form *viz.*, physical or mental, nevertheless encouraging healthy interaction between the freshers and seniors.[15]

Note:—Author does not support the principle of consensual ragging because how can a crime be consensual?

---

7. *Ibid.*
8. *Ibid.*
9. *Ibid.*
10. AIR 2001 SC 2814.
11. *Supra note* 6.
12. Coalition to Uproot Ragging from Education (CURE), available at http://noragging.com/index.php/Table/CURE/About/, last accessed on 16th February, 2014.
13. *Ibid.*
14. *Ibid.*
15. *Ibid.*

Cure mission[16]

- To establish public opinion against ragging.
- To dispel the myths about ragging through research and advocacy.
- To present a platform for every individual who wishes to share his or her opinion against ragging.

Achievements of cure[17]

- The CURE web-site is the first online dedicated forum to condemn ragging.
- CURE has evolved from an initial membership of just 4 to more than 340 members.
- Anant Asthana, CURE, Aligarh facilitated issuance of religious injunction against ragging in year 2004.
- CURE recently published its second periodical completely focusing on the theme of ragging. The idea of the periodical is to make people aware about ragging incidents, ragging psychology and its ills, thus garner support against ragging. The 2004 periodical was freely distributed in many colleges around India including the ones in Delhi, Bangalore, Pune, Chennai, Bombay, etc. CURE also provides free copies of the newsletters.
- Apart from this periodical, CURE's slogan stickers have become part of many college workshop coursewares, which constantly remind students about the ills of ragging.
- CURE has established contact with noted psychiatrist, Dr. V.M. Sharma, VIMHANS for online counselling of victims. Any victim can contact Dr. Vikas Mohan Sharma directly through e-mail or through web-site of CURE.
- CURE has presented seminars at Unnati (NGO) and joined the panel on Sab TV Show 'Kuchh Dil Se'.
- CURE members had conceptualised and hosted DD-Bharati's show 'Meri Baat' for facilitating a constructive discussion on ragging in the year 2004.
- CURE had actively pursued *Harsh Agarwal's* case through letters, e-mail campaigns and publication in the magazines to serve as an eye-opener for the society.

Raghavan Committee and CURE

CURE also worked as a consultant body with the Raghavan Committee set up by Supreme Court to curb the menace of ragging. It suggested an alternate definition of ragging. According to CURE, "Ragging is an act of aggression committed by an individual or a group of individuals over another individual or a group of individuals where the former, by virtue of their being senior to the latter, somehow gets the authority and audacity to commit the act and

16. *Ibid.*
17. *Ibid.*

the latter, by virtue of their being new to the institution, are automatically the victims".[18] The Raghavan Committee has appreciated the co-operation rendered by this NGO.

CURE has also made available the findings of the 'CURE Comprehensive Research Report' to the Committee. In its report CURE defined ragging by identifying the menace with three kinds of abuse: verbal, physical and sexual. The problem has been analyzed from various dimensions such as psychological, group dynamics, sociological, stereotypes and so on.[19] In its approach to solutions, the CURE report has identified the core issues to be; denial of ragging, lack of clear guidelines, complete helplessness of freshers, casteist and regional colouring of the incidents etc.[20]

During its association with the Committee, CURE through a random survey, took 64 ragging cases reported since 2005 and classified these cases into five categories *viz.* (i) physical, (ii) physical and sexual, (iii) sexual, (iv) verbal and (v) 'not known'.[21] The report de-mystified the popular myth that sexual and physical ragging is no more prevalent after the Supreme Court judgment of 2001.[22] It also questioned the oversimplified argument that ragging is an ice-breaker for the 'fresher' and claimed that ragging is not a harmless fun, but cuts deep into the mental health of the ragged.[23] It broke several stereotypes prevalent in the society about ragging. The CURE report tried to underline the fact that the stakeholders such as seniors, freshers, college/university authorities, law enforcing agencies, media and other social organisations, civil society groups must be collectively involved in eradicating this malice.[24]

3. Society Against Violence In Education (Save)

Young professionals and students from diverse academic fields (viz. medicine, engineering and IT, law, film, media and journalism, architecture, management etc.) conceptualized and set up Society Against Violence in Education (SAVE) to facilitate the eradication of ragging.[25] These youths joined their hands to share the pain and offer help to the victims. Their vision is to create a ragging-free society.[26] Born in Kolkata, currently SAVE has its presence in Delhi, Bangalore and Mumbai. It is trying to spread to several other cities at the earliest. They encourage every conscientious individual to join them and to strengthen the Anti-Ragging Movement in her/his area.[27]

---

18. *Supra note* 5, para 4.19.
19. *Ibid*, para 2.06.
20. *Ibid*, para 2.08.
21. *Ibid*, para 2.07.
22. *Ibid*.
23. *Ibid*.
24. *Ibid*.
25. Available at http://www.no2ragging.org/aboutus.html, last accessed on 16th February, 2014.
26. *Ibid*.
27. *Ibid*.

Supporting the victims, whatever and whenever possible!

They try their best to provide support to the victims. When approached for necessary support, they try to arrange medical help, including psychiatric/ psychological consultation (which is often required), whenever possible. However, for this and for other medical help, they are dependent on the kind of support offered by the concerned professionals supporting the cause.[28] They also try to provide legal guidance to the victims and/or their families. Again, they are dependent on the kind of support offered by the lawyers. However, they have also started their own legal cell in Delhi, headed by Mrs. Meera Kaura Patel, who has co-founded their Delhi chapter along with Mr. Ajay Govind, an independent film-maker.[29]

Plans to reach the goal[30]

- To initiate Pan-India movement against ragging.
- To spread awareness against ragging in educational institutions.
- To pro-actively promote measures to eliminate ragging, through the formation of anti-ragging campus units.
- To urge print and electronic media, cinema halls/multiplexes, State and civil society to share responsibility for spreading anti-ragging awareness.
- To provide counselling, medical and legal support to ragging victims.
- To promote healthy and positive learning environment in educational institutions.
- To create statistics on ragging to effectively monitor and research the incidents of ragging.
- To assist in creation of a uniform Central legislation in place of different State legislations.
- To co-operate with the government and with statutory bodies in curbing ragging in every possible way.
- To monitor implementation of various government orders, circulars, regulations etc., against ragging.
- To ensure rehabilitation and restoration of the victim with dignity in her/ his campus.
- To urge TV Channels/Filmmakers to refrain from making serials/reality shows/movies that eulogize ragging.

4. Society for People's Action, Change and Enforcement (Space)

SPACE is an NGO engaged in advocacy and research campaign to curb ragging since May, 2004 through both field based interaction with institutions and victim students as well as over the internet (www.stopragging.org and http://groups.yahoo.com/group/stopragging).[31] The Raghavan Committee

28. Available at, http://www.no2ragging.org/activities.html, last accessed on 16th February, 2014.
29. *Ibid.*
30. *Supra* note 25.
31. *Supra note* 5, para 2.09.

benefited from the presentation made by the SPACE, which debated over the issue of the definition of ragging and focused on the nature and the implications of definition of ragging given in the Vishwa Jagriti Mission matter.[32] SPACE suggested that the Apex Court's definition did not cover all the aspects of ragging. According to SPACE, ragging is a systemized form of human rights abuse in educational institutions of South Asia, the worst forms of which are found in engineering, medical and military colleges. It is committed by 'senior' students (those in second year or higher) upon 'freshers' or first-year students.[33] The forms and traditions of ragging may vary from one place to another, but the greatest common factor in ragging in any educational institution is the creation of an environment of constant fear and intimidation in the minds of 'freshers'.[34]

According to the SPACE, Supreme Court's order seems to imply a zero-tolerance approach against ragging but students and college administration use words like 'mild-ragging' and have found alternative words such as 'interaction' and 'introduction' to justify the continuance of the practice.[35] Thus, SPACE report recommended a uniform law against ragging to be enacted by the Parliament. SPACE advocates that a monitoring mechanism should be put in place to enforce compliance with the Supreme Court guidelines and the relevant applicable laws.[36] Society also suggested to establish one or more full time anti-ragging cells at the Central level; anti-ragging cells to start 'Helpline'; and to arrange for the counselling of the victims.[37] This may take the form of an independent authority or may be a part of institutions such as the UGC/AICTE/or other affiliating authorities, HRD Ministry or the National Human Rights Commission. One function of any such anti-ragging cell would be to act as a 'Helpline'.[38] Complaints against ragging should be received by such a cell from across the country *via* post or e-mail.

It was pointed out to the Committee by SPACE that the Directorate of Medical Education in Andhra Pradesh had successfully tried a web-format, where ragging victims file their complaints.[39] If a victim is particularly disturbed, the cell could quietly arrange for the counselling of the victim. Such a cell would, however, have to be sensitive to the victim's desire for anonymity so that the victim does not run the risk of ostracism from the campus community. However, if the complainant explicitly demands an inquiry in a particular ragging incident, files an FIR, takes legal action etc., she/he would obviously not ask for anonymity. In respect of anonymous complaints, an enquiry targeting particular seniors may not be fair as such a complaint could be fake or motivated therefore, such a cell

---

32. *Ibid.*
33. *Ibid,* para 4.19.
34. *Ibid.*
35. *Ibid,* Notes on the interactions of the Committee with various stake holders, annexure III.
36. *Ibid,* para 2.09.
37. *Ibid.*
38. *Supra note* 35.
39. *Ibid.*

should undertake independent investigations as to the prevalence of ragging in that institution.[40]

It suggested that each education institution should present to the National Assessment and Accreditation Council (NAAC) and the National Board of Accreditation (NBA), as the case may be, an annual report about the compliance and the status of ragging in its institution, including the number and nature of ragging complaints received, and how they were handled and solved. Bodies like the NAAC of the University Grants Commission and the NBA or the All India Council of Technical Education should take into account the status of ragging in educational institutions before awarding ratings.[41]

5. Sathee

Sathee a social organisation is waging war against ragging. The President of organisation, Dr. S.S. Shilwant, Ph.D. in Law, offers legal help to fight this menace. Sathee organises lectures, seminars, workshops etc., in order to motivate student communities. It also organises debates and essay competitions in educational institutions on the issue. It publishes literature against this menace. Organisation is planning to take the help of audio-visual medium in a grand manner.[42]

NEED OF CIVIL SOCIETY & NGO

Raghavan Committee viewed the absence of civil society initiatives on the issue of ragging as a matter of serious concern.[43] Unless, the wider part of society gets involved in the crusade of eradication of the ragging, the problem cannot be curbed or prevented by educational institutions alone. The Committee recommended that at each level, the active involvement of media and the civil society is essential in tackling the problem of ragging.[44] Non-Government initiatives in anti-ragging movements need to be supported in order to bring about qualitative improvement and efficient outcomes.[45] The Committee recommended that the Central Government and State Governments should support such organizations to widen and intensify their activities.[46] They could be helped to launch awareness programmes either on their own or in collaboration with the media. Such efforts by the civil society may encourage parents and freshers to exercise their various rights including the Right to Information for ascertaining the real situation in college campuses.[47]

---

40. *Ibid.*
41. *Ibid.*
42. Gulshan Naveen, Ragging – The Red Alert, 1st Edn., 2010, p. 55.
43. *Supra note* 5, para 4.03.
44. *Ibid*, para 5.01.
45. *Ibid*, para 5.38.
46. *Ibid.*
47. *Ibid.*

Chapter XI
Alarming State

In the last 57 years, at least 250 cases of bullying related deaths have been reported in the English newspapers from other parts of the world. The majority (62.3%) of the reports of bullying-related deaths have originated in Europe, with majority (93%) of them occurring in the United Kingdom.[1] As far as the problem of ragging in India is concerned, it is widespread but hardly reported. An anti-ragging NGO, SAVE has brought to the light 7 incidents of the death caused by ragging in the year 2007 alone and 31 in the period between 2000-2007.[2]

How deplorable the consequences of ragging have become in recent years can also be gauged from the incidents of ragging reported by the media. Statistics gathered by CURE, based on the media reports, indicate the number of cases in 2008-09 as 88 while they were as high as 164 in the year 2009-10 across India.[3] According to the organization, in the academic session 2009-10 (July 2009 - June 2010) out of 164 cases of ragging, 19 cases were related to death. There have also been reports related to suicide attempts.[4] The maximum number of deaths due to ragging was recorded in Maharashtra (4), West Bengal (4) and Punjab (3).The highest number of incidents was reported from Uttar Pradesh (26), Andhra Pradesh (18), Tamil Nadu (14), Kerala (13) and West Bengal (11). There were 56 cases of ragging that had led to major and minor injuries to the students including several incidents leading to hospitalization and even permanent disability to young students.[5] 22% of the total cases involved sexual abuse of freshers. Twenty-four cases of ragging were related to serious group clashes, protests and strikes and violence between students. Elements of drug abuse, alcoholism, extortion, caste difference or regionalism were noted in 19 cases of ragging.[6]

---

1. Jorge Sabstein, 'Deaths Linked to Bullying and Hazing', Int J Adolesc Med Health 2008;20:235-9.
2. Rajesh Garg, Ragging: A Public Health Problem in India, Indian J Med Sci, Vol. 63, No. 6, June 2009, p. 269.
3. Ragging: March Against A Social Menace, p. 89-90, available at http://www.gnit.ac.in/pdf/Anti-RaggingHandbook.pdf, last accessed on 16th February, 2014.
4. *Ibid.*
5. *Ibid.*
6. *Ibid.*

RAGGING COMPLAINTS[7]

In the past 5 years, *i.e.*, from June, 2009 to April, 2014, a total of 2484 complaints were registered by the National Anti-Ragging Helpline. The problem is found to be severe in UP, West Bengal, Orissa, Bihar and Madhya Pradesh. In the below, total number of complaints registered by helpline since 15th June, 2009 to 14th April, 2014 have been given in a tabular form:—

1. YEAR WISE DISTRIBUTION OF COMPLAINTS

2009	345 (From 15th June, 2009)
2010	435
2011	577
2012	375
2013	641
2014	111 (As of 14th April, 2014)
Total number of Complaints received	**2484**

2. STATE-WISE DISTRIBUTION OF COMPLAINTS

State	2009	2010	2011	2012	2013	2014	Total
Andaman & Nicobar	0	0	0	0	0	0	0
Andhra Pradesh	11	9	10	11	14	3	58
Arunachal Pradesh	0	0	0	0	1	0	1
Assam	3	6	6	4	15	2	36
Bihar	10	15	27	27	33	5	117
Chandigarh	0	0	0	0	1	0	1
Chhatisgarh	5	8	6	4	4	1	28
Dadra & Nagar Haveli	0	0	0	0	0	0	0
Daman & Diu	0	0	0	0	0	0	0
Delhi	13	15	11	3	10	1	53
Goa	0	0	1	0	0	0	1
Gujarat	1	2	9	2	12	5	31
Haryana	9	10	18	5	9	1	52
Himachal Pradesh	1	2	0	3	5	1	12
Jammu & Kashmir	14	6	5	3	6	2	36
Jharkhand	7	11	17	13	24	4	76
Karnataka	18	15	17	10	23	1	84
Kerala	8	12	27	18	26	4	95

7. Data is taken from report prepared by Mr. Raj Kachroo, founder trustee of Aman Satya Kachroo Trust and from Aman Movement website.

Lakshadweep	0	0	0	0	0	0	0
Madhya Pradesh	40	33	37	32	80	15	237
Maharashtra	9	30	40	15	27	14	135
Manipur	1	0	1	0	1	0	3
Meghalaya	0	0	0	0	1	0	1
Mizoram	0	0	0	0	0	0	0
Nagaland	0	0	0	0	0	0	0
Orissa	36	41	54	44	71	6	252
Pondicherry	1	3	1	0	4	1	10
Punjab	12	18	5	12	12	4	63
Rajasthan	18	15	32	19	39	6	129
Sikkim	3	0	0	0	1	0	4
Tamil Nadu	17	20	33	17	32	5	124
Tripura	0	0	0	4	4	1	9
Uttar Pradesh	64	105	120	85	94	12	480
Uttarakhand	1	5	11	6	11	3	37
West Bengal	43	54	89	38	81	14	319
Grand Total	**345**	**435**	**577**	**375**	**641**	**111**	**2484**

3. SEX WISE DISTRIBUTION OF COMPLAINTS

As expected, the number of complaints from girls is less than those of boys. Girls have reported about 10% of the complaints compared to those of boys.

STATE	**MALE**	**FEMALE**
West Bengal	277	42
Uttar Pradesh	452	30
Orissa	229	23
Madhya Pradesh	220	17
Maharashtra	117	19
Andhra Pradesh	44	14
Rajasthan	118	11
Bihar	104	13
Tamil Nadu	116	9
Uttarakhand	29	8.
Delhi	47	6
Gujarat	27	6
ALL Other States	456	50
Total	**2236**	**248**

4. UNIVERSITIES/COLLEGES-WISE DISTRIBUTION OF COMPLAINTS[8]

Colleges affiliated to (i) Biju Patnaik University of Technology in Orissa, (ii) West Bengal University of Technology, (iii) Rajiv Gandhi Proudyogiki Vishwavidyalaya in MP, (iv) Gautam Buddh Technical University, in UP are amongst the most notorious colleges in the country as far as Ragging is concerned. Likewise, Banaras Hindu University (BHU) has a deep rooted tradition of Ragging. Unfortunately, the administration of BHU is in denial. Out of 1880 Complaints filed from around 439 Universities, there are more than 100 Complaints that are from medical and associated professional colleges. While it might seem like a small number but it is serious because the number of medical and associated colleges are also small. Roughly 10,000 Colleges are associated with AICTE. 23,000 colleges are affiliated to UGC. Colleges affiliated to MCI and associated regulatory authorities are only about 1500.

Reduction in Ragging is noticed in institutions that are located in metro cities like Delhi, Mumbai, Kolkata, Bangalore, Chennai etc. Among these, Delhi University is virtually Ragging Free. There are 3 possible explanations for this. (i) Students of these institutions are more exposed to national main stream media. (ii) The administration in these institutions has zero tolerance to Ragging. (iii) Students themselves have moved on to a better intellectual level. Ragging does not stimulate them any longer.

Sr. No.	Name of University	State	No. of Complaints Received
1	Biju Patnaik University of Technology	Orissa	116
2	West Bengal University of Technology	West Bengal	91
3	Rajiv Gandhi Proudyogiki Vishwavidyalaya	Madhya Pradesh	72
4	Gautam Buddh Technical University	Uttar Pradesh	66
5	Board of Technical Education	Uttar Pradesh	50
6	Rajasthan Technical University	Rajasthan	47
7	Uttar Pradesh Technical University	Uttar Pradesh	47
8	Anna University	Tamil Nadu	40
9	Banaras Hindu University	Uttar Pradesh	36
10	Punjab Technical University	Punjab	31
	Total of 10 Universities.		**596**
	From Remaining 429 Universities		**1284**
	Total from 439 Universities		**1880**

8. Data available for this part has been for the period of 4 years *i.e.*, from 15th June, 2009 to 15th June, 2013.

Sr. No.	Name of the College	State	Number of Complaints
1	Banaras Hindu University	Uttar Pradesh	28
2	Government Polytechnic Jhansi	Uttar Pradesh	22
3	National Institute of Technology, Durgapur	West Bengal	15
4	Birla Institute of Technology	Jharkhand	12
5	IITT College Of Engineering	Punjab	12
6	Indira Gandhi Institute of Technology	Orissa	10
7	Muzaffarpur Institute of Technology	Bihar	9
8	Rewa Engineering College	Madhya Pradesh	9
9	Purshotam Institute of Engineering & Technology	Orissa	9
10	Rajendra Institute of Medical Sciences	Jharkhand	8
	Total of 10 Colleges.		**134**
	From Remaining 1231 colleges		**1746**
	Total of 1241 Colleges		**1880**

The complete data set comprising 1241 colleges has been stored on the web at **www.amanmovement.org.**

There are several other incidents which have not come to the attention of the media *i.e.*, have not been reported or that the reports appearing in the vernacular sections of the press have not been reached to the whole society. It seems that the number of cases of ragging is very low, but what we see in the media is nothing but an *"iceberg phenomenon"*.[9] RTI queries have revealed that only 1% of the actual number of cases gets registered with the helpline because students are too scared to complain, fearing a backlash.[10] Unfortunately, only the murders, rapes and suicides get the attention of the media and society. If the daily humiliation was reported, we could have realized the extent to which this disease has crept into the educational institutions.

---

9. *Supra note 3.*
10. http://articles.timesofindia.indiatimes.com/2014-02-05/lucknow/47048287_1_national-anti-ragging-helpline-overall-complaint-status-aman-satya-kachroo-trust.

Chapter XII

Live Cases on Ragging

It is generally believed that ragging no more exists in the present society and if it exists anywhere then it is not that serious. But it is just a myth because practice of ragging is still rampant and increasing day by day, using new and different methods which are totally unimaginable. Following live cases show the real picture of this menace:—

LIVE CASES

YEAR – 2014

Case – 1

Name of the Institution – National Institute of Technology

Name of the Student – Unknown, A first year student

Incident - National Institute of Technology (NIT) cracked the whip on nine erring students who physically abused a first year student at the hostel.[1]

YEAR – 2013

Case – 1

Name of the Institution – Navi Mumbai College

Name of the Student – Unknown, A second year engineering student

Incident – One student committed suicide after allegedly being ragged. The 19-year-old jumped in front of a local train. He has named two of his fellow students in his suicide note for harassing him for several months.[2]

Case – 2

Institute – Ramrao Adik Institute of Technology, Navi Mumbai

Name of the Student – Unknown, a Second Year Student

Incident – A second year student committed suicide allegedly due to ragging by fellow students.[3]

Case – 3

Institution – Jawahar Lal Nehru Medical College at Aligarh Muslim University

1. http://www.thehindu.com/todays-paper/tp-national/tp-andhrapradesh/nit-suspends-9-students-for-ragging/article5629081.ece.
2. http://ibnlive.in.com/news/mumbai-19yearold-boy-jumps-in-front-of-a-train-after-he-was-ragged/391106-3-237.html.
3. http://timesofindia.indiatimes.com/city/mumbai/Familys-hopes-dashed-after-ragged-students-suicide/articleshow/20010466.cms.

Name of the Student – Unknown

Incident - Twelve students have been booked for allegedly ragging a junior. The case was registered by Jawed, a third-year student of the college on the basis of a complaint, containing that accused had confronted junior inside the hostel earlier in the week and ragged him causing great mental agony.[4]

Case – 4

Institution – MC Saxena College of Pharmacy

Name of the Student – Shumbul Ishaq, a first-year student

Incident - A first-year student, jumped off the third floor of her college building following "harassment by college staff and students and succumbed to her injuries".[5]

Case – 5

Institution – Pondicherry University

Name of the Student – Unknown

Incident – The University suspended two girl students for six months who lodged a ragging complaint against a senior student. The University also suspended the senior student and his friend against whom ragging charges were levelled. It suspended five other students for extending support to the two ragging victims and staging anti-ragging protests on the university premises.[6]

Case – 6

Institution – Extol College, Shahpura

Name of the Student – Unknown

Incident - A student has filed an FIR against three other students of the same college at Shahpura police station. Though college management suspended the accused students, they tried to downplay the incident, terming it a fight between students.[7]

Case – 7

Institution – Kurukshetra University

Name of the Student – Unknown

Incident - The incidents, which have been taking place at night in girls' hostel, were not brought to the attention of the authorities as the juniors were scared. A group of B Pharmacy students summoned all the first year students at night and posed indecent questions for hours together. The fear-stricken

---

4. http://zeenews.india.com/news/uttar-pradesh/12-amu-medical-students-booked-for-ragging_871630.html.
5. http://archive.indianexpress.com/news/harassed-by-teachers-students-girl-who-jumped-off-building-dead/1165894/.
6. http://timesofindia.indiatimes.com/city/puducherry/Pondicherry-University-suspends-alleged-ragging-victims/articleshow/25268923.cms.
7. http://articles.timesofindia.indiatimes.com/2013-11-23/bhopal/44389493_1_3-students-senior-students-bu-committee.

victims did not report the matter. However, it came to light when one of the girls informed her parents who in turn complained to the Pharmacy College principal. In 2008-2009, similar incidents took place at the girls' hostel leading to the suspension of girls.[8]

Case – 8

Institution – Jadavpur University.

Name of the Student – Unknown.

Incident – Two students were suspended after they were found guilty of ragging a junior student. The victim has alleged that he was beaten up by his seniors who also broke the window panes of his room at the University hostel.[9]

YEAR – 2012

Case – 1

Institute: College of Engineering and Management, Kolaghat.

Name of the Student: Subhro Samanta, a first-year student of electronics and instrumentation.

Incident: Victim was allegedly assaulted by his seniors outside the college campus while the West Midnapore boy was on his way back home. Seniors with their faces covered slashed the boy's arm, neck and back and threatened him with dire consequences if he ever returned to the college.[10]

Case – 2

Institution: Visva Bharti University, West Bengal.

Name of the Student: Unknown.

Incident - Uma Poddar, the warden of Karabi Girls' Hostel of the University, who allegedly forced a young girl student to drink her own urine as a punishment for bed wetting has been arrested and was also suspended.[11]

YEAR – 2011

Case – 1

Institute – Bengal Engineering and Science University (BESU).

Name of the Student – Unknown.

Incident – Five students were suspended from the hostel and fined for ragging a junior student through social networking web-site Facebook.[12]

---

8. http://www.thehindu.com/news/national/andhra-pradesh/ragging-rears-its-ugly-head-again-on-ku-campus/article5352431.ece.
9. http://www.thehindu.com/todays-paper/tp-national/tp-newdelhi/two-students-of-jadavpur-university-suspended-for-ragging/article5122259.ece.
10. http://articles.timesofindia.indiatimes.com/2012-09-04/kolkata/33580762_1_kolaghat-seniors-razor.
11. http://archive.indianexpress.com/news/warden-arrested-for-making-girl-student-drink-urine/972093/.
12. http://www.indianexpress.com/news/ragging—facebook-five-fined-and-also-the-complainant/826822.

YEAR – 2010

Case – 1

Institute: Post Graduate Institute of Medical Education and Research, Chandigarh.

Name of the Student: Nagedra AV.

Incident: The police said he jumped to death from the hostel building, his father said he had been pushed. His father said that he had said he was finding it difficult to continue there due to ragging.[13]

Case – 2

Institute: Sarabhai Institute of Science and Technology.

Name of the Student: Ajub Ajith.

Incident: He had told his mother that he was being ragged badly, but prevented her from complaining to the principal as, he said, that would make matters worse for him. Then he hanged himself to death from the ceiling fan in his house in Thiruvananathapuram.[14]

Case – 3

Institute: Advanced Training Institute, Mumbai.

Name of the Student: Satwinder Kumar.

Incident: Satwinder committed suicide. In his suicide note he named seven seniors who had ragged him so much that he left for home for Kurukshetra rather than taking mid-term exams. Before he could reach home, he committed suicide by throwing himself before a goods train in Rajasthan's Jhalawar district.[15]

Case – 4

Institute: B.S. Abdur Rahman Crescent Engineering College.

Name of the Student: Premlatha.

Incident: She committed suicide by consuming sulphuric acid in the chemistry lab. Her brother singled out one senior, Yogesh, 22, a fourth year student, as the person ragging her the most.[16]

Case – 5

Institute: Unknown.

Name of the Student: Sinmoi Debroy.

Incident: He was found hanging from the ceiling fan, dead, in his hostel room. During the investigation police found that his cell phone contained 42 messages, most of them allegedly abusive and threatening in nature.[17]

---

13. http://news.outlookindia.com/items.aspx?artid=679794.
14. http://newindianexpress.com/cities/thiruvananthapuram/article265198.ece.
15. http://ibnlive.in.com/news/ragged-to-death-student-jumps-in-front-of-moving-train/110988-3.html.
16. http://www.mumbaimirror.com/article/3/201002122010021202095461261052faf/Student-kills-herself-after-being-%E2%80%98ragged%E2%80%99.html.
17. http://newindianexpress.com/cities/chennai/article190921.ece.

YEAR – 2009

Case – 1

Institute: Rajendra Prasad Medical College, Tanda, Kangra, HP, India.

Name of the Student: Aman Kachroo, a first year student.

Incident: He had repeatedly complained to his parents about the brutal ragging that took place on the Medical College campus — often by completely drunk third-year students. On March 6–7, 2009, the boy was beaten so badly that he died of brain haemorrhage.[18]

YEAR – 2008

Case – 1

Institute: Institute of Management Technology, Ghaziabad.

Name of the Student: Unknown.

Incident: He was ragged by 3 of his seniors, namely, Ravi Shankar, a resident of Vadodara; Naveen Tomar, from Hisar; and Ajmer resident P.C. Gupta. The victim (name withheld) complained that three fellow management students at IMT-Ghaziabad forced him to undress and threw lit matchsticks at his private parts in the campus.[19]

YEAR – 2007

Case – 1

Institute: Pioneer College, Bhopal.

Name of the Student: Durgesh Shukla.

Incident: The victim hanged himself from a ceiling fan in his hostel room. He blamed seniors in his suicide note.[20]

Case – 2

Institute: Government Medical College, Chandigarh.

Name of the Student: Manjot Singh, an MBBS student.

Incident: He committed suicide by consuming a poisonous substance. He did so at his residence in Chandigarh, due to ragging in his hostel.[21]

Case – 3

Institute: Unknown.

Name of the Student: Chetan Raj.

Incident: He committed suicide in Mysore. His body was found hanging from the roof of his lodge room. He had already complained to his parents that he was being ragged in his college.[22]

---

18. http://articles.timesofindia.indiatimes.com/2009-03-10/india/28034755_1_aman-kachroo-senior-students-first-year-students.
19. http://expressindia.indianexpress.com/latest-news/3-management-students-from-imt-booked-in-ragging-case-68-days-after-complaint/395262.
20. http://articles.timesofindia.indiatimes.com/2007-09-20/india/27959212_1_hostel-room-senior-students-first-year-student.
21. http://www.hindustantimes.com/Punjab/Chandigarh/Ragging-drives-medical-student-to-suicide/SP-Article1-241115.aspx.
22. http://zeenews.india.com/znnew/articles.asp?aid=396228&sid=REG&sname.

Case – 4

Institute: Anand Engineering College, Agra, U.P.

Name of the Student: Abdul Wahab (21) a 2nd year student.

Incident: When the victim denied paying Rs. 2000 for seniors' drinks, he was brutally beaten up and was pushed off 4th floor hostel balcony. He got multiple fractures in legs and injuries in spinal cord which made him unable to speak any more.[23]

Case – 5

Institute: Sahara Arts & Management Academy, Lucknow, U.P.

Name of the Student: Sanjoy Singh, student of management.

Incident: When Sanjoy Singh was going to college, he was ragged, beaten and humiliated in the bus by senior students from Lucknow University. Later he disappeared from hostel.[24]

Case – 6

Institute: Kandi Raj College, West Bengal.

Name of the Student: Unknown, 14 first year students.

Incident: Juniors were asked to do sit-ups at least a hundred times and touched feet of seniors every night and were forced to dance in underwear. They were also made to write indecent things about their families. They were beaten up with sticks when they protested.[25]

Case – 7

Institute: Bengal Engineering & Science University, Shibpur, West Bengal.

Name of the Student: Soumik Basu, a 3rd year student.

Incident: Soumik was thrown out of balcony resulting in his death. University saw as many as 9 incidents of serious campus violence within a period of 3 years requiring a series of enquiry commissions and even police camp inside campus.[26]

YEAR – 2006

Case – 1

Institute: Mahatma Gandhi Institute of Technology, Hyderabad.

Name of the Student: S.P. Manoj.

Incident: He committed suicide in his hostel room due to ragging.[27]

---

23. Ragging: March Against a Social Menace, p. 91, available at http://www.gnit.ac.in/pdf/Anti-RaggingHandbook.pdf, last accessed on 16th February, 2014.
24. *Ibid.*
25. *Ibid, p.* 93.
26. *Ibid,* p.94.
27. http://www.hindu.com/2006/11/11/stories/2006111118640500.htm.

YEAR – 2005

Case – 1

Institute: Unknown.

Name of the Student: C Abraham, a first year engineering student.

Incident: He hanged himself to death at his residence in Hyderabad. In his suicide note, he mentioned that he was not interested in studies. His parents suspected his suicide to be a result of ragging.[28]

Case – 2

Institute: Unknown.

Name of the Student: Kamlesh Sarkar,

Incident: He committed suicide in a Private Hotel, Management Institute in Kalyani, Nadia district, West Bengal. Family members of the deceased insisted that he was a victim of ragging.[29]

Year – 2004

Case – 1

Institute: Madan Mohan Malviya Engineering College, Gorakpur, U.P.

Name of the Student: Sushil Pandey.

Incident: Sushil commited Suicide after being haunted by seniors.[30]

YEAR – 2002

Case – 1

Institute: Institute of Engineering and Technology, Lucknow.

Name of the Student: Anup Kumar.

Incident: Committed suicide by hanging himself from a ceiling fan at his residence in Kanpur. In his suicide note, Anup said that he was going through mental agony due to the sexual harassment by second-year students in the name of ragging.[31]

YEAR – 2000

Case – 1

Institution: All India Institute of Medical Sciences (AIIMS).

Name of the Student: Honhar Singh Meena, a first year MBBS student.

Incident: He was severely ragged in the undergraduate students' hostel. Then he went back to his native place.[32]

---

28. http://stopragging.org/2005/12/30/engineering-student-commits-suicide-was-it-ragging.
29. http://www.mail-archive.com/stopragging@yahoogroups.com/msg00139.html.
30. *Supra note* 23, p. 92.
31. http://articles.timesofindia.indiatimes.com/2002-09-14/lucknow/27326589_1_anup-kapoor-kanpur-student-iet.
32. The Ragging Menace, Issue of ragging raised in Rajya Sabha, available at http://www.educationobserver.com/College-Ragging-in-India.HTM, last accessed on 16th February, 2014.

Case – 2

Institution: Ravenshaw College, Orissa.

Name of the Student: Sushree Bijeta Mohanty, daughter of a CPI (M) leader and lawyer in Rourkela.

Incident: She was subjected to brutal 'welcome party' the seniors convened for ragging.[33]

LIVE CASES DISCUSSED BY RAGHAVAN COMMITTEE[34] :—

- Engineering student S.P. Manoj is reported to have hanged himself in Hyderabad, according to his parents, after ragging;
- Vipin Lal of Kozhikode, a student of Teachers' Training Institute was severely manhandled and forced to consume alcohol;
- A student of the Orissa University of Agriculture Technology was pushed down from the terrace by seniors resulting in spinal injuries and broken legs;
- Mukesh of Andhra Pradesh was sexually assaulted during ragging and his mother could not bear the ignominy leading to her suicide;
- In Bhagalpur, an altercation over ragging is reported to have led to bomb-blasts;
- A college student in Indore jumped in front of a running train after he was caught and detained for ragging other students;
- A first year medical student of Pune had to be hospitalized in the Intensive Care Unit after being ragged severely by seniors;
- Rohit Vijay Rane of Mumbai suffered severe swelling of chest and skull injuries after being hit with belts;
- Stripping and branding of junior students has been reported from Gujarat Vidyapeeth, ironically, an institution founded on Mahatma Gandhi's call;
- In Hyderabad, three students were paraded naked and to add to the humiliation, the entire episode was recorded through cell-phone camera;
- Two senior students of the Institute of Hotel Management at Hyderabad were reportedly killed in retaliation by a junior who had been subjected to ragging humiliation;
- Girl students of Viswa Bharati at Shanti Niketan allegedly forced a junior to undergo group sex;
- A. Naga medical student was found hanging in his hostel room at his institute in Imphal after he had been ragged;
- Swapnil Sharma of NIT, Durgapur was traumatized after being forced to kneel down for two hours.

---

33. *Ibid.*
34. The Menace of Ragging in Educational Institutions and Measures to Curb it, Report of the Committee constituted by the Hon'ble Supreme Court of India, in SLP No. 24295 of 2006, headed by R.K. Raghavan, para 3.23.

PERSONAL EXPERIENCES OF CELEBRITIES ON RAGGING

1. Amitabh Bachchan: The legendary bollywood actor Amitabh Bachchan shared his experience and said that *"I really can't tell you guys what kind of ragging I have been through. Please don't ask me."* It seems like Bachchan had a bad time in his college days.[35]

2. Arjun Rampal: According to Arjun Rampal, *"The actor was subsequently ragged for a long time and vowed never to rag his juniors in turn. Rampal is admittedly very much against ragging and considers it to be equal to a full-fledged crime."*[36]

3. Arindam Chaudhury: The management guru writes about his IIT Delhi friends, *"Well, their first months in IIT were traumatic to say the least. They would cry in front of me. They couldn't take in the humiliation of ragging. The humiliation of being stripped totally naked and being made to run around the IIT Delhi campus... The engineering and medical colleges of India are the havens of the worst possible ragging in this country."*[37]

4. Sujit Saraf: A California based filmmaker and playwright reveals, *"we crawled on all fours and barked like dogs; we brought cigarettes and Coca Cola for our seniors; we cleaned their rooms; we dropped our trousers so they could measure our penises; we formed human trains — each car holding the penis of the car in front — and whistled our way through hostel corridors; we simulated orgies; stripped naked"*.[38]

5. Imtiaz Ali: A well known filmmaker Imtiaz Ali shared his experience that, *"In college (Hindu College, Delhi), a lot of guys had stripped me naked during the ragging... At that time it was terrible....Craziest thing I've ever done – we've all walked naked...in those days ... it was part of mass ragging that everyone had to do"*. [39]

6. Prakash Rajpurohit: Top rank holder in IIT-JEE and IAS examinations, ran away from IIT Delhi hostel hitting the headlines. In his complaint lodged with the police, Rajpurohit had said students were asked among other things to enact a honeymoon scene, strip and consume alcohol.[40]

7. Manish Gupta: Movie Director, says *"I was a day-boarder in an engineering college in Bandra and my friends who stayed in the hostels were forced into sodomy with other boys as part of a ragging ritual"*.[41]

8. Rahul Dev: Movie actor says, *"I did my engineering from Bangalore and stayed in a hostel there. Though the seniors with their presence sparked off fear telling us to jump around holding our crotches, we challenged them and did not give in to their*

---

35. Available at http://www.no2ragging.org/celebs.html, last accessed on 16th February, 2014.
36. *Ibid.*
37. Prof. Arindam Chaudhuri (2010-12-09). "It's We Parents and Teachers Who Create Raggers out of Our Children". [Business and Economy]. Retrieved 2011-10-26.
38. Sujit Saraf (2006-10-14). "'Ten minutes into campus life, I was on my knees with a leash round my neck'". [Tehelka]. Retrieved 2011-10-26.
39. http://articles.timesofindia.indiatimes.com/2011-07-11/delhi/29758414_1_hostel-hindu-college-college-days.
40. Amba Batra (2004-07-22). "Victim of IIT ragging prepares to help freshers". [Indian Express]. Retrieved 2011-10-26.
41. http://articles.timesofindia.indiatimes.com/2013-01-08/parenting/36162148_1_student-case-colleges-educational-institutions/3.

unreasonable demands. But I can't describe the tension that we went through at that moment. There were times when juniors were made to wear kurta-pyjama and rubber slippers and roam around the college campus. Let me tell you that is not a good feeling and can damage your esteem for life".[42]

9. Sona Mohapatra: Singer reveals, *"I was horribly ragged in my engineering college in Odisha. Ragging is deplorable, and must be banned. Be it physical, mental, minor or major, ragging is a very perverted show of power, control and humiliation, and not way of getting anyone to join a community and blend into it. There are more interesting ways of doing that".*[43]

Disclaimer – These cases and experiences have been taken from the reports of leading NGO's like SAVE, CURE & SPACE, Dr. Raghavan Committee, newspapers & other media sources. Author does not own any responsibility for the authenticity of these incidents. Author's intention is not to harm the reputation of any prestigious institution or individual, but to explain how the menace of ragging is getting more dreadful day by day.

---

42 http://articles.timesofindia.indiatimes.com/2013-01-08/parenting/36162148_1_student-case-colleges-educational-institutions/2.

43. http://articles.timesofindia.indiatimes.com/2013-01-08/parenting/36162148_1_student-case-colleges-educational-institutions.

Chapter XIII

Ragging in Sri Lanka

There are some countries like Canada and Japan where ragging has been completely eradicated but it is still prevalent in South Asia. According to a research conducted by CURE, India and Sri Lanka are the mainly two countries in the world where ragging still exists and Sri Lanka is the most affected country in the world.[1] That is why I have analysed the situation of ragging in Sri Lanka in this chapter:—

A HISTORICAL PROFILE

Ragging in Sri Lanka is not a home-grown occurrence, but a direct result of the British colonialism like in India. There is no record to prove that such an act had prevailed in the ancient Sri Lankan educational institutions. The concept of ragging came into existence in the post-World War II era with the re-entrance of the soldiers into the college. In its initial phase ragging was fun-oriented and was done with the aim to instill team-spirit among the students. Gradually, ragging lost its primary objectives and became a violent and hazardous exercise.

PRESENT SCENARIO

Currently most of the government universities and several private institutions are affected by the menace of ragging. First few months in the universities, are commonly known as the *ragging period.*[2] During this period seniors are found mocking and jesting at the newcomers.

ADVERSE CONSEQUENCES

In Sri Lanka, several types of ragging can be observed like physical, behavioral, emotional, social etc. It has caused an increase in the suicidal tendencies among the ragged students. Innocent lives are crucified due to the unbearable ragging.[3] Ragging isn't merely a socio-legal problem, it has psychological dimension too.

POLITICS ON RAGGING

It has been pointed out by the various academicians in the Sri Lanka that ragging has direct influence of politics which has taken control of the student

---

1. Harsh Agarwal, Evolution of Ragging, available at http://noragging.com/index.php/Research/Ragging-The-Phenomenon/Evolution-of-Ragging.html, last accessed on 16th February, 2014.
2. http://www.dailynews.lk/2009/06/24/fea02.asp.
3. http://www.lankanewspapers.com/news/2007/2/12522_image_headline.html.

unions.[4] Student leaders controlling the movements against ragging have become members of the political parties and have become politically oriented.[5]

LATEST INCIDENTS

Freshers asked to use smart phones against raggers, December 29, 2013 – The Sunday Times[6]

Students at State-run universities and higher education institutions should use smart phones to record incidents of ragging so that action can be taken against the perpetrators, University Grants Commission (UGC) Chairman Prof. Kshanika Hirimburegama has advised. "They (students) can use their smart phones and take pictures or videos to prove incidents of ragging and immediate steps will be taken to punish those who are found guilty, she said."

Ragging drives student to suicide, July 21, 2013 – The Sunday Times[7]

Ragging of students in schools continues to take a heavy toll on their lives, with one victim, unable to bear the harassment, deciding to end her life. The student had managed to gain admission into HaliEla MV, but her dreams of higher education were shattered after incidents of ragging.

Ragging students assaults teachers, June 18, 2012 – The Daily Mirror[8]

Four AL students on charges of having assaulted several teachers of the Buttala Uva Pelwatte Maha Vidyalaya, when the teachers had intervened to stop the ragging of the newly admitted students. This incident had happened when several teachers had attempted to stop some senior students from ragging new students who had arrived at the school to begin their AL classes. A student who was also injured and admitted to hospital had left the hospital.

Peradeniya fresher allegedly stripped, hung from a beam and sexually abused, January 29, 2012 – The Sunday Times[9]

A fresher at the Peradeniya University was ordered to eat 10 parcels of rice, stripped and hung on a beam and later sexually abused, a Criminal Investigations Department (CID) probe into an incident of inhumane ragging has revealed. Twenty five students of the University, including three who sexually abused a male fresher, have been identified in the probe.

MAJOR INCIDENTS

These incidents will show how the monster of ragging crosses its limits and in the worst conditions can even take the precious worthy lives of the ragged.

---

4. http://www.priu.gov.lk/news_update/EditorialReviews/erev200011/20001113editorialreview.html.
5. http://www.asiantribune.com/?q=node/14294.
6. http://www.sundaytimes.lk/131229/news/freshers-asked-to-use-smart-phones-against-raggers-78193.html.
7. http://www.sundaytimes.lk/130721/education/ragging-drives-student-to-suicide-53477.html.
8. http://www.dailymirror.lk/news/19534-ragging-students-assault-teachers.html.
9. http://www.sundaytimes.lk/120129/News/nws_40.html.

- In 2011, a female student of Faculty of Humanities and Social Sciences, University of Ruhuna, was semi-paralysed in one limb as a result of ragging in the canteen.[10]
- In 2006, Prof. Chandima Wijebandara, the Vice Chancellor of University of Sri Jayewardenepura resigned as a result of students failing to comply with his orders to eradicate ragging from the university.[11]
- In 2002, Samantha Vithanage, a third year Management student at the University of Sri Jayewardenepura, pioneer of an anti-ragging campaign in an attempt to stop the practice, was murdered at a meeting.[12]
- In 1997, a first year female student of University of Ruhuna committed suicide following severe ragging by senior students.[13]
- In 1997, Kelum Thushara Wijetunge, a first year student at the Hardy Technical Institute in Ampara who was forced to do tough exercises and drink excessive quantities of liquor died from a kidney failure.[14]
- In 1997, 21 year old S. Varapragash, an Engineering student of University of Peradeniya, died from a kidney failure as a result of ragging.[15]
- In 1975, V.W. Kularatne Commission in its report to the Governor General recommended ban on ragging in the universities and enforcement of better security measures with wide powers to the Board of Regents. Twelve undergraduates were expelled from a university as a result of his findings and three more were suspended. Four officials were penalised for their failure to take an appropriate action against the ragging. This was the first major step taken against ragging in a university by the Sri Lankan Government.[16]
- In 1975, University of Peradeniya reported the first ragging related death when a 22 year old female student of the Faculty of Agriculture, Rupa Rathnaseeli was paralyzed as a result of jumping from the second floor of the hostel "Ramanathan Hall" to run off the physical ragging carried out by her seniors. It was reported that she was about to have a candle inserted in her vagina just before she had jumped out of the hostel building.[17]

LEGAL FRAMEWORK TO PREVENT AND PUNISH RAGGING

Constitution of the Democratic Socialist Republic of Sri Lanka, the supreme law of Sri Lanka provides for the protection of the human rights of the citizens of Sri Lanka. Any citizen can produce a petition to the Supreme Court in case of a human right violation or a case closer to the infringement.[18] In Constitution

10. http://www.sundaytimes.lk/111225/News/nws_11.html.
11. http://www.rivira.lk/2010/02/07/rivinetha6.htm.
12. http://groundviews.org/2009/11/30/ragging-in-our-universities-a-symptom-or-a-disease.
13. http://www.tamilnet.com/art.html?catid=13&artid=174.
14. http://www.sundaytimes.lk/980104/news2.html.
15. http://noragnofear.com/index.html.
16. http://www.island.lk/2002/11/17/news10.html and http://www.island.lk/2003/11/13/opinio07.html.
17. http://www.thesundayleader.lk/2011/03/27/ragging-%E2%80%93-my-experience.
18. Article 126 of Constitution of the Democratic Socialist Republic of Sri Lanka.

ruthless, brutal or contemptuous treatment to any party by another is considered as a violation of human rights[19], and in an instance of violation of such rights committed by university students, they shall be produced before the relevant Court and subject to suitable punishment that is followed by the trial. In order to curb the menace of ragging, *Prohibition of Ragging and Other Forms of Violence in Educational Institutions Act,* 1997 was enacted.[20] The Act, includes all the Higher Educational Institutions established under the Universities Act No. 16 of 1978.

PROHIBITION OF RAGGING AND OTHER FORMS OF VIOLENCE IN EDUCATIONAL INSTITUTIONS ACT (NO. 20 OF 1998)

This act was enacted to eliminate ragging and other forms of violence, cruelty and inhuman degrading treatment, from educational institutions.[21] The Act covers, ragging committed both within and outside an educational institution. Any student found guilty would be subject to imprisonment for a term not exceeding ten years and may also be ordered to pay compensation of an amount determined by court, to the person in respect of whom the offence was committed for the injuries caused to such person.[22] The Act provides for penalty on acts done by any person who, within or outside an educational institution, threatens, verbally or in writing, to cause injury to the person, reputation or property of any student or a member of the staff, of all educational institution or to the person, reputation or property of some other person in whom the victim is interested, with the intention of causing fear in the victim or of compelling the victim to do any act which the victim is not legally required to do, or to omit to do any act which the victim is entitled to do.[23] Such person shall on conviction after summary trial before a Magistrate be liable to rigorous imprisonment for a term not exceeding five years.[24] Further, such student shall be expelled or dismissed from such institution as the case may be.[25] The Act has made such offence bailable but with the discretion of the judge.[26] Offences under this Act are deemed to be cognizable offence.[27]

UNIVERSITY GRANTS COMMISSION[28]

It was observed by UGC that the powers vested or the provisions of the above Act had not been properly utilized by the Universities to curb ragging. In view of the alarming increase of incidences of ragging of various

19. http://www.sundayobserver.lk/2008/06/29/fea01.asp.
20. http://www.commonlii.org/lk/legis/num_act/poracfovieia20o1998797, last accessed on 16th February, 2014.
21. Preamble of Prohibition of ragging and other forms of violence in educational institutions Act 1997.
22. *Ibid*, section 2.
23. *Ibid*, section 3.
24. *Ibid*.
25. *Ibid*, section 8.
26. *Ibid*, section 9.
27. *Ibid*, section 11.
28. Commission Circular No. 919 of University Grant Commission, given on 15th January, 2010.

forms that were reported and observed in all Universities/Higher Education Institutions (HEIs), in spite of having introduced the above Act in 1998, the following guidelines were prepared in order to facilitate implementation of the provisions of the above Act by UGC. Thus, Universities/Higher Education Institutions are required to adopt the following measures in three phases, namely Prevent, Perform and Punish in addition to the strategies suitable to the respective Institutions.

1. PREVENT

1.1 The students should sign a declaration, countersigned by the parent/guardian stating that they shall not initiate, aide, abate, perform or participate in any form of ragging or violence inside or outside the premises of the HEIs during the period of their registration at the HEI.

1.2 Appoint an Anti Ragging Committees (ARC) in all Universities/HEIs consisting of the Vice Chancellor and/or DVC, Deans, One Council Member representing the UGC nominees, Proctor if any, University Medical Officer, Student Counsellors, sub-wardens, and SAR/AR Student welfare as the convener. This committee should meet at least twice a month during the preparatory and peak period and regularly report to the Council. Universities/HEIs are encouraged to establish faculty level Anti-Ragging Committees depending on the needs of the individual Universities/HEIs.

1.3 Prepare a handout detailing the acts that could be considered as ragging together with the punishments that could be meted out under the provisions of the above Act.

1.4 Appoint Academic Staff of Senior Lecturer Grade II and above at least for a period of three months or more as Temporary Student Counsellors (TSC) on the basis of one TSC not exceeding per 20-25 students.

1.5 Educate all heads of departments and other responsible unit heads on all aspects of ragging including the provisions of the Act.

1.6 Posters on all measures taken on ragging should be displayed in prominent places such as the libraries, student canteens, hostels and on the relevant notice boards.

1.7 All security staff should be detailed on the preventive measures.

1.8 All parents and new entrants should be informed about the features of the Act.

1.9 Educate the seniors on the consequences of ragging.

1.10 Admit the fresher students while the senior students are on vacation.

1.11 Conduct an orientation/familiarization programme for fresher students educating them on the strategic locations and procedures to be followed if subjected to any form of ragging.

1.12 All relevant officials should be encouraged to be present after working hours or during weekends to take part in vigilant activities round the clock within and in the immediate vicinity of the HEI.

1.13 Keep the local police informed of the places and period in which ragging could likely to occur.

1.14 Keep the mass media informed on the measures taken to curb ragging and create public awareness especially targeting the neighborhood.

1.15 Encourage the presence of Student Counsellors and sub-wardens within the University premises for longer hours, may be on voluntary and roster basis.

1.16 Initiate innovative University specific programmes or activities that could provide a safer and student friendly environment for the fresher students to get familiarized with the University environment and culture.

2. PROCEDURES TO BE FOLLOWED IN THE EVENT OF RAGGING

2.1 Record all complaints related to ragging and provide facilities to lodge open complaints or under 'confidential' basis if needed.

2.2 Encourage submission of evidence as much as possible, written forms of complaints, material evidence, witnesses, tape-recorded (audio) and photographs or videos.

2.3 Report all cases of ragging to the relevant Police Station to be followed under the Ragging Act No 20 of 1998.

2.4 Refer for medical or psychiatric examination of the victim and request medical reports if necessary.

2.5 In case of grievous injuries or on punishable acts as prescribed in the Penal Code and the Convention against Torture and Other Cruel, Inhuman or Degrading Treatment or Punishment Act No 72 of 1994, report to the police.

2.6 Obtain details of the damages caused to University or public property as a result of ragging.

2.7 Follow the procedures prescribed in the Prohibition of Ragging Act No 20 of 1998.

2.8 Report all incidences of ragging and the punishments meted on the basis of the Ragging Act No 20 of 1998 to the University Grants Commission on a weekly basis during the period of the first three months of the enrollment of fresher students.

3. PUNISHMENT

It is emphasized that many of the offences listed under the above Act are non-bailable and liable to rigorous imprisonment, up to ten years. It is also possible that a student if found guilty under the provisions of the said Act could be expelled from the Institution and also liable to pay compensation for any damages to property or injuries caused on the victims.

TEMPLATE OF THE DECLARATION

According to UGC guidelines as mentioned earlier, the students should sign the following declaration, countersigned by the parent/guardian stating that they shall not initiate, aide, abate, perform or participate in any form of ragging or violence inside or outside the premises of the HEIs during the period of their registration at the HEI.

1. DECLARATION BY THE CANDIDATE OR STUDENT

1. I...have carefully read and fully understood the law prohibiting ragging referred in the Prohibition of Ragging and Other Forms of Violence in Educational Institutions Act, No. 20 of 1998 and the Commission Circular No:.......of 15th January, 2010.
2. I hereby undertake that;
   - 2.1 I will not indulge in any behavior or act that may come under the definition of ragging.
   - 2.2 I will not participate in or abet or propagate ragging in any form.
   - 2.3 I will not hurt anyone physically or psychologically or cause any other harm.
3. I hereby agree that if found guilty of any form of ragging, I may be punished as per the law enforced and by-laws of the University.

Signed this on the..................... day of the month of........................in the year.........

....

Signature of the student

Name .

Admission No..............

Address:...

....

....

2. UNDERTAKING BY THE PARENT/GUARDIAN

1. I ....have carefully read and fully understood the law prohibiting ragging referred in the Prohibition of Ragging and Other Forms of Violence in Educational Institutions Act, No. 20 of 1998 and the Commission Circular No: ....of.............15th January, 2010.
2. I assure you that my son/daughter/ward will not indulge in any form of ragging.
3. I hereby agree that if he or she is found guilty of any form of ragging he or she may be punished as per the law in force and by-laws of the University.

....

Signature of Parent or Guardian

Name.............

Relationship to the student..........

Address...

....

ANTI-RAGGING MOVEMENT

After so many endeavors by the government of Sri Lanka to stop the menace of ragging, the situation is even getting worse year by year. That is why there is a dire need of official anti-ragging movements across the whole nation but internal clashes have been the biggest hurdle between ragging and anti-ragging movements. Best suitable example of it is – Samantha Vithanage, a third year management student at the University of Sri Jayewardenepura, who pioneered an anti-ragging campaign, was killed by the student council of the same university who defended the practice, at a meeting while in a discussion to stop ragging.

On the positive node despite all this, slowly and gradually anti-ragging movements have started to appear in all other universities. Hopefully, over a period of time rag-free culture will increase in several universities due to these movements.

Chapter XIV

Steps to Be Followed – If Ragged

"I was always looking outside myself for strength & Confidence.
But it comes from within. It is here all the time."

— Anna Frend

Generally, an innocent victim of ragging who might not even know the first place where he should go if ragged, feels helpless in the circumstances, due to her/his lack of awareness about the law and procedure. It becomes even difficult for her/him to contemplate the right line of action; therefore, she/he needs to be educated about steps which should be taken, in case of ragging. But, before all other legal steps to be taken, one must necessarily take the required medical treatment to prevent the injuries suffered from taking the bad shape. .

[A] MEDICAL STEP TO BE TAKEN

1. If Injuries are not grave then:-

If physical/mental injuries caused due to ragging are not grave then Reiki and Pranic therapies are the magnificent tools to remove or cope up with the negative emotions of ragging. These therapies scan the energy field, identify the blockage, remove the diseased energy and charge the area with positive divine energy. These therapies are important because one feels light and relaxed after doing this.

Pranayam therapy:- In a traumatic situation, it is a matter of fact that the normal breathing rate alters and oxygen fails to reach millions of cells in the body. *Pranayam*, a form of yoga exercise, supplies fresh oxygen to the body and calms the mind. Practicing the following breathing exercise helps the students to get rid of the accumulated toxins in the body:-[1]

- Sit in a chair, close your eyes,
- Keep your hand on the arms of chair or your lap,
- Just inhale deeply imagining that white divine light is entering with each breath to the count of 3,
- Hold your breath to the count of 3 imagining that white light is cleaning your body,

1. Naveen Agarwal, Tips for Overcoming Ragging Trauma, available at http://noragging.com/index.php/Research/Finding-a-CURE/Tips-for-Overcoming-Ragging-Trauma.html, last accessed on 16th February, 2014.

- Exhale to the count of 3 imagining that the white light has turned gray as it departs taking away negative energy with it,
- Repeat the exercise for 5 minutes. Regular practice will make one feel comfortable and confident.

Alternatively, sharing of the traumatic experience with the person you trust or with friends or with relatives can also improve one's mood. In case, if student stays away from home, she/he may write down the traumatic event or the feelings on a paper and tear it.[2]

2. If Injuries are grave then:

If Injuries are grave then the injured student should be rushed to the nearest hospital for the medical treatment. It is better, if the first-aid treatment is locally available which would prevent any further deterioration in the condition of the injured. This first-aid should be made available in the college campus or with the office of the superintendent/warden of the hostel.[3]

If at all the victim is still advised by the doctor-on-duty, then she/he should be immediately admitted to the hospital. Doctor-in-charge of the hospital should be notified about the incident of the ragging to ensure that the word 'assault' is mentioned by him in the prescription sheet of the hospital and the medical certificate.[4] The victim should leave the hospital only when she/he is declared fit and gets a 'fit certificate'[5] along with all the treatment papers, x-ray plates and reports which should be preserved for the future purposes.

[B] LODGE A COMPLAINT WITH THE COLLEGE AUTHORITY

After getting the preliminary medical treatment, a written complaint should be filed with the college authority immediately. It may be addressed to the head of the college seeking disciplinary actions against the culprits. Complaint must contain the detailed information about the incident of ragging.

Draft Copy of Complaint[6]

Dated............

To

The Principal

(Add name & address of college)

Respected Sir,

Subject: Lodging of complaint for the incident of ragging on .... in the campus.

I do hereby lodge a complaint with you as detailed below and request you to take immediate action against the culprits.

That on .... at about .... am/pm, my son/daughter namely Mr./Miss ...., a student of your College/University

2. *Ibid.*
3. Ragging: March Against a Social Menace, p. 39, available at http://www.gnit.ac.in/pdf/Anti-RaggingHandbook.pdf, last accessed on 16th February, 2014.
4. *Ibid.*
5. *Ibid.*
6. *Ibid*, pp. 43-45.

studying B.Tech/B.E./Medical/Hotel Management/Law/Other (specify the name & year of the course) and staying at college hostel namely .... (delete if ragging incident happened in college premises) was ragged by some senior students of the college/university/hostel when she/he was in the college/hostel and she/he was hurt grievously and seriously injured so much so that her/his life is in danger.

She/he was (beaten, abused, forced to utter filthy languages, kept physically confined for hours, forced to uncover body, made to dance as per their wishes or nature of injury whichever is applicable) .... She/he was rushed immediately to a hospital namely, ... in a critical condition where she/he has been treated by the attending doctors. The attending doctors on duty hospitalized her/him due to major injuries for treatment and medical care. She/he was released after making necessary investigation by the attending doctors with advice for complete bed rest/to be examined by a Psychologist whichever is applicable). She/he needs a few more days of observation and prolonged treatment by the doctors.

That the names of the assaulters who ragged Mr. /Miss .... are

(1) Mr./Miss .... alias ...., a student 2nd/3rd/4th/5th year

(2) Mr./Miss .... alias ...., a student 2nd/3rd/4th/5th year

(3) Mr./Miss .... alias ...., a student 2nd/3rd/4th/5th year

(Keep whichever is applicable and delete others. Add names & other details as available)

Further kindly note that some other students, namely Mr./Miss .... Mr./Miss .... and Mr./Miss ....(Add names who had also been assaulted) were also tortured, abused, humiliated, made to stand for hours/sexually assaulted/knelt down on floors (or any other specification) .... by those senior students.

Sir, ragging in educational institute is a punishable offence and the culprits are liable to be punished and to face disciplinary actions as per the rules and regulations of the college/university and law of the land. Therefore, I kindly request you to take immediate necessary disciplinary actions so that justice prevails and the campus is freed from the menace of ragging.

Thanking You,

Yours faithfully,

(Name & signature of father/mother)

Address: ....

Telephone No./Mobile No. : ....

*Enclosure: Documents/papers related to treatment in hospital (Photo copies)

X-Ray Report (Photo copy)

* add or delete as per documents available.

[C] LEGAL STEPS TO BE TAKEN

If college authority does not take cognizance of the matter or if one feels dissatisfied with the decision of the authority then one should take proper legal steps and file/register a complaint against the offender.

HOW TO FILE A COMPLAINT

- Individual has the right to complain against any offence.
- The complaint can be made
  1. At the police station
  2. In the court

1. At the Police Station

(a) Non-cognizable offence [Section 155 of the Cr.P.C.]

- If one is a victim of non-cognizable offence then the police will enter a brief statement of facts into the register of non-cognizable offences.
- To investigate the offence, the police require the permission of a magistrate.
- If the police do not take steps to get permission for investigation, one can her/himself go to the court for such permission.
- Examples of non-cognizable offences: Criminal intimidation, voluntarily causing hurt, etc.

(b) Cognizable offence [Section 154 of the Cr.P.C.]

- If the offence is a cognizable one, the police will register it in their register of cognizable offences.
- Since it is the "first piece of Information" that pertains to the commission of a cognizable offence, it is called a **First Information Report or F.I.R.**
- The police can investigate the complaint on their own without the permission of a Magistrate.
- Examples of cognizable offence: murder, sexual assault etc.

Where can one file the F.I.R.

- Register the F.I.R. at the police station within whose jurisdiction the offence occurred.
- If you are not sure of which police station exercises jurisdiction, register the F.I.R at the nearest police station. They must take down your complaint and forward it to the police station exercising the jurisdiction. The police cannot refuse to register the F. I. R. on the ground that the offence was not committed within their jurisdiction.

Note: Recently, a Constitution Bench of the Hon'ble Supreme Court in ***Lalita Kumari v. Govt. of U.P.,***[7] held that registration of FIR is mandatory under Section

7. Writ Petition (Criminal) No. 68 of 2008, decided on 12/11/2013.

154 of the Code of Criminal Procedure, if the information discloses commission of a cognizable offence and no preliminary inquiry is permissible in such a situation. If the information received does not disclose a cognizable offence but indicates the necessity for an inquiry, a preliminary inquiry may be conducted only to ascertain whether cognizable offence is disclosed or not.

Procedure of lodging the F.I.R. at the Police Station

- Go to the police station and meet the officer-in-charge.
- Narrate step-by-step in an orderly sequence to the officer every information about the offence.
- An FIR may be given orally or in writing.
- The officer should reduce the information given orally into writing.
- If given in writing, it should be in the format of a formal letter, addressed to the senior police inspector of the concerned police station.
- Carry a Xerox/carbon copy of the letter and take an acknowledgment of receipt from the police station after you have handed over the original one.
- The information given should be entered in a register kept by the officer.
- The written information should be read over to you.
- The information given should be signed by you.
- One is entitled to get a copy of the F.I.R. (free of charge, immediately after the registration of the F.I.R.)[8]

The FIR should be specific about-

- What happened - The facts which make out the offence.
- Sequence of events.
- Name and description of the offender. Additional information regarding offender *viz.*, year of study, stream, name of hostel, room no. etc. should be noted in FIR to avoid any future confusion towards identification of guilty.
- Date and time of offence.
- Place of offence.
- Description of weapons used (if any).
- Description of injuries sustained (if any).
- Attach medical certificate (if any).
- Do not forget to mention that you have been given first aid at the hostel/college and subsequently at hospital, duly examined and treated by the doctor-on-duty. In case the fresher is still admitted in hospital/nursing home due to severe injury, the matter needs to be noted in FIR.

---

8. Section 154 (2) of CrPC.

- Names of all others who were present at the time of ragging/assault and had promoted/encouraged assaulters instead of saving the victim.

All important facts are to be noted in FIR as any lapses in FIR may help accused to give a slip and to get away easily without any punishment.

Who can file the F.I.R.

- F.I.R. as the name suggests is the first Information regarding an offence, so any person who has first-hand knowledge of facts can file an FIR.
- An F.I.R. can also be filed by a person who has just heard/read about commission of the offence but does not have first-hand information of facts. So, in case if student her/himself is sick enough due to injury, FIR may also be lodged by parents and/or local guardians or by friends at the local police station.

When can one file the F.I.R.

- An F.I.R. should be registered at the earliest possible opportunity.
- Delayed F.I.R. - any delay in lodging the F.I.R. must be properly explained.
- Effect of unexplained delay – it may cast doubt on you.

DRAFT COPY OF FIRST INFORMATION REPORT (FIR)[9]

To

The Officer –In – Charge Dated............

Police Station: ....

Distt: ....

Respected Sir,

Subject: Lodging of FIR on the incident of Ragging on ....

I, do hereby lodge a complaint with you as detailed below and request you to treat it as an FIR for taking immediate action against the culprit(s): That on.................. at about .... a.m./p.m., my son/daughter namely Mr./Miss .... a student of .... College/University and staying at hostel namely .... was ragged by some senior student/s of the college/ university/ hostel and was seriously injured so much so that her/his life is in danger.

She/he was beaten, abused, forced to utter filthy languages, forced to uncover her/his body, made to dance, commit nuisance, sexually abused, hurt in private parts (specify the nature of injury) ....

She/he has been rushed immediately to a hospital namely,........................ in a critical condition where she/he has been hospitalized with grievous injuries for treatment and medical care by the attending doctors on duty. She/he needs a few days observation and prolonged treatment.

9. *Supra note* 3, pp. 41-42.

That the names of the assaulters who ragged Mr. /Miss .... are

(1) Mr./Miss .... alias .... , a student 2nd/3rd/4th/5th year

(2) Mr./Miss .... alias .... , a student 2nd/3rd/4th/5th year

(3) Mr./Miss .... alias .... , a student 2nd/3rd/4th/5th year

(Keep whichever is applicable and delete others. Add names & other details as available)

Further, note that some other students, namely Mr./Miss.................... .... Mr./Miss .... and Mr./Miss .... (Add names who had also been assaulted) were also tortured, abused, humiliated, made to stand for hours/sexually assaulted/knelt down on floors (any other specify here) .... by those senior students.

You are aware that ragging is a punishable offence in the educational campus and the culprits are liable to face criminal charges as per the law of the land. I would request you to treat this complaint letter as the FIR and please take necessary actions so that justice prevails.

Thanking You,

Yours Faithfully,

(Name & Signature of father/mother)

Address : ....

Telephone No./Mobile No. : ....

Enclosure: Documents/papers related to treatment in hospital (Photo copies)

X-Ray Report (Photo copy)

Procedure to be followed if police do not register the F.I.R.

- Go to the D.C.P. (Deputy Commissioner of Police) or D.S.P. (Deputy Superintendent of Police). If the D.S.P./D.C.P. is satisfied that such information discloses the commission of a cognizable offence, he shall either investigate the case himself or direct an investigation to be made by any police officer subordinate to him.
- If no action is taken at this level, approach the higher authorities in the police hierarchy, first the A.C.P. (Additional Commissioner of Police) of the area and then the C.P. (Commissioner of Police) or the S.P. (Superintendent of Police) as the case may be.
- At each level, when submitting the letter to the Police/DCP/DSP/ACP/CP or SP take an acknowledgement of receipt on a xerox/carbon copy of the letter and attach the xerox copy of this receipt to all future communication with the same authority or a senior authority. If they

do not accept the letter, send it by registered post acknowledgement due [R.P.A.D.]

- If all levels of the police hierarchy do not take any action, then write to the Magistrate within whose jurisdiction the police station lies. Attach copies of receipts/AD slips of all communications with the police and describe the lack of action or negligent action which made it necessary to approach the Magistrate.[10]

2. Approaching the Courts

A complaint can also be filed in the court directly.[11]

Jurisdiction

- All complaints are to be made to a Magistrate within whose local jurisdiction the offence was committed.
- If the offence was committed within the jurisdiction of more than one Magistrate, it may be tried by any such Magistrate in whose jurisdiction the offence or a part of the offence was committed.

Grounds for Initiating the Proceedings[12]

Proceedings before a Magistrate may be initiated:

- On receiving a complaint of facts which constitute an offence.
- On receiving a police report of facts which constitute an offence.
- On receiving information from any person that an offence has been committed.
- On his own knowledge that an offence has been committed.

Examination of complainant[13]

On receiving a complaint and taking note of the offence made out from the complaint, the Magistrate shall:

- Examine the complainant and any witnesses on oath.
- The substance of such examination shall be reduced to writing.
- It shall be signed by the complainant and the witnesses.
- The Magistrate can then do one of two things:
  a. The Magistrate can postpone the issue of process and either inquire into the case himself or direct an investigation to be made by the police.
  b. Issue process (summons/warrant) against the accused.

PROCEDURE: Once the process is issued, and the accused appears or is brought before the Magistrate, the case will proceed as a warrant case or summons case depending on the kind of offence.

---

10. Section 156 (3) of CrPC.
11. Section 190 of CrPC.
12. Section 190 (1) of CrPC.
13. Section 200 of CrPC.

BRIEF INTRODUCTION OF SOME USEFUL CONCEPTS OF CRIMINAL LAW -

Ignorance of law is no excuse in eyes of justice. But, one should know that our laws are not uncomplicated to be understood by a lay man; so, here short description of some useful concepts of Criminal law are given which would help during legal proceedings.

STAGES OF A CASE-[14]

Filing an F.I.R. is the first stage of any case which sets criminal law in motion. Here below, short notes on further stages of criminal cases are given, so that one can get an idea that what would happen after lodging an F.I.R.

1. Investigation

The Police/Magistrate/any other person authorized by the court makes inquiries and investigation into the matter.

2. Arrest of the Accused

A person is arrested in connection with the offence.

3. Remand – Police/Judicial Custody

- The accused is produced before the Magistrate.
- The accused may be remanded to police custody.
- The accused may be remanded to judicial custody.

4. Bail

- The accused may be granted bail.
- If the accused can furnish the bail amount, he will be released from custody.
- If bail is denied or the accused is unable to furnish the bail amount, he will continue to remain in custody.

5. Discharge of Accused by Police

- The accused may be discharged by the police themselves, if they do not find any evidence against him.
- In such a case the accused is free to go and if in custody, he is released.

6. Filing of the Chargesheet[15]

- If the police find enough evidence against the accused, they will file a charge-sheet against him in court.
- If the accused is on bail, a summon is issued to him, informing him that the charge-sheet has been filed against him and asking him to attend the court.
- The charge-sheet includes all the documents relied on by the police.
- A copy of the charge-sheet along with all the documents that form a part of it must be furnished to the accused.

---

14. After lodging an FIR.
15. Section 173 of CrPC.

7. Committal of the Case to the Sessions Court[16]

- If the case is triable by the Sessions Court, the Magistrate will commit the case to the Sessions Court.
- The case papers will be sent to the Sessions Court.
- The case will be tried by the Sessions Court.

8. Discharge of Accused by Court[17]

- If the court finds on the basis of the material in the charge-sheet that there is no ground for proceeding against the accused, the court can discharge the accused.
- In such a case the accused is free to go, and if in custody, he is released.
- However, if during the trial any material appears on the record against the accused, the court may order the discharged accused to be re-arrested and tried.

THE TRIAL

9. Framing of Charge[18]

- If the judge finds that there is enough evidence against the accused, he will frame the charges against him.
- The accusation is explained to the accused in a language that he understands.
- He is asked whether he pleads guilty or not guilty.
- The judge records the plea in writing.

10. Accused Pleads Guilty[19]

- The judge may convict him, and sentence him or
- The judge may proceed with trial.

11. Accused Pleads Not Guilty

The judge will fix a date for the examination of witnesses.

12. Summons/Warrants to Prosecution Witnesses[20]

- Summons are issued to the prosecution witnesses to attend the court and give evidence in the case.
- If the witness does not attend the court on receiving the summons, the judge can issue a warrant against him.

13. Examination of Prosecution Witness[21]

- Examination-in-chief - The witness will be questioned by the prosecutor.
- Cross Examination- The witness will be questioned by the advocate of the accused.

---

16. Section 209 of CrPC.
17. Section 227of CrPC.
18. Section 228 of CrPC.
19. Section 229 of CrPC.
20. Section 230 of CrPC.
21. Section 231 of CrPC.

- Re-Examination - The witness may be again questioned by the prosecutor and cross-examined by the advocate for the accused.
- Recall of witness - A witness, who has already been examined, may be recalled by the court, for any reason in the interest of justice.

14. Statement of the Accused[22]

- The statement of the accused is recorded to enable him to explain what the prosecution witnesses have said against him in court.
- This statement is not taken on oath.

15. Examination of Defence Witnesses[23]

- The accused may examine himself and any other witnesses in his defence.
- Examination-in-chief - The witness will be questioned by the defence advocate.
- Cross-examination- The witness will be questioned by the prosecutor.
- Re-examination - The witness may be again questioned by the defence advocate and cross-examined by the prosecutor.

16. Final Arguments[24]

- Arguments from both the prosecution and the defence are heard.

17. Judgement/Sentencing[25]

- The judge records his findings in the form of a judgement.
- If the judge finds the accused to be innocent he passes an order of acquittal.
- If the judge finds the accused to be guilty, he hears the accused on the question of sentence and sentences the accused.

RIGHT TO APPOINT A 'WATCHING' ADVOCATE [SECTION 301 OF THE CR.P.C.]

- The complainant/victim in a police case may appoint his own lawyer, who may apply to the court to assist the prosecution. Such a lawyer is known as a 'watching' advocate.
- At the stage of remand, the complainant/victim may oppose the grant of bail to the accused by filing an intervention application in the court, either personally or through his lawyer.
- The Public Prosecutor, Assistant Public Prosecutor or Special Public Prosecutor or in-charge of the case shall conduct the prosecution.
- The 'watching' advocate does not have the right to examine prosecution witnesses or cross-examine defence witnesses. As the term itself suggests, he can only assist the prosecutor and can act only under his directions.

---

22. Section 313 of CrPC.
23. Section 233 of CrPC.
24. Section 234 of CrPC.
25. Section 235 of CrPC.

- The watching advocate may submit written arguments at the end of the trial with the permission of the court.
- When the court imposes a sentence of fine, the court may while passing a judgement orders the whole or any part of the fine recovered to be paid to the complainant/victim in payment of compensation for loss/injury caused by the offender.
- When the court does not impose a sentence of fine, the court can order the accused to pay an amount as compensation to the complainant/victim. There is no limit on the amount of compensation payable to the complainant under this clause.
- An order for compensation may also be made by the appeal court or by the Sessions Court or High Court in the revision.
- The complainant can also file a separate civil suit for compensation. The amount of compensation awarded by the court shall be considered by the civil court at the time of awarding the compensation to such person.

WITNESS

Witness is an important constituent of the administration of justice. If one is a witness of any ragging incident then understanding of following concepts would help:-

Who is a witness?

Any person acquainted with the facts and circumstances of a case is a witness.

At the police station [Section 160 Cr.P.C.]

- Any witness may be called to the police station for interrogation.
- No woman, or boy under 15 years of age can be called to the police station for the purpose of interrogation. They can be interrogated only at their residence.
- The witness can be called to the police station by an order which must be in writing.
- The witness must be within the limits of that police station or any adjoining one. If not, he cannot be called to the police station.
- The witness is entitled to be reimbursed the reasonable expenses incurred in attending any place other than his residence.

REMEMBER

- Your statement may be taken down in the local language.
- Once you have given the statement to the police, read it over yourself or if it is in a language you do not understand, ask the police officer taking the statement to read it to you.
- Make sure that what has been recorded matches with the oral statement given by you. For this purpose, try to keep a person with you who knows the local language.

- If the witness does not attend the police station as required, he can be prosecuted for disobedience of the order of a public servant under section 174 of the I.P.C. (simple imprisonment for 1 month or a fine of Rs. 500, or both).[26] So, if you are called by police, please go to police station.

Interrogation at the police station

- The witness will be examined orally by the investigating officer.
- No oath/affirmation is required to be administered.
- The witness is bound to answer truthfully all the questions put to him except the questions, answers to which may expose her/him to a criminal charge/penalty/forfeiture.
- This oral examination may be reduced to writing.
- Written statement is not required to be signed by the person making it.
- The police cannot prevent a person from making any statement which she/he wants to make out of her/his own free will.
- However, they cannot cause the witness to make a statement by any inducement, threat or promise.

Use of the statements of witnesses

- The statement of the witness so recorded, if found to be material, will be included in the charge-sheet filed against an accused person after completion of the investigation by the police.
- The witness may then be called to the court to testify when the trial begins.
- The court will issue a summons to the witness.
- If the witness does not attend the court, the judge may issue a warrant for her/his arrest in order to compel her/his attendance in the court.
- If the court considers the production of a document or thing necessary for any trial, it may issue a summons to the person in whose possession it is, requiring her/him to attend and produce it in the court.

---

26. Section 174 of IPC - Non- attendance in obedience to an order from public servant.— Whoever, being legally bound to attend in person or by an agent at a certain place and time in obedience to a summons, notice, order, or proclamation proceeding from any public servant legally competent, as such public servant, to issue the same, intentionally omits to attend at that place or time, or departs from the place where he is bound to attend before the time at which it is lawful for him to depart, shall be punished with simple imprisonment for a term which may extend to one month, or with fine which may extend to five hundred rupees, or with both; or, if the summons, notice, order or proclamation is to attend in person or by agent in a Court of Justice, with simple imprisonment for a term which may extend to six months, or with fine which may extend to one thousand rupees, or with both.

Illustrations

(a) *A*, being legally bound to appear before the High Court at Calcutta, in obedience to a subpoena issuing from that Court, intentionally omits to appear. *A* has committed the offence defined in this section.

(b) *A*, being legally bound to appear before a District Judge, as a witness, in obedience to a summons issued by that District Judge intentionally omits to appear. *A* has committed the offence defined in this section.

- If the summons is issued merely for the production of a document or a thing and not for the personal attendance of the person, it is sufficient if the person causes only the document or thing to be produced, instead of producing her/himself.

Deposing in the court

- The oath will be administered to the witness.
- Examination-in-chief – The witness will first be examined in-chief by the prosecutor.
- Cross-examination – The witness will then be cross-examined by the advocate appearing for the accused.
- Re-examination – The witness may then be re-examined by the party calling him.
- A witness must answer truly all the questions put to him.
- The witness is not excused from answering any question on the ground that the answer to the question will incriminate him or expose him to a penalty or forfeiture of any kind.
- A witness can be prosecuted for giving false evidence.
- Inconsistencies between the statement given to the police and the deposition of the witness in court would render the evidence of the witness doubtful.
- The witness can apply for a certified copy of his deposition recorded by the court. He will have to pay a certain nominal charge for the same in the court office.

REMEMBER

- Remember clearly the version of facts in the statement given by you to the police, and your deposition in the court must be consistent with your statement.
- Be brief in your answers and answer the prosecutor's questions to the point.

Costs, etc.

- The witness may be paid the reasonable expenses of attending the court to testify.[27]
- She/he must be paid proper diet money when he attends the court, even if the matter is adjourned and his evidence is not recorded.[28]
- If a witness is present in court, she/he must be examined. The matter can only be adjourned for special reasons.[29]
- Under section 311 of the Cr.P.C., any person may be summoned as a witness by the court, even if her/his statement has not been taken by the police/not been included in the charge-sheet filed by the police.

---

27. Section 312 of Cr.P.C.
28. *Swaran Singh* v. *State of Punjab*, 2000 Cr LJ 2780 (SC).
29. Section 109 of Cr.P.C.

- The evidence of the witness must be essential for the just decision of the case.
- The court may call such a person as a witness at any stage of the trial.

Examination of witnesses by the Commission

- If the examination of a witness is necessary for the ends of justice and his attendance cannot be procured without delay, expense or inconvenience, the court may dispense with the attendance of the witness, and issue a Commission for the examination of the witness under section 284 of the Cr. P.C.
- The court may, when issuing a Commission for the examination of a witness for the prosecution direct that, such amount as the court considers reasonable to meet the expenses of the accused including the pleader's fees, be paid by the prosecution.[30]
- The Commission will summon the witness before him or proceed to the place where the witness is and record his evidence in the same manner as the trial court does.
- Any party to the proceeding may appear in person or by pleader and may examine, cross-examine and re-examine the witness.
- Pending the examination of the witness on Commission, the proceedings in the trial court may be adjourned for the amount of time necessary for the execution and return of the Commission.
- The deposition of the witness shall form a part of the record and proceedings in the case.
- The court may also issue a Commission in order to examine as a witness any person confined or detained in a prison.

APPEALS, REVISION AND LIMITATIONS

Appeals

- An appeal can be filed either against an order of conviction or acquittal.
- It is filed to decide whether the order of a lower court is correct or not.

Appeals from convictions (Section 374 of the Cr.P.C.)

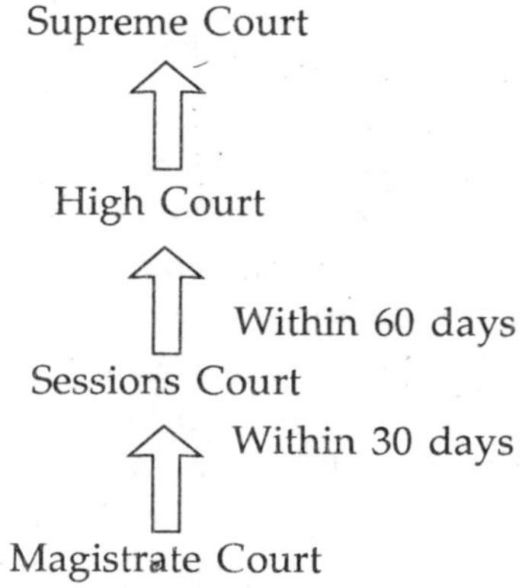

30. Section 284(2) of CrPC.

- A person convicted on a trial held by a judicial Magistrate or an Assistant Sessions Judge can appeal to the Sessions Court.
- A person convicted on a trial held by a Sessions Judge, Additional Sessions Judge or any other court in which a sentence of imprisonment of more than 7 years has been passed can appeal to the High Court.
- A person convicted on a trial held by the High Court can appeal to the Supreme Court.

No appeal where the accused pleads guilty [Section 375 of the Cr.P.C.]

- There can be no appeal in cases where the accused has pleaded guilty and has been convicted.
- In such cases, the person can appeal only with regard to the extent or legality of the sentence.

No appeal in petty cases [Section 376 of the Cr.P.C.]

There can be no appeal by a convicted person in the following cases:

- Where the High Court passes a sentence of not more than 6 months imprisonment or fine upto Rs. 1000 or both.
- Where the Sessions court or a Metropolitan Magistrate passes a sentence of not more than 3 months imprisonment or fine upto Rs. 200/- or both.
- Where the judicial Magistrate First Class passes a sentence only of fine upto Rs. 100.
- Where in cases tried summarily the fine imposed is not more than Rs. 200.

Appeal against inadequacy of sentence [Section 377 of the Cr.P.C.]

- The State Government can direct the Public Prosecutor to file an appeal in the High Court in a case of conviction on the ground of inadequacy of sentence.
- The accused must be given a reasonable opportunity to show cause against enhancement of sentence and can even plead for his acquittal or reduction of sentence.

Appeal in case of Acquittal [Section 378 of the Cr.P.C.]

- An appeal against an order of acquittal can only be filed in the High Court.
- It can be filed by the Public Prosecutor or by the Complainant.

Appeal by Public Prosecutor

- The State Government can direct the Public Prosecutor to file an appeal in the High Court from an order of acquittal.
- The appeal can only be filed with the leave of the High Court. Therefore, first an application for leave to appeal must be filed.

Appeal by Complainant

- If the case is instituted on a private complaint, the complainant can file an appeal against the order of acquittal.

- The complainant must first file an application for leave to appeal.
- If the application for leave to appeal by the complainant is refused, no appeal can then be filed by the State.

REVISION

- A revision application can be filed against any final order.
- It is filed to decide whether the order of a lower court is correct or not.
- It cannot be filed against an order rejecting a bail application which is an interim order.
- The revision application may be filed either in the Sessions Court under section 397 of Cr.P.C. or in the High Court under section 401 of Cr.P.C. If the revision application is rejected by the Sessions Court, then another revision application cannot be filed in the High Court.
- It must be filed within 90 days from the date of the order challenged.

Session Court/High Court	High Court
↑ Within 90 days	↑ Within 90 days
Magistrate Court	Session Court

LIMITATION

The period of limitation means the period specified for taking cognizance of an offence. In simple language, this means the period of time within which a person can file a complaint regarding an offence. It is also the period of time within which an appeal or a revision application can be filed.

Period of limitation

The period of limitation is as follow:

- 6 months, if the offence is punishable only with fine.
- 1 year, if the offence is punishable with imprisonment for a term not exceeding 1 year.
- 3 years, if the offence is punishable with imprisonment for the term between 1 year to 3 years.
- For an offence punishable with more than three years, there is no limitation.

Commencement of the period of Limitation

The period of limitation in relation to an offence shall commence;

- On the date of the offence; or
- If the commission of the offence was not known to the person aggrieved by the offence or to any police officer:-
    a. On the first day on which the person aggrieved by the offence comes to know about the offence, or
    b. On the first day on which any police officer comes to know about the offence, whichever is earlier.

- If the offender is not known:
    a. On the first day on which the person aggrieved by the offence comes to know about the identity of the offender, or
    b. On the first day on which the police officer comes to know the identity of the offender, whichever is earlier.

[D] COMPLAIN TO EXTERNAL AUTHORITY

You may also complain to the Chairperson of the Human Rights Commission about the incident. For female students, a complaint may also be submitted to the Chairperson of Women Rights Commission for immediate intervention and protection.[31]

[E] CREATE PUBLIC OPINION AGAINST RAGGING

One should also create a public opinion against ragging by taking the help of media. The only requirement is to send them important documents like photocopy of the complaint/FIR, medical certificate etc. Then the media would prepare a suitable 'story' which may force the college authorities or administration to take the necessary actions without any further delay due to the fear of negative publicity.[32]

Online media: - Since, it is not possible for the media to cover all the incidents of ragging, so you can write a detailed article about the incident of ragging on sharing/networking/blogging web-sites. You can also make a short film on it and then you can post the video on sharing/networking/blogging web-sites such as youtube.com. Such initiatives will definitely pressurize the college authorities to perform their obligations. This step would be beneficial as the college authorities would be concerned about the reputation/prestige of their institution.

[F] OTHER STEPS[33]

- Parents are the best friends to discuss this issue. Talk to them frankly; do not feel that you will burden them. They will understand that it is not your fault.
- Your college administration is there to help you. Please do not hesitate to ask for help. They will definitely help you. The local police and the local administration is also there to help you.
- Anonymous complaint of ragging can also be registered if you do not want your identity to be revealed in the public. However, this option should be avoided because without knowing the details it becomes difficult to take the necessary action, but in such cases confidentiality is assured.
- Anyone can register a complaint of Ragging. Complainant need not to be the victim only. It is one's moral duty to inform the respective authorities about the incident of ragging when any such case comes to your knowledge.

---

31. *Supra note* 3, p. 43.
32. *Ibid.*
33. Available at, https://antiragging.in/upload/Infopack/where_can_I_get_help.pdf,last accessed on 16th February, 2014.

- Ragging Prevention Programs are always there to help you. These can be called any time on 1800 180 5522. It is a toll-free number. The matter can also be notified by writing them an e-mail on helpline@antiragging.in.
- For knowing the progress of your complaint you can log on to the Anti-Ragging Portal: www.antiragging.in or visit www.amanmovement.org.

USE OF RTI AS WEAPON:[34]

The Right to Information Act (RTI) is an act of the Parliament of India *"to provide for setting out the practical regime of right to information for citizens"*. Under the provisions of this act, any citizen may seek information from a public authority (a body of government or instrumentality of State) of any Government department, agency or institute and the reply of the same has to be given by them within 30 days, otherwise a fine of Rs. 250 per day is levied on the responsible officer.

Public Information Officers (PIOs) have been appointed in every government department/agency/institute to provide the information that has been sought in the RTI. The PIO acts as the Nodal Officer for the implementation of this act. Here, it is important to mention that only government entities come under the purview of RTI Act, so for the private colleges one has to file the RTI application to the UGC/AICTE/MCI or the university to which the private college is a part of.

Any person who wants information should apply in writing to the concerned PIO. One needs to deposit Rs. 10 as the application fee. This could be deposited either in cash or through DD or a postal order. However, these rules and fees differ from State to State.

How to write the Application:

- Don't ask vague questions. Be very specific.
- Ask the information always by mentioning your name and signature and not by your designation, as only the citizens have the right to information.
- Do not ask questions which contain 'Why', because it is not obligatory on PIOs to reply to such type of questions. So in this condition you can re-frame your questions, for example in place of asking "Why no action has been taken yet by the college/police against the raggers", you can ask "Please furnish the reasons for not taking actions against the raggers till now".
- Your RTI should not be in more than 500 words.
- You do not need to mention the reasons for asking the information.
- Mention the payment details like DD/PO number, date, name of issuing bank/post office, cash receipt details etc., towards the end of your application.

---

34. Gaurav Singhal, Head, RTI cell of Society against Violence in Education (SAVE), available at http://www.no2ragging.org/morerti.html, last accessed on 16th February, 2014.

- You should keep the copy of the application and the DD for the record.
- If information involves providing photocopies of any document, then the PIO will charge you extra (generally at a maximum rate of Rs. 2 per page) for the cost of those photocopies. But they will have to inform you about the amount and when you submit the amount, you will get the information.

How to submit the RTI Application:

There are four methods to submit an RTI application:

1. **Personally, by hand**: You can go to the concerned authority and give them your RTI, but ensure that you get your copy of the application and proof of the payment duly stamped, signed and dated, either by the PIO or by the department.
2. **Registered Post Acknowledgement Due [R.P.A.D.]:** If you can't go to the concerned authority then you can send a registered post with an AD card and after the delivery it will be returned to your address with a signature of the department/institute which has received it. The AD card will act as a proof of the submission.
3. **Speed Post (A postal department service):** You can also send a Speed Post with a proof of the delivery card attached on it. You can track your speed post on, http://www.indiapost.gov.in/Speednew/track.aspx and keep a print record of the delivery status carefully with you.
4. **Online:** A web portal namely 'RTI Online' with url https://rtionline.gov.in has been launched recently. This portal is a facility for the Indian Citizens to file online RTI applications and first appeals and also to make online payment of RTI fee. The prescribed fee can be paid through Internet banking of State Bank of India and its associate banks as well as by Credit/Debit cards of Visa/Master, through the payment gateway of SBI linked to this site.

One should try to avoid an ordinary post, private courier companies etc., because these will not provide you the proof of delivery of your RTI. One can file RTIs with the colleges/universities and ensure that they fully comply with the anti-ragging laws. Use of RTI by the freshers/victims to ensure that the institutions follow the rules to curb ragging has been advocated by many RTI activists. One of the main reasons for ragging to happen is that the wrong doers are damn sure that their parents would never ever get to know about their heinous acts.

According to the guidelines of UGC every parent is supposed to file an affidavit in college/universities. The affidavit filed by parents to the institution has their name, address and telephone numbers. So a fresher can use the tool of RTI here by getting a copy of this affidavit and then can talk himself or make his parents talk to the ragger's parents. Also, through this tool the college and the UGC can be made to follow the anti-ragging measures strictly.

SAMPLE RTI APPLICATION[35]

[A] If delay in investigation of any ragging case by college authorities

To

The PIO/CPIO Date:

Xyz University

City name.

Respected Sir,

Application for Information under the Right to Information Act, 2005

The undersigned applicant wishes to seek the following information:

The section 7 of the UGC REGULATIONS ON CURBING THE MENACE OF RAGGING IN HIGHER EDUCATIONAL INSTITUTIONS, 2009 says that

"on receipt of any information concerning any reported incident of ragging, the Head of institution shall immediately determine if a case under the penal laws is made out and if so, either on his own or through a member of the Anti-Ragging Committee authorized by him in this behalf, proceed to file a First Information Report (FIR), within twenty four hours of receipt of such information or recommendation, with the police and local authorities..."

Provided that the Head of the institution shall forthwith report the occurrence of the incident of ragging to the District Level Anti-Ragging Committee and the Nodal officer of the affiliating University, if the institution is an affiliated institution"

In this context please refer to the incident of ragging of your college/ university student XYZ, in whose case the FIR to the police was filed after several months/weeks by the college/university administration.

I therefore seek information under section 6(1) of RTI Act; please provide the following information for this case:

1. Please provide the reasons for the Head of College/University not complying with the section 8 of the aforesaid UGC regulation and took much more than 24 hours to file the FIR in the case.
2. Please provide a copy of the report of the occurrence of the ragging sent to the District Level Anti-Ragging Committee and the Nodal Officer, if applicable.
3. If the report has not been sent yet, please provide the reason for the same.

I have attached a postal order for Rs. 10 (bearing No.) towards payment of application fee as per DoPT circular No. F. 10/9/2008 – IR dated 05.12.2008. Kindly intimate me for the additional fees payable, if any.

Note: In case, the application is not received by the appropriate PIO the same should be transferred to the concerned PIO within 5 working days of the receipt of this application and the applicant shall be intimated about the same.

35. Based on Sample RTI application prepared by Gaurav Singhal, Head, RTI cell of Society against Violence in Education (SAVE), available at http://www.no2ragging.org/morerti.html, last accessed on 16th February, 2014.

Sincerely,

Name of applicant: ....

Father's Name: ....

Information Required by: Post

Place: Signature of applicant

Date:

Address:

....

....

Phone number: ....

E-mail address: ....

[B] General information from college

To

The PIO/CPIO Date:

Xyz University

City name.

Respected Sir,

Application for Information under the Right to Information Act, 2005

The undersigned applicant wishes to seek the following information:

1. Please provide brief point-by-point information on how each clause of section 6 of UGC REGULATIONS ON CURBING THE MENACE OF RAGGING IN HIGHER EDUCATIONAL INSTITUTIONS, 2009 was complied with by XYZ University during January 1st, (Year) to December 31st, (Year).
2. Please provide the name of the police officer(s) who attended the meeting and also the date of the meeting as detailed in the section 6.1(h) of the above UGC regulation.
3. Are freshers stayed separately in XYZ University as per the clause 6.2(j) of the above mentioned UGC regulation?
4. Please mention the number of students who are allowed to attend the classes in college/university name even after not submitting the affidavits as mentioned in the clause (m) of the regulation 6.2 of the above mentioned UGC regulation.
5. Please provide the copy of the first of the fortnight report as mentioned in the clause (o) of the regulation 6.4 submitted during January 1st, (year) to December 31st, (year).
6. Please provide the dates, timings and places of the surprise raids made by the Anti-Ragging Squad as per clause (d) of the regulation 6.3 of the above mentioned UGC regulation during January 1st, (year) to December 31st, (year).

Sincerely,

Name of applicant: ....

Father's Name: ....

Information Required by: Post

Place: Signature of applicant

Date:

Address:

....

....

....

Phone number: ....

E-mail address: ....

Chapter XV

Do's and Dont's[1]

"Never let your sense of morals prevent you from doing what's right"

— Issac Asimov

Awareness is a necessary step in order to eradicate ragging. Unless and until, one is aware of the issues and concerns of ragging, it is difficult to lead a successful movement against it. So, this is very necessary for everyone to know that what should and shouldn't be done (given below) in order to prevent the evil practice of ragging.

1. Do's and Don'ts for Fresher

- Be courteous to all. It will make a favourable impression of yours on the others.
- Even if you are an introvert or a laid back, ensure that you are in constant touch with your batchmates/roommates.
- Never be alone in those places of the college and the hostel premises which are more prone to the incidents of ragging.
- Always keep the mobile phone with you. A mobile phone with camera is more preferable for the obvious reasons.
- Save all the important contact numbers like, the Principal of college, the Registrar of college, the Hostel Superintendent/warden, the Security officer, the Medical officer, Parents/Guardian, Local guardian, the Local Police Station, the Superintendent of the Police of the district, the District Magistrate etc.
- A fresher must share every problem with her/his parents/local guardian.
- Keep a standard SMS in your cell phone ready for a rapid and an instant communication with your parents/guardians. For example – Ok (everything all right), LNPW (last night passed well), NP (No Problem) or SOS (save our souls indicating possible ragging) etc.
- Save the contact numbers and residential addresses of your class mates/ room-mates.
- Save the contact number and the complete address of the office and the residence of your local guardian in case you stay in the hostel.

1. This Chapter is Based on Ragging: March against A Social Menace, available at http://www.gnit.ac.in/pdf/Anti-RaggingHandbook.pdf last accessed on 16th February, 2014.

- Ensure that your telephone number and the full address are known to your friends.
- Each day is a new day – look at it with hope and enthusiasm.

2. Do's and Don'ts for the Seniors

- Welcome freshers in a true sense.
- You are the torch bearer. The new comers look upon you as a mentor and approach you for guidance, so you must help them in the new environment.
- Don't act over smart.
- Don't bend the rules for your own advantage.
- Don't take pleasure in violating the human rights of juniors.
- Do not rag. Just interact in healthy and friendly manner with the new comers because ragging creates a dreadful image in the minds of the juniors which may have disastrous effect on their lives.
- Enjoy the college and hostel life in a healthy manner and let the juniors also enjoy it.
- Seniors should promote co-operation, joint efforts and group work with juniors which will open gates of new ideas and may help them in achieving a common goal.
- Remember the initial days of yours in the college when you had joined as a fresher and used to remain anxious and intimidated by the idea of ragging at the hands of your seniors. This would be like repeating the same mistake again, if you indulge in the same crime.
- Welcome juniors to the campus with warm regards, love and affection to make them feel comfortable and happy in a totally new environment.
- Act with maturity and respect human dignity of your junior fellows.
- Be loving, compassionate, optimistic and have a high self-esteem. This will help to get rid of the feeling of cruelty, selfishness, hatred and animosity.

3. Common Do's & Don'ts

- Always carry positive attitude and be mentally and physically enriched.
- Be sensitive and show sympathetic reactions to each other's problems.
- Be disciplined and dutiful.
- Be good to others.
- Always try to engage yourself in productive activities.
- Try not to act impulsively.
- Be careful about other's welfare.
- Be reasonable in your expectations.
- Be self confident.
- Communicate effectively.
- Try to be more social and harmonious.
- Be self introspective.
- Understand other's problems and help them.

4. Do's and Don'ts for Parents/ Guardians

- Save all the important contact numbers like, the Principal of college, the Registrar of college, the Hostel Superintendent/warden, the Security officer, the Medical officer, Parents/Guardians, Local guardians, the Local Police Station, the Superintendent of the Police of the district, the District Magistrate etc.
- Save and keep the contact numbers of your ward's close friends.
- Parents should meet regularly and maintain a flow of frank and easy communication with the wardens and college authorities.
- Parents should encourage their wards to share every problem whether it is grave or trivial.

5. Do's and Don'ts for the College Authorities

- Ensure and enhance the security services in the college and the hostel campuses, particularly during night hours.
- Maintain discipline in the college campuses.
- Constitute an Anti-Ragging Committee based on the Supreme Court guidelines to prevent the incidents of ragging in the college.
- This Committee must suggest action plans to promote a cordial relationship amongst the students and must also investigate the ragging complaints received from the students/guardians and suggest remedial prescription.
- Constitute an Anti- Ragging Squad consisting of the faculty members, the non- teaching staff members, the senior students, the representatives of the student unions etc.
- There should be separate accommodation for the freshers under the full time supervision and care of the hostel superintendents/wardens.
- Filling up the vacant post of the hostel superintendent (if any) by a full time qualified and competent person with an experience to handle typical situations.
- Organizing pro-active cultural activities throughout the year, like arranging football, volleyball and cricket competitions, quizzes, debates, dance and songs on socio-educative values.
- Colleges should conduct awareness campaigns among the students on the evil effects of ragging through various competitions like poster making, essay writing etc.
- Colleges should organise orientation programmes against ragging.
- Ensuring publicity of the contact numbers of all the important functionaries like the head of the institution, the faculty members, the hostel wardens/ superintendents, the district administration etc.
- File an FIR with the local police station as soon as the incident occurs. Confidentiality of the source of complaints/ information should be strictly maintained.

Chapter XVI
Ways to Stop the Menace of Ragging

Ragging is a very inhuman crime against one's human rights, so there should be strict punishment for those who are involved in ragging, which may include expulsion or suspension from the university, hostel or mess, fine, public apology, withholding scholarships or other benefits, etc. If the individuals committing or abetting the ragging are not identified or cannot be identified then collective punishment can be awarded that can act as a deterrent.[1] University Grants Commission (UGC) should also act against the colleges and universities, with action against the erring dean/principal along with de-recognition of that college or university and suspension of grants if college authorities were found unable to curb ragging in the campus. In the wake of the recent Aman Kachroo ragging case in Himachal Pradesh, UGC said that the universities and the colleges under it will have to implement a strict anti-ragging regulation from the next academic session.[2] This is indeed a step in the right direction.

CORRECTIVE MEASURES TO CONTROL RAGGING IN COLLEGES[3]

1. On the commencement of new academic session, the students must be addressed personally by the head of the institution and informed about the ban on ragging.
2. Contact numbers of the senior faculty members should be displayed in the college campus and a printed copy thereof should be given to the freshers at the time of admission.
3. Counselling sessions must be in place to counsel the students that indulge in ragging.
4. At the time of admission, an affidavit should be submitted by the students stating that they would not indulge in or support, any form of ragging.

---

1. Anti-ragging policy, Chitkara University, Himachal Pradesh 2009, available at http://chitkarauniversity.in/dnn/Admissions/AntiRagging/tabid/94/Default.aspx., last accessed on 16th February, 2014.
2. UGC's anti-ragging regulation from next academic session, Economy and Policy: Business Standard 2009, available at http://www.businessstandard.com/india/news/ugc%5Cs-anti-raggingregulationnext-academic-session/57526, last accessed on 16th February, 2014.
3. Based on, views of different authors and from "Notes on the interactions of the Committee with various stake-holders" & "Recommendation by the Group of Consultants" of Raghavan Committee.

5. Mentoring Programme – It might help to stop the menace of ragging, for example - IIT Bombay has a mentoring programme from past some years under which there are 40 or so mentors spread across 13 hostels; who have been made responsible for 15 freshers each. There is also a mentor coordinator who is a faculty member. To promote this programme a certificate is issued after every year to the mentors.
6. Promote alternative methods of interactions between juniors and seniors *e.g.*, dramas, community work, adventurous sports, short trips, evening games etc., keeping in mind that these gatherings should be done in the presence of hostel wardens. Dance competitions, name game and various other activities devised by psycho synthesis and human behaviour experts may also be used for interaction.
7. The issue of warden:
    a. Warden is a specialized post which should be occupied by qualified people after giving proper training through orientation programmes. Warden's power, authority and responsibility to be clearly defined. Emolument and perks to be determined in an appropriate manner to attract competent and qualified people.
    b. Hostel warden should be drawn from the faculty members as they are more familiar with the attitude of different students which may be crucial and helpful in preventing the commission of the crime.
    c. Surprise checks should be undertaken from time to time by the hostel wardens especially during the nights.
    d. There should be an additional staff (teaching or non-teaching) temporarily assigned to assist the wardens during the initial months of the session.
8. There should be a system of registration of private hostels so that a watch can be kept on them too.
9. There should be appointment of one teacher for every 10 students as their local guardian so that the problems can be shared.
10. Faculty members should stay in close contact with the freshers and instill in them a sense of confidence.
11. The students' union should be encouraged and involved in the fight against ragging.
12. Complaint boxes should be placed at the dean's office, library, college canteen, wherein the juniors can drop their complaint letters (as most of them are reluctant to come into the open for lodging a complaint because of the fear of being thrashed or boycotted by the seniors). It would make system of complaint friendlier and safer for the freshers.
13. A complainant may not have enough evidences to support that the person was ragged, so instead of the victim having to prove himself, the burden of proof should be on the alleged senior.
14. Protection should be provided to the witnesses of ragging incident.

15. Alcohol and smoking should be strictly banned within the college and hostel premises.
16. Seniors' identity is not known to the juniors; therefore, wearing of ID cards must be made compulsory.
17. Exemplary punishment should be given to deter its (ragging) recurrence.
18. Enrolment in the academic pursuits or a campus life should not immunize any student from penal provision of the laws of the land.
19. Intervention of the police must be defined. Only in extra-ordinary cases of ragging like sexual abuse, death or grave injury or violence, police should be allowed to intervene.
20. First Information Report (FIR) should be filed with the police as soon as possible. No evidence is required while filing an FIR, however, evidence is looked into once the investigation in a case gets start. Institution shall also continue with its own enquiry and remedial action to be completed within seven days. If any college authority refuses to take action when a case of ragging comes to their knowledge, they shall be considered as abetting (encouraging) the crime. Also a complaint can be filed against them in a similar manner as any offender who commits the crime of ragging.
21. Anti-ragging Committee:—
    a. Should be constituted at every level of governance *i.e.,* Central level, State level, District level and even at lower level of administration.
    b. Should be constituted in the colleges comprising of not just seniors but also juniors and other administrative staff.
    c. Majority of the membership should comprise of parents, police and outsiders (such as NGOs, media persons etc.,) rather than the insiders.
22. An independent statutory body outside the institution should also be constituted with representation from various sections of that university and civil authorities, where a victim may approach directly if local institution is hostile to her/his complaint.
23. Disciplinary committee to instill the value of discipline in the minds of students and cultural and creative committee to channelize the energy of students in right direction should be formed in the colleges.
24. Proctor office, within educational institution, should be made primary agency to work for elimination and prevention of ragging.
25. There should be provision for appointing most senior students as 'floor prefect' on each floor of every hostel for prompt reporting of ragging incidents.
26. Migration certificates issued by every institution should mention whether the student had indulged in the crime of ragging or not.
27. Each educational institution should present an annual report to the National Assessment and Accreditation Council (NAAC) of the University Grants Commission (UGC) and the National Board of Accreditation (NBA) of the

All India Council of Technical Education (AICTE), as the case may be, about the compliance and status of ragging, including the number and nature of ragging complaints received, and how they were handled and solved.

28. NAAC and the NBA should take into account the status of ragging in the educational institutions before awarding ratings.
29. Incentives should be made available to the institutions for curbing the menace and there should be disincentives for the failure to do so.
30. The Medical Council of India (MCI), University Grants Commission (UGC), All India Council for Technical Education (AICTE) etc., must act against the erring principal and the college.
31. Accountability of the management or concerned authority in the institution must be defined by the law.
32. Government should ensure its support for building anti-ragging activism in India. It should give financial and institutional support for advocacy and research in this field. For example UGC should be asked to prepare and publish an annual report on ragging. Such report will serve as a database on ragging related issues.
33. Responsible people from the society like academicians, artists and social organizations must be actively involved in the fight against ragging.
34. Efforts to be made to highlight ragging as a social evil by showing its ill-effects and thus establishing a public opinion against it.
35. Advocacy programmes focusing on the ill effects of ragging should be arranged in each campus by engaging important personalities/public figures.
36. Issue of ragging should be introduced as a matter of human rights in education and human right activists and NGOs should introduce appropriate initiatives in this regard.
37. Ragging needs to be perceived as a failure to inculcate human values in a student during the school life itself.
38. On the whole, the best way to stop ragging is the realization by the senior himself. He should understand that it is his weakness which instigates him, not his strength. He is not respected but feared and he embosses bad memories than sweet moments.
39. Sensitization Programme:- It intends to monitor and facilitate personal, moral and ethical growth of students and create awareness on the part of the parents and the teachers regarding the overall growth of students. According to this programme:-
    - (i) Parents, teachers and students need to undergo some mandatory counselling sessions over a year with the help of experienced psychologists.
    - (ii) Doctors, both from the government and the private sector, should be sensitized to report any injury suspected to have occurred due to ragging.

(iii) A formal paper to be introduced in the curriculum at all levels of study which deals with the acquisition of life skills and civic culture.

(iv) Participation in sensitization programmes for teaching/non-teaching staff to prevent ragging/sexual harassment should be made mandatory in consideration for their promotion.

(v) The mass media needs to stop projecting ragging as a fun and frolic activity and instead act as a significant watchdog to take on the responsibility of checking this vicious practice. The State should intervene to regulate media projections/pictures which glorify/ glamorize ragging.

(vi) Democratization of student bodies and institutions should be encouraged to promote student-student and student-faculty interactions.

(vii) The Sensitization Programme must necessarily be a continuous on-going process. CDs and other specialized information packages developed by people who have interest in anti-ragging spirit can be used to disseminate information and raise awareness throughout the country.

Corrective steps as enumerated above and some more novel ideas must be implemented without any delay. In the present time, the problem of ragging needs more attention from our leaders and intellectuals than in the past as it disturbs the harmony in the educational institutions and society. Isn't it the right time to declare ragging as a public health problem because it involves the physical, mental and social exploitation of not only an individual but her/his family and society as a whole? So international organizations like UNHRC and WHO should consider ragging as a public health hazard and frame guidelines for its prevention and control in collaboration with the governments of the respective countries.[4] Concrete action is required at the level of the school, higher educational institution, district administration, State and Central Government to make any curb effective. Also, all State Legislations and circulars should be replaced by a Central Legislation on ragging, whereby UGC should be made the main agency to devise ways of proper implementation of the Supreme Court guidelines and provisions of such legislation.

---

4. Rajesh Garg, Ragging: A Public Health Problem in India, Indian Journal of Medical Sciences, Vol. 63, Issue No. 6, June, 2009, pp. 269-270.

Chapter XVII

Scope of Ragging

It is the common and popular perception that Ragging is generally practised only in educational institutions. Even the Hon'ble Supreme Court and other regulatory bodies have issued anti-ragging guidelines only with regard to educational institutions and have ignored or left the other spheres where ragging is rampant. As defined by the apex Court and other State laws, ragging is done by senior students on the freshers or junior students in educational institutions. But everyone needs to understand this fact that menace of ragging is not limited to only educational institutions but it is done in one or other forms at workplaces, in prisons etc., also. Even 'educational institutions' have limited scope and barely cover schools under its purview for prevention of ragging. Following analysis proves this fact that wherever there is a concept of senior-junior or senior-fresher; junior or fresher has to go through the pain and sufferings of the evil of ragging.

RAGGING IN SCHOOLS

Schools are temples of education where children learn the good values of life, but scourge of ragging did not even spare this place. The practise of ragging starts from the very base *i.e.*, from the schools. In schooling period itself, students get accustomed to this evil to a great extent, but still, it does not come into the limelight because most of the ragging incidences are mediated by the teachers or parents themselves and thus, die down within a short boundary. Very rarely such incidents are reported outside the immediate family of the victim, and the traumatized victim is labelled as a poor student who lacks the power to stand up for himself.[1] Although in schools, teachers have greater degree of control over student activities and behaviour, even then ragging is able to spread its leg in schools. It is unseen truth that schools especially boarding schools are breeding grounds for this evil.

School ragging not only gives rise to mentality of ragging in higher education institutions; it also changes a child into a hard core criminal, which is evident by the following examples:-

> '1. India's first school shooting took place in early December, 2007, in an elite school named Euro International School at Gurgaon where Abhishek Tyagi, an eight class student was shot from point blank range by two of his school mates. This instance was a planned murder provoked by ragging of

1. K. Jaishankar and Debarati Halder, "Cyber bullying among school students in India", in K. Jaishankar (Ed.), International perspectives on crime & justice, 1st Edn., 2009, p. 581.

the victim. The Gurgaon Police Commissioner Mohinder Lal said that "the two boys allegedly killed Abhishek Tyagi as he was physically stronger than both and had been beating them up for the past two months, and the two carried a grouse against Abhishek as he used to "tease them" at every opportunity so they decided to take "revenge" (TOI, December, 2007).'[2]

'2. It is quite similar to previous school shoot out case in Gurgaon. On 3rd January, 2008 a student of seventh standard was shot dead by a tenth standard student in Chorbari village, Satna district of Madhya Pradesh. They both had heated arguments and ragged each other. The elder student had shot the junior in a spate of anger. (Staff correspondent, The Hindu, February, 03, 2008).'[3]

Despite all this the problem of school ragging has been less understood or poorly neglected in this country unlike many developed countries. Although, the Raghavan Committee, which was the first to note the menace of ragging in schools in our country, had included schools in its definition of educational institutions but in a very narrow sense, which is not enough to deal with the problem that is much more grave.

However, on the positive node, in the light of recent reported cases of ragging in schools, Central Board of Secondary Education [CBSE] issued a circular to all the Heads of the institutions affiliated to CBSE showing the serious concern towards this bad practice. In this circular, it defined ragging and laid down the guidelines which should be followed in order to prevent the menace of ragging in schools.[4]

LIVE CASES

Here are some reported incidents which will corroborate the need to address the problem of ragging in schools also:-

Case – 1

Name of the School –Christ Church School in Dum Dum of North 24-Parganas district.

Name of the Student – Oindrila Das.

Incident –A Class V student died, a week after she was allegedly locked inside a school toilet by some of her seniors who demanded money from her as part of ragging.[5]

Case – 2

Name of the School - Madharpakkam Government Higher Secondary School, Tiruvallur, Chennai, Tamil Nadu.

Name of the Student – K Thilagavathi.

2. *Ibid*, p. 584.
3. *Ibid.*
4. CBSE notification, on subject "Violence and Ragging in Schools affiliated to CBSE", Circular No: 24, dated 14th July, 2009, available at http://cbse.nic.in/circulars/cir24-2009.pdf
5. http://zeenews.india.com/news/west-bengal/kolkata-ragging-case-probe-oindrila-death-punish-the-guilty-says-father_877543.html.

Incident - A 16-year-old girl student, committed suicide by hanging, allegedly after being ragged by senior boys.[6]

Case – 3

Name of the School – St Xavier's School, Raiganj.

Name of the Student – Unknown.

Incident –The school had witnessed demonstrations by parents. They protested the principal's alleged refusal to take action against seniors who physically harmed the juniors.[7]

Case – 4

Name of the Institution – Jawahar Navodaya Vidyalaya in Chirang district, Assam.

Name of the Student – Unknown, around sixteen students.

Incident – The incident happened at the canteen. Altogether 16 students of Classes VII and VIII were severely beaten up by their seniors of Class XII. The assault was a result of a minor scuffle between the two groups that soon took violent turn.[8]

Case - 5

Name of the School – Shigally Hill International Academy, Dehradun.

Name of the Student – Unknown.

Incident – A class VI student has alleged sexual harassment by seniors.[9]

Case - 6

Name of the School – Bhavan VM Public School, Vadodara.

Name of the Student – Unknown.

Incident – A class VIII student complained of ragging and left the institution.

Case - 7

Name of the School - Delhi Public School, R.K. Puram

Name of the Students - Deepak Sharma and his friend.

Incident - Deepak Sharma and his friend were told to lift eggs with their buttocks by some seniors.

RAGGING IN SAINIK SCHOOLS

The practise of ragging takes severe form in Sainik Schools where juniors are subjected to very cruel, physical and mental torture due to which sexual abuse, physical harassment and verbal teasing becomes the standard norm for the hostel life.

It is justified on the name of making them tough for the reason that they will have to protect the country in future, and thus need to be strong. Even,

6. http://timesofindia.indiatimes.com/city/chennai/Ragging-drives-schoolgirl-to-commit-suicide/articleshow/11214333.cms.
7. http://www.telegraphindia.com/1130916/jsp/siliguri/story_17353820.jsp#.Uw3chvmSzVs.
8. http://timesofindia.indiatimes.com/city/guwahati/Students-union-protests-against-ragging-in-Kokrajhar-school/articleshow/21530383.cms.
9. http://www.ndtv.com/morenews/showmorestory.asp?slug=Student+alleges+sexual+harassment&id=91694&category=National.

Ministry of Defence has admitted this fact in its sixteenth report[10] that such indiscipline is increasing in Sainik schools. It stated in its report that strict action has always been taken against the perpetrators in all reported and observed cases of ragging based on the gravity of the matter. It was also stated in this report that suitable action is taken such as counselling, community service, revocation of appointment, suspension and in extreme cases expulsion. In consequence of this, during 2009-2012, 13 students had been expelled as punishment for ragging and 15 students suspended from school for 1-2 months.

INCIDENTS OF SAINIK SCHOOL RAGGING

Case – 1

1. Name of the School –Sainik School, Tilaiya, Koderma, Jharkhand.

Name of the Student – Shankar Xalxo.

Incident– In 2009, he cracked the tough entrance exam of Sainik School, Tilaiya, in Jharkhand's Koderma district, about 160 km from Ranchi. Two years later, the 14-year-old Class VIII student sneaked out of the school of his dreams and returned to his father's tea stall. Sustained ragging by his senior hostel-mates for over two years forced the boy to run away.[11]

Case – 2

Name of the School – Sainik School in Jhumri Telaiya, Koderma, Jharkhand.

Name of the Student – Rohit Murmu.

Incident–A 14 year old, class VIII student tried to commit suicide by slashing his wrists after being repeatedly ragged by senior students. The senior students used to compel him to wash their clothes and press them. Whenever he defied them, they beat him up.[12]

Case – 3

Name of the School – Sainik School in Kapurthala, Punjab.

Name of the Student – Lovepreet Singh.

Incident– In an incident of ragging, a ninth class student of Sainik school was allegedly beaten up severely by his seniors with sticks and belts resulting in fracture on his left arm and injury on his back after which four students were suspended.[13]

Case – 4

Name of the School - Telaiya Sainik School, Hazaribagh.

Name of the Student - Anand Kumar, class X student.

Incident – Saurabh Kumar, class XII student, was sent back home in the presence of police on the pretext of ragging of Anand Kumar of class X.

---

10. Critical review of functioning of sainik schools, 16th Defence Ministry report presented to Lok Sabha on 22-08-2012,available at http://164.100.47.134/lsscommittee/Defence/Critical%20Review%20of%20Functioning%20of%20Sainik%20Schools.pdf.
11. http://indiatoday.intoday.in/story/jharkhand-ragging-victim-quits-sainik-school/1/160071.html.
12. http://archive.indianexpress.com/news/-ragging--sainik-school-student-tries-to-kill-self/474574/.
13. http://www.deccanherald.com/content/18616/seniors-thrash-student-sainik-school.html.

Case – 5

Name of the School - Sainik School, Lucknow.

Name of the Student - Unknown.

Incident - 35 class VIIIth students fled from the school and went to their homes. The parents said that this was due to the fact that the children were being brutally ragged and harassed. The children also named 4 seniors.

The only way required to get rid of this problem is a concerted action at school stage itself because this menace gets seeded during this period only which bears its repercussions later in college life. It can be done *via* imparting school education that would inculcate feelings of brotherhood and encourage school children to appreciate diversity in the society and think beyond social identities. For this, respect for human rights, consciousness against violating others' rights, and respect for privacy, diversity and equality should be discreetly grafted into the lessons and exercises right from the primary and elementary stages of schooling in order to inculcate the desirable value system from the formative years of every child. For example, a chapter on ragging can be introduced in NCERT, SCERT school books. Also, Ragging and sexual intimidation in schools should be brought into the ambit of the Juvenile Justice Act.

RAGGING AT WORKPLACE

Recently, a 19-year-old girl, a trainee with a German MNC in Pune, Maharashtra, committed suicide after having been repeatedly ragged by fellow apprentices[14], which is one of the numerous incidents that show existence of ragging at workplaces also. Whenever a new recruit joins the work, she/he is overloaded with the work by seniors, made to stay till late hours for the work and is left to suffer the physical and mental agony. Specially, young people, who come from extremely disadvantaged backgrounds, are more vulnerable to harassment because they can less afford to exit a hostile work site. Although, the term 'bullying' is used commonly at workplaces in place of 'ragging' but it is much wider term than ragging, as it can be even done by a junior of her/his senior. So, ragging can be called a subpart of 'bullying', but it is not given the due recognition and just ignored. It is a matter of concern that being such a grave problem, nobody has paid attention to it in our country. Although we now have Prevention of Sexual Harassment at Workplace Act, 2013 which is very crucial in preventing sexual harassment at workplaces but the thing to focus on is that sexual harassment is not the only way of harassing the victim.

So, the bigger evil is ragging which is practised at workplaces unhindered, due to absence of any law regarding it. That is why this plight of new recruits needs to addressed as soon as possible in the interest of that person and the company/workplace itself, because it will ultimately harm the interests of company, if, the victim employee does the less productive work or leaves the job itself. Also, everyone requires a healthy environment to work efficiently and happily.

---

14. http://www.thehindu.com/news/national/other-states/ragging-at-work-drives-girl-to-suicide/article5090407.ece.

RAGGING IN PRISONS

It is very strange but harsh truth that Ragging happens in prisons also. There is evidence that new entrants (known as Naya Ahmads in prisons) in prisons or in new cells and wings are harassed by ragging, bullying, taunting, intimidation, insults, provocations, or overt invitations to fight.[15] One may find several types of ragging in prisons like sexual, mental, physical etc. Most Naya Ahmads are taken to the After Barrack, where they spend a night or two before being assigned to a fixed barrack. This waiting period allows the jail staff, convict-warders, in house extortionist gangs and other sharks to assess what they can extract from her/him. Middle and upper class entrants are easy targets. They are softened up with dark stories of prison-life horrors and not-so-veiled threats. Young people are targeted for free labour and as sex toys.[16]

There is a horrifying truth that has been unaddressed for decades *i.e.*, sodomy and rapes are done in jails, not just in India, but across the world. It happens in very corner of the world, even in the most rights-sensitive and well-equipped jails because it is part of prison-behaviour, particularly when so many criminals are together at one place fighting for supremacy, space, sex, food, entitlements and even mere survival. Interestingly, this has nothing to do with general homosexual behaviour in people. The most affected are the new prisoners, because they are 'fresh' and are subjects that need to be subjugated and controlled. And this trend is not new. The People's Union of Civil Liberties had this to say about Tihar way back in 1981: "When a young boy enters, the prisoners have been known to have bid a price for the boy. The price offered is in terms of 'bidis', soap or 'charas'. Often prisoners have been divided into camps and the groups have fought each other on the issue of who shall have the new entrant."[17] Also, there are cases which show about rampant corruption in the prisons and extortion by jail mafias, from new entrants to the jail by threat and torture.[18]

Time has come to break the shackles of mind which has kept the concept of ragging limited to Educational institutions, and that too, to only colleges or universities, leaving aside all the equally important spheres, where there is as much need of preventive steps as in colleges or universities. As it is now clear that ragging has sewn much wider web of spheres under its scope. So, there is need of an umbrella law keeping in mind the need of present societal conditions, which would address the concern of ragging not only in educational institutions, workplaces, prisons but everywhere where this evil has its reach.

---

15. Diego Gambetta, Codes of The Underworld: How Criminals Communicate, 1st Edn., 2009, p. 98.
16. Arun Ferreira, Prison Diaries, available at http://www.openthemagazine.com/article/nation/prison-diaries, last accessed on 16th February, 2014.
17. G. Pramod Kumar, Ram Singh's death: Rape and ugly sexual violence in Indian jails, available at http://www.firstpost.com/india/ram-singhs-death-rape-and-ugly-sexual-violence-in-indian-jails-657071.html, last accessed on 16th February, 2014.
18. PUCL Bulletin, Jan. 2001, available at http://www.pucl.org/reports/WestBengal/2001/nhrc.htm, last accessed on 16th February, 2014.

Conclusion

From what was intended to provide good humour and harmless fun to students, ragging today has assumed torturous, vulgar and inhuman forms that defy all norms of decency and morality.[1] Millions of students are brutally abused in the name of introduction every year. Historically originated, probably, to generate fellow-feelings, camaraderie and the ability to work in a team, it has metamorphosed to a blood sucking vampire![2] The practice of ragging has cost many young lives and many more have been traumatised by the wanton aggression and suffered permanent mental disability.[3]

Ragging is like an *entry fee* or *a toll tax* to enter the hostel.[4] It is a criminal problem which has psychological roots and a social ignorance around it. It has taken the shape of a serious human rights violation and even the most reputed and disciplined educational institutes are falling prey to it. It is imperative to say that under the garb of 'welcoming' new students to college, ragging, in reality, is an infamous practice. The society is equally responsible to a large extent for this because it has not yet taken this issue seriously and ragging, hazing etc., is still seen as a *'growing up pill'* for the youngsters. It has never been portrayed as a social evil.[5]

College life is a very important phase in everybody's life. Most of the students carry fond memories of the best days of their life, but for some, the years may bring about unpleasant memories because of the menace of ragging and for them the trauma remains whole life affecting their self esteem, leaving a scar on the victim forever. The Aman Kachroo incident at the Rajendra Prasad Medical College, Tanda (Himachal Pradesh) and many other severe incidents of ragging are still afresh. Ragging related deaths, suicides and homicides have become common. The practice is reported from colleges of all disciplines like agriculture, fashion, law, technical specialities etc.

1. Madhavi Chopra, Ragging in Educational Institutes: A Human Rights Perspective available at http://www.legalserviceindia.com/articles/ragging.htm, last accessed on 16th February, 2014.
2. What is Ragging?, available at http://www.no2ragging.org/ragging.html, last accessed on 16th February, 2014.
3. R.K Raghavan., Campus menace, Frontline, Volume 26, Issue No. 16, Aug. 01-14, 2009.
4. Mohit Garg, What is ragging? available at http://noragging.com/index.php/Research/Ragging-The-Phenomenon/-What-is-Ragging.html, last accessed on 16th February, 2014.
5. Conversation happened between Harsh Agarwal and Michael Britton in 2007 that began with Harsh's research report on "ragging" in colleges in India, available at http://www.humiliationstudies.org/documents/BrittonAgarwalConversationonRagging.pdf, last accessed on 16th February, 2014.

It has been revealed by sample surveys that awareness about the existence of ragging among the members of general public is very low and in some cases zero. It is surprising that even the people of relatively higher strata of society cut out a sorry figure as they are simply non–committal about the menace of ragging in educational campuses. Thus, we may term this as *Zero research on the issue of ragging*. The foremost reason behind unawareness is that incidents of ragging at various college campuses are not reported in the print and electronic media with due importance. People still believe ragging as form of joke and merry-making at the beginning of academic sessions by some handful merry loving seniors in the college class rooms, canteens or at the hostels to get themselves acquainted with the newly admitted students.

Further, the executive ideology is that since there is no prospect of stern anti-ragging measures winning them votes in an election, therefore it is a waste of time and energy on an exercise that would hardly bring major political gains because students, who live in residential college, generally do not cast vote. Government prioritise its political concerns over such a serious matter.[6] All these reasons combined together are largely responsible that these atrocities are still hidden and the perpetrators of the crime don't consider it wrong but rather see it as a tradition.[7]

Presently, Sri Lanka is the worst affected country in the world.[8] Even India continues to have undeniable tension of ragging because of demographic, religious and socio-economic factors. Various instances of suicides, violence, physical injuries, sexual abuse and psychological disorders, resulting because of ragging have been reported by the media but, in reality, the number of unreported cases of ragging are much more than the cases reported by the media. But still the issue of ragging has not been given the proper attention that it deserves. It is yet to be recognized as a traditional and systematic human rights violation in the field of education. The moot question is that why in India the menace of ragging still prevalent? Is it the case that the guidelines of the Supreme Court are ineffective to deal with the situation? If so, what can be the reasons? Is it that some of them are impractical? Or, is it merely the case that the guidelines have not been adequately publicized? Is it that the institutions have not taken the problem to be serious enough? Is it that the problem being seasonal at the time of admissions, petering out later in the academic session, does not last in the institutional memory? Is it that the moral edge in educational administration has extinguished so much that no one has the courage to bring about order in campuses? Is it the failure to co-opt all the stake-holders? Is it the unwillingness or neglect of governments to implement the guidelines? These questions are necessarily to be answered to solve this problem.

Ragging is a sociological problem more than a law and order issue. Harsh Agarwal rightly says "Ragging is a complex issue that cannot be tackled just

6. *Supra note* 3.
7. *Supra note* 5.
8. Harsh Agarwal, Evolution of Ragging, CURE Report CR2005/07-27, available at http://noragging.com/index.php/Research/Ragging-The-Phenomenon/Evolution-of-Ragging.html, last accessed on 16th February, 2014.

by punitive measures or by passing a law." The law has been there since 1989, but it is not producing desired results. It is difficult to implement a law without addressing and changing the mind-set of society. We need something more than laws to eradicate the menace that ragging or hazing has become. One has to think of ragging in the context of a psycho-social problem. The solution, apart from punishment as deterrence to ragging, must also suggest ways to build up confidence in the relationships of juniors, seniors and the authority.[9] It is often argued that measures to eliminate ragging should go beyond law. We must understand that unless the society condemns it, ragging cannot be eliminated. We require a focused and concentrated effort to educate the masses[10] and educational institutions need to take responsibility to prevent ragging.[11] We have to give students a chance to think and question the reasons that support this menace because solution lies in thinking.

Ragging is a problem of the students, by the students and for the students; and therefore, the solution to it also lies with the students. It is high time that the student community awakens its conscience to this inhuman practice before more and more students and more and more educational institutions become victims of it.

If education, and particularly Higher Education, is to serve as the lever to the great surge of the Indian nation, the scourge of ragging which corrodes the vitals of our education system needs to be curbed. It is noteworthy to say that if one has no regard for the human rights of other fellow students, it will be a foolhardy to expect one to be a responsible citizen of tomorrow's India.[12] How can we believe that a student who is cruel and sadistic enough to torture someone will magically transform her/himself into an empathetic and caring doctor, lawyer, engineer etc.?

It is hoped that in a few years of time with our earnest efforts, we all together can eradicate the social scar called ragging. We are sure a new enlightened India is waiting for us at the end of this dark tunnel.

"Hold your head high; stick your chest out, you can make it.

It gets dark sometimes, but morning comes KEEP HOPE ALIVE"

— Jesse Jackson

---

9. Rajesh Garg, Ragging: A Public Health Problem in India, Indian Journal of Medical Sciences, Vol. 63, Issue No. 6, June, 2009, p. 267.
10. Ragging in India, A Summary Report on Incidents, Social Perceptions and Psychological Perspectives, CURE REPORT: CR2007_05-16, May 16, 2007, p. 17, available at http://www.noragging.com/analysis/CR2007_05-16_RaggingInIndiaSummary.pdf, last accessed on 16th February, 2014.
11. Dr. Ch. Venkateswarlu and N. Satyasri, Effects of Ragging on Human Dignity-A Critique, International Journal of Multidisciplinary Educational Research ISSN: 2277-7881, Volume1, Issue 4, September, 2012, p. 240.
12. *Ibid.*

HELPLINE

24 Hour Help: UGC Helpline: Toll Free Number

1800-150-5522

Mail - helpline@antiragging.net

AMAN MOVEMENT

689, Sector 23, Gurgaon, Haryana- 122017, India

Phone: 0124-4017168

Mobile No.-: 0-9650587168, 0-9871170303, 0-9818400116

E-mail - info@amanmovement.org

CURE

Coalition Uproot Ragging Education

E-mail: cure@noragging.com

SAVE

Society Against Violence in Education

E-mail: mail@no2ragging.org

SPACE

Society for People's Action, Change and Enforcement

E-mail: help@stopragging.org

SATHEE

E-mail: dr.s.s.shilwant@gmail.com

CASE LAWS

SUPREME COURT

1. *Inspector of Police, Tamil Nadu* v. *John David*, (2011) 2 SCC (Cri) 647

Dalveer Bhandari, Mukundakam Sharma, JJ.

Facts: In this case, the accused was alleged to have committed the murder of the deceased-Navarasu, junior student of MBBS in Raja Muthiah Medical College, Annamalai University, Annamalai Nagar. It was contended that the deceased was subjected to severe ragging as accused severed his head and limbs with the help of stainless steel knives and removed his gold ring, watch and gold chain and caused his death when the latter did not subjugate himself to the accused.

Lower Court's judgment: The Principal Sessions Judge found that there are enough circumstantial evidence and motive on the part of the accused for committing such a crime and held the accused guilty.

High Court's Judgment: HC erroneously set aside the judgment of trial court by giving reasoning of lack of evidence.

SC' Judgment: Supreme Court, on the matter placed before it, held that accused nurtured ill feeling against deceased as deceased refused to write record note for accused, deceased was last seen with accused and he was searching for him very eagerly, the conduct of the deceased was very weird and strange and the bags/suitcases kept by him also produced stinking smell, recovery of crime objects on basis of information given by accused provides link in chain of circumstances. Failure to explain one of the circumstances would not be fatal for prosecution case. Minor loopholes and irregularities in the investigation process cannot form crux of case when there were strong circumstantial evidences deduced from said investigation which logically and rationally point towards guilt of accused.

The Apex Court concluded that the recovery of crime objects on the basis of information given by the accused provides a link in the chain of circumstances. Also failure to explain one of the circumstances would not be fatal for the prosecution case and cumulative effect of all the circumstances is to be seen in such cases.

SUPREME COURT

2. *Mahatma Gandhi University* v. *S. Sherin*, Civil Appeal No. 5894 of 2010

D.K. Jain and H.L. Dattu, JJ.

Facts: On initiation of disciplinary proceedings against few students on account of their involvement in ragging, they were suspended by the University.

High Court's Judgment: They challenged the suspension order before the High Court. HC decided in favour based on the reasoning that the disciplinary proceedings as well as trial in the criminal case would take considerable time, and directed University to permit students to attend the institution from which they were suspended or any other institution offering the same course.

SC' Judgment: The decision of HC was challenged by the University in the Supreme Court. The Apex court held that the High Court was not justified in interfering with the decision of the University. It is for the University authorities to decide whether or not any disciplinary action against the students. Supreme Court held that the High Court should not have interfered in the matter as it is for the University to decide matters affecting discipline of the students and the High Court showed misplaced sympathy to the errant students.

SUPREME COURT

3. *State of Himachal Pradesh* v. *A Parent of A Student of Medical College, Shimla,* (1985) 3 SCC 169

A.N. Sen, P.N. Bhagwati and Ranganath Misra, JJ.

Facts: In this case HC of Himachal Pradesh, on the writ petition filed by the guardian of a student of the Medical College in Shimla complaining about the ragging of freshers by senior students within and also outside the college campus and the hostel, came to the conclusion that the practice of ragging was prevailing in the Medical College, Shimla on a noticeable scale and that ragging took the form of subjecting freshers including female students to inhuman and humiliating treatment degenerating even into physical violence and that the college authorities had not been able to effectively control ragging with the result that the college administration had lost confidence of a sizeable section of student, parents and well-wishers as regards its capacity to deal with the problem of ragging.

High Court's Judgment: The Division Bench accordingly gave various directions which included a direction to the State Government to constitute a committee consisting of the Vice-Chancellor of the Himachal Pradesh University and the Secretary to the Government, Health Department, *inter alia*, to make "recommendations in regard to the curative, preventive and punitive measures to be adopted by the college authorities to control and curb the evil of ragging and the machinery to be set up to enforce these measures."

The High Court directing the Chief Secretary to the Government of Himachal Pradesh to file an affidavit setting out what action has been taken by the State Government towards implementation of the recommendation of the Report of the Anti-Ragging Committee, recommended introduction of a bill to prevent ragging.

SC' Judgment: Supreme Court disapproved the HC's decision as it was an indirect attempt to direct the Executive to initiate legislation with a view to curbing the evil of ragging, hence a matter falling, outside the functions and duties of the Judiciary which is not permissible under the Constitution of India.

Any member of the Legislature could also introduce legislation but the Court could not mandate the Executive or any member of the Legislature to initiate any legislation and supervise the action of initiation.

It was pointed out that public interest litigation is a weapon which has to be used with great care and circumspection and the Judiciary has to be extremely careful to see that under the guise of redressing a public grievance it does not encroach upon the sphere reserved by the Constitution to the Executive and the Legislature.

HIGH COURT/TRIBUNAL CASES

1. CENTRAL INFORMATION COMMISSION

***Maulesh G. Shah* v. *Ministry of Health and Family*,**
CIC/LS/A/2013/001352 SS

Sushma Singh, Chief Information Commissioner

The Appellant through an RTI application dated 17.11.2012, filed before the CPIO, Medical Council of India, New Delhi, sought to know the action taken on certain complaints, which were mainly related to the alleged violation of Rules and Regulations (relating to the Prevention of Ragging in Medical Colleges) by the Baroda Medical College in relation to his daughter, a PG student in the said college.

The Appellate Authority, *inter alia*, observed that the issues raised by the Appellant are primarily legal issues pertaining either to interpretation of MCI Regulations or the procedure followed by the College and Government of Gujarat to implement judgment of Supreme Court and the relevant Rules and Regulations of MCI which cannot be answered by PIO or FAA. He, however, with regard to the action taken on representations (dated12.08.2012) filed by the Appellant's daughter, recorded that the MCI had sought information from the college on the matter which has not been received by the Council till date. He accordingly directed that a reminder be issued to the college seeking report on the issue.

Aggrieved by the decision of the Appellate Authority the Appellant filed the present appeal before the Commission reiterating his complaint/grievance against non-implementation of Anti-Ragging Guidelines by Medical College, Baroda.

During the hearing, the Respondents informed the Commission that they had conducted an enquiry into the complaint in question (regarding harassment and ragging), but had not found any merit in the same. The Appellant, on his part, while reiterating his complaint regarding non-implementation of Anti-Ragging Guidelines by Medical College, Baroda, also complained that the Respondents have not complied with the Commission's decision No. CIC/SG/A/2011/003627 dated 13.02.2012 by which they had been directed to display the list of all the complaints received by them and action taken thereon on their web-site. The Respondents, however, denied the Appellant's allegation and stated that the said order of the Commission dealt with the complaints regarding professional misconduct which they have already complied with. However, in the present case the complaints in question are on different subject viz., non-implementation of Anti-Ragging guidelines.

Considering the importance of the issue, the Commission directed the Respondents to file a written submission on the implementation of Anti-Ragging Rule/guidelines by the Medical Council of India.

In exercise of its powers under section 33 of the IMC Act and in light of the incidents of ragging prevalent in medical colleges the MCI has framed the Medical Council of India (Prevention and Prohibition of Ragging in Medical Colleges/Institutions) Regulation, 2009 for curbing the menace of ragging in order to ensure maintenance of standards of medical education in the country.

That Clause 3.3 of the aforementioned Regulations of 2009 defines 'ragging' and Clause 4 gives ingredients (acts) of ragging. Clauses 5 and 6 of the Regulations provide for measures to be taken for prevention of ragging, including at the institutional level which includes the provisions of constituting Anti-Ragging squads and University Monitoring Cells. Clause 7 provides for verification by MCI that colleges are following the anti-ragging norms. Further, Clause 8 of the Regulations talks about 'Punishments'; Clause 8.1 relates to 'punishments' to those who are found guilty of 'ragging', whereas Clause 8.2 provides for Penal consequences for the heads of the institutions/administration of the institution who do not take timely steps in the prevention of ragging and punishing those who rag; Clause 8.3 provide for institutional punishments against the Medical College/Institution/University by the MCI itself on failure to curb the menace of ragging which might go to the extent of declaring the erring Medical College/Institution/University to be ineligible for preferring any Application under section 10A of the IMC Act for a minimum period of one year, extendable by such quantum by the Council as would be commensurate with the wrong.

That the Medical Council of India has laid down a detailed structure of Anti-Ragging Committees and Squads in its regulations namely "the Medical Council of India (Prevention and Prohibition of Ragging in Medical Colleges/Institutions) Regulations, 2009"

It is the Medical College/Institution/University who are primarily responsible for implementation of the provisions of these regulations. In addition to the framework MCI has also introduced the concept of 'regulatory measure' by time to time inspection of the Colleges by teams of MCI to ensure that the Regulations are being followed in their letter and spirit and further by way of providing for 'institutional punishments' the MCI has put in place a deterrent as well as penal provision for Medical Colleges/Institutions/University in form of Clause 8.3 of the Regulations if a medical college/institution/University fails to carry out its duty under the said Regulations.

The Commission is of the view that the disclosure requirement under the RTI Act in the present case would be completed if the Appellant is apprised of the final outcome/present status of complaints listed out in his RTI application. The CPIO is accordingly directed to provide this information to the Appellant within 2 weeks of receipt of this order.

Appeal is disposed of with the above directions.

---

2. HIGH COURT OF KOLKATA

Tapas Kumar Bhanja v. *State of West Bengal*, W.P 26971 (W) of 2013

Arun Mishra, C.J. and Joymalya Bagchi, J.

The petition has been filed by way of public interest litigation by an Advocate practicing in this court with the prayer that the grievance with respect to ragging in colleges. Following prayers were made before the Hon'ble Court –

1. Prayer has been made to direct the State Government to implement the West Bengal Prohibition of Ragging in Educational Institution Act, 2000 and the provision of sections 7 and 8 of the aforesaid Act with special emphasis.
2. Prayer has also been made to direct the State Government to pay compensation to the victim of ragging to the tune of Rs. 25 lakhs.
3. The final prayer was made to take steps to prohibit mobile camera phone in any educational institution's hostel to protect humiliation of the students.

Learned counsel of petitioner has submitted that though the provisions of the Act of 2000 have been enacted by the State Government but the same remains on paper and are not actually implemented. Sections 7 and 8 of the Act of 2000 enjoin the duty upon the State to form a Committee whose decision shall have to be taken as final in such matter. No such committee has been constituted.

Learned counsel appearing for the State has submitted that State is complying with the provisions of sections 7 and 8 of the Act of 2000 and thus, the Committee shall be constituted within a reasonable time.

Judgment – Directions are issued for scrupulous compliance of provisions of Act of 2000 and in case Committee as contemplated under sections 7 and 8 of the Act of 2000 has not been constituted to take care of the grievance, the Committee should be constituted within a period of three months to see the grievance. However, the prayer made with respect to grant of compensation of Rs. 25 lakhs, no such relief can be granted by way of public interest litigation. The prayer made is misconceived and it is the duty of the State Government/ authorities to ensure that mobile camera phones are not misused or used for illegal purpose.

The authority/State also to consider the decision of the Hon'ble Supreme Court as well as the direction issued by other bodies in the matter.

---

3. HIGH COURT OF JHARKHAND

Court on its Own Motion v. *State of Jharkhand*, AIR 2012 Jhar 146

Prakash Tatia, C.J. & Aparesh Kumar Singh, J.

Facts: This Court shocked to read the news items published in the newspaper "DainikBhaskar" dated 14th November, 2011 about the ragging of the students and, therefore, *suo motu* cognizance was taken and this Public Interest Litigation was registered, on the basis of photographs where large number of students have been shown to be tortured by the senior students of the same school *i.e.*, Sainik School Tiliaya and it was ordered by this Court to hold an enquiry upon which, the Principal Secretary, Human Resources Department, Government of Jharkhand conducted the enquiry and submitted its report, which is taken on record.

Judgment: Since the school diary for the academic year 2012-13 has been shown containing the some guidelines and it nowhere provides and permits anybody in the school to give beating to the junior students by the senior students, therefore, now the school administration will proceed to take all corrective measures which they themselves suggested in their report and written submission and will effectively implement their schemes to prevent such type of illegal activity and take steps for safety of the students.

The State of Jharkhand may also take steps for preventing the ragging in the schools for which the State Government may also come with its proposal so that no further incident may occur. The proceeding against the Sainik School Tiliaya is dropped because of the fact that this writ petition will be covering all educational institutions including Sainik School Tiliaya also, so far as issue of ragging is concerned. It is an issue of public importance and for which even personal hearing is not required. However, if Sainik School Tiliaya wants to proceed with the proceeding, they may continue to participate in the proceeding, but it will be at their, choice. At this juncture, the State' Government may take steps so that such incidents may not occur in any of the schools or colleges including technical education institutes in the State of Jharkhand because of ragging so many brilliant students left the school, even technical courses and further some of them have also committed suicide and because of such incidents the students have to suffer mental agony.

4. HIGH COURT OF PATNA

Vivek Kumar S/o Shri Chandeshwar Pandit, R/o. Village Fatehabad, P.O. Sehduari, P.S. Hajipur, District-Vaishali* v. *State of Bihar through the Principal Secretary, Department of Science and Technology, Government of Bihar, Patna,

2012 (2) PLJR 261

Navin Sinha, J.

Facts: The petitioners are stated to be second year students in the discipline of Mechanical, Electrical and Electronics stream respectively at the Motihari College of Engineering, a Government College under the Department of Science & Technology. They are aggrieved by the order of expulsion dated 23.12.2011 passed by the Officer on Special Duty on allegations for having indulged in ragging a first year student as held on enquiry by the Anti-Ragging Committee.

They are alleged to have ragged a first year student, Monika Shailesh. No statement of the victim was ever recorded much less furnished to the petitioners with an opportunity to defend. No show cause notice of any allegations was ever given to the petitioners. The procedure followed by the Anti-Ragging Squad and Anti-Ragging Committee was completely unilateral and *ex parte* in nature. At no stage of the alleged enquiry, the petitioners were associated with it in any manner to present their defence of having been falsely implicated in the matter. It was their alleged conduct which was the subject of enquiry. Yet they were not considered relevant to be associated with the enquiry.

Issue: Whether or not the Anti-ragging squad acted in just and fair manner and following the principle of natural justice?

Judgment: For commencement of the enquiry by the Anti-Ragging Squad, there had to be a statement of the alleged victim recorded first. No such statement has been brought on record. The First Information Report has also not been lodged by the alleged victim. There is no explanation for lack of any statement of the alleged victim. The First Information Report is vague and only states that report had been received of her being ragged causing harassment and mental trauma. What was the nature of ragging and the kind of harassment and mental trauma has again not been mentioned. The order of expulsion by the Officer on special duty referring to his powers under the Disciplinary rules is therefore held to be without jurisdiction and vitiated in law. The role of the Anti-Ragging Squad was to enquire. The decision making authority was the Anti-Ragging Committee. A person holding the enquiry could not be part of the decision making body. That would make them the judge and executioner both, a concept fundamentally flawed.

So, the petitioners are entitled to a monetary compensation of Rs. 1,00,000/- (One lakh only) each.

5. HIGH COURT OF MADRAS

Rahul Sadasivan, S/o. K. Sadasivan Kuruvath House, Manakulangara P.O. Kodakara Thrissur, Kerala* v. *Indira Gandhi National Open University, rep. by Director, The Office of The Regional Centre, Chennai-35,
(2012) 7 MLJ 880

D. Hariparanthaman, J.

Facts: The petitioners have joined the two year Diploma Course *viz.*, Tool and Dye making in the second respondent institution during April, 2010. The Course came to an end in April-May, 2012. The Course comprises two semester examinations in each year. In the first year, they appeared for two semester examinations and in the second year, they appeared for third semester examinations. While they were in the fourth semester, some incident took place on 25-1-2012. Two first year students *viz.*, Shaffaf and Ashwin D. made a complaint on 25-1-2012 stating that the petitioners and others attacked them with lethal weapons and caused severe injuries to them. It was stated that the petitioners used deadly weapons like iron chain, iron rod, steel pipe, wooden stick, and curtain strip, etc., during the incident. However, there was no police complaint against the petitioners for the alleged incident of ragging. The petitioners were placed under suspension by order dated 27-1-2012 based on the preliminary enquiry conducted with the complainants. Thereafter, on 4-3-2012, an external enquiry was conducted by a team of two persons *viz.*, Dr. S.M. Ravichandran, Professor and Head, Deptt. of Tamil, Bharathiyar University, Coimbatore-46 and Dr. O. Balakrishnan, Asst. Professor, Deptt. of Tamil, Bharathiyar University, Coimbatore-46.

Judgment: The enquiry report does not reveal the details of the witnesses and also deposition of the witnesses. No records, more particularly, medical records were produced. In fact, in the enquiry report, nowhere it is stated that lethal weapons were used. There is nothing on record about the injuries caused to the complainants. The enquiry report simply states that the petitioners indulged in ragging of the first year students. Whereas, the complaint made against the petitioners was that the petitioners used lethal weapons and caused serious injuries on the complainants. However, there was no such finding in the enquiry report. Based on the same, termination order, dated 30.3.2012 was passed.

As already stated, the enquiry was a farce one. The enquiry was conducted in violation of principles of natural justice, for the reasons stated above. Furthermore, the petitioners have already lost one year.

For the aforesaid reasons, the termination order is liable to be quashed and accordingly quashed. The petitioners shall be permitted to pursue fourth semester in the second respondent institution. The petitioners shall pay necessary tuition fees and other fees applicable for the fourth semester examinations which will commence in January, 2013. The second respondent is directed to admit the petitioners in fourth semester during January, 2013 after collecting necessary fees.

6. HIGH COURT OF KERALA

***Ahammed Manaf E.* v. *Sub-Inspector of Police*, 2011 Cr LJ 789**

Sasidharan Nambiar, J.

Facts: Petitioners are the accused in Crime No. 668/2010 of Medical College Police Station, Kozhikode. They are students of AWH Engineering College, Kuttikkattoor, Kozhikode. Crime 668/2010 was registered and complaint sent to Sub-Inspector of Medical College Police Station, by the Principal of the College, based on an enquiry conducted on receipt of a complaint forwarded an e-mail by helpline@antiragging.net on 1-9-2010. The Committee reported that Petitioners were involved in asking the junior students to button up Shirts, asking irrelevant questions, asking to tuck shirts inside and asking them to march on the road, after getting down from the bus. Petitioners were suspended as provided under section 6 of the Kerala Prohibition of Ragging Act, 1998 and the Principal forwarded complaint to the police Station as provided in the section.

Judgment:

Before parting with the case it is necessary to caution Government on the deficiency of Kerala Prohibition of Ragging Act, 1998 enacted for a laudable purpose. The Act was enacted to prohibit ragging in Educational institutions in the State of Kerala as it has become a menace to the civilized society. Though under section 4 of the Act, a penal provision is enacted, providing imprisonment for a term which may extend to two years and also fine which may be extend to ten thousand rupees, the offence is not made cognizable. Though under section 6, a direction is issued to the head of the Educational institution, to suspend the student immediately and to forward the complaint to the police station, having jurisdiction over the area in which the educational institution is situated, for further action, it will serve no purpose when the offence is not made a cognizable offence. The Station House Officer on receipt of such a complaint can only refer the informant to the concerned Magistrate as provided under Sub-section (1) of section 155 of the Code of Criminal Procedure. The police cannot even investigate such a non-cognizable offence, without the orders of the Magistrate. In such circumstances, the Act would serve no purpose. Public Prosecutor is directed to bring it to the notice of the Government, to make appropriate amendment to the Act making the offence under section 4, a cognizable offence.

---

7. HIGH COURT OF KERALA

***Suresh P. and Musfar Muneer* v. *Sub Inspector of Police*, Crl. M.C. No. 722 of 2011**

Thomas P. Joseph, J.

Facts: Petitioners are accused Nos. 1 and 2 in Crime No. 542 of 2006 of Thrikkakkra Police Station and C.C. No. 2768 of 2007 of the Court of learned Judicial First Class Magistrate-I, Aluva for offences punishable under sections 323, 294(b) and 506(i) read with section 34 of the Indian Penal Code (for short, "the IPC") and sections 4 and 6 of the Kerala Prohibition of Ragging Act, 1998 (for short, "the Act"). The *de facto* complainant is impleaded as additional second Respondent. Petitioners originally wanted to quash proceeding against them on the contention that registration of the case, submission of final report and cognizance taken are illegal being in violation of provisions of section 6 of the Act. After the additional second Respondent was impleaded, he has filed an affidavit stating that the matter is settled between the parties. Learned counsel for Petitioners submitted that in the circumstances stated above, proceeding against Petitioners may be quashed.

Judgment: In the present case, complaint was preferred by the second Respondent on 20-12-2006 and the next day *i.e.*, on 21-12-2006 the head of the institution has forwarded the complaint to the Sub Inspector, Thrikkakara. Under section 6 of the Act, head of the institution is to forward a complaint (of the student, parent, guardian or the teacher as the case may be) only after conducting an enquiry in the matter and being *prima facie* satisfied that allegations in the complaint are true. No such enquiry was conducted by the head of the institution. At any rate, no such report is even referred to. It is revealed that the head of the institution has merely confirmed receipt of the complaint and forwarded the same to the police. That is not in accordance with the mandatory requirement of section 6 of the Act. Hence registration of the case for offence under the Act is illegal, not to say about submission of final report and cognizance taken thereon.

In the affidavit of the second Respondent it is stated that he has settled the dispute with Petitioners and does not want to proceed in the matter. In the affidavit additional second Respondent has specifically stated that the dispute between additional second Respondent and Petitioners has been amicably settled and that they are staying together as friends. In the circumstance the additional second Respondent does not want to continue the proceeding. I am inclined to accept the composition.

Resultantly, in the light of the composition referred to above and non-compliance of section 6 of the Act as explained in the decision referred (supra), this criminal miscellaneous case is allowed.

---

8. HIGH COURT OF KERALA

Derric Joy v. *Director, Technical Education Trivandrum,* 2011 (4) KLJ 625

Hon'ble Mr. Justice Thottathil B. Radhakrishnan

Facts: The petitioners, students of a Government Polytechnic College, face Ext. P2 order imposing removal from certain semesters. Petitioners 1 and 7 are barred from attending classes for 4 semesters spreading through the academic years 2009-2010 and 2010-2011. The other petitioners are barred for 2 semesters spreading over the academic year 2009-2010. All of them, except two, are also barred from appearing in the examinations, while two are permitted to appear in the supplementary examinations. Petitioners challenged it. The plea of the petitioners is that the allegations against them, of having indulged in ragging a deaf and dump student, is unfounded and there is no provision in the college calender to dismiss a student from the college. They plead that the Kerala Prohibition of Ragging Act, 1998, hereinafter referred to as the 'Kerala Act', does not contain any provision authorising dismissal but provides for only suspension of students against whom accusation of ragging is made.

Judgment: AICTE Regulations were issued in exercise of statutory power under the AICTE Act, 1987 and with the objective to root out ragging in all its forms from technical institutions, Universities, including deemed to be Universities imparting technical education in the country, by prohibiting it by law, preventing its occurrence and to punish those who indulge in ragging in spite of the prohibition. It also provides for preventive action. In Regulation No. 8, that, the punishment to be meted out to the persons indulging in ragging has to be exemplary and justifiably harsh to act as a deterrent against recurrence of such incidents and the students who are found to have indulged in ragging should be debarred from taking admission in any technical institution in India. Without, exception, the institutional authorities are to report every single incident of ragging to the police authorities for registration of First Information Report, Depending upon, the nature and gravity of the offence as established by the Anti-Ragging Committee of the institution, the possible punishments for those found guilty of ragging at the institution level shall be any one or any combination of the different punishments enumerated in those regulations. They include 'rustication from the institution for a period ranging from 1 to 4 semesters. It needs to be, therefore, noticed that the punished handed down to the petitioners are within that frame. With that the mere fact, that the Kerala Act- provides for dismissal only on the basis of conviction under that Act is of no consequence and the mere reference made to the Kerala Act in the impugned order, in no manner, takes away the jurisdiction of the Principal to have imposed the impugned punishment.

---

9. HIGH COURT OF MADRAS

C.N. Vasantha Raja* v. *The Registrar, Tamil Nadu Dr. Ambedkar Law University, The Controller of Examinations and The Principal, Dr. Ambedkar Government Law College,

MANU/TN/2956/2011

D. Hariparanthaman, J.

FACTS: The Petitioner is a law student. He joined five year Law course in Dr. Ambedkar Government Law College, Chennai during 2005-2006. During 9th Semester, a girl student, namely, Dhanalakshmi, studying in Dr. Ambedkar Government Law College, Chennai, gave a complaint that the Petitioner teased her. Based on that complaint, the Petitioner was placed under suspension by the 3rd Respondent by an order dated 10-08-2009. The 3rd Respondent, on 14.08.2009, requested the Inspector, Esplanade Police Station, to take action under the provisions of Harassment of Women Act, 1998. Accordingly, a case was registered in Crime No. 480 of 2009 on the file of Esplanade Police Station, Chennai. Since the complainant appeared both before the Inspector of Police as well as 23rd Metropolitan Magistrate, Saidapet, Chennai and gave a statement that the Petitioner did not tease her and somebody in the crowd teased her, the criminal proceeding was dropped on 26-11-2009. However, the 3rd Respondent did not revoke the suspension order.

As the Petitioner was not admitted in the 10th Semester class citing the suspension as the reason, though the criminal proceeding was dropped, he was constrained to file W.P. No. 25402 of 2009 to quash the suspension order. This Court, on 31-06-2010, set aside the suspension order taking into account the aforesaid subsequent development. The matter was remanded to the 3rd Respondent for passing appropriate orders.

In these circumstances, the Respondents permitted the Petitioner to write 10th semester examinations during October - November 2010. However, he was not permitted to appear for *viva-voce* test. The Petitioner wrote all the theory examinations and the practical written test except the *viva-voce* test. The Petitioner made a representation dated 16-03-2011 seeking permission to appear for *viva-voce* test. Since no order was passed, he has filed the present writ petition, seeking for direction to the Respondents to conduct 10th Semester *Viva-voce* test to the Petitioner and also to publish his result without insisting admission for 10th Semester.

Judgment: The Petitioner has stated in affidavit that the rules framed under section 8 of the Tamil Nadu Prohibition of Ragging Act, 1977, a student, who was placed under suspension based on the complaint of ragging is ultimately not convicted, the Management shall revoke the suspension and the period of suspension of such student shall be treated as if the student had attended the classes.

In this case, the Petitioner was not convicted. Hence, he is deemed to have attended the classes. Furthermore, he was also permitted to write 10th semester examinations by the Respondents. In these circumstances, the Respondents could not prevent the Petitioner from taking the *viva-voce* test on the ground that he did not attend 10th semester classes. For all the aforesaid reasons, I am inclined to allow the writ petition and the 3rd Respondent is directed to conduct *viva-voce* test for the Petitioner within a period of six weeks from the date of receipt of a copy of this order and Respondents 1 and 2 are directed to publish the result of 10th semester examinations which the Petitioner had written.

---

10. HIGH COURT OF JHARKHAND

***Kandarp Jha* v. *State of Jharkhand*,**

MANU/JH/0775/2010

Sushil Harkauli, J.

Facts: By the impugned order dated 18-02-2010 the guardians of the petitioners have been informed that the petitioners had indulged in beating up two of their junior students on 16-02-2010, with regard to which an F.I.R. was lodged. The order says that considering the incident and on the recommendation of the disciplinary committee of the college the Management of the College has decided to expel the petitioners from the college.

Judgment: The "reasonable" opportunity of hearing, obviously in the light of the nature of the incident and the time available in hand, requires clear indication of the allegation against the person noticed and grant of a reasonable time to submit a reply in writing. A mere oral hearing can suffer from the vice of non-notice in the impugned order, about what has transpired during the hearing that is to say what defence the person noticed has taken. This would make it difficult for the superior authorities or Courts to judge whether the defence has been considered in its proper perspective or not.

I am of the opinion that the extreme punishment awarded without affording an adequate and reasonable opportunity of hearing cannot be sustained and is hereby set aside.

Ratio: Considering the overall facts and circumstances, the extreme punishment awarded without affording an adequate and reasonable opportunity of hearing cannot be sustained and is thereby liable to be set aside.

---

11. HIGH COURT OF ANDHRA PRADESH

Nadiminti Triveni* v. *State of Andhra Pradesh, rep. by its Public Prosecutor, High Court of Andhra Pradesh,
2010 (2) ALD (Cri) 697

Gopala Krishna Tamada, J.

Facts: The petitioner, by name, Nadiminti Triveni has joined the 1st year B. Tech (Agriculture) in Acharya N.G. Ranga Agricultural University, College of Agricultural Engineering, Bapatla, during October, 2008 and she was staying in one of the hostels attached to the university. As she was a new comer and was staying in the hostel, she was subjected to severe prolonged ragging by her seniors *i.e.*, the accused Nos. 1 to 5. Unable to bear the said torture which is in the nature of ragging the petitioner tried to commit suicide by consuming hair dye and tablets on 27-02-2009 and when she became unconscious she was taken to a private hospital where she was treated for about 25 days and after her recovery she was discharged from the hospital on 21-03-2009. As the petitioner by name Triveni tried to commit suicide, initially a case in Crime No. 48 of 2009 of Bapatla Police Station was registered under section 309 of IPC, but after recording her statement, the same was altered and the said crime was registered against the accused Nos. 1 to 5 for the offences punishable under sections 4(i)(ii)(iii) and 7(1) of the Andhra Pradesh Prohibition of Ragging Act, 1997 (for short - 'the Act'). After investigation, charge sheet was filed before the Judicial First Class Magistrate, Bapatla, against the accused Nos. 1 to 5 for the offence punishable under section 4(i)(ii)(iii) of the Act only. As there was pressure on the *de facto* complainant *i.e.* Triveni/LW1 to withdraw the case, she took transfer certificate from the College of Agricultural Engineering, Bapatla, and joined in B.Sc., at Srikakulam. As she is residing at Srikakulam and it is causing inconvenience to her, she approached this Court and filed the present transfer application. This matter was admitted and stay was granted.

Judgment: In the light of the compromise entered into between the parties as advised by the Court, and the present application is filed under section 482 of Cr.P.C. to get the proceedings quashed by way of compounding the offences, this Court looked into the various provisions of the Andhra Pradesh Prohibition of Ragging Act, 1997.

This is an enactment which has come into force in the year 1997 and this Act is silent as to whether the offences falling under section 4 of the Act are compoundable or not. In the instant case, the Act has come into force in the year 1997 only to curb the said menace of ragging and, on the ground that the said offence is not included in section 320 of Cr.P.C., it is not proper for this Court to refuse to interfere and invoke its extraordinary jurisdiction conferred under section 482 of Cr.P.C. After all, the Courts have to look after the welfare of society and so, keeping in view the peculiar circumstances of the case *i.e.* the involvement of the students, their future, their career etc., this Court is of the considered view that this Court can definitely exercise its inherent powers conferred under section 482 of Cr.P.C. and quash the said proceedings.

There is no provision in the Act to the effect that the said offences are not compoundable. All accused are young girls aged less than 20 years coming from middle class background and if convicted their career would get spoiled - Under its inherent jurisdiction Court orders compounding of offence and hence quash proceedings.

---

12. HIGH COURT OF JHARKHAND

***Jharkhand High Court Legal Services Committee through its Secretary* v. *State of Jharkhand*,**
MANU/JH/0716/2010

Sushil Harkauli, A.C.J. and Dhirubhai Naranbhai Patel, J.

Facts: This public interest litigation (PIL for short) has been initiated by the Jharkhand High Court Legal Services Committee seeking directions to the State Government and its officials to prevent ragging of fresher students in various colleges.

Issue: Whether this kind of PIL can be initiated by the petitioner as a statutory body.

Judgment: Hon'ble Court said that despite the Regulation 12, it is beyond the scope of the functions of the Jharkhand High Court Legal Services Committee to become a litigant itself. Regulation 12(a) only empowers the Committee to "recommend" filing of Public Interest Litigation. It does not empower the Committee to itself file a Public Interest Litigation.

Thus, court declined to entertain this Public Interest Litigation from the side of the Jharkhand High Court Legal Services Committee, leaving it open to the petitioner to "recommend" in accordance with Regulation 12, to the appropriate person or body to file a PIL on this count.

---

13. HIGH COURT OF RAJASTHAN (JAIPUR BENCH)

***Manmohan Machra* v. *University of Rajasthan*, RLW 2010 (3) Raj 2249**

Raghvendra S. Chauhan , J.

Facts: The petitioners were studying in B.Sc. III year at Maharaja College, in the University of Rajasthan. They alleged that they were falsely implicated in two criminal cases due to politics amongst the college students. According to them, they were suddenly served with a letter dated 12-12-2009 wherein they were informed that due to the FIRs registered against them, they were being rusticated from the college. They further received an order dated 30-12-2009 wherein it was stated that on 12-12-2009, the Anti-Ragging Committee has decided to cancel their admissions in the college. Therefore, their admissions stand cancelled. Hence, they filed petition before the High Court.

Issue: The main issue in the case was that whether or not opportunity of hearing was granted to the petitioners by the respondents?

Judgment: It was revealed that the petitioners have not come with clean hands and have hidden some facts from this Court. They were given an opportunity of hearing before the Anti-Ragging Committee on 21-12-2009. At the meeting, the petitioners were heard and a decision was taken. According to the Committee since the petitioners had indulged in indisciplined activities even on earlier occasions, their admission should be cancelled from the college and T.C. should be issued to them. Hence, the petitioners are not justified in claiming that no opportunity of hearing was given to them. Thus, he has supported the impugned orders.

The contention that the principles of natural justice have been violated is absolutely baseless. Since the petitioners have not approached this Court with the clean hands, on this ground alone, the writ petition deserves to be dismissed.

Further, it was stated that although the State of Rajasthan may not have an Anti-Ragging Law, yet the University Ordinance does prescribe the procedure and the consequences for indulging in indisciplined behavior as educational institutions are temples of learning. In educational institutions, students are not only educated, but they also learn about life in general. In the temples of learning, sanctity, discipline, decorum and serenity have to be maintained. Students are expected to excel in their studies and to perform well in their extra-curricular activities. They are expected to train and discipline their mind and body. No educational institution can permit its students to be rowdy, to be indisciplined and to be uncouth. For, the peace and tranquility of the campus, the prestige and goodwill of the institution has to be preserved and protected at all times. Thus, one of the responsibilities of an educational institution is to enforce and maintain discipline among its students. Likewise, the students owe a duty towards an education institution to be on their best behaviour during their student life.

The Petition was dismissed accordingly.

---

14. HIGH COURT OF PUNJAB AND HARYANA

Baldev Raj v. _Registrar, Panjab University,_
2010 (6) SLR 603

Permod Kohli, J.

Facts: The petitioners are the students of M.A. 2nd year, Indian Theatre in Punjab University, Chandigarh. They are also allotted accommodation in the Hostel No. 2. Three students of M.A. 1st year, Indian Theatre namely Manish Kumar, Pankaj and Kailash who staying in the same hostel, were summoned by the petitioners and some passed out students of the same discipline to Room No. 5/38 in Hostel No. 2 allotted to one Gurcharan Singh, an M.A. 2nd year student *i.e.*, petitioner No. 4, where the petitioners and some passed out students were present in inebriated condition. After the introduction, the freshers were forced to put off their clothes and they were asked to perform objectionable activities *i.e.*, some obscene sexual acts. They were photographed naked with the mobile phone. The freshers named above lodged a complaint with the university authorities on the following day *i.e.*, 10-8-2008 narrating the incident of ragging and also apprehended danger to them. They also named the petitioners and some passed out students who indulged in ragging these freshers. On the receipt of the complaint, the Vice Chancellor of the university constituted an Anti-Ragging Committee to probe into allegations of ragging. The Committee after listening to the complainants and the petitioners recorded its findings and made recommendations to the university *vide* its report dated 30-7-2008. Based upon the recommendations of the Committee the petitioners have been expelled *vide* the impugned order.

While challenging the order of expulsion the petitioners have sought parity with some other students of the departments of U.I.E.T and D.C.E.T of Punjab University, Chandigarh, who were also accused of indulging in ragging but were expelled for only few days. The petitioners, however, alleged violation of the principles of natural justice.

Judgment: In instant case, the petitioners have admitted their guilt. The nature of their behaviour during the ragging where the freshers were forced to unclothe themselves and indulge in obscene acts in presence of a number of persons is sufficient to draw an inference that the petitioners are not normal human beings. Such actions demonstrate their perverted thoughts. The petitioners deserve no compassion from this Court. The plea of the petitioners for parity and discrimination with some students of U.I.E.T and D.C.E.T of Punjab University, who were allegedly involved in ragging and have been let off with expulsion of only few days also deserves to be rejected. No material has been placed on record to even suggest the nature of allegations against them to enable this Court to appreciate the contention of the petitioners of the allegation of discrimination. It depends upon the act and nature of ragging to attract the mild or harsher punishment. Though, ragging *per se* deserves punishment. In absence of any relevant material, the allegations cannot be looked into.

From the above regulation it appears that expulsion is for a minimum period of two years. The petitioners will have to suffer this punishment for their indecent acts.

Ratio: Punishment depends upon the act and nature of ragging and thereby varies accordingly. Though, ragging *per se* deserves punishment, in absence of any relevant material, the allegations of violation of principles of natural justice cannot be looked into.

---

15. HIGH COURT OF KERALA

***Shefiq Youseph* v. *State of Kerala*,**
2009 Cr LJ 3148

V.K. Mohanan, J.

Facts: Brief facts of the prosecution case are as follows. PW2 was a student of School of Medical Education. Gandhi Nagar, Kottayam who had just joined for the 1st Year B.Sc. Nursing course in the said institution. The classes for the 1st Year course started on 5-9-2005 and initially, she was a day scholar till 18-9-2005 and on 19-9-2005, she joined in the Santhinikethan hostel situated adjacent to the School of Medical Education. According to the prosecution, PW2 was in need of leave on 22-10-2005 and thus, on 21-10-2005 at about 4 p.m., she met accused No. 7, the Principal at her office in the second floor of the institution and submitted the leave application and while she was coming down, she found accused Nos. 1 to 6 standing on the steps. It is the specific case of the prosecution that when PW2 passed the accused, accused No. 1 called her back and asked whether she did not know that junior would wish the seniors whenever they see them and thereupon accused Nos. 1 to 6 ridiculed, humiliated and ragged her at the steps and then accused No. 1 told her to come to nearby room and after wishing them, she can go. Thus, according to the prosecution, accused Nos. 1 to 3 including the petitioner/appellant took her to the Histo-pathology lab situated at the first floor of S.M.E., the School of Medical Education. Thereafter, accused No. 1 bolted the door from inside and directed PW2 to sit on a chair. Thereafter, he gave a laddu like item mixed with a stupefying substance and told her to eat the same. Obliging the direction, PW2 ate the same and became physically and mentally exhausted. Then, they directed her to remove her dress and when she refused, they forcibly removed her dress and laid her on a work bench. Thereafter, accused Nos. 1 to 3, after undressing, looked at her and made insinuating comments. Thereafter, accused Nos. 1 and 2 committed rape on her. According to the prosecution, the petitioner/appellant, who is accused No. 3, did not commit rape on her, but he kissed on her face and chest and fondled her body parts and thus outraged her modesty. By this, PW2 was terribly shocked and exhausted and was unable to object or react. Further, after such sexual assault, the accused told her to wear her dress, but she was unable to do so. Thus, they dressed her up and first accused then criminally intimidated her by saying that if she divulged the incident to anybody, they will pour acid on her face. Then they opened the door and PW2 came out of the room. At that time, accused Nos. 4 to 6 were standing outside and guarding the Histo-pathology lab to ensure that nobody entered the lab room and thereby they rendered aid and support to A1 to A3 in accomplishing their illegal acts.

On the basis of the above allegation, Crime No. 513 of 2005 was registered in the Gandhi Nagar Police Station for the said offences and investigation was undertaken which culminated in filing the report. During the trial, PWs. l to 27 were examined and Exts. Pl to P108 documents were marked from the side of the prosecution. Material objects such as MOs.1 to 30 were also identified and marked. The incriminating circumstances, which emerged during the evidence of prosecution, when put to the accused under section 313 of the Cr.P.C, they denied the same. The accused took a defence of total denial and maintained the plea of innocence. During the defence evidence, DWs. 1 to 7 were examined and Exts. DI to D4 and C1 series (a to s) were marked. Based upon the rival pleadings and the materials on record, the trial court formulated 13 points for its consideration and finally, pronounced the above judgment, which is being challenged in this appeal.

Judgment: On a reading of the proviso which is newly introduced to section 389(1) of the Cr.P.C., it can be seen that the criteria to be adopted, while dealing with an application by the appellate court, at the instance of the convicted person is not the period of imprisonment awarded by the trial court, but the nature of the offences contemplated in that provisions. While introducing the proviso to Sub-section (1) of section 389, the same legislative authority, who incorporated Clauses (i) and (ii) to Sub-section 3 of section 389, in exercise of their legislative wisdom deliberately omitted to prescribe any such period of imprisonment awarded or the fact whether the offence is bailable or non-bailable one. By using the words 'punishable with' in the above provision, it is crystal clear that the legislative intention is to restrict the releasing of convicted person on bail, ignoring the period of imprisonment awarded and also ignoring the offence whether bailable or non-bailable. At that point of time, the only consideration must be the seriousness of the offence alleged and proved, especially the category of offences, which are "punishable with" sentence of death or imprisonment for life or imprisonment for a term of not less than ten years. In other words, in order to attract the above restriction, the convicted person need not be punished with the entire period of imprisonment contemplated and awardable. So the contentions of counsel for the petitioner/appellant, that the appellant is sentenced only for three years and the trial court has granted bail, are untenable. Therefore, in view of the above new provision, though the sentence awarded is only for three years or less, on application of the above criteria while dealing with a petition under section 389(1) of Cr.P.C., the petitioner is not entitled to get relief as sought for in this petition.

Even otherwise on a reading of Sub-section (1) of section 389, it can be seen that in an appeal, suspension of execution of sentence and bail cannot be claimed as a matter of right and it can only be considered and granted in exercise of the discretionary power of the Appellate Court. It is also relevant to note that by employing the terms namely, "for reasons to be recorded by it in writing', for issuing an order of suspension of sentence, the court must satisfy with the reasons for passing such orders. The proviso, introduced as per the amendment mentioned above, is only in consonance with the above stipulation contained in Sub-section (1) of section 389. Before the amendment, giving of such an opportunity in favour of prosecution was not contemplated. Thus, it can be seen that before the amendment mentioned above, it was incumbent upon the appellate court to state the reasons for passing such order in favour of a convicted person. By introducing such proviso, the Legislature specifically intended to impose duty on the prosecution to file a statement of objection in writing against the grant of such order where offences are found against the convicted person in such a nature and thus, it is heavily burdened with the Appellate Court to overrule such objection with adequate reason in granting an order in terms of section 389(1) of the Cr.P.C. The above restriction is introduced through the above provisions for two reasons. *First* reason is in respect of consideration of the seriousness and gravity of the offences referred in that section and *secondly*, the fact that the trial court., being a fact finding authority, has come to a conclusion regarding the guilt of the accused. Thus, the presumption of innocence of the accused is replaced by said convictions and unless there are substantial reasons to be recorded, such convicted person cannot be released on bail.

In the present case, unless the finding of the trial court is reversed or set aside, what proved against the petitioner is that along with accused Nos. 1 and 2, he took the poor girl to the place of occurrence from where she was subjected to sexual intercourse, outraging her modesty and humiliated her. Therefore, at present. I find no reason to suspend the execution of the sentence and to release the petitioner on bail as contemplated by sections 389 and (2). So, a heinous crime was committed under the guise of ragging - a social menace which has to be depreciated. Therefore, if the prayer is allowed, as observed by this Court in order, a wrong message is being given to the society. Hence, according to me, in the light of the approach of the Honourable Apex Court and this Court against the ragging, a correct message can be given to the society, including the parents of students like the victim in this case, only by rejecting the prayer.

In the result, there is no merit in the petition and the petitioner's prayer is accordingly rejected.

16. HIGH COURT OF KERALA

M.R. Arunraj v. *Kerala Agricultural University*, AIR 2009 Ker 54

H.L. Dattu, C.J. and A.K. Basheer, J.

Facts: Appellants who are studying in the College of Veterinary and Animal Science under the Kerala Agricultural University were suspended from the college on the charge of ragging junior students. After holding an enquiry, the University imposed certain minor punishments, one of which was that the period of suspension from October 31, 2007 to March 4, 2008 shall be treated as absence for all "academic programmes of the University". After revocation of suspension, appellants approached the University seeking permission to write the supplementary examinations in some papers which they could not write during the period of their suspension. The University did not accede to the above request.

It was in the above circumstances that appellants had filed the writ petition under article 226 of the Constitution of India praying for issue of a writ of *certiorari* to quash the order of revocation of suspension to the extent it treated the period of suspension as absence for all academic programmes of the University. The other prayer was to issue a writ *mandamus* to permit them to write the supplementary examinations and to regularise the period of suspension. The learned single Judge dismissed the writ petition declining to interfere with the stand taken by the University.

Judgment: The head of the educational institution is empowered to suspend a student if a complaint of ragging is received against him from any student, parents, guardian or a teacher of an educational institution and if the complaint is *prima facie* found to be true. More significantly, if the head of the institution fails or neglects to take action under section 6 on receipt of a complaint he shall be deemed to have abetted the offence of ragging punishable under section 4 of the Act. Treating the period of suspension as absence for all academic programmes of the University is not arbitrary and illegal - Thus university justified in refusing to grant permission to appellants to write the supplementary examinations.

It may be true that the appellants might have missed some of the mid-term and internal examinations during the period when they were placed under suspension. The suspension was for valid and justifiable reasons. The Enquiry Committee had categorically stated that the victim had identified the appellants as his tormenters in unambiguous terms on more than one occasion. One or two inappropriate phrases or terminologies used by the Enquiry Committee in its report cannot decide the issue as to whether or not the appellants were *prima facie* responsible for the alleged acts of ragging. Proving the charge against the appellants under the Act is within the domain of the Criminal Court. The enquiry in question was confined to the action to be taken against the appellants at the institutional level. The University had accepted the report and expelled the appellants from the hostel. They were permitted to continue their studies subject to the result of the criminal case pending against them. The appellants were also asked to give an undertaking that they would not indulge in any such activity in future. It was made clear that violation of any of the above conditions would result in expulsion from the college. Viewed from the above angle, it cannot be said that the University had committed any illegality in treating the period of suspension of the appellants as absence for all academic programmes of the University. Admittedly the appellants could not attend the classes during the period of suspension. They had not participated in any of the academic programmes during that period. Though the University is vested with the power to conduct supplementary examinations for students who could not attend the examination for genuine reasons, such as accident, hospitalization, contagious diseases etc., the case of the appellants was totally different. As rightly pointed out by the University, the appellants did not have the minimum percentage of attendance for the subjects concerned because of suspension, as envisaged under rule 26.1 of the Academic Regulations and therefore they had not successfully completed the course, either in theory or practical classes.

Viewed from the above angle, it cannot be said that the University had committed any illegality in treating the period of suspension of the appellants as absence for all academic programmes of the University.

The Writ Appeal fails. It is accordingly dismissed.

---

17. HIGH COURT OF JHARKHAND

Avinash Bhaskar v. *Birla Institute of Technology*, 2009 (57) BLJR 342

Facts: The petitioner had been admitted in BHMCT course (Hotel Management) a 4-years degree course in Birla Institute of Technology (BIT Mesra), Ranchi in the year 2003 and came out successful in all the semester examination including 6th semester by securing first class marks. While the petitioner was in the 6th semester, he underwent six months' training in Seven Star Hotel at Goa from 5-12-2005 to 6-5-2006. After completing training when he returned home, he took admission in 7th semester on 18-7-2006. On 10-8-2006, the Superintendent of Hostel No. 7 and also Associate Deans when came to know that the students of 1st semester of BHMCT course have been subjected to ragging by the senior colleagues from 24-7-2006 to 10-8-2006, the matter was enquired into whereupon seven students of the 1st year of BHMCT course including Gaurav Bhardwaj, Amit Kumar Verma and Satyajeet Srivastava made a complaint in writing that ragging has been going on in the 5th lobby of Hostel No. 7 regularly. Thereupon the matter was reported to the Vice-Chancellor who asked the Associates Dean to issue notice to all the students of 5th lobby of Hostel No. 7 to vacate the Hostel. Thereafter students of the 1st year BHMCT course met with the Vice-chancellor on 30-8-2006 and disclosed the name of three persons including the petitioner who had indulged themselves in the illegal act of ragging. Thereupon, all those three persons including the petitioner were suspended along with one Gilbert Michael Linda and notice to that effect was issued by the Registrar of the Institute.

After following proper procedure, the office order dated 18-10-2006 was issued by the Registrar under the order of the Vice-Chancellor, Birla Institute of Technology informing therein that all the three students including the petitioner, who had earlier been suspended are expelled from the Institute and the mid-semester examination papers of the above students were cancelled.

Issues: Whether punishment imposed seems to be justified and proportionate to the act committed by Petitioner?

Judgment: One can easily understand that act of ragging includes various acts indecent to moral values such as abuses, physical torture, mental torture putting the students to indulge in obscene act etc. Each such act has got degree of its severity and among all these acts 'abuse' seems to have lesser severity but still the petitioner who came out successful in his all the 6th semester has been expelled from the Institute which, in the facts and circumstances of the case, never seems to be justifiable rather imposition of lesser punishment would have been appropriate as it would have telling effects upon the career of student and if one such act ruins a career of student, it would certainly be too harsh when the petitioner had to take only two examination to finish the course. Thus, punishment imposed never seems to be justified nor proportionate to act committed by the petitioner. On other counts also the impugned order of punishment as contained in suffers from illegality as the order seems to have been passed in violation of the principles of natural justice as the petitioner was not given any opportunity of being heard at the time of enquiry nor copy of the enquiry report was submitted before infliction of the punishment, though no such rule is there for providing copy of the enquiry report or allowing the culprit to participate in the enquiry but equity demand that petitioner should have been given opportunity of being heard before infliction of the punishment.

In the result, this application is allowed.

---

18. HIGH COURT OF KERALA

***Berin P. Varghese* v. *State of Kerala*,**

2008 (2) ALT (Cri) 278

R. Basant, J.

Facts & Issues involved:

A young student with a rural background born of parents from the economically weaker section of the community achieved the dream of himself and his family. He secured admission to a State run professional college. This proved achiever with a lot of idealism in his young mind with trepidation walked into the professional college - the Government Veterinary College, Mannuthy. He joined the college on 9-10-2007. He was subjected to harrowing, humiliating, embarrassing and harassing acts of his senior students. He was subjected to the most inhuman methods of physical and mental torture that goes in the name of ragging. He went back to his house at the first available opportunity - on the 18th. He was forced to come back to the college on 22-10-2007 as he could not continue to be away any longer.

A person attempts to commit suicide. He is culpably abetted by another to so commit suicide. Providentially he escapes and he does not die. Is the law helpless against the one, who abets the commission of suicide (I mean the attempt thereof) merely because the attempt was unsuccessful? Is he guilty of the offence punishable under section 306 read with 511 I.P.C. or at least under section 309 read with 116 I.P.C.? Or, is the law to throw its hands up and say that you can go on abetting; you can go on attempting to persuade or goad a person to commit suicide; you may succeed in your attempt to abet; he may attempt to commit suicide also; but if he does not die, you can go scot free. Can that be the law? How serious is the law in its attempt to prevent ragging? Do we lack the societal, political, legislative and administrative will to prevent ragging? Do we accept ragging as not serious enough that it can be left entirely to the managements, principals and Wardens to tackle the problem? Why does ragging continue to be a non-cognizable, and bailable offence in the statute book, fettering considerably the effectiveness of the preventive action possible and the deterrence against commission of such offence of ragging?

These sets of questions, the former legally interesting and the latter socially disturbing, do arise for consideration in this bail application.

Judgment: Under the general principle of law embodied in section 511 I.P.C. every offence can be attempted also. In jurisprudential theory intention, preparation, attempt and commission are the four specific stages of commission of every crime, from principle and precedent I am unable to accept the theory that so far as the offence under section 306 I.P.C. is concerned, this third step/ phase must be held to be absent and non-existent in all cases. I take the view that an attempt to commit the offence under section 306 I.P.C. is certainly possible and there is no warrant for the presumption that there cannot ever be a conviction for an offence under section 306 read with 511 I.P.C. If a person abets the commission of suicide and the abetment does not succeed and fructify into a completed offence under section 306 I.P.C. it must, according to me certainly, be held to fall within the sweep of section 306 read with 511 I.P.C. The miscreants, against whom allegations are raised under section 306 read with 511 I.P.C. that they attempted the abetment to commit suicide by the unfortunate victim in this case can legitimately be proceeded against under section 306 read with 511 I.P.C. and there is no inherent legal defect, infirmity or impossibility in such prosecution. The history of the war against ragging in the campus reveals that there has been no determined and positive action. I have gone through the provisions of Kerala Prevention of Ragging Act. The offence is non-cognizable and bailable. The system cannot expect the impossible from the police force. If you expect them to fight against ragging on behalf of the sublime polity of this country, they have to be equipped with necessary legal weapons. It passes my comprehension as to why ragging continues to be a non-cognizable and bailable offence as per the schedule to the Code of Criminal Procedure without any specific provision in the Act itself. Determined action is required and the Legislature must not be found wanting in arming and equipping the police with necessary legal weapons. The arms of the State – Legislature, Executive and Judiciary, cannot be found wanting in the efforts to prevent such *vice* in our campuses.

In the above view of the matter, I am of the opinion that the miscreants, against whom allegations are raised under section 306 read with 511 I.P.C. that they attempted the abetment to commit suicide by the unfortunate victim in this case can legitimately be proceeded against under section 306 read with 511 I.P.C. and there is no inherent legal defect, infirmity or impossibility in such prosecution. This bail application is, in these circumstances, dismissed.

---

19. HIGH COURT OF KERALA

Alpha Jose v. *State of Kerala*, 2006 (3) KLT 886

C.N. Ramachandran Nair, J.

Facts: The two petitioners, who are Third Year B.Sc. Nursing students in the School of Medical Education run by the Mahatma Gandhi University at Kottayam are challenging their suspension from the institution on account of the criminal case pending against them before the Judicial Magistrate of the First Class, Ettumannur, for ragging punishable under section 4 of the Kerala Prohibition of Ragging Act, 1998, hereinafter called the "Act". FIR is filed against the petitioners based on Ext. P4 complaint filed by a first year B.Sc. Nursing student of the same School by name Ms. Supimol on 19-11-2005 before the District Superintendent of Police stating that the two petitioners were supporters of two boys by name Ranjith and Sherine who ragged and sexually assaulted the complainant. The main allegation against the petitioners in Ext. P4 which led to filing of FIR is that they along with other girls ragged the complainant in the ladies hostel by compelling the complainant to sing, dance, jump, etc. Even though Ext. P4 does not contain the date on which petitioners ragged the complainant in the hostel, in the FIR filed by the police, the date of ragging by the petitioners was stated as 23-10-2005. However, later, additional report was filed by the police changing the date of ragging as 23-9-2005. Petitioners, in support of their denial of the charges, have produced copy of the attendance register and clinical rotation plan for third year Nursing degree students maintained by the Medical College Hospital which show that petitioners were on night duty in the hospital on the alleged date of ragging that is on 23-9-2005 from 6 P.M. to 7.30 A.M., whereas the alleged ragging under the final police report took place at 8.30 P.M. on that day. I do not think it either proper or required for this Court to consider the merits of the pending criminal complaint in this proceeding wherein petitioners are only challenging their continued suspension from college for more than six months.

Judgment: Section 6 of the Act authorises suspension only if there is written complaint by the student, parent or guardian or teacher of the educational institution. Admittedly neither the victim nor any of the persons referred to in section 6 has lodged a complaint against the petitioners before the University demanding their suspension. University admittedly suspended the petitioners purely based on the criminal complaint.

Even though statute does not authorise the educational institution to initiate *suo motu* action for suspension, I am of the view that an educational institution has inherent authority to take note of ragging from any source of information and can initiate disciplinary proceedings against the students involved as part of discipline in the institution, without any statutory power authorising it. Suspension authorised under section 6 of the Act is only when there is a *prima facie* case.

I do not think even in exercise of the inherent power of the educational institution assumed by this Court, students can be suspended on allegation of ragging without establishing a *prima facie* case about the allegation. In the circumstance, I feel the continued suspension of the petitioners is unjust, arbitrary and unauthorised by the Act.

---

20. HIGH COURT OF ANDHRA PRADESH

***News Item (Paper Clipping, The New Indian Express dated 27-10-2005 at page No. 5)* v. *Principal, Bapatla Engineering College,* 2006 (2) ALD 172**

T. Meena Kumari and K.C. Bhanu, JJ.

Facts: This is a taken up writ petition based on an article under the caption "Ragging drives student to suicide", in the "Paper clipping" dated 27-10-2005 of the New Indian Express daily news paper, and the report *inter alia* reveals that a first year student of Bapatla Engineering College, Bapatla Guntur District, namely Sri Katuri Alexander committed suicide by consuming pesticide at his residence in Chintgumpalli of Chinaganjam Mandal. As per Police, the said Alexander returned home a couple of days ago and informed his parents that the college is unsuitable for him, that on the same day the family members found him lying in unconscious condition and that he later died at a private hospital. Hence, this Court, *suo motu* took the same on file as taken up W.P. and proceeded further.

Judgment: Under the above facts and circumstances, apart from the Acts, Rules and the guidelines already framed and issued by the State Government, but in the interest of student community at large, we thought it fit to direct the Secretary of Home department, District Collectors, the D.G.P and also the Registrars of Universities, the Director of Higher Education, the Director of School Education and the Board of intermediate Education, the following guidelines;

(a) that every educational institution should notify the disadvantages of ragging and also the consequences thereof and the punishments for violation of the same in this regard in their prospectus for admission;

(b) That as soon as the admissions of the freshers have started all the educational institutions must see that the students are made aware of the disadvantages of the ragging either by conducting classes or by way of lectures by the concerned teachers of the institution at least for a group of students as identified allotting one class in each week/month for bringing to the notice of the students about the disadvantages of the ragging;

(c) All the communications of media like the Televisions, News papers, Open circulars, Suitable posters at colleges and hostel premises etc., by the Principal/head of the institution and the Public Address system should be utilized to bring to the notice of the students that ragging is a serious offence and wide publicity should be given mostly in the places where educational institutions are situated and at the traffic junctions through the public address system, at least, in the specified hours;

(d) Strict surveillance should be maintained in such locations for prevention of ragging;

(e) The educational institutions, who are able to afford, can also utilize the channels of media to give adequate publicity to the negative aspects of ragging and also narrating the past incidents of suicides, so that public awareness and aversion can be built up against ragging, as once life is lost, it is lost for ever in view of the fact that the agony of the parents cannot be explained in words as they would be sending their children with a hope that their children would come out of the portals of educational institutions with good education in near future;

(f) As the matter relates to the students at large, the authorities *i.e.*, District Collector and the Police department should co-operate with the educational institutions to bring awareness amongst the student community by arranging group meetings between the students of certain institutions at specified times and at specified places in the same college campus about the 'disadvantages of ragging', so that the students, if any, have an idea of indulging into ragging, would definitely change their minds, if they are properly taught;

(g) Whenever any student complains of ragging to the Head of the Educational Institution, such head shall enquire into the same forthwith and if the complaint is found true, shall take serious action against such doer of the act in view of the fact that no educational institution is taking serious view on the ragging till it becomes very serious in nature;

(h) The Head of the institution shall constitute anti-ragging squads involving teachers and students to prevent ragging and keep continuous watch and vigil over ragging so as to prevent its occurrence and recurrence;

(i) The Principal/Head of the institution shall obtain an undertaking in writing from the students at the time of admission that they shall not resort to ragging inside or outside the institution;

(j) As soon as fresh admissions are over, Principal/head of the institution should see that there should be an assembly of the students of all classes including the freshers and seniors wherein the lecturers should take part with regard to the interaction amongst them and also the lecturers, teachers, staff and the students should be requested to take oath that they will not resort to ragging and that they will move friendly with all the freshers and juniors, and if that is done, we are hopeful that the students community at large would definitely understand the disadvantages of ragging;

(k) At the commencement of the Academic session, the Review Committee headed by the District Collector and the Superintendent of Police of the concerned Districts should ensure that there should be an interaction with the students at large at least periodically may be twice in a month till the students *i.e.*, freshers are settled down in their colleges to see that the act of ragging comes down and the freshers feel confident and secure in their college campus;

(l) The Universities and the institutions shall at a reasonable time before the commencement of an academic year, and at frequent intervals, deliberate over and devise such positive and constructive activities to be arranged by involving the students generally so that the seniors and juniors, and the existing students and the freshers, interact with each other in a healthy atmosphere and develop a friendly relationship so as to behave like members of a family in an institution;

(m) To stop the ragging, awareness should be brought amongst the students, teachers and parents that ragging is a reprehensible act which does no good to any one and by simultaneously generating an atmosphere of discipline by a clear message that no act of ragging shall go unnoticed and unpunished.

---

21. HIGH COURT OF CALCUTTA

***Sk. Nur Alam* v. *Director, College of Engineering and Management*, 2006 (3) CHN 291**

Jayanta Kumar Biswas, J.

Facts: Alleging that on the night of October 20, 2003 the petitioner along with five other students of the college indulged in ragging to six junior students of the college, proceedings were initiated against him and his companion students under provisions of the West Bengal Prohibition of Ragging in Educational Institutions Act, 2000. After giving the petitioner reasonable opportunity to defend himself, and after making necessary inquiry, the authority found the petitioner and his companion students guilty of the charges of ragging, and recommended permanent expulsion of the petitioner from the college. Accordingly, the Director of the College issued the order dated October 28, 2003 expelling the petitioner from the college with immediate effect. The writ petitioner is aggrieved by this order.

Issue: Whether or not the order contains imposition of disproportionate punishment and question of the petitioner's future was not considered by the authorities?

Judgment: Section 6 of the Act provide that if the allegation of ragging is found to be true, then the only punishment that is to be imposed is to expel the student from the educational institution. Exactly such punishment has been imposed in the present case. Provisions of the Act did not contemplate imposition of any lesser punishment. Hence simply because the authorities were soft with the other guilty students on whom a lenient punishment was imposed, though it was contrary to provisions of the Act, the petitioner is not entitled to allege discrimination.

As far as the question of the petitioner's future is concerned, the transfer certificate should be issued by the college to the petitioner, if according to rules and regulations he is entitled to get a transfer certificate. I only say that at the time of issuing the transfer certificate the college shall keep in mind that at a very young age the petitioner has already suffered a very harsh punishment.

---

22. HIGH COURT OF MADRAS

R. Karthik* v. *The Dean, Stanley Medical College, The College Council, Stanley Medical College and The Chairman, Enquiry Committee, Stanley Medical College,

2004 Writ LR 423

A. Kulasekaran, J.

Facts: The facts of the case is one Nithyanandam, first year MBBS Student sent a complaint to Class representative stating that the petitioner ragged him severely during the month of August, 2003. On receipt of the said complaint, the respondents have furnished photographs of 15 students including the petitioner herein. Nithyanandam, after seeing several photographs stated that "I am not sure which one of the photo is the correct person. If this photo identified by me is Karthik it is okay otherwise I am not sure. I do not want to identify the wrong one. I have seen the person only two or three minutes in the dark in the terrace". The petitioner was also examined on 03-12-2003 and the petitioner denied the charges of ragging.

The Enquiry Committee submitted the report to the Dean wherein it is stated that 11 students have not seen the petitioner Nithyanandam. The Dean forwarded the enquiry report to the DME for further direction. The DME ordered for another enquiry based on the statement of the petitioner that there was severe ragging in the hostel and almost all seniors have indulged in ragging by striking them with hockey sticks, sexual harassment etc., and he could identify them. On 23-12-2003, the Dean ordered the same Committee to re-enquire the petitioner regarding the statement given by him during the previous enquiry. I have perused the files. On 27-12-2003, statement of the petitioner was recorded. The petitioner answered that "I have seen them (seniors) ragging but I do not know the names". For question about his memory, he answered 'the question appears stupid and teasing my mental health". While giving statement on 27-12-2003, the petitioner requested the Committee to furnish the copy of the complaint of Nithyanandam. On the same day, the petitioner's father stated to have misbehaved with the members of the Enquiry Committee, with the result, a complaint was lodged against him with the Dean. It is stated in the complaint that the petitioner's father abused the Committee members with unparliamentary words. After receipt of the Committee's report, the Dean has placed the matter before the College Council on 30-12-2003. The College Council unanimously passed the impugned order of suspension.

Judgment: Though the petitioner was absolved from all charges, his behaviour before the College Council is not appreciable. Moreover, relying on his wrong statement, second enquiry was conducted which caused inconvenience to the respondents. Similarly, the petitioner's father also not conducted himself properly, which is evident from the complaint made by the Council Members to the Dean. Of course, they could have acted unwittingly, however, in order to realise their mistake, I feel that both shall be directed to submit an affidavit of apology before the Dean, the first respondent herein.

Hence, the impugned order is set aside on condition that the petitioner and his father shall file an affidavit of apology to the Dean/first respondent herein within a period of seven days from today.

The campus of educational institution is the place where the virtues of discipline and non-violence should be written as with a sun beam on every student's mind. Maintenance of standards of decency dictated by high moral sense is impossible unless the citizen have a sense of discipline. Where self-discipline and self-restraint do not prevail, Law has to step-in and adjudication by Court is compulsory. The educational institutions like professional colleges facing the situation of raging year-after-year. We shall not allow educational institutions bid farewell to discipline. The authorities concerned should take all preventive steps in advance to avoid the brutal act of ragging.

---

23. HIGH COURT OF BOMBAY (NAGPUR BENCH)

***Rahul Pandurangji Khadatkar* v. *State of Maharashtra*,**
AIR 2002 Bom 312

Facts: The facts, giving rise to the instant petition, stated in briefly, are that: the petitioners, who are senior students of the Government Polytechnic College, Gadchiroli, in violation of the provisions of the Maharashtra Prohibition of Ragging Act, violated personal sanctity of one Mr. Ravikumar s/o Baliram Dakhane, respondent No. 4 herein, a 19 years old student of the Polytechnic College, by subjecting him to ragging, which resulted in physical and mental injury to the said student, who and his parents complained of about it to the Police and the Police, after investigation into the matter, have filed Charge-sheet in the Court for prosecuting the present petitioners under the provisions of section 323 of Indian Penal Code and other related offences. After having noticed the charge-sheet filed against the petitioners, the respondent No. 3 - Principal of the College, issued an order of suspension dated 26-5-2000 under section 6 of the Act, thereby suspending the petitioners. The petitioners have, therefore, challenged the order of suspension in this Court by way of this writ petition under article 226 of the Constitution of India. On behalf of the petitioners, the order was challenged mainly on the ground that order of suspension is outside the scope of section 6 of the Act and, therefore, it is without jurisdiction and deserves to be quashed. The argument on behalf of the petitioners is that there is no proof of any complaint, in writing, filed with the Educational Institution by the student or his parents, as the case may be, and, therefore, there is no case before the respondent No. 3- Institutional head, to exercise his power under section 6 of the Act.

Issues: Whether or not section 6 of Maharashtra Prohibition of Ragging Act, 1999 empowers the Principal of college to make order of suspension?

Whether or not written complaint with the educational institution is mandatory ?

Judgment: The provisions of section 6 of the Act are very clear. It provides that whenever *prima facie* case of ragging being practised, is brought to the knowledge of the head of the institution, he shall, without prejudice to foregoing provisions, within seven days of the receipt of the complaint, enquire into the matter and if it is found true, suspend the student The provisions of section 6, therefore, mandate the institutional chief to suspend the student, who is found *prima facie* guilty of having practised ragging. The mandate of Legislature is very clear. The head of the institution is empowered to take action of suspension of a student, if *prima facie,* he is of the opinion, after due enquiry, that ragging has been practised. Existence of complaint, in writing, with the educational institution, is not mandatory. The purport of the section is that whenever head of the institution comes to know of practice of ragging in his institution, he shall take action. Whether the complaint is received by him, or whether it is received by the Police is immaterial. What is the mandate by the section is his taking of action of *prima facie* existence of practice of ragging.

Ratio: Existence of complaint, in writing, with the educational institution not mandatory.

---

24. HIGH COURT OF KARNATAKA

Sawen Ramesh* v. *Yenepoya Dental College,
MANU/KA/0257/2002

H.L. Dattu, J.

Facts: Petitioner, who has suffered an order of suspension of his Educational carrier, and was allowed to attend the classes only on the condition that his parents/guardian would give a necessary undertaking for good behaviour on or before 16-3-1998 and after leaving the first respondent college for good, is before this Court for the following reliefs. They are :

I. To quash the impugned order dated 3-3-1998 *vide* Ref. B/504/98/YDC dated 3-3-1998 passed by the respondent.

II. For a direction to the respondent to return the amounts paid by him for pursuing his carrier in the respondent College after deducting the tuition fee for the Ist and IInd year B.D.S. course *i.e.*, deducting Rs. 1,03,850 out of Rs. 7.5 lakhs *i.e.*, Rs. 6,46,150

Issue: Whether the Committee constituted by the respondent management is a valid Committee as required under section 42 of the Karnataka Education Act, 1983 for the purpose of holding an enquiry against the petitioner and others for an act of indiscipline and to have been committed by them in the first respondent college?

Judgment: In the Instant case, an act of indiscipline is alleged against a student studying in a particular course. The management intends to hold an enquiry into that allegation. For that purpose, the management need not have to fall back on section 42 of the Act in constituting an Enquiry Committee. Further, the allegation against the petitioner is with regard to verbal ragging of a student. The management feels that, that act of indiscipline should be enquired into by a Committee consisting of Lecturers of the college. In a Committee of that nature, in my opinion, the representatives of the teachers, representatives of the parents, representatives of the members of the teaching staff, etc., are absolutely unnecessary. Therefore, the Committee that is constituted by the respondent management may not be in accordance with the provisions of section 42 of the Act, but the same has not prejudiced the case of the petitioner in any manner whatsoever.

---

25. HIGH COURT OF KERALA

***Principal, College of Engineering, Trivandrum* v. *P.S. Anoop*, MANU/KE/0506/2001**

K.S. Radhakrishnan and K. Balakrishnan Nair, JJ.

Facts: The Principal of the College of Engineering, Trivandrum is the appellant herein. Writ Petition was preferred by respondents 1 to 5 challenging Ext. P5 order passed by the Principal suspending them from the college with effect from 31-1-2001 to 31-5-2001. The order also stated that they would not be re-admitted to the college hostel in future.

In the instant case as soon as Principal received complaint from the student as well as from the father of the student, the Principal constituted an Enquiry Commission consisting of three Professors and it is on the basis of the report of the Commission and the statement recorded from the student and the Principal decided to suspend the writ petitioner for a period of five months. As per the Act petitioners have necessarily to undergo the said punishment.

Learned single Judge passed an order on 11-4-2001 permitting them to appear for those examination on condition that the results would not be published without further orders. Original Petition was later disposed of by the learned Single Judge regularising the examination taken on the basis of the interim orders of this Court. Aggrieved by the same Principals has filed this appeal.

Judgment: We are convinced that Principal was only discharging his statutory duty by initiating action on the basis of the report of the Commission and in the best interest of the institution. We have therefore no hesitation to set aside the judgment of the learned single Judge interfering with the orders of the Principal. We do so. However, we may direct the Principal to give writ petitioners opportunity to complete their course at the earliest. We also note the Principal has also stated that the petitioners can be given opportunity to appear for the internal examinations and do the laboratory work at the next immediate chance when the subject is offered. Principal has also stated that the students could attend to experiments and submit assignments only when a particular semester is on. Third petitioner can complete his pending laboratory work if he registers as per the University norms for the semesters when the particular courses are offered.

---

26. HIGH COURT OF KERALA

***Regarding Ragging of Freshers in Thiruvananthapuram Government Engineering College* v. *State of Kerala*, AIR 2000 Ker 245**

Arijit Pasayat, C.J. and K.S. Radhakrishnan, J.

Facts: On the basis of a grievance made to the High Court that student pursuing their studies in various educational institutions of the State are subjected to ragging by senior students the petition was registered as a *suo motu* writ petition and notice issued to the State of Kerala. After hearing the counsel who appeared for the Petitioner and for the State, considering the matter and disposing of the Writ Petition;

Judgment: State has taken the right direction by enacting the Act. But enactment of stringent laws without effective implementation is meaningless. Not only those who indulge in ragging but also those who directly or indirectly aid and/or abate it have also to be penalised. In many instances, authorities, in order to protect image of the institution by cajoling, intimidating threatening and doing such other reprehensive acts, prevent affected students from making complaints which would necessitate action under the Act. Some times friends/ relatives of persons involved in ragging do such acts in order to save them from statutory consequences. Suitable provisions are required to be made in respect of them also. They are as much guilty for ragging as those who do it.

We, therefore, close this petition with the further following directions :

(i) In addition to the action taken as provided under the Act, the Cells shall take steps which are not in any way repugnant to the statutory provisions and continue to monitor the anti-ragging efforts;

(ii) In the case of those against whom cases have been registered and are produced before Magistrate, necessary orders shall be passed in line with the directions given regarding the daily attendance before police officer. After two months from the first date of attendance it shall be twice a week *i.e.,* on Wednesday and Sunday and after four months, it shall be once a week *i.e.,* on Sunday. This arrangement shall continue till completion of trial, if any. If the concerned Court feels that more stringent conditions, including remand to custody, are necessary, it shall be free to pass such orders;

(iii) Cases registered for ragging shall be taken on a priority basis considering its social impact; and

(iv) State Government shall examine desirability of having legislative measures in the line indicated above. Notwithstanding closure of the case, reports shall be submitted quarterly by concerned authorities for consideration by this Court. Same shall be placed before a Bench presided by Chief Justice.

---

27. HIGH COURT OF MADRAS

M. Lakshmanan* v. *The Principal, Government Arts College (Autonomous) and The Registrar, Bharathiar University,
MANU/TN/0998/1999

P. Shanmugam, J.

Facts: The case against the Petitioners is that they had indulged in ragging the 1st Year students and assaulted another student one A. Ganesan on 5-7-1999. The said fact was witnessed by two Professors S. Tamilmani of Commerce Department and G.S. Durai of Sanskrit Department. The said Ganesan gave a complaint in writing, counter-signed by 43 students of the college who were present at that time. In the said complaint, he has stated that while he was going out of the class, the Petitioners Lakshmanan and Rajesh picked up a quarrel under the influence of liquor and assaulted him. Hence, he requested that action may be taken against them. Both the professors have explained the incident directly to the Principal, The injured student Ganesan was found suffering from pain due to the assault made by the Petitioners. Therefore, the Principal immediately asked the Head of Department of the Political Science Thiru Prof. K. Mohd. Razzaq to enquire into the matter. Thiru Prof. K. Mohd. Razzaq enquired the injured student as well as the other students who were witness to the incident. Those who have seen the incident have signed the statement. Thiru Prof. K. Mohd.Razzaq reported after a due enquiry that Ganesan was assaulted and serious injuries have been caused to the said student. Thereafter, a decision was taken by the College Council after a long deliberation to issue Transfer Certificates to the Petitioners. However on 9-8-99, the complaint given by the Ganesan counter signed by 43 students was withdrawn and by a separate letter, it was requested that no action need be taken. The writ petition is filed against the order of dismissal and the issue of Transfer Certificates.

Issue: Whether the summary dismissal of the Petitioners without following the normal rule of issuing notice and enquiry is sustainable or not.

Judgment: I have gone through the files which were placed before me as to the conduct of the enquiry and I am satisfied that the authorities have come to the conclusion based on the evidence that the Petitioners were involved in ragging. In the light of this finding and the instructions that persons involved in ragging should be summarily expelled from the University, as directed by the Supreme Court of India in W.P. (Civil) 656/99, the question of framing charges against the Petitioners does not arise for consideration. I am of the view that in the interest of justice and due to the lapse of the time, it is just and necessary that the Respondents are directed to issue the Transfer Certificates without any remark of dismissal against the Petitioners to enable the Petitioners to join a different institution and to continue and complete their studies.

Ratio: It is clear that if the students are found indulging in ragging, they are liable to be summarily dismissed from the college. There is no question of enquiry and notice in such cases of ragging.

---

28. HIGH COURT OF ALLAHABAD

***Vivek Kumar* v. *Vice Chancellor, B.H.U.*,**
AIR 1998 All 218

S.R. Singh, J.

Facts: When the impugned action against the Petitioner came into existence, he happened to be a student of last semester, *i.e.*, VIIIth semester of B. Tech. Chemical Engineering. The Petitioner was selected for the aforesaid B. Tech. Chemical Engineering course in the Institute of Technology in the Banaras Hindu University on his performance in the admission test conducted on all India basis. Petitioner states that he has a good academic record as in the High School and Intermediate examinations conducted by the U.P. Board, he has secured 79% and 76% marks respectively. Petitioner claims that he has passed out all the semesters regularly with good performance. It is in respect to an incident which is said to have taken place in the night of 24/25th March, 2001, in which the Petitioner and one Gaurav Anand committed a misconduct with a fellow student, namely, Siddharth Sinha, on a complaint having been made by the aforesaid Sri Sinha, the disciplinary proceedings started, which has resulted into expulsion of Gaurav Anand for one year from the university and expulsion of the Petitioner for all the time to come. It is this action of the Respondents which is under challenge before this Court.

Court felt that the acts of ragging have to be severely dealt with. It is a matter of common knowledge, as has been and is being published also from time to time that on account of the severe ragging and even on its threats to the freshers by the seniors, large number of innocent students including the boys and the girls having their bright future/career, having got a seat in specialised courses by sheer dent of their merit, have to leave their course/study and even in some of the cases may be in very less number but innocent boy/girl has to commit even suicide. This causes great frustration among the freshers as well as to their parents. The senior students of any college, hostels are supposed to behave like an elder, like a guardian of the freshers treating them to be a junior member of the family and they are expected to teach them, guide them in respect to various kinds of disciplinary things which may be befitting to the dignity in the society. Senior students in the name of ragging *i.e.*, an introduction of the freshers normally involve themselves in various kinds of serious misconducts including manhandling, physical assault and even encroachment on personal liberty of the innocent boy/student.

In view of the aforesaid , so far act of ragging is concerned if any student is found to be indulged in it, he has to be dealt severely. Here in the case in hand, there is no dispute about the fact that the victim, namely, Siddharth Sinha is concerned, he was not a fresher or junior than the Petitioner. Admittedly, both happened to be fellow students, running in VIIIth semester. Both of them had taken admission in B. Tech. Chemical Engineering course at a time, continued together for more than 3-1/2 years, by completing seven semesters and both happened to be inmates of the same hostel, *i.e.*, Dhanrajgiri Hostel. The ragging in the strict sense has to be taken as an indecent act of a senior with a fresher or even with a junior fellow. But so far the indecent act, behaviour or any kind of misconduct with the fellow student on completion of about four years, *i.e.*, in the VIIIth semester, it cannot be brought within the purview of the ragging although it can be called a serious misconduct on the part of that student.

Looking into the past academic record of the Petitioner, his brilliance, completing seven semesters in the same university and peaceful tenure of the hostel for all the aforesaid times, it appears that loss of more than 1-1/2 years, is enough punishment for the Petitioner as during this period of 1-1/2 years, he must have suffered great mental strain besides humiliation from various corners having become junior in various respects from large number of candidates. There also appears to be another reason for taking this view, *i.e.*, so far as awarding the punishment for any indiscipline or any crime is concerned, the approach of the Courts should be to think that whether the quantum of punishment will result in a reformation and will be a kind of warning to improve the habits and misdeeds of the person involved or it will cause and create a more serious situation and will aggravate the feelings of that man to cause and commit more serious acts of indiscipline and the crime. Here so far as the case in hand is concerned, admittedly, the Petitioner is neither a criminal nor he happened to be an indisciplined boy, which is clear from his past record as well as an admitted situation that even up to VIIth semester, there happened to be no complaint of any kind from any quarter and, therefore, this solitary incident in the given set of facts, *i.e.*, annoyance with the victim Siddharth Sinha on account of earlier complaint and at the time of incident, the Petitioner being in drunken state, has certainly crossed the limit but the punishment which he has already received, *i.e.*, loss of his 1-1/2 year career, besides mental strain and for all this time a hanging pendulum and a fear pinching him that whether he will get any relief in relation to the impugned action of his expulsion from the Court or not, this Court feels, is enough for the present case.

In view of the foregoing discussion, this writ petition succeeds in part. The impugned order of the Respondent No. 1 dated 20.4.2001, as contained in is hereby quashed to the extent that instead of Petitioner's expulsion from the university for all the times to come, it is directed that in the next coming examination, Petitioner will be permitted to appear and complete his VIIIth semester, in accordance with law.

29. HIGH COURT OF ALLAHABAD

Pankaj Srivastava* v. *Principal, MotiLal Nehru Regional Engineering College, Allahabad,
1998 (2) AWC 1473

D.K. Seth, J.

Facts: the petitioner was rusticated for one year and his re-admission was also directed not to be considered till the period of rustication. However, he was permitted to appear in the supplementary examination of B.E. first year class but he was directed not to enter hostel or college premises. By the second order dated 24th September, 1991, a notice was issued in which the petitioner's name was Included at serial No. 4, whereby it was directed that petitioner will not be allowed admission until rustication period is over and that in case of further complaint, the period of rustication will be extended beyond one year.

It is not disputed that the Principal has power to rusticate students on account of indiscipline. Ragging is surely an indiscipline. The culture of ragging has been imported from England along with English education system. But now it has attained dangerous proportion. The disease of ragging is polluting the campus atmosphere. In the name of ragging, freshers are subjected to severe psychological and physical sufferings, sometimes resulting into psychological and mental disorder and physical harms even death. It is a situation that is causing concern to educationists. The parents are afraid of sending their wards in hostel. Many of the students left their studies having failed to withstand ragging. It is, therefore, necessary that adequate steps should be taken so as to create an impression in the mind of the students that undertaking of ragging or participation in the act of ragging may jeopardise their career and end their student life. In order to contain this disease, strict discipline is to be imposed. It cannot be overlooked. But at the same time, if punishment on account of ragging is inflicted, it has to be inflicted with proper care and caution only when it is established that the student is responsible and the authority has reasons to believe that he had participated in ragging and was responsible for the same. Such conclusion can only be arrived at after giving an opportunity of hearing and holding proper enquiry in the matter. It is not dependent on the whims and caprice of the authority concerned.

Thus, the contention that the authority cannot impose such a punishment on account of ragging, cannot be sustained. The authority has every power and jurisdiction to take proper steps for enforcing discipline and preventing spread of ragging and to maintain conducive atmosphere in the campus in order to restore confidence of the freshers. It is expected that the educational authorities will take proper care and caution in the matter so that the system of ragging is uprooted altogether and is prevented by all means including imposition of any kind of discipline and means and methods bestowing responsibility on the persons in-charge of such hostel and senior students, if necessary by forming a committee for monitoring the relations between the freshers and seniors.

Judgment: In the present case, it was alleged that neither any charge-sheet was issued nor show cause notice was given nor any enquiry was held against the petitioner before inflicting the punishment. It is further mentioned that no enquiry was held neither any notice was issued to the petitioner. The petitioner has denied his participation in the alleged ragging. No counter-affidavit appears to have been filed. There is no material to show as to how the authority had come to the conclusion that the petitioner was involved in ragging. Though in the order, it is pointed out that on account of ragging and some other acts of serious indiscipline, but no particulars in respect of acts of serious indiscipline have been mentioned. Therefore, the impugned order appears to be wholly vague and indefinite and that too without any enquiry and opportunity of hearing to the petitioner. Thus, solely on the ground that the order is vague and has been passed without adopting proper procedure, the order of rustication contained are liable to be quashed and the same are accordingly quashed. Let a writ of *certiorari* to issue. Since there was an interim order, it appears that the petitioner must have continued his study. Since the two orders have been quashed, the petitioner's result that might have been or may be declared, shall be without any stigma.

The writ petition thus succeeds and is allowed. No order as to costs.

---

30. HIGH COURT OF DELHI

Narender Singh v. *University of Delhi,*
1998 (II) AD 321 (Del)

Cyriac Joseph, J.

FACTS: According to the petitioner, he successfully cleared the IInd year of the B.A. (Pass) Course in August, 1996 and he was entitled to be admitted to the IIIrd year (final year) of the said course On 21st August, 1996 the petitioner went to deposit his fee for admission to the IIIrd year. However, he was prevented from depositing the fee and was told that the Principal of the college had issued instructions that fee should not be accepted from the petitioner. The petitioner was not given any reason for the said decision. The father of the petitioner went and met the Principal on 22nd August, 1996. He was advised to withdraw the name of the petitioner from the college. It was also threatened that in case he did not do so the Principal would see to it that the petitioner would not be admitted to the IIIrd year. On 26th August, 1996, the petitioner and certain other students were summoned to the office of the Principal where they were man-handled by the Principal and the college staff. Thereafter when the father of the petitioner went to see the Principal to enquire about the above incident, a show cause notice dated 23rd August, 1996 was given to him wherein it was mentioned that a complaint had been received from one Mr. Sanjay Kumar, a IInd year student of B. Com. (Hon.) against the petitioner. The said show cause notice referred to a complaint received from Mr. Sanjay Kumar on 30th July, 1996 alleging that the petitioner indulged in ragging students in the canteen premises and that in the course of ragging the petitioner had severely beaten up the complainant. The petitioner was asked to explain latest by 29th August, 1996 why disciplinary action should not be taken against him. On 29th

August, 1996 another show cause notice was issued to the petitioner wherein it was alleged that the petitioner alongwith 15 other students had forcibly entered the Principal's office, disrupted some classes and assaulted the employees. The petitioner was asked to show cause why disciplinary proceedings be not initiated against him. The replies to both show cause notices were submitted by him on 29th August, 1996. No personal hearing was ever given to him. Thereafter in a meeting held on 3rd September, 1996, the Disciplinary Committee of the college decided that the replies of the petitioner were unsatisfactory and recommended that the petitioner should not be admitted to the next course *i.e.*, IIIrd years B.A. (Pass) course. The said recommendation of the Disciplinary Committee was submitted to the Principal for his approval. By a letter dated September 10,1996, respondent No. 2, informed the petitioner that as per the recommendations of the Disciplinary Committee his involvement in the incident of beating Mr. Sanjay Kumar had been found to be proved and that he was not permitted to deposit the fee for admission to the next course *i.e.*, B.A. (Pass) IIIrd year course. Being aggrieved by the said action of respondent No. 2, the petitioner submitted a detailed representation dated 19th September, 1996 to respondent No. 1 contending that the recommendations of the Disciplinary Committee be set aside and that he be permitted to deposit fee for admission to the B.A. (Pass) IIIrd year course. The said representation was forwarded by respondent No. 1 to the Dean of Students Welfare for enquiry into the contents of the same. The Dean of the Students Welfare by his letter dated 11th October, 1996 requested the Principal to persuade the Disciplinary Committee of the college to reconsider the matter sympathetically. The petitioner also submitted another application to respondent No. 2 and the Disciplinary Committee of the college seeking sympathetic reconsideration of his case. However, the petitioner did not receive any reply to the said application. Thereafter, the petitioner made repeated requests to respondent No. 2 as also the Disciplinary Committee to reconsider their stand and to permit him to deposit his fee for attending the IIIrd year B.A. (Pass) course. But there was no favourable response. Thereupon the petitioner filed C.W. No. 4343/96 in this Court praying that he be permitted to deposit his fee and attend his classes for the B.A. (Pass) IIIrd year course. When the said writ petition was listed on 21st March, 1997, the petitioner sought leave to withdraw the writ petition since the examinations were scheduled to commence from 22nd March, 1997. He also sought a direction to the respondent college to permit the petitioner to appear in the B.A. (Pass) IIIrd year examination and also offered to seek admission elsewhere thereafter. The prayer was not opposed by the Counsel for the college and accordingly by order dated 21st March, 1997 this Court permitted the petitioner to withdraw the writ petition and directed that the petitioner would be allowed to take the examinations by respondent college subject to completion of formalities prescribed under the Rules. Pursuant to the directions contained in this Court's order dated 21st March, 1997, the petitioner approached the college on 21st March, 1997 and sought to deposit his admission fee and take the admission Roll Number. However, the college authorities refused to accept the fee and informed the petitioner that the Principal had specifically directed not to accept the fee of the petitioner. The petitioner was forcibly ejected from the college premises. Thereafter on 22nd March, 1997, the petitioner approached the college with a copy of this Court's order dated 21st March, 1997 and sought permission to deposit the fee. However, he was not permitted to enter the college even though he succeeded in serving a copy of the order through the watchman of the college. The petitioner, through his Counsel, sent a representation dated 31st March, 1997 to respondent No. 2 and also to the Counsel for respondent No. 2. Still the petitioner was not permitted even to enter the college. Therefore, the petitioner filed C.M. No. 2659/97 in C.W. No. 4343/96. The said application was disposed of by this Court on 9th April, 1997 directing respondent college to reconsider the case of the petitioner on the basis of the directions contained in the order dated 21st March, 1997 as well as on the basis of the relief granted to similarly situated students. Thereafter the petitioner received a letter dated 10th April, 1997 from the Principal intimating that he could not be permitted to take IIIrd year examinations on the ground that the petitioner had not been admitted as a regular student in the IIIrd year and that he had not submitted the examination fee and form before the due date and that he did not have the requisite attendance. Even though the reasons given by the Principal were erroneous the petitioner did not pursue the matter any further as the examinations had already been commenced and he resigned himself to the fact that he lost out one entire academic year without any fault or lapse on his part. On 5th June, 1997 *i.e.*, in the fresh academic session the petitioner once again approached the college and sought to take admission in the IIIrd year course since the period for which he had been denied admission had already lapsed. However, once again he was prevented from entering the college let alone depositing the free. Hence the petitioner submitted a representation dated 6th June, 1997 to respondent No. I as well as to respondent No. 2 pointing out that while directing not to admit the petitioner to the IIIrd year course, the Disciplinary Committee had not specified any period and hence the necessary inference was that the said recommendation was to remain in force only for one academic year. It was also pointed out that there was not plausible reason for not permitting the petitioner to deposit the fee in the next academic year commencing from June, 1997. Since no reply was received to the said representation for one entire month, the petitioner sent a legal notice dated 30th June, 1997 to respondent Nos. I and 2 calling upon them to permit him to take admission to the IIIrd year B.A. (Pass) course for the academic year commencing from June 5,1997. Since no reply was received, the petitioner was constrained to file this writ petition praying for a direction to respondent No. 2 to permit the petitioner to deposit his admission fee and to admit the petitioner to the IIIrd year B.A. (Pass) course in the Maharaja Agrasen College.

Judgment: Learned Counsel for the petitioner submitted that if the petitioner is not permitted to be admitted to the IIIrd year course in respondent No. 2 college, he will not be able to complete the course and his studies for the first and second year would be wasted. The petitioner alone is to be blamed for the said unfortunate situation. Though one may have sympathy for a young person whose educational career is being lost, such sympathy cannot be allowed to influence the Court to impose on a college a student whose presence in the campus is perceived by the college authorities as a potential threat to the discipline and peaceful functioning of the college especially when such perception is justifiably based on the past conduct of the student. Between sympathy and concern for an individual and the larger interests of an institution and its students as a whole, the Court can only choose the latter view of what has been stated above, I hold that the writ petition is devoid of merit and is liable to be dismissed. Accordingly the writ petition is dismissed. There will be no order as to costs.

---

31. HIGH COURT OF ANDHRA PRADESH

Matter Taken Up as* Suo motu *on the News Item Published in Deccan Chronicle News Paper* v. *Principal, Manpower Development College, Maredpally, Secunderabad,
1998 (1) ALD 270

P.S. Mishra, C.J. and D.H. Nasir, J.

Facts: As per Newspaper report which appeared in Deccan Chronicle dated 3-12-1996, one Ms. Padmaja, Aged 24 years, student of Post Graduate Master of Computer Applications Course at the Manpower Development College, Marredpally, Secunderabad committed suicide in her house as she was unable to bear the 'ragging' in the college. The deceased joined the college during the last week of November, 1996. She was subjected to ragging by her seniors in the college, who asked her to sing or dance in front of others. She was pinched and pushed by the students when she refused to yield to their demand. She complained to the Lecturers, but the same was of no avail and no steps were taken to protect her from ragging, and she became too emotional and suddenly took the extreme step of hanging herself. The members of her family hesitated to lodge a complaint with the police. A neighbour reported the matter to the police and the body was eventually moved to hospital for post-mortem examination.

This matter was taken up as Public Interest Litigation and was registered as Writ Petition No. 26132/1996, and the same was heard by a Division Bench of this High Court.

Judgment: In this background of the present PIL, we believe that positive steps are required to be taken in the direction of ameliorating the conditions for fearlessly prosecuting studies in the college campuses. Before laying down any guidelines for that purpose, we must take into consideration the Bill already introduced in the Legislative Assembly on 13th September, 1996 which calls for the enactment of a statute under the name and style of "Andhra Pradesh Prevention of Ragging in Educational Institutions and Public Places Act, 1996" which is proposed to extend to the whole State of Andhra Pradesh. In the statement of objects and reasons, it is envisaged that the practice of ragging by old students on new entrants had become very common in colleges, hostels attached to it and other places of public resort and there had been several instances of brilliant students committing suicides unable to bear insults by old students and to prohibit such evil practices. Section 2 of the Bill defines

"Ragging" as including "decking", teasing by which any person is insulted and put to mental agony by anything done against his/her wishers or consent. Section 3 provides for prohibition of Ragging in Educational Institutions and Public Places and hostels of any Educational Institutions. Ragging in whatever form indulged into is prohibited. Section 4 provides for penalty for indulging in the acts of ragging laying down that whoever indulges in such activities as stated in the said section shall be punished with imprisonment for a period of two years or with fine or with both. Section 5 enables the Educational Institutions to debar such persons from studies in Educational Institutions and lays down that notwithstanding the punishment that may be inflicted on persons indulging in ragging, the head of the Educational Institution or the Manager of any Hostel or other places of public resort, may debar such persons from continuing their studies or remaining in the hostels with immediate effect.

The Bill restricts its scope only to the extent as stated above, which in our opinion is grossly insufficient for curbing and controlling the menace of ragging. An Ordinance has been promulgated in the State of Tamil Nadu being Ordinance No. 10 of 1996. Apart from what is included in the Bill introduced in Andhra Pradesh Legislative Assembly, the Ordinance of Tamil Nadu also provides for immediate suspension of the student from the Educational Institution, who is alleged to have committed the offence under the said Ordinance and the decision of the Head of the Educational Institution or the person responsible for the management of the Institution, under sub-section (1) of section 6 of the said Ordinance is to be treated as final.

We are also of the considered opinion that the following guidelines should also be complied with, while endeavouring to deal with ragging.

(1) The Educational Institutions should provide for the constitution of a committee consisting of the parents and guardians of the students taking education in their institute, as well as two representatives of the students' union, if any, apart from the Principal and a representative of teaching staff in that institute for establishing the code of conduct for the students as well as the members of the teaching staff of the Educational Institute and to review the same by regularly calling a meeting of the committee of parents etc., which may be constituted for this purpose. The committee should recommend to the management whether any steps are required to be taken against any student who may have violated the code of conduct and the school management should take necessary remedial measures as expeditiously as possible, but not later than four weeks from the date of the recommendation so made by the parents' committee.

(2) No person who is not a student of the concerned Educational Institution shall be allowed to enter the premises of that Educational Institution or its hostel without obtaining prior written permission of the Principal of that Institute.

Provided that the parents or the guardian of the students shall not be required to take such permission in writing.

(3) Any student found to be indulging in any ragging activity shall be suspended immediately after communication is sent to him under the signature of the Principal of the concerned Educational Institution stating that he is alleged of indulging in ragging activity. Such student shall be debarred from entering the campus of the Educational Institution or its hostel, except on any day at any time when he is called upon by the authority of the school or by the parents committee for tendering explanation or for defending his case.

(4) No person who is not studying in the given Educational Institution shall be allowed to enter any hostel of boys or girls attached to the concerned Educational Institution. However, by obtaining prior written permission of the Warden of the hostel, he may be so allowed;

Provided, however, that in case of girls' hostel, no male student or any male person shall have any access to a girl inmate of the hostel except in the presence of the Care Taker of the ladies' hostel apart from obtaining advance permission of the Warden for that purpose.

(5) Any girl inmate of the hostel who has gone out of the hostel premises for a personal errand shall return to the hostel latest by 9.00 p.m. if she is delayed, she should render written explanation there and then to the Care Taker of the hostel, who shall allow her to enter the hostel and occupy her seat in the room allotted to her on such written explanation submitted by her. The written explanation so submitted shall be forwarded to the Warden of the hostel by the Care Taker as soon as possible, but not later than 9.00 a.m. on the next day.

(6) Any boy or girl student should keep the identity card issued by the concerned Educational Institution in his/ her possession and offer the same for verification as and when demanded by any authority of the school or hostel or any member of the staff of the school or hostel who is authorised to verify the identity of the concerned student.

(7) Teachers taking the 1st year classes will leave the class at the end of the period only after the next teacher arrives.

(8) Teaching staff and Warden will be at liberty to check and inspect the hostel area at any time during night.

With regard to the criminal liability arising out of the incident of the suicide having been committed by Ms. Padmaja, we are given to understand that prosecution against the persons accused in the crime has already been initiated and, therefore, we do not consider it desirable to intervene at this stage in that proceeding.

32. HIGH COURT OF KARNATAKA

***M. Rajesh* v. *State of Karnataka*,**
AIR 1998 Kant 165

V.P. Mohan Kumar, J.

Facts: The petitioners herein are students of M.B, Patil Medical College, Bijapur. A complaint was lodged on 21-1-1997 in the A.P.M.C. Police Station, Bijapur, alleging that an incident of ragging took place on 18-12-1996 in the said college. Accordingly, it is alleged that an FIR was lodged alleging that 4 persons were involved in the ragging incident, namely, (1) Prashant Desai, (2) Mayank Kumar, (3) Shakil Ahmed, and (4) Abdul Aziz. These 4 students and 11 others were suspended from the college. Thereafter proceedings were initiated to rusticate the students involved in the ragging incident from the college. It is alleged that a notice was served on the petitioners on 17-3-1997 calling upon them to appear before the Principal on 26-3-1997. Thereafter rustication order was passed on 27-3-1997 after hearing the petitioners; sixteen students are rusticated. The said order is impugned in these proceedings.

Judgment: It is clear from section 62(1) of the Karnataka State Universities Act, 1976 that the final authority responsible for maintenance of discipline among the students is the Vice-Chancellor and his directions in that behalf shall be given effect to by the heads of colleges/hostels and other institutions. In other words, his will be the final order in the matter of maintaining discipline among students of the University. Derivatively any order passed by any other authority responsible for maintaining discipline in any of the institutions referred to in the section is amenable to his supervisory jurisdiction.

In the light of the circumstances stated above, it is only proper to direct the petitioners to move the Vice-Chancellor to re-examine the impugned order in exercise of the power conferred on him under section 62(1) of the Karnataka State Universities Act, 1976. In such circumstances, it is not proper for this Court to examine the propriety or correctness of the said order at this stage. All contentions urged by the petitioners in the writ petitions can be examined by the Vice-Chancellor if revision is filed by the respective aggrieved students against the order of rustication issued against them.

In the light of the said circumstance, I direct the petitioners in all the writ petitions to approach the Vice-Chancellor by filing an appeal/revision under section 62(1) of the Act, challenging the rustication order and seek appropriate orders. The Vice-Chancellor may dispose of the same after hearing the affected persons if deemed fit and proper.

Ratio: Court cannot in its writ jurisdiction re-appreciate the evidence tendered by the students.

33. HIGH COURT OF MADRAS

A. Kumaran v. *The Government of Tamil Nadu rep. by its Secretary, Education Department, The Registrar, Tamil Nadu Dr. M.G.R. Medical University and The Principal, J.K.K. Muniraj Medical Research Foundation College of Physiotherapy,* MANU/TN/1619/1998

S.S. Subramani, J.

Facts: Petitioner joined Bachelor of Physiotherapy Degree Course at the 3rd Respondent-College on 15-10-1997 in the category of payment seat and he paid the necessary fees of Rs. 65,200 at the time of admission. According to the Petitioner, in the third Respondent-College, right from the time of admission, there was heavy ragging by Senior students and the behaviour of the students was also not upto the standard. The Senior students often used to rag the Petitioner and his friends. According to Petitioner, though he brought this to the notice of the Principal, he was asked to bear the same for some more days and that action will be initiated against the Senior students. Even in the Hostel of third Respondent-College, he was ragged by senior students. According to the Petitioner, on 22-3-1998 his seniors, namely, (1) Balamurugan, (2) Krishna Kumar, (3) Ashok Kumar, (4) Ashok Venkatesh and (5) Rajendran along with two other henchmen, who were not students of third Respondent-College, ragged the Petitioner, and made him naked and asked him to go around the Hostel in night hours, which resulted in great shame and mental agony to the Petitioner. He was forced to do all sorts of obscene and vulgar movements. He was even subjected to do unnatural sexual deeds and his seniors attempted to have homosexual relationship with him. With the help of his other friends and Warden, he prevented his Senior students from indulging in such ragging. According to the Petitioner, immediately on the next day he made a complaint to the third Respondent. Third Respondent called the five students and warned them. They were also asked to pay a fine of Rs. 5,000. Petitioner has further stated in the affidavit that when he was doing his Second Year, on 15-7-1998, the said five persons came to his hostel and tortured him by adopting all sorts of indecent behaviours and took him to the terrace and threw him from the terrace. Due to this, he sustained severe stomach pain and also injuries all over his body. Immediately, his friends took him to the nearby Bhavani Karthik Hospital and admitted him. The said incident was also published in 'Dinamani' of Salem Edition. Thereafter, his friends contacted his father and narrated the said incident, and thereupon, his father contacted the third Respondent and made a complaint. But the third Respondent failed to initiate any action against the said five senior students and prevented his father from lodging police complaint against them. According to Petitioner, after the incident, his father took him to his native place at Kancheepuram and gave him medical treatment after obtaining two months medical leave from third Respondent. On 20-7-1998, Petitioner's father sent a representation to the second Respondent and first Respondent, narrating the said incident and also reported that there was every possibility of danger to Petitioner's life in the College campus. He, therefore; requested the third Respondent to transfer the Petitioner to any one of the self-financing colleges in and around Madras and Kancheepuram, or in particular College of Physiotherapy, Savitha Dental College at Poonamallee. On receipt of the said letter, first Respondent forwarded the same to the second Respondent. On 11-8-1998, second Respondent sent a letter to Petitioner stating that they can transfer him provided the Petitioner furnished (1) No Objection Certificate from the third Respondent-College, (2) No Objection Certificate from any other College which can accommodate him, (3) Demand Draft for Rs. 500 and (4) Original Mark sheet of the First Year Degree Course. Immediately, Petitioner approached the third Respondent and sought for no objection certificate, but the third Respondent told him that such incidents will not happen in future. According to Petitioner, he has no belief in the words of third Respondent, since she failed to take any action in spite of the Petitioner's three complaints on three occasions earlier and also about the incident on 15-7-1998 which made him hospitalised for two months. Petitioner has stated that having no other alternative remedy, he has filed this writ petition for the aforementioned relief.

Judgment: From the records available before this Court, it could be seen that the third Respondent has made earnest attempt to find out the truth and it is after taking evidence, the Principal of the third Respondent-College has come to the conclusion that the allegations made by the Petitioner are not true, and under the guise of falsely alleging that there was some ragging in which he was alleged injured, the Petitioner is trying to get a transfer from the College.

Ragging is considered to be the most uncivilised thing, and nobody will support if in fact such incident had taken place in any Institution. Severe action also will have to be taken in such cases. Public opinion is badly against ragging and the Government has also taken necessary action to prevent such instances. But that public opinion should not be used by the Petitioner for achieving a selfish end by making false allegations, and thereby tarnishing the image of a meritorious Institution. In my opinion, it is worse than ragging.

I do not find any merit in the writ petition and consequently the same is dismissed, with costs.

Ratio: "Court shall not allow anybody to tarnish image of meritorious Institution, by making false allegation to meet selfish end."

---

34. HIGH COURT OF MADRAS

S. Suhasini* v. *The Director of Legal Education, The Principal, Central Law College and The Registrar, University of Madras,
MANU/TN/1666/1998

S.S. Subramani, J.

Facts: Petitioner is a Law Student doing B.L. Course in the second Respondent College in Evening Course. According to Petitioner, she was short of attendance and hence she paid condonation fee for the shortage in attendance and did abide by the other Regulations of College and University. Petitioner also Produced

Medical Certificate as required by authorities but the same was not forwarded by second Respondent. Examination was fixed on 5-5-1998 and till 3-5-1998, Petitioner could not get her hall ticket. On 4-5-1998, third Respondent directed second Respondent to permit Petitioner to sit for examination. The results of the examinations are yet to be published.

Petitioner again approached second Respondent and wanted to attend third year course. But second Respondent did not permit her and hence Petitioner again approached third Respondent and by letter dated 10-8-1998 third Respondent gave directions to second Respondent to permit the Petitioner to Join College for third year course and attend classes, and the question of loss of attendance is to be dealt with separately. Subsequent to this direction also second Respondent did not permit Petitioner to join College is the grievance of the Petitioner.

In the letter written by University addressed to the College, a reference is made to ragging of Petitioner by one Paul Jayaseelan, who is also a student of same College. Paul Jayaseelan was asked to explain his conduct and he denied the same and at the same time he also enclosed a copy of letter from the very same Petitioner where she has disapproved the ragging story, in her letter dated 17-5-1998 to the Registrar. In that letter Petitioner had stated that the story of ragging by Paul Jayaseelan as alleged by her cousin is not true and she absented herself only because of illness.

When Petitioner herself admitted that reason submitted by her cousin was false, University was wrong in permitting such candidate to write examinations and therefore University had committed illegality and flouted its own Regulations, no directions should be given to Second Respondent College to permit Petitioner to continue course for third year.

The direction issued by University dated 10-8-1998 is *per se* illegal and it is declared that the second Respondent is not bound to obey the same. Likewise, second Respondent is also not bound to publish the results of the second year Examinations of Petitioner since she has not fulfilled her second year attendance requirement. In fact, the order dated 4-5-1998 permitting Petitioner to attend Examination is itself subject to the fulfilment of attendance requirement. Once it is admitted that she has not attended the College as required, she will not be entitled to have the results also declared.

In the result, the Writ Petition is dismissed.

---

35. HIGH COURT OF MADRAS

A. Suresh Babu* alias *Suresh* v. *State By Inspector of Police,
1998 Cr LJ 3411

M. Karpagavinayagam, J.

Facts: This case relates to the sorry state of affairs, in which one Arivudai Nambi, a First year B.Sc. (Chemistry) student studying in A.M. Jain College Meenambakkam, is subjected to the suffering at the hands of two students studying in the same College on the pretext of ragging and one among those two is the petitioner.

Arivudai Nambi was sleeping in his room in the Hostel. At that time, the petitioner Suresh, staying in room No. 121 of the same Hostel, entered into his room in a drunken mood carrying a liquor bottle in his hand. Arivudai Nambi woke up from his bed and went to room No. 85 and took rest there along with his friends.

Half-an-hour later, the petitioner came to that room and compelled Arivudai Nambi to come to his room. When he went to his room, the petitioner slapped on his cheek repeatedly. He also abused the first informant by stating and again beat and so saying he kicked on his stomach. He further exclaimed by saying and he pushed him on the ground. Another student by name Vinod Khanna joined him and he also repeatedly beat him. Then both of them removed the lungi and baniyan of the first informant and he was made to stand with only underwear on a chair. Then, they asked him whether he had got "sex feelings"? He sobbed and said "No". Thereafter, both of them slapped him.

After this horrible experience, the first informant immediately left the Hostel and reached his native place and informed this to his father.

Immediately, the father of the first informant sent a telegram to the Principal requesting action. The father of the first informant, Kuppusamy, who is the Vice President to Thamizhaga Aasiriyar Koottani sent letters to Chief Minister and higher authorities. Thereafter, this complaint was preferred by the first informant, which was registered against the petitioner and Vinod Khanna.

Judgment: The present education develops the intellect and skill but does little to develop good qualities. Of what avail is all the knowledge in the world, if one has not got good character? It is like water going down the drain. Education should help to make the students the embodiments of human values such as Truth, Love, Right Conduct, Peace and Non-violence. Academic knowledge alone is of no value. There is no point in blaming the students alone. If parents and teachers set the right example, the students will automatically blossom into models of excellence. Mahatma Gandhi said : "Knowledge without character is a powerful evil". Today's education is knocking off the "s" from "skill", with the result that the knowledge is "killed" with disastrous results for mankind. The students should be given the combination of knowledge, skill and character. So, the teachers and parents should take a pivotal role in the cultivation of human values in the minds of younger generation, which alone is education. If the education does not teach the students to love all and serve all, the education would become meaningless.

It is quite shocking to see that this sort of inhuman incident is being taken place inside the Hostel by the students in which the comforts have been provided to them for the purpose of study. But the above incident would indicate that some of the students have used the Hostel facilities for committing various offences. If this sort of incident is taken place in the College Hostel, the parents would be very much reluctant to send their children for study for the reason that some children may become criminals and others may become victims. If these things to be corrected, the introduction of the penal statutes alone is not sufficient. But, the younger generation must be made to feel that what they are doing is quite wrong. In order to create these feelings, the Teachers, Hostel Wardens and parents have to play an important role and the students must be inculcated of the human values. If we do not make any effort in teaching human values for the students, then this Nation, which has got a spiritual tradition will have no future.

In view of the serious allegations made against the petitioner, especially when the petitioner is stated to be highly influential being a son of a former M.L.A., I am not inclined to grant anticipatory bail, which could be granted in deserving cases. In my opinion, the petitioner does not deserve this special privilege. Therefore, the petitioner could surrender before the Police and seek for regular bail after some progress is made in the investigation. The petition is dismissed.

---

36. HIGH COURT OF MADRAS

***The Principal, Noorul Islam College of Engineering* v. *The Mononmaniam Sundaranar University*,**
1996 (1) CTC 393

K.A. Swami, C.J. and Kanakaraj, J.

Facts: In the writ petition, the order dated 13th October, 1995 passed by the Principal, Noorul Islam College of Engineering was challenged.

The Principal of the College passed the following order:-

"Mr. J. Jagan, 93 ECE, is expelled from the College for the rest of the academic year 1995-96 with effect from 18.9.1995 as he was proved to be the main culprit in ragging first year students on 13.9.1995."

The contention of the learned counsel appearing for the College is that the aforesaid order did not attract the provisions contained in Regulation 9(c) of Chapter 17 of the statutes of the University, in as much as in effect, there was no expulsion, but it was only debarring of the student from attending the rest of the academic year 1995-1996 with effect from 18th September, 1995.

Judgment: We may also point out here that Regulation 9(c) of Chapter 17 of the statutes is intended to serve a great purpose, *viz.*, to ensure that the Principal of the College or the Authorities of the College affiliated to the University does not or do not act arbitrarily and take vindictive actions against a student and no student is put in any undue hardship or injustice. The University having been vested with the authority of controlling the functioning of the College, is entitled to have such a control over the affiliated College as otherwise, the possibility of the students being harshly dealt with by the College and its Authorities cannot be controlled.

Hence, we see no reason to admit title appeal.

---

37. HIGH COURT OF CALCUTTA

Pratul Kumar Sinha v. *State of West Bengal*, (1995) 1 Cal LT 223 (HC)

Mukul Gopal Mukherji and Gitesh Ranjan Bhattacharjee, JJ.

Facts: This public interest litigation was initiated by Sri Pratul Kumar Sinha, an Advocate and a social activist before the Supreme Court by way of writ application under article 32 of the Constitution of India. He referred, to the age old practice of ragging prevalent in Engineering, Medical Colleges and also in some other Colleges in India where the fresher 1st year students had to face ragging by the senior students in the shape of mental and physical cruelty and acts of violence. He submitted that usually the period of ragging continued in between 1 and 3 months from the very beginning of the session of the new entrant in the institution. Because of the phychological pressure and even physical violence many students have to give up their studies. He wanted that this evil system of ragging should be eradicated from the education system altogether. He was of the view that neither the Government nor the college authorities took adequate and proper or effective steps for combating the evil of ragging.

He prayed *inter alia* that the directions be issued so that (i) a Commissioner may be appointed to enquire over the matter and (ii) adequate necessary police arrangements be made during the time of ragging in such institutional campus and (iii) that a direction be issued for creating congenial atmosphere so that the fresher students may be alleged of the apprehension of facing ragging in the college hostel, (iv) He further advocated the framing of a scheme for eradication of the evil of ragging, (v) He further urged upon the Hon'ble Court to issue directions so that the actual culprits, despite their being students, be ousted from the college and be not admitted over again and (vi) suitable such other or further direction or directions be issued as may be deemed fit and proper.

Judgment: The Supreme Court sent the case to this Hon'ble Court with a direction to hear out the matter as a public interest litigation deleting the Principal of Ramjas College, New Delhi from the category of respondents. The writ application was registered as an application under article 226 of the Constitution of India before this Hon'ble Court and allotted to this Division Bench.

Taking into account the recommendations of various authorities, HC made the following remarks:

(1) The State Government may appoint a high level Commission or an Anti-Ragging Committee comprising of academicians, civil servant-cum-administrators including high ranking police officers, sociologists and psychologists to frame a uniform policy to meet the problem of eradication of ragging in the various institutional campuses including medical and engineering colleges.

(2) It is on the basis of the report of the Commission or the Anti-Ragging Committee that the Government may think of introducing a proper legislation in the field.

(3) All educational institutions who have already taken out a programme for eradication of ragging may continue the same in the future.

(4) We would be content in present state of affairs to direct the Education Department (Technical Branch) of the State of West Bengal to appoint an Anti-Ragging Committee or a Commission to find out the ways and means for eradicating the problem and may only humbly request the Legislature to take into consideration, our suggestions to introduce "ragging" as a criminal offence and to provide punishment therefore by way of a suitable amendment in the penal statute and nothing beyond, treating the same as a cognizable offence, if deemed fit and proper, irrespective of its magnitude.

(5) We would direct All India Radio (Akashvani) and the Doordarshan Authorities to continue their programmes on the problem of eradication of ragging every year at the time of admission of the freshers in the Engineering and Medical Colleges preferably in the months of July to October.

(6) We may direct a copy of our Judgment to be sent to the Speaker of the West Bengal Assembly, the Leader of the Opposition and the Chief Whip as well as the Hon'ble Chief Minister of West Bengal and the Minister for Higher Education and a copy to the Union Ministers for Human Resources and for Education for giving the matter a considerable thought for a proposed all India legislation.

---

38. HIGH COURT OF GAUHATI

***Bhabendra Kumar Kalita* v. *Union of India*,**
AIR 1995 Gau 121

D.N. Baruah, J.

Facts: The petitioner's son Dhruba Jyoti Kalita who is aged about 14 was admitted in Class-VI of Sainik School, Goalpara of which the respondent No. 2 is the Principal. The school is a member of the Indian Public Schools'. Conference and affiliated to the All India Central Board of Secondary Education, New Delhi. The school is directly functioning under the Ministry of Defence, Government of India. It is a residential school. Dhrubajyoti Kalita was promoted to Class-VIII in the year 1994. He was thereafter shifted to a hostel known as Lachit House meant for the senior students from Class-VIII to Class-XII. Class-VIII students are the junior-most in the said hostel. According to the petitioner in the first part of December, 1994 Dhrubajyoti Kalita had his 2nd phase test (of class-VIII). It has been averred by the petitioner that on the night of 8-12-94 his son was subjected to severe ragging by the senior students of the said hostel, which made impossible for his son to prepare for his examination scheduled for the next day. The 3rd respondent was in-charge of the said hostel.

3. On 9-12-94 the petitioner's son some how could appear in his paper. However, being subjected to severe ragging compelled him to leave the school on

9-12-94 and came to his parents. On 24-12-94 the petitioner received letter from the 2nd respondent whereby he was informed that his son has withdrawn from the school on gross disciplinary grounds as he left the school on 9-12-94 without permission of the school authority leaving an objectionable note. According to the petitioner this action was taken by the 2nd respondent on his own without giving any opportunity to his son or to the petitioner to explain the position. On receiving the order the petitioner submitted a representation to the 2nd respondent, that is, the Principal of the school on the day, *i.e.*, 23-12-94. However, nothing was heard from the 2nd respondent. Situated thus, the petitioner submitted yet another representation dated 30-12-94. In his representation he informed the 2nd respondent that he was busy with the medical treatment of his son who sustained injuries on his nose and ears when he arrived home on 11-12-94. He also explained the situation and requested the 2nd respondent by letter dated 5-1-95 replied to the representation submitted by the petitioner. However, in the said letter the petitioner's first representation dated 23-12-94 was referred to. In the said representation the 2nd respondent informed that the petitioner's son left the school in the past many times without permission. This time he "flouted all norms and (Code) of conduct of school by adopting unfair means and left the school leaving behind a note". On receipt of letter the petitioner submitted yet another representation dated 28-1-95 reiterating his earlier prayer. However, nothing was done. Hence the present petition.

Issue: Whether or not the impugned order is arbitrary and violative of the principles of natural justice?

Judgment: In the present case petitioner's son a minor student left the school and he was caught on the next day by the House Master of the School and some others and he was asked to write a statement and he wrote it. In such circumstances there is every possibility of threat or some pressure. At least he was under severe mental pressure. Therefore, a charge ought to have been framed against him and the authority ought to have given notice calling for explanation. The boy ought to have been given some time to get over from the fear psychosis he might have been having under the fact and circumstances.

Hence, in my opinion, the impugned order is arbitrary and violative of the principles of natural justice.

Ratio: Principles of natural justice have to be complied with in case of expulsion order by the principal of school.

---

39. HIGH COURT OF DELHI

***Ashish Bhateja* v. *Indian Institute of Technology*,**
1993 III AD (Del) 689

D.P. Wadhwa and Vijender Jain, JJ.

Facts: The incident alleged against the petitioner happened on 16 August, 1993 at early hours at 1.00 A.M. at the Karakoram Hostel in the campus. He was informed of the charge against him on 18 August, 1993 by the Dean of

Students. It was mentioned therein that the incident took place in the early morning of 16th August, 1993 at about 1.00 a.m. and continued for a period of over one hour." The petitioner was told that he had appeared before the Hostel Honours Committee and he was informed about his involvement in the incident. The Hostel Honours Committee provided him an opportunity to make a written statement regarding his involvement in the incident which the petitioner did. The petitioner was further told that on the recommendation of the Hostel Honours Committee the case was then to be examined by the Institute Disciplinary Committee of the Institute on 19 August, 1993 at 2.30 P.M. By this letter of 18 August, 1993 of the Dean, the petitioner was informed his direct involvement in the incident and was given opportunity to make his submissions, if any in addition to his written submission already submitted by him to the House Honours Committee. He was told to give the written submissions latest by 10.00 A.M. on 19 August, 1993. The petitioner did represent. He denied his involvement and said that he had come from his residence at 10.30 P.M. on 16 August, 1993. He said around 1.30 A.M. there was a lot of noise in the corridor outside his room due to very loud music being played. He said he was disturbed in his sleep. He opened the door of his room and retired back to sleep when the deafening music was switched off after 10-15 minutes. That is all what the petitioner said about the incident and then he said about his excellent academic career in the Institute.

The petitioner said that proper opportunity was not granted to the petitioner and that the petitioner should have been allowed to cross-examine the students naming him. We do not think right of cross-examination is a part of rule of natural justice in every case.

Judgment: It is a matter of common knowledge that menace of ragging is assuming alarming proportion and it has to be curbed with a heavy hand. The incident alleged in the present case required an immediate action, and this is what the authorities have done. Ms. Anand appearing for the petitioner said that proper opportunity was not granted to the petitioner and that the petitioner should have been allowed to cross-examine the students naming him. We do not think right of cross-examination is a part of rule of natural justice in every case.

---

40. HIGH COURT OF MADRAS

S. Bright Singh* v. *Bharathiar University, Coimbatore by its Registrar, Karunya Institute of Technology, Coimbatore, by its Principal and Director of Technical Education,

MANU/TN/0891/1994

K.A. Swami, C.J. and Somasundaram, J.

Facts: The Appellant joined the Second Respondent college in the B.E. Degree course in August, 1991. The second Respondent college is affiliated to the first Respondent - University. According to the Appellant, he joined the second Respondent college on payment of Rs. 60,000 as capitation fee and he underwent the first year B.E. Degree course during 1991-92 and passed all the subjects in the first year examination held in April, 1992. On 8-9-1992 when the Appellant was in the second year of the course, was served with a memo/ order of the Principal of the second Respondent college dismissing him from the college.

Aggrieved by the said order dated 8-9-1992, the Appellant filed W.P. No. 19131 of 1992 praying for the issue of a Writ of *certiorarified mandamus* to quash the order passed by the second Respondent, dated 8-9-1992 dismissing the Appellant from the college and expelling him from the hostel of the second Respondent and to direct the Respondents to reinstate the Appellant in the college and hostel of the second Respondent and to permit him to appear for the examination and to complete the B.E. Degree course. The Appellant challenged the order dated 8-9-1992 on the ground that no charge memo was served on him with regard to the allegations made against him and that no enquiry whatever was conducted before the order challenged in the Writ Petition was passed and that the order dated 8-9-1992 is invalid and liable to be quashed as it is violative of the principles of natural justice. The Learned Single Judge who heard the Writ Petition took the view that the minutes recorded by the Committee of enquiry sufficiently indicate that a fair enquiry that is possible with reference to the nature of the charges and the peculiar circumstances of the case has been conducted and that there is no violation of the principles of natural justice.

Judgment: Admittedly, in the present case, no charge was framed against the Appellant, not to speak of handing over the same to the Appellant and that no opportunity was given to the Appellant to state whatever he had to say in writing. The Appellant was not put on notice about the acts of misconduct alleged against him and he was not given an opportunity to state his case. Another significant fact which cannot be lost sight of in the present case is that the impugned order does not even refer to the enquiry conducted by the enquiry committee appointed by the second Respondent on 7-9-1992 and the finding of the enquiry committee. Also, the enquiry committee first recorded the statements of three affected students who were subjected to ragging and harassment that thereafter the Appellant was sent for by the enquiry committee and he was identified by the three affected students and that when the Appellant was asked to give a statement by the enquiry committee admitting the guilt, he refused to give any statement before the enquiry committee. As already pointed out that in the present case, on the basis of the statements recorded from the three affected students the Appellant was not served with any charge memo and he was not asked to state his case by submitting his explanation. We are of the view that the minimum and basic requirements of the principles of natural justice (a) notice of the case not be met and (b) reasonable opportunity to explain was not given. Hence, we are inclined to hold that both the basic requirements of the principles of natural justice referred above, are not fulfilled by the second Respondent before passing the order dated 8-9-1992, because the second Respondent admittedly failed to secure reasonable opportunity to the Appellant and serving a charge memo on the Appellant and asking him to state his case with regard to the allegations levelled against him. Therefore, it has to be held that the enquiry in the present case and the punishment of expulsion imposed on the Appellant by the order dated 8-9-1992 is clearly vitiated by violation of the principles of natural justice.

The Writ Appeal is allowed and the order under appeal is set aside.

Ratio: When no charge was framed, notice about acts of misconduct is not put, and no opportunity to state the case is given proceedings, enquiry in such case and punishment of expulsion imposed on person is said to be clearly vitiated by violation of principles of natural justice.

---

41. HIGH COURT OF ORISSA

Srinibas Kar* v. *Orissa University of Agriculture and Technology represented by the Registrar of the University,
58 (1984) CLT 272

B.K. Behera and R.C. Patnaik, JJ.

Facts: This is an application by the Petitioners under article 226 of the Constitution of India for the quashing of the decision of the Orissa University of Agriculture and Technology expelling them for a period of two years for their alleged misconduct.

The Petitioners are students of third Semester of B.V. Sc. and A.H. course under opposite party No. 1. They were alleged to have indulged in ragging on Kishori Mohan Biswal, a student of first year class.

Issue: Whether or not the punishment has been awarded following the principles of natural justice?

Judgment: The principles governing disciplinary action against students are by now well settled. While it is no doubt true that the authorities have to maintain discipline in the institution, it is at the same time fundamental that before punishment is inflicted on a student, he should be given adequate opportunity to defend himself. The principles of natural justice mandate that a student against whom disciplinary proceeding has been started should be afforded an opportunity of being heard. In short, the proceeding should be just and fair. We find some offending features in the proceeding. We are of the opinion that howsoever reprehensible the conduct of the Petitioners might be, they were not afforded adequate opportunity in the proceeding; the proceeding has not been just and fair.

Despite our quashing as aforesaid, it is open to the authorities to take such measure or start fresh proceedings against the Petitioners as they may be advised. In case it is decided to start fresh proceedings, the same should be completed within two months from today after complying with the principles of natural justice.

The writ application is accordingly, allowed.

---

42. HIGH COURT OF KERALA

R.C. Thampan* v. *Principal, Medical College, Calicut,
AIR 1979 Ker 171

V.P. Gopalan Nambiyar, C.J. and M.P. Menon, J.

Facts: These writ petitions are directed against the disciplinary action taken by the Managing Committee of the Medical College, Calicut, against the writ petitioners, students of the College, resulting in their suspension from the College for varying terms. The reason for the action was the "ragging" indulged in by the petitioners who may be broadly referred to as the senior students of the College, against the "freshers" or the junior students. "Ragging" has passed so much into popular parlance that we feel that any elucidation of the term would be unnecessary.

Issue: The action has been impugned on the ground that the Principal of the College (or, we believe, for that matter, the Managing Committee) had no jurisdiction to take disciplinary action against the petitioners.

Judgment: The inherent right and the quasi-parental authority of a teacher to proceed by way of disciplinary action against a pupil under his charge has been well-recognised over the years; and it is ingrained in the habits of thought and philosophy of our country. Moreover, the College Calendar commences by stating that the College is administered directly by the Government through the Principal who is responsible to the Government for everything connected with the College and that the administration and internal management of the College is vested with the Principal. Rule 11 of the calendar again repeats that the Principal will be in-charge of the administration of the College; and rule 23 provides that "students of the College conducting themselves in any activity in such a way as to interfere with the corporate life and educational work of the College will be liable to be suspended or expelled from the College by the Principal...." In the face of these, there is little force or merit in the plea, strongly urged, that the Principal had no disciplinary powers over the students.

---

43. HIGH COURT OF KERALA

Principal, Government Engineering College, Trichur* v. *John K. Kurien,
AIR 1979 Ker 150

V.P. Gopalan Nambiyar, C.J. and G. Balagangadharan Nair, J.

Facts: The appeal is against the judgment of a learned Judge of this Court to quash the order of suspension from the College passed against the two writ petitioners and the order of expulsion from the hostel passed against them, in view of their involvement in the ragging incidents at the Government Engineering College, Trichur during the year 1975.

The ragging incidents complained of were on the 5th and 6th Nov. 1975. A preliminary enquiry was made by the Warden of the hostel who was a Professor to the College. Charge was framed and served on the students concerned and their statements in answer to the charge framed were also taken. An enquiry was conducted by two Professors of the College, one of them being the warden himself. Victims of ragging were examined in the presence of the writ petitioners and were cross examined by them. At the end of the enquiry a report was submitted which was considered by the College Council and by Ext. R. 2 proceedings the College Council accepted the enquiry report and passed the proceedings leading to the suspension of the petitioners till the next semester in June, 1976, and to their expulsion from the College hostel.

Judgment: We are unable to sustain the reasoning or the judgment of the learned Judge. We think that in the circumstances and against the background of the facts which we have detailed the College Council's reference to the Commission's Report and "other evidence" can only have reference to the Enquiry Report and to the evidence collected at the enquiry. We do not think it is reasonable to understand that the College Council referred to and acted upon certain undisclosed and secret evidence. There is no foundation in the pleadings for coming to such a conclusion. The files were made available to us by the learned Government Pleader.

An order of interim stay of suspension of the judgment of the learned judge for three weeks was passed on 9-3-1976. But the stay ordered on 9-3-1976 and continued by this order will not preclude the respondents from moving the Calicut University for permission to sit for the examination fixed to commence on the 8th April, 1976. This was on 29-3-1976. We felt difficulty to understand as to how the writ petitioners against whom the order of suspension and expulsion became effective by reason of the stay order of this Court, could write the examination.

We allow this appeal, set aside the judgment of the learned Judge.

---

44. HIGH COURT OF CALCUTTA

***Ashoke Kumar Sharma* v. *The State of Calcutta*,**
(1973) ILR 1 Cal 13

R.N. Dutt, J.

Facts: The prosecution case is in short as follows:

One Subrata Bose was admitted in the Marine Engineering Training Course in August, 1967. On August 9, 1967, at about 8.30 a.m. he reported himself at the College. Some others candidates admitted to the training course also reported themselves at that time. Subrata was allotted to the Calcutta Port Commissioners' workshop for practical training along with several other such fresh cadets. Subrata and some twenty others went to the Port Commissioners' workshop gate at about 9 a.m. where they were received by one senior cadet Pradip Knmar Biswas, Appellant No. 4, who took them inside the workshop and then inside a room marked 'D.M.E.T.' where he found some 12 senior cadets. The other Appellants and Sujit Bagchi, Sanjoy Chatterjee and Anil Vohra were amongst them. The senior cadets greeted the fresher saying that they were welcome, but this welcome would not make them laugh; this welcome would make them cry. Thereafter, the senior cadets divided the fresher into several groups and the Appellant Ashoke Sharma took Subrata and some other fresher to a corner of the room and ordered them to make fifty sit ups, that is, sitting on the toes and standing up. This done, they were asked to box each other's ears and to move like a piston engine. Then Sanjoy Chatterjee caught hold of Subrata, made him sit on his toes with arms stretched holding a brick on both hands. Sanjoy then put his legs on the brickbat and asked Subrata to sing a song. Sujit Bagchi slapped him and directed him to make vulgar gesture and recite obscene songs. Anil Vohra too asked Subrata vulgar questions and directed him to recite obscene songs. Subrata protested when Anil Vohra, Sujit Bagchi and Sanjoy Chatterjee and the Appellant No. 2 Ranganathan assaulted him with fists and blows. Ranganathan made him lie on a table in a bow-like fashion and put the burning side of a lighted cigarette into his mouth. Subrata was then taken to an adjacent room and Sujit Bagchi and Sanjoy Chatterjee asked him to put off his trousers, but on his refusal he was kicked and slapped by the Appellants Ahsoke Sharma, Ranganathan, Nayer and Anil Vohra. Thereafter, they laid him flat on the floor when Sanjoy poured inside his mouth some white sticky liquid. Sujit Bagchi pressed his mouth and the Appellant Pradip Biswas squeezed a few drops of liquid into his mouth which smelt like urine from a soaked handkerchief. This continued till about 12 noon and, thereafter, the fresher were directed to respect the seniors and not to disobey them. Subsequently, they were taken around the workshop and that was followed by lunch-break at 1 p.m. when the fresher returned to the hostel, Subrata felt very bad and on some pretext he took leave and returned to his house and went straight to his room and vomited lying on the carpet in the floor. The parents came there, a doctor was called; some friends and relatives also came. Subrata told them what had happened in the workshop. Subrata's father Jyotish Bose made a complaint before the Police on August 23, 1967.

Judgment: The facts are all proved. But then, I have my doubts about the conviction under section 355/34 of the Indian Penal Code. For a conviction under section 355 of the Indian Penal Code it must be proved that the accused had intended to dishonour the person hurt. Here true, what was done was dishonorable. But then, the intention of the senior cadets was just to show their supremacy so that the fresher obey them unquestionably in future. It is doubtful whether they had the intention to dishonour the fresher and, in that view of the matter, I think the conviction under section 355/34 of the Indian Penal Code should be set aside. But, there is no reason to interfere with the conviction under section 323/34 of the Indian Penal Code. The sentence appears to me to be rather light in view of break in the boy's career and the public importance of the matter. But, when the appeal was admitted no Rule was issued for enhancement of the sentence.

In the result, the appeal is allowed in part. The conviction and sentence of the Appellants under section 355/34 of the Indian Penal Code are set aside and they are acquitted of that charge. But, their conviction under section 323/34 of the Indian Penal Code is upheld and each of them is sentenced to a fine of Rs. 200 (Rupees two hundred), in default, rigorous imprisonment for one month.

---

45. HIGH COURT OF JAMMU AND KASHMIR

***Surindra Pal Trikha* v. *Principal Govt. Medical College*, AIR 1965 J&K 23**

Janki Nath Bhat, J.

Facts: This writ petition has been presented by Surindra Pal Trikha, a student, of the Government Medical College Srinagar, against the Principal of the College and the University of Jammu and Kashmir on the following allegations:

That the Principal by his order No. 7391-92 dated 14th August, 1963 rusticated the Petitioner from the college for a period of one year on the ground that he had been engaged in activities of a subversive kind and had been using ragging measures and language which was unthinkable," That the Principal by his order No, 8187-97 MC dated 28-8-63 expelled him from the College for all time from the date of the aforesaid order due to his taking a second year student Kumari Simianlata Samyal in the Mens' Hostel at Bemina through a window of one of the rooms. The University had confirmed these orders of the Principal on 23-11-63. That both the orders were passed by the Principal without holding an inquiry in his presence, nor was any notice or opportunity of showing cause against the orders made against the Petitioner given to him, and the Petitioner was condemned unheard. The principles of natural justice had been violated; the effect of the orders was to place a permanent stigma on the life of the Petitioner and to blast the whole of his career.

The Petitioner's father 'was asked through a messenger to bring the Petitioner on the day of the inquiry in his office, but the Petitioner deliberately stayed away and did not come to his office along with his father. This is what is termed by the learned Advocate General as notice to the Petitioner. It is interesting to note that information was not sent to the Petitioner but to his father. Further, the information was sent through a messenger. Who that messenger was is not at all disclosed. Whether that messenger actually conveyed the information to the Petitioner's father is also not at all mentioned in the affidavit or the objections. All this is suggested to have happened verbally. There is no allegation that any such communication was addressed to the Petitioner's father in writing. Nor is it disclosed what kind of information was sent on to the Petitioner's father.

Judgment: In the instant case, the presence of the father of the Petitioner during the inquiry would be neither here nor there, as it is nobody's case that he was acting on behalf of or as an attorney for the Petitioner. Nor is this fact at all material that; the inquiry was conducted in the presence of some respectable doctors and others. What was necessary in the eye of law was that the inquiry should have been held in the presence of Petitioner. Other people's presence, however important they might be, would not affect the legal aspect of the case.

The Petitioner, therefore, in my opinion had no legal notice of any proceedings taken against him for his alleged misbehavior.

In this case, in view of what has been stated above, the order of the principal expelling the Petitioner from the College for all time to come dated 28th August, 1963 as confirmed by the University is set aside.

Ratio: In disciplinary proceedings head of institution does not act as a judicial or a *quasi*-judicial tribunal and has no right to examine witnesses.

ANNEXURES

Annexure 1
Committee Reports

(a) Report of Committee to Curb the Menace of Ragging in Universities/Educational Institutions – 1999 (Prof. K.P.S. UNNI Committee Report)

Table of Contents

Report of Committee Constituted by the University Grants Commission to Frame Guidelines to Curb the Menace of Ragging in Universities/ Educational Institutions

1. Constitution of the Committee

The University Grants Commission was made one of the respondents in a Public Interest Litigation case filed in the Supreme Court of India by the Vishwa Jagriti Mission highlighting the adverse impact of ragging of freshers in educational institutions all over the country. During the hearing of the case held on 16th July 1999, the learned Judges had indicated that it would be appropriate if the UGC takes a more pro-active view in the matter and frame guidelines with regard to combating the menace of ragging in the universities and other educational institutions. Accordingly, the UGC constituted the following Committee to frame the guidelines in the matter:

1. Prof KP.S. Unni, (Former Registrar, JNU), Dean, School of Language, Literature & Culture Studies, Jawahar Lal Nehru University, New Delhi-110067 **-Chairman**
2. Dr. J.L. Gupta, Principal, Sri Ram College of Commerce, Delhi University, Delhi. **-Member**
3. Prof. R.P. Hooda, Deptt. of Business Studies, Kurukshetra University, Kurukshetra-136119. **-Member**

4. Dr. R.P. Gangurde, Additional Secretary, University Grants Commission, NewDelhi-110002. ,

-Member Secretary

Dr. (Mrs.) Pankaj Mittal, Deputy Secretary, UGC assisted the Committee in its deliberations. The Committee met on 13th September, 11th October and 29th October, 1999.

2. Introduction

The word 'ragging' means the acts of teasing, taunting, playing a practical joke upon someone or holding comic parades and other activities during certain period of a college term to raise money for charity.

Ragging has therefore, both positive and negative manifestations,

Ragging could be considered positive if it is done within decent limits and if:

- It aims at raising funds for charity,
- it helps ease the pen(~up tensions of modern students without harming anyone, it helps freshers to shake themselves out of inhibitions and inferiority complex
- and to smoothen their angularities,
- it helps dispelling the tendency among newcomers to remain isolated- it is fun which is enjoyable by all, including the freshers:'

But over the years the word 'ragging' ceased to denote the healthy practice it used to be and has acquired more negative connotations and notoriety. Nowadays 'ragging' may include;

Display of noisy, disorderly conduct, teasing, excitement by rough or rude treatment or handling, indulging in rowdy, indisciplined activities which cause or likely to cause annoyance, undue hardship, physical or psychological harm or raise apprehension or fear in a fresher, or asking the students to do any act or perform something which such a student will not do in the ordinary course and which causes him/her shame or embarrassment or danger to his/her life.

The Karnataka Education Act, 1983 (Karnataka Act No. 1 of 1995) Section 2(29) defines ragging as:

> "causing, inducing, compelling or forcing a student, whether by way of a practical joke or otherwise, to do any act which detracts from human dignity or violates his person or exposes him to ridicule or forbear from doing any lawful act, by intimidating, wrongfully restraining, wrongfully confining, or injuring him or by using criminal force to him or by holding out to him any threat of such intimidation, wrongful restraint, wrongful confinement, injury or the use of criminal force."

It is generally observed that such perverse forms of ragging is more prevalent in professional colleges and institutes mainly because of large number of students staying in hostels.

3. Forms of Ragging

Ragging is found to take the following forms (the list is only indicative and not exhaustive)

Crisp orders

- to address seniors as 'Sir',
- to perform mass drills,
- to copy class notes for the seniors;
- to serve various errands,

- to do menial jobs for the seniors;
- to ask/answer vulgar questions
- to look at pornographic pictures to 'shock the freshers out of their innocence';
- to force to drink alcohol, scalding tea, etc.,
- to force to do acts with sexual over tones, including homo sexual acts;
- to force to do acts which can lead to physical injury/mental torture or death, to strip, kiss, etc.;
- to do other obscenities.

It can be seen from the above that most of them, except the first few, constitute perverse forms of ragging.

4. Causes for Ragging

The main causes for indulging in ragging are:

- Eagerness of seniors to show off their power, authority, superiority, An attitude of backlash: a "do-unto-others what others did to you" (similar to mother-in-law *Vs* daughter-in-law syndrome);
- Importance the seniors get in the initial stages of admission by helping and guiding the freshers for various things in the absence of or ineffectiveness of institutional mechanism to help the freshers at that point, resulting in the freshers getting indebted to seniors and thereby feeling compelled to do their biddings.

5. Vulnerable Locations for Ragging

Ordinarily, places which are most vulnerable for ragging are:

Hostel blocks and messes

Vacant class rooms

Canteen

Stadium or play ground

Student activity centres

6. Causes for the Increase in the Incidence of Ragging and ineffectiveness of Measures Against it

Among the main causes, one can cite the following:

The powers and moral authority of the Wardens and other functionaries have eroded over the years, as many of them may not be committed to their work, but take up such responsibilities for the sake of perks attached to those offices;

Lack of interest and involvement in such matters among majority of faculty members;

Fear that the Head of the Departments and others may be pressurised later on for withdrawal of complaints or for revocation of the orders of punishment;

Fear that they and/or their family members may be harassed and victimised,

It must be admitted that most of these causes are the direct result of politicisation of educational institutions and the resultant erosion of standards of behaviour. If there is no political interference, the concerned authorities will be able to take effective measures to curb ragging.

7. Existing Governmental/Institutional Efforts in Curbing Ragging

The Committee came across a reference to a formal Government of India Notification banning ragging in the aftermath of the death of two freshers in a Regional Engineering

I College in the late 1970's. The Committee also studied the following documents on the subject to enable it to formulate certain guidelines:

Ordinance regarding prevention of ragging in Colleges and Hostels, University of Mysore, 1982,

The Karnataka Education Act, 1983 (Karnataka Act No. l of 1995), Section 116 Penalty for Ragging;

Order passed by the Hon'ble High Court of Himachal Pradesh in CWP No. 153/84 dated 30-V1984;

Report of the Committee constituted by the Director, IIT, Delhi, to examine and make recommendations on issues related to 'Ragging', 1993;

The Tamil Nadu Prohibition of Ragging Act, 1997;

The Kerala Prohibition of Ragging Ordinance, 1997 (Ordinance No. 16 of 1997),

Ordinance XV-C. Prohibition of and Punishment for Ragging. University of Delhi;

Booklet entitled; "Ragging Problems and Solutions", Pon Naavarasu Publications, 1998.

8. Recommendations

On the basis of detailed deliberations, the UGC Committee suggests a three-pronged system to curb the menace of ragging in educational institutions, namely:

PROHIBITION - PREVENTION - PUNISHMENT SYSTEM (PPS SYSTEM);

that is, prohibition by Law, prevention by following a set of guidelines and punishment in case ragging takes place in spite of prohibition and prevention. The Committee is of the view that punishment for the offenders should be balanced by some incentives for non-offenders and those who help check the menace of ragging. The details of the PPP System are given below.

8.1 Prohibition

1. The Central Government and the State Governments may be requested to enact a law (where-ever no such law exists) prohibiting ragging in the educational institutions, which, *inter-alia*, should also contain provisions; to treat ragging as a cognisable offence. Since ragging in its perverse forms have the effect of dehumanisation of the individual affecting his/her self-esteem, ragging should be treated more or less at par with rape and other atrocities against women, ill-treating persons belonging to reserved categories, etc. Fresh students, like other weaker sections of the society, need and deserve protection, to identify the perverse forms of ragging under the law (some of them a real ready mentioned under para 3 above), to prescribe suitable punishments keeping in mind the gravity of the offence committed, providing for a maximum punishment of rigorous imprisonment upto-three years, or a fine upto Rs. 25000, or both. The educational institutions may prescribe other punishments such as suspension from classes, from the hostel, rustication, etc. (A list of possible punishments is given below in para 8, 3); to ensure that the Films Censor Boards and other agencies do not allow films to be screened with scenes which make heroes out of youngsters who indulge in ragging.

2. Till such time as the Governments ban ragging by law as above, the universities and other educational institutions which have any Ordinance or Rule for banning ragging may make such Ordinance detailing the guidelines, rules, punishments, etc, They may amend their Statues and/or, Ordinances accordingly.

8.2 Prevention

The Committee recommends the following guidelines to prevent ragging in the educational institutions:

1. Anti-ragging movement should be initiated by the institution right from the time of advertisement for admissions. The advertisement must clearly mention that ragging is banned in the institution, and anyone indulging" in ragging is liable to be punished appropriately, including expulsion from the institution and/or imprisonment up to 3 years, and/or fine up to Rs. 25,000.
2. The brochure of admission/instruction booklet for candidates must print in block letters the Prohibition of Ragging Act/Ordinance in full along with other details of punishments for ragging. It also must mention in clear terms that the institution considers ragging a cognisable offence and really means business and will not hesitate to take stern action against the offenders.
3. The application form for admission/enrolment should itself have a printed undertaking to be filled up and signed by the candidate to the effect that he/she is aware of the law regarding ragging as well as the punishments, and that he/she, if found guilty of ragging, is liable to be punished appropriately.
4. The application form must also contain a written undertaking to be signed by the parent/guardian of the applicant stating that he/she is also aware of the law in this regard and agrees to abide by the punishment meted out to his/her ward in case the latter is found guilty of ragging.
5. Undertakings of similar nature as in 3 and 4 above should be made mandatory in the application forms for admission to the hostels as well.
6. A printed leaflet detailing when and to whom one has to turn for information, help and guidance for various purposes, addresses and telephone numbers of such persons, etc., should be given to each fresher at the lime of admission, so that the freshers need not look up to the seniors for help in such matters and get indebted to them and start doing things, right or wrong, at their behest. This will reduce their dependence on their seniors and the latter will loose the moral authority to command.
7. The leaflet mentioned above can also tell the freshers about their rights as *bona fide* students of the institution, that they should desist from doing anything against their will even if ordered by the seniors, that they have nothing to fear as the institution cares for them and will not tolerate any atrocities against them.
8. A letter from the Controller of Exams./Principal/Dean of Students must be sent at the end of the academic year to the parents/guardians of the students who are getting promoted to the 2nd/3rd year informing them about the law regarding ragging and the punishments, and appealing to them to impress up on their wards to desist from indulging in ragging when the new academic session starts.
9. A similar appeal from the Dean of Students/Principal should be, sent to all 2nd and 3rd year students (to be handed over to them when they come to pay the fees) at the commencement of the academic session.
10. Undertakings as in 3 and 'A above should be mandatory also at the commencement of academic session each year, that is, such undertakings should be given even by the students of 2nd and 3rd years as well as their parents/guardians. If there is no provision for filling application forms for registration at that stage (unlike for the first year admissions), the receipt for the fees paid for 2nd/3rd year should be issued only after receiving such undertakings.
11. The commencement of the academic session the Head of the Institution (Vice-Chancellor/Director/Principal, etc.) may address a meeting of various agencies like Wardens, representatives of students, parents/guardians, faculty, police and

other law and order machinery with an appeal to help eradicate the menace of ragging in the institution completely.

12. At the commencement of the academic session, the institution should constitute a Vigilance Committee consisting of senior faculty members, some hostel authorities like Wardens and a few responsible senior students to have an in-built mechanism for checking the incidence of ragging. The Committee should monitor the events involving ragging, enquire into them and make recommendations in this regard to the institution authorities. The Committee can draw up its modalities of functioning, frequency of visits/meetings, etc.

13. The community at large and the students in particular must be made aware of the dehumanising effect of ragging inherent in its perverse forms. For this, big posters (preferably multi coloured, in different colours for the provisions of law, punishments, etc.) should be prominently displayed on all Notice Boards of all departments, buildings/hostels as well as at all vulnerable places. A few of them may be of permanent nature (like the anti-drug use posters in some campuses, bus-stops, etc.) These posters can also be used to send the message across that ragging is a cognisable offence and the institution means business and shall not fail to take strict action against the offenders. The posters may also (optionally) include the names of those punished for ragging during the previous year and the nature of punishments

14. The media may be requested to give adequate publicity to the negative aspects of ragging mainly during the months of July and August every year so that public awareness and a version can be built up against ragging.

15. All vulnerable locations have to be identified a list of a few of them, (please see para 5 above), properly illuminated and manned, posters as mentioned in para 13 above put up prominently. The members of the Vigilance Committee should visit such locations frequently during the first two-three months of the academic session.

16. Security may be tightened in the premises of the institution, especially at the vulnerable places If necessary, intense policing should be resorted to at these points at odd hours during the first two-three months of the academic session.

17. The powers of Wardens and other authorities should be suitably enhanced. Some of them may be vested with a kind of magisterial powers, so that they can take immediate action in certain situations.

18. The security personnel posted in hostels must be under the direct control of the Wardens and assessed by them.

19. A Disciplinary Committee may be setup at the institution level to consider the recommendations of the Vigilance Committee and spell out the punishments. If considered necessary, this Committee can further investigate the events, recommendations for which were brought before it.

20. The Head of the institution (Vice-Chancellor/Director/Principal, etc.) should take immediate action on receipt of the recommendation of the Disciplinary Committee. He can also take action *suo motu* if the circumstances so demand.

21. Freshers should be encouraged to report incidents of ragging. Those who do not do so even when being witnesses or victims, should also be punished suitably.

22. When the persons committing or abetting the crime of ragging are not identified, collective punishment could be resorted to as a possible deterrent measure, as it would ensure community pressure on the potential raggers not to indulge in ragging.

23. For speedy disposal of cases involving ragging, the institution should continue with the disciplinary proceedings, even if a FIR has been filed and a case is pending before a court of law.
24. The Migration Certificate issued by an institution should have an entry, apart from those of general conduct and behaviour, whether the student had participated in and/or punished for the offence of ragging, or not.
25. If an institution fails to curb ragging, the UGC7 funding agency should stop financial assistance to such an institution till such time as it achieves the same.
26. A university may disaffiliate a college or institution for failing to curb ragging.

Apart from the above, the institutions may think up and formulate certain positive actions and a system of incentives broadly on the following lines

Positive Actions

27. Appropriate committee(s) may be setup including the course-in-charge, student advisor, Warden and some senior students to actively monitor, promote and regulate healthy inter-action between freshers and senior students.
28. The student-faculty inter-action may be increased to involve the students in all matters of the institution, except in actual processes of evaluation and in faculty appointments. Such involvement will make the students feel that they are responsible partners in managing the affairs of the institution, and the credit due to the institution for good work performance is due to them as well.
29. Freshers' welcome parties may be organised soon after admissions by senior students and the faculty together, where they can be properly introduced to one another. Such parties can bring out the talents in the freshers without the element so indecency normally occurring during ragging. Mass participation has its own built-in checks, as an overzealuus person could often be prevailed upon by sober elements. In the presence of the faculty, even the miniscule of misguided students, who are otherwise compulsive raggers, will be forced to behave properly and not cross the limits of decency. Exhibiting their talents in the open will help the freshers to shed their inferiority complex, remove their inhibitions and bring out the best in them.

Incentives

30. The institution should give due weightage tc the contribution made by Wardens and other functionaries to the institution's administration when assessing them for higher posts The perks for the Warden's and all such functionaries should be suitably enhanced to attract committed persons for these posts. The perks may include providing accommodation in the campus, telephone rental charges and suitable honorarium. Raised to the status that is their due and with increased powers and perks their ability and commitment to the cause of curbing ragging can be expected to be enhanced.
31. The Institution may work out allocating some marks or grade for those students who actively helped the institutions in curbing-ragging, This may be added to the total at the end of the programme, which might change the final division to be recorded in the certificate.
32. "Good conduct" and, "Not found indulging in any form of ragging" during the semester must also be one of the elements to be graded for sessional evaluation during the third and fifth semesters (*i.e*, during the first thalf of second and third years)

8.3 Punishments

The following could be the possible punishments for those who are found guilty of participation in or abetment of ragging. The quantum of punishment shall, naturally, depend upon the nature and gravity of the offence as established by the Disciplinary Committee or the court of law.

1. Cancellation of admission.
2. Suspension from attending classes.
3. Withholding/withdrawing scholarship/fellowship and other benefits.
4. Debarring from appearing in any test/examination or other evaluation process.
5. Withholding results
6. Debarring from representing the institution in any national or international meet, tournament, youth festival, etc.
7. Expulsion from hostels
8. Rustication from the institution for periods varying; from 1 to 2 semesters
9. Expulsion from the institution and consequent debarring from admission to any ether institution
10. Fine upto Rs. 25,000.
11. Rigorous imprisonment upto three years.

While the first 10 types of punishment can be awarded by the appropriate authority of the institution itself, the last punishment can be awarded only by a court of law.

(b) The Menace of Ragging in Educational Institutions and Measures to Curb it

(Dr. R.K. Raghavan Committee on Prevention of Ragging in Educational Institutions)

5. Recommendations

5.01. Based on its interactions and the elaborate methodology followed by it, the Committee is convinced that the society at large considers ragging as a definite menace. We are equally convinced that softer options have not worked and therefore it is time for tough measures. The Committee's recommendations, in terms of actions necessary, fall in six levels, namely, schools, higher educational institutions, district administration, universities, State authorities and Central authorities. At each level, we recommend that the active involvement of media and the civil society is essential in tackling the problem of ragging.

5.02. At the School level, the Committee recommends that on the same lines as topics on environment education were introduced in the school curriculum, the National Council of Educational Research and Training (NCERT) and the respective State Council of Educational Research and Training (SCERT), should devise methodologies and content for introducing Human Rights education of which awareness against ragging should be a compulsory part. Where inputs in Human Rights already exist, the same should be reviewed to ensure that awareness and exposure to the evil of ragging are highlighted in the syllabi. In the lower classes, respect for human rights, consciousness against violating others' rights, and respect for privacy, diversity and equality should be discreetly grafted into the lessons and exercises right from the primary and elementary stages of schooling in order to inculcate the desirable value system from the formative years of every child.

5.03. At the secondary and senior secondary stages of schooling, every school should be required to arrange regular and periodic psychological counselling sessions for every student till the time he/she passes out from the school. Parents and teachers should also be involved in such sessions. Every year there should be a certain number of mandatory counselling sessions with experienced psychologists. The Committee was informed by experts that 20 counselling workshop/sessions were desirable each year. Since it may not be immediately possible to avail the services of a vast number of trained psychologists, it is recommended that the B.Ed. and Teacher training programmes should be mandated to provide for anti-ragging and human-rights appreciation inputs so that every teacher is equipped to provide at least the rudiments of the counselling approach.

5.04. What would be desirable is that the school leaving certificate and the character certificate categorically mentions the status of the student in terms of his/her behavioural pattern; which should be mandatory to be submitted at the time of admission at the institute of higher learning. This certificate should mention whether the student has displayed persistent violent or aggressive behaviour or any desire to harm others. It is recommended that each State should create a pool of professional counsellors at the level of the district, who visit each and every school in every State to fill the obligation stated above. The District Institutes of Educational Technology (DIETs) should be reoriented for the purpose.

5.05. The Committee endorses the view that bullying and corporal punishments at the school level legitimize ideas of power abuse, harassment, violation of dignity and privacy, and as such may prepare the ground for ragging at the college level. Bullying is a phenomenon in which the students tease and humiliate other students in various ways. Corporal punishment has been banned by some States *viz.* Goa, Delhi and Tamil Nadu. Therefore, teachers at the school level must be made conscious of this fact. The curriculum for B.Ed. and other teacher-training courses, as well as in service training courses for the teachers, should include topics on sensitization against corporal punishment and checking of bullying amongst students.

5.06. At the level of the Higher educational institutions, it should be mandatory for the student at the time of admission to submit documentation in respect of (i) the school leaving certificate/character certificate which will include a report on behavioural pattern; (and, in due course include the report by a professional counsellor). The institution may thereupon keep intense watch upon a student who has a negative entry in this regard. (ii) an annual undertaking to be signed by each student, whether fresher or senior, and his/her parent(s) jointly stating that each of them have read the relevant instructions/regulations against ragging, as well as punishments, and that if the ward has been found guilty he/she will be proceeded against. The UGC Committee (1999) had also recommended so and the directions of the Apex Court also included this. While endorsing these recommendations, we emphasize specifically the following: *First,* we strongly recommend that such an undertaking should be provided in English as well as in the vernacular (mother tongue of the parent); *second,* the undertaking should be furnished at the beginning of each academic year by every student; *third,* the undertaking should be obtained every year from each student admitted to the hostel; and *finally,* the undertaking should be appended to a brochure containing the guidelines and other relevant instructions in regard to ragging and consequences of indulging in ragging – so that there is no denial of the responsibility on the one hand, and there is also a clear understanding of the requirement by all concerned, including parents who may be otherwise deficient in their facility with the English language. Merely getting an undertaking signed from students and parents, without linking it with the information relevant to ragging in our opinion would be ineffective, and hence our modified recommendations.

5.07. We feel that it is extremely important that this requirement of a binding undertaking is complied with by all institutions, and some superior level bodies must cross-verify and vouch that there is strict compliance thereto. This has to be ensured by the affiliating university and also verified by bodies such as the National Assessment and Accreditation Council (NAAC), the UGC Expert Committees, including those which visit institutions for recognition under section 2(f) and 12(B) of the UGC Act, AICTE's Committees, and Committees of other statutory councils or authorities such as the Medical Council of India (MCI), the Dental Council of India (DCI), the Nursing Council of India (NCI) etc. At present these bodies appear to perceive ragging merely as a disciplinary issue in which the regulatory authorities have little or no role, and in the context of curbing the menace of ragging appropriate directions must be given defining their role and responsibility. Indeed, without the active involvement of the multitude of bodies and authorities, a continuous vigil cannot be maintained. We are constrained to remark that while ensuring a ragging-free environment in campuses has a direct bearing on the standards of higher education, none of the bodies responsible for co-ordinating/establishing or maintaining standards of higher education (technical and medical etc., included) with whom we interacted, radiate the confidence that they consider the continuing practice of ragging as contributing to lowering of the standards.

5.08. The University Grants Commission and the statutory bodies such as the AICTE, MCI, DCI, NCI, ICAR as well as affiliating universities and Directorates of Higher, Technical, Agricultural and Medical etc. Education of State Governments, must make it mandatory and ensure that each institution compulsorily incorporates in the 'prospectus' and in other admission related documents, the earlier directions or any future directions of the Apex Court and/or of the Central or State Governments as applicable, so that candidates and their parents are sensitized in respect of the prohibition and consequences of ragging. Non-compliance with the directives against ragging in any manner whatsoever shall be considered as lowering of academic standards by the errant institution. The regulatory authorities must proceed against such errant institutions by imposing the prescribed penalties already provided under their respective statutes/regulations etc., which they would otherwise have exercised in matters of lowering of academic standards.

5.09. Just as there ought to be disincentives as mentioned in paragraph 5.08 above for failure to prevent ragging, there should be incentives to institutions for curbing it. By way of incentives, the Central Government, State Governments, University Grants Commission and other funding bodies such as the AICTE and the Indian Council of Agricultural Research etc., should provide special/additional annual financial grants-in-aid to those of the universities and colleges, which report a blemish-less record in terms of there being no incidents of ragging. These bodies should also institute another category of financial awards or incentives for colleges or universities which take stringent action against those responsible in respect of ragging incidents. This would overcome the present problem of institutions covering up incidents for fear of adverse impact on reputation.

5.10. The Committee notes that while there have been some isolated efforts at publicizing the concern and ban in respect of ragging, it could not come across any meaningful advertisement campaign through the various news media, either nationally or regionally, despite the 2001 direction of the Apex Court. This indicates a general apathy and a failure to sensitize society. The entire approach to ragging appears to be viewed as a seasonal issue, to be attended to only during the admission time and put on the back-burner after the heat and dust of admissions settle down. We recommend that there has to be a concerted effort on the part of Central and State Governments as well as the universities in publicizing the ills of ragging and in sensitizing and building public opinion.

5.11. We have described the need to launch effective advertisement campaigns at the national and regional level – the Central Government through the Directorate of Audio Visual Publicity (DAVP) and the State Governments through their Directorates of Information or Public Relations have the primary responsibility in this regard. This apart, multi-pronged campaigns have to be launched and sustained by universities as well as the institutions, locally. Extensive publicity must be undertaken by the institution by means of creative posters, audio-visual aids, by holding counselling sessions, workshops, painting and design competitions among students and other methods as it deems fit. We came across a number of initiatives by institutions, one such effort forms the back cover of our report.

5.12. The Committee recommends that it is critical that institutions promote a sense of confidence among every student entering the portals of higher education. It is important that the natural anxiety among the 'freshers' is addressed by institutional authorities. We recommend that there should be a clear gap of one to two weeks between the date of joining of 'freshers' and the seniors, classes for the seniors should commence later. This would enable the 'freshers' to familiarize themselves with the campus environment and adjust to the sudden changeover from schools to higher education. In addition, this period would be critical in building and consolidating a definite sense of bonding among the 'freshers' who would be better equipped to deal with the seniors with confidence acquired during the interim. It must be ensured that senior students are not allowed to enter the campus, including the hostels, under any pretext. The only exception to this rule may be for a few senior students who have been appointed by the institutional authorities for assisting in the orientation programme. We recommend that it should be mandatory for institutions to inform parents of senior students to send their wards only on the due date and not earlier. This system is in practice in some institutions and the Committee recommends that this must be implemented in all institutions. We further recommend that every university – whether established by Central law or State law or declared by the Central Government as an institution deemed to be university – must compulsorily amend its relevant Ordinances or bye-laws to ratify the schedule of the first two weeks described above as well as in the following paragraphs. We acknowledge that in some professional programmes – medicine and engineering in particular – there could be some practical difficulties in ensuring that senior students are not present on the campus when freshers join, however we feel that if the respective Councils make a sincere effort to adapt their academic calendar suitably this should not be such an insurmountable problem.

5.13. We further recommend that social events such as 'welcome parties' or 'freshers'' day celebrations in honour of 'freshers' is a sound tradition that needs to be encouraged by institutions. However, what is lamentable is that such events which often mark the ending of ragging and beginning of bonhomie among seniors and 'freshers', is scheduled only after a prolonged bout of ragging. Therefore, we recommend that in every institution, the 'freshers'' day or ' welcome party' shall be concluded within the first two weeks of the beginning of the academic session, that is not later than one week after the commencement of classes for the seniors in the context of our recommendation in 5.12 above. In any such event, celebrating the 'freshers'' day or party, college faculty must be present and must ensure that no ragging or untoward incident takes place on the occasion.

5.14. We also recommend that every institution should engage or seek the assistance of professional counsellors at the time of admissions to counsel 'freshers' in order to prepare them for the life ahead, particularly for adjusting to the life in hostels. The Committee feels that preparing students in this manner would enable them to cope with the stresses of the hitherto unknown life in the campus.

5.15. The Committee recommends that each institution, and where required the affiliating university, should lay down a calendar of events and activities to facilitate and complement familiarization of juniors with the academic environment of the institution. This calendar must be automatically ratified under the relevant Ordinances of the affiliating university. There should be an introductory interaction with faculty members, members of the staff and senior students as was suggested by the UGC Committee (1999) as well. The breakup of the orientation programme should be as follows: (i) the head of the institution must address all fresh students on the first day of the academic session, and the address must amongst other issues educate them about their rights against harassment of any kind including ragging; and all faculty members must invariably be present on the occasion; (ii) the second orientation programme for fresh students should be held for each course/class, during which all the respective departmental faculty must be present. The main purpose of this orientation would be to inculcate a sense of bonding and a feeling of fraternity among the freshers, as well as to develop an affinity towards the teaching faculty; (iii) the third orientation programme for fresh students should be conducted at the level of the class/section/division; (iv) one or more counselling sessions must be arranged through out the first week as part of the orientation sessions, during which a professional counsellor should address 'freshers' and motivate them to confidently deal with strangers/seniors; (v) during this week each institution should organize cultural events, sports and other activities, for 'freshers' to get to know each other; there should be very little or no 'serious' academic activity which digresses from the familiarization and sensitization programmes chalked out by the institution; we also recommend that the UGC and other funding bodies must make special allocations for the purpose of enabling institutions to engage counsellors and organize various events that contribute to the building of confidence among the 'freshers'. (vi) the institution must not only work out a variety of alternative methods of interactions, but should also publicize the details of the orientation programmes described above.

5.16. We recommend that on the arrival of senior students after the first week or after the second week as the case may be, further orientation programmes must be scheduled as follows (i) joint sensitization programme and counselling of both 'freshers' and seniors by a professional counsellor; (ii) joint orientation programme of 'freshers' and seniors to be addressed by the Principal/Head of the institution, and the anti-ragging committee; (iii) organisation on a large scale of cultural, sports and other activities to provide a platform for the 'freshers' and seniors to interact in the presence of faculty members; (iv) in the hostel, the warden should address all students; may request two junior colleagues from the college faculty to assist the warden by becoming resident tutors for a temporary duration; and, the UGC and other funding bodies should provide financial grants for meeting the expenditure on resident tutors (v) It is strongly recommended that as far as possible faculty members should dine with the hostel residents in their respective hostels to instill a feeling of confidence among the fresh residents.

5.17. The Committee agrees with the views expressed by student leaders of various ideological affiliations with whom it interacted that a thriving and active students' association of comprising of genuinely enrolled students helps in minimising incidents of ragging, as each competing student group during elections to the student body would have a vested interest in 'protecting' target group of fresher voters from being subjected to ragging by others. As a matter of fact, it was repeatedly brought to the notice of the Committee that one of the reasons for engineering and medical or professional colleges being highly ragging prone is due to the absence of genuine student election activity. Although much can be said in this regard, including the evidence that ragging has slowly spread to other types of institutions as well, we recommend that the reforms in student body elections approved by the Hon'ble Supreme Court on the basis of the recommendations of the J.M. Lyngdoh Committee should be implemented expeditiously and the students' union election must be held within 15 days of the beginning of the academic session. This will undermine the nexus, reported in some places, between campus politics and ragging.

5.18. We recommend that every institution must have an Anti-Ragging Committee and an Anti-Ragging Squad. It is essential to have a diverse mix of membership in terms of levels as well as gender in both the Anti-Ragging Squad as well as the Anti-Ragging Committee. The Anti-Ragging Committee at the level of the institution should consist of the representatives of civil and police administration, local media, Non-Governmental Organizations involved in youth activities, representatives of faculty members, representatives of parents, representatives of students belonging to the freshers' category as well as seniors, non-teaching staff and should be headed by the Head of the Institution. The Anti-Ragging Squad, in contrast, should be a body with vigil, oversight and patrolling functions and should appropriately be a smaller body which should be nominated by the Head of the institution with such representation as considered necessary to keep it mobile, alert and active at all times. The Squad may be called upon to make surprise raids on hostels and other hot spots and should be empowered to inspect places of potential ragging. The Squad should work under the overall guidance of the Anti-Ragging Committee. The Squad should not have any outside representation and should only consist of members belonging to the various sections of the campus community.

5.19. We recommend that there should also be a 'Mentoring Cell' in each institution to oversee and involve senior students as Mentors for the 'freshers'. The Mentoring Cell should be formed at the end of every academic year where applications should be invited from students to join the Mentoring Cell as Mentors for the succeeding academic year. There should be as many levels or tiers of Mentors as the number of batches in the institution. The Anti-Ragging Squad of the institution and the Head/Principal should be involved in selecting the first level of Mentors who would be chosen from among the batch of students immediately senior to the 'freshers'. A diverse mix of Mentors would be desirable who would be selected at the ratio of one student for a certain number of 'freshers'. It has been observed that a ratio of 1:6 is optimal. There should be a hierarchy of Mentors, that is, for every group of six Mentors chosen from the 2nd year or the batch immediately senior to the 'freshers', there should be one second level Mentor. Then there would be one third year student per six Mentors of the second level and so on. At every level of Mentors, there should be a Faculty Adviser. The warden and faculty would directly deal with the highest level of Mentors, which is not to say that they would not interact with the other tiers of Mentors, but such interaction would be more indirect. Every Mentor at the first level should be allowed in to the hostel when 'freshers' join and, 'freshers' and Mentors should be introduced to each other. The Mentors would help 'freshers' in settling down. This makes sure that 'freshers' have some seniors to fall back on without the fear of ragging and would serve by way of "peer counselling". This model has been implemented in some places and has been successful. The third year Mentors and the faculty in-charge should oversee the working of the Mentoring Cell and make sure that the Mentors don't misuse their powers.

5.20. We also recommend that anonymous random surveys must be conducted by each institution, across the entire 1st year batch of students ('freshers') every fortnight during the first three months of the academic session in order to verify and cross-check whether the campus is indeed free of ragging or not. The institution may design its own methodology of conducting such a survey. It is extremely important that the institution does not compromise the anonymity of the whistle blowers.

5.21. The job requirement for the warden calls for a dedicated cadre of trained and specially qualified professionals. In a situation of shortage of teachers in higher education, sparing academics for the duties of wardens also needs to be reviewed. We feel that it is unfair to thrust this specialized responsibility on teachers and other academics who have to discharge the functions in addition to the demands of teaching or research. This is not, however, to suggest that academics can not discharge the obligations of the warden, indeed a large number of them are already doing it successfully, but this arrangement is not desirable in all cases. We recommend that the UGC and other regulatory bodies should lay down the eligibility of the post of warden reflecting both the command and control aspects of maintaining discipline, as well as the softer skills of counselling and communicating with the youth outside of the class-room situations. The post of warden must carry the necessary incentive to attract the right type of eligible candidates, and motivate the incumbent.

5.22. We recommend that in the light of the increasing number of private commercially managed lodges or hostels outside campuses, such hostels and management must be registered with the local police authorities and permission to start such hostels or register them must necessarily be recommended by the Heads of educational institutions. It should be mandatory for both local police, local administration as well the institutional authorities to ensure vigil on incidents that may come with in the definition of ragging. Managements of such private hostels should be responsible for non-reporting of cases of ragging in such premises. Local authorities as well as the institutional authorities should be responsible for action in the event of ragging in such premises, just as they would be for incidents within campuses. The Committee also recommends that besides registering private hostels as stated above, the towns or cities where educational institutions are located should be apportioned as sectors among faculty members, as is being done by some institutions, so that they could maintain vigil and report any incidents of ragging outside campuses and enroute while 'freshers' commute.

5.23. The Committee respects the autonomy of academic institutions and believes that to the extent possible incidents of harassment of 'freshers' by seniors should be dealt with under the prevalent ordinances or statutes and the procedures prescribed thereunder or under the provisions of the relevant State law. However, where the victim or his/her parent/guardian is not satisfied with the action taken by the Head of the institution or by other institutional authorities, or where the Head of the institution is of the opinion that the incident ought to be so reported, it must be mandatory for the institution to file a First Information Report with the local police authorities. Such reports should also be made to the civil Authorities (such as Sub-Divisional Magistrate, Deputy Commissioner or District Magistrate), the higher Police Authorities (Commissioner or Superintendent of Police or his Deputies) and also to the media for wider dissemination. In incidents of extreme sensitivity or grave consequences, such reports should also be made to the appropriate State Authorities. Media reports may at times kindle the interest of civil society activists and Non-Governmental Organizations, whose involvement in tackling incidents of ragging or the prevention of such incidents must be welcomed and not looked upon as any hindrance. Universities and State or Central Governments should also encourage institutional authorities to share information in respect of ragging, rather than sweeping any incident under the carpet; we believe that reporting information about incidents of ragging contributes to the prevention and recurrence of such incidents, while attempts to cover up only result in more unreported incidents taking place and matters getting out of control for the authorities. The Committee expects the sub-divisional, district and divisional or State level authorities also to share information rather than prevent access to information for the media and the civil society.

5.24. The Committee recommends that institutions must adhere to complaints in regard to ragging or any *suo motu* information in respect thereof, which its authorities may come across promptly, and all relevant and necessary action must be attended to with great despatch. The complaints or information in regard to ragging could be oral or written and even from third parties and the confidentiality of the source of information must be protected at all costs. Remedial action must be initiated and completed with in the week of the incident itself so that complaints do not linger on and allow either interest in pursuing the matter to vane or enable the culprits to tamper evidence or influence witnesses.

5.25. The Committee recommends that preventing or acting against ragging should be the collective responsibility of all levels and sections of authorities or functionaries with in the institution *i.e.*, administrative head, teaching faculty and non-teaching employees and not merely that of the specific body constituted for prevention of ragging. In case of any incident taking place all the sections must co-ordinate with the sense of moral propriety and share the responsibility and accountability.

5.26. The burden of proof must, in the opinion of the Committee, lie on the perpetrator and not on the victim to prove that ragging did not take place. As mentioned earlier in the previous Chapter, dealing with the Observations of the Committee, we did not come across any significant instance of implementing the earlier directions of the Apex Court in regard to collective punishment in those cases where the perpetrators could not be identified. Nevertheless, the concept of collective fines or punishment is a time-tested method of making both active as well as passive participants or abettors pay for the crime and therefore we recommend that collective punishment must continue to be in force, with a more effective monitoring at higher levels.

5.27. Wardens must be accessible at all hours and therefore it is important that they be available on telephone and other modes of communication – therefore, we recommend that wardens must be issued mobile phones by the institutions and the details of their telephone number must be widely publicised. Similarly, the telephone numbers of the other important functionaries – Heads of institutions, faculty members, members of the anti-ragging committees, district and sub-divisional authorities and State authorities where relevant, should also be widely disseminated for the needy to get in touch or seek help in emergencies. The Committee recommends that brochures or booklet/leaflet distributed to each student at the beginning of each academic session for obtaining undertaking not to indulge or abet ragging, shall contain the blueprint of prevention and methods of redress.

5.28. At the level of the District, we recommend a District level Anti-Ragging Committee, which should consist of the Heads of Higher Education Institutions as members. It should be headed by the District Collector/Deputy Commissioner/District Magistrate and should also have the Superintendent of Police/ SSP of the District as member. The Additional District Magistrate should be a member-secretary of the Committee, which should also have representation of the local media and district level Non-Governmental Organizations actively associated in youth development programmes, as well as representatives of all student organizations. The District level Committee should hold preparatory meetings during the summer vacation meetings to take stock of the state of preparedness of each institution and their compliance with the policies and directions or guidelines of the appropriate bodies, the university/State/Central authorities; and the Apex Court's guidelines in regard to curbing the menace of ragging. We have already emphasized on the need for publicity campaigns, summer months may be appropriate to launch such campaigns. Some of the role expectations from the District level Committees have already been mentioned in the preceding paragraphs dealing with activities at the level of Schools as well as higher educational institutions and therefore are not being repeated.

5.29. We have thought through the suggestion that the District level Committee should function as some sort of an appellate forum to the action taken by the institution level Anti-Ragging Committee. We feel that this is neither necessary nor desirable. It is not necessary in the context of the recommendation that we propose to make in respect of the scheme of penalty later in this Chapter. It is not desirable from the point of view that such a mechanism lends an extra-campus dimension to the tackling of intra-campus disciplinary matters All matters of discipline within teaching institutions, in our opinion, must be resolved within the campus-except those impinging on law and order or breach of peace or public tranquillity, all of which should be dealt with under the penal laws of the land; fortifying of which is being suggested by us later on.

5.30. At the level of the University, we recommend that there should be a Monitoring Cell on Ragging, which should coordinate with the affiliated colleges and institutions under its domain. The Cell should call for reports from the Heads of institutions in regard to the activities of the Anti- Ragging Committees, Anti-Ragging Squads, Mentoring Cells at the level of the institution, the compliance with instructions on conducting orientation programmes, counselling sessions, the incidents of ragging, the problems faced by wardens or other officials. It should also keep itself abreast of the decisions of the District level Anti-Ragging Committee. This Monitoring Cell should also review the efforts made by institutions to publicize anti-ragging measures, soliciting of undertaking from parents and students each year to abstain from ragging activities or willingness to be penalized for violations; and should function as the prime mover for initiating action on the part of the appropriate authorities of the university for amending the Statutes or Ordinances or Bye-laws to facilitate the implementation of anti-ragging measures at the level of the institution.

5.31. At the State level, we recommend that there should be a Monitoring Cell at the level of the Chancellor of the State Universities, who may also co-ordinate with those of the Central Government institutions located in the State in which the Governor has a defined role under the relevant law. Governors, in their capacity as Chancellors of State Universities, can leverage the influence of their office to ensure that the State Government as well as the university authorities are suitably instructed to be alert in regard to ragging. The involvement of Governors would also ensure that the autonomy of institutions of higher learning is not compromised. In addition, Governors of States are associated with Central Universities in their role as Chief Rector/Chancellor etc., and can oversee the function of co-ordination where required *vis a vis* the office of the President of India in his capacity as the Visitor of the Central Universities and also the Central Government in the Ministry of Human Resource Development. The State level Monitoring Cell should receive periodically, and at such frequencies that it may lay down, status reports from the University level Monitoring Cells and District level Anti-Ragging Committees.

5.32. The Heads of institutions should be required to submit, to the Vice-Chancellor of the University, weekly reports during first three months of the reopening of the institution and there after reports each month on the status of compliance with anti-ragging measures. The Vice-Chancellor should submit fortnightly reports of the University level Monitoring Cell to the State level Cell under the Chancellor. The fortnightly reports as well as the weekly reports should be compulsorily shared with the media, so that 'nil' reports if any are also in the public domain. Wide publicity, including mandatory hosting of information on the institutional web-site, should be given to such 'nil' reports so that the media acts as a 'watchdog' for feedback and citizens exercise their Right to Information, in case false claims are made by institutions with a view to protect their "reputation".

5.33. At the National level, we recommend that the University Grants Commission should be responsible for co-ordinating and monitoring the anti-ragging movement across the country and should constitute a Board for Coordination consisting of the following : (i) representative of the AICTE (ii) a representative of the IITs (iii) a representative of the NITs (iv) a representative of the IIMs (v) a representative of the MCI (vi) representative of the DCI (vii) a representative of the NCI (viii) a representative of the ICAR (viii) a representative of the Veterinary Council and such other representatives as have to do with higher education and are not represented in the categories mentioned above. The Committee has already expressed its disappointment that despite the passage of over six years since the directions of the Apex Court, neither the UGC nor any of the statutory authorities in the different sectors of higher education have focussed their attention in dealing with the menace of ragging. The UGC should constitute an institutional mechanism – such as a Cell within the Commission to provide secretarial support for collection of information and monitoring. There should be no delay on this account for any reason, the Cell should be carved out of its existing secretariat and should co-ordinate with the State level and University level Committees for effective implementation of anti-ragging measures. The UGC and the other statutory authorities should intervene wherever their existing guidelines or academic instructions come in the way of implementation of the recommendations being made in this report. The Commission and the other funding bodies should also provide adequate funds to universities and colleges for carrying out the mandate of curbing incidents of ragging. It should co-ordinate with the other statutory authorities (AICTE, MCI, DCI, ICAR, NCTE, NCI etc.) so that timely instructions are sent by such authorities for enabling or mandating institutions to prevent and prohibit ragging as well as to take action against institutions that tolerate or do not report incidents of ragging. The UGC and the other funding agencies should also work out a mechanism of providing grants-in-aid where institutions successfully prevent occurrence of ragging or where stern action is taken by institutions against ragging incidents.

5.34. The UGC and the statutory bodies must issue the necessary guidelines or regulations prescribing the qualifications and eligibility of persons for holding the post of wardens in hostels. They should work out a suitable scale of pay for the post of wardens and also assist institutions to create sufficient number of posts in the cadre of wardens during the XIth Plan period for which allocations should be provided by the Commission. Just as the UGC must ensure that every hostel in the academic institutions must have a professional warden as stated above the AICTE, MCI etc., and State Governments should be responsible for the appointments of the respective Cadre of wardens. The necessary facilitating amendments must be carried out in the statutes of universities and other institutions for the purpose of creating the new Cadre. The UGC may also consider encouraging universities to start specialized courses and programmes of study in Hostel Administration.

5.35. One class of institutions not covered under our recommendations above is that of the institutions deemed to be universities, which come under the purview of the UGC and the Central Government. These institutions, commonly referred to as "deemed universities" consist of constituent units which impart all types of higher education including professional education in engineering, medicine etc. Ragging is stated to be as prevalent in several of them as in other public institutions or universities established by Legislatures of States or by Parliament. Monitoring the status of anti-ragging measures and prevention of incidents of ragging in these institutions would logically be the responsibility of the University Grants Commission's national-level Monitoring Cell. It should be ensured that the directions in regard to the setting up of Anti-Ragging Committees, Anti-Ragging Squads, Mentoring Cells recommended by us in respect of institutions are complied with by the constituent units of deemed universities as well. The anti-ragging mechanism at the level of such constituent units of deemed universities must coordinate its activities *vis a vis* the district-level mechanism recommended by us in earlier paragraphs. Similarly, each deemed university should constitute the university level monitoring cell which should co-ordinate the anti-ragging activities at the level of the constituent units and should also report to the Monitoring Cell at the UGC.

5.36. Compliance with anti-ragging measures recommended and required to be brought in to affect by institutions of higher education, universities as well as deemed universities, should be adequately recognized by the UGC and other statutory authorities while earmarking financial assistance to them as well as while according them academic recognition or while granting expansion in capacity of seats in various branches of study or while sanctioning new programmes of study.

5.37. What should be the role of the State Governments and the Central Government in the efforts to curb the menace of ragging? We recommend that the responsibility of generating mass awareness and public opinion against ragging is a function which the appropriate Governments through the machinery at their disposal and through intelligent use of the media as well as co-option of civil society activists can accomplish efficiently. We recommend that there should be media advisory committees at the level of each State Government and at the national level with the Central Government which should chalk out campaign strategies and prepare effective messages for propagation. The Press Information Bureau of the Central Government should cull out all reported incidents of ragging and forward the same to the MHRD/UGC for monitoring – the fact that the Committee had to depend on the assistance provided by Non-Governmental Organizations for documentation in regard to the reported incidents of ragging over the years, points to the absence of any centralized mechanism to monitor such incidents in an authentic manner.

5.38. Non-Governmental initiatives in anti-ragging movement need to be supported in order to bring about qualitative improvement and efficient outcomes. The Committee recommends that the Government of India, and State Governments support such organizations to widen and intensify their activities. They could be helped to launch awareness programmes either on their own or in collaboration with the media related efforts of the Central or State Governments. Such efforts by the civil society may encourage parents and other well-wishers of 'freshers' to exercise various rights including the Right to Information for ascertaining the real situation in our campuses.

5.39. Similarly, the Directorates of Information and Public Relations of State Governments should ensure that there is widest possible publicity to anti-ragging measures adopted in each State or what is prescribed under national guidelines. In States with anti-ragging laws in place, the responsibility of enforcement also lies squarely with the State Governments, including the responsibility to make rules under the Act. There is a larger reason for launching a sustained media campaign to sensitize the public, with less than 10% of the population in the relevant age group of 18 years to 23 years enrolled in all sectors of higher education, due to the low access to higher education, even less in professional colleges, lower still in hostels, the public at large being too distanced from the problems that beset higher educational campuses. The problem of ragging may therefore seem too exclusive to most and too remote to happen to oneself – precisely why it needs to occupy centre stage in public debates on higher education.

5.40. Yet another role of the Central Government, through its agency for censoring and certifying films, would be to ensure that appropriate directives are in place so that films which have a deep impress on young minds do not eulogize ragging; we recommend that such directives should be issued by the Centre Board of Film

Certification, similar to the instructions on alcoholism, smoking or in regard to vulgarity.

5.41. We also recommend that the policy in regard to migration of students from one university or institution to another whether in the same State or outside the State needs to be reviewed by the UGC and the appropriate statutory authorities. While victims of ragging would find it helpful to be 'evacuated' from a notorious institution, the misuse of such a facility by students trying to gain transfer to institutions of their choice, pretending to be victims of ragging can also not be ruled out. This issue needs to be approached with circumspection. Also, it is not necessary that the institution to which a student victim of ragging is migrated would be less trouble prone than the one being left behind. In any case there has to be a case to case approach based on the merit of each.

5.42. We recommend that the National Assessment and Accreditation Council (NAAC) or other accrediting bodies should factor any incident of ragging while accrediting institutions in different grades. Thus an institution which has been unable to prevent ragging or where incidents of ragging do not abate should be given a negative rating appropriately so that its overall grading is affected.

5.43. The Committee recommends that at the national level, the UGC should fund a toll-free Helpline which could be accessed by students in distress owing to ragging related incidents. The Ministry of Communication and Information Technology should facilitate the establishment, infrastructure and operation of the proposed Helpline. Any distress message should be simultaneously relayed to the Head of the Institution, warden or officer of the Hostels, District authorities including the Superintendent of Police, and should be web-linked so as to be in the public domain simultaneously for the media and citizens to access it. A genuine message of distress from the victim of ragging should make it obligatory for the Head of the institution and civil authorities to initiate action on the lines already suggested by us.

5.44. Timely communication being the key to attending to distress signals from victims of ragging, we recommend that access to mobile phones as well public phones should be unrestricted in hostels and campuses with reasonable restrictions on the use of mobile phones in class rooms or other prohibited places in the Campus through the use of technology (using jammers) rather than banning the use of cell phones by students. If necessary the UGC or the universities/institutions should issue appropriate instructions in this regard.

5.45. The Committee recommends that rather than subjecting each incident of ragging to a different penal treatment under various sections of the Indian Penal Code, a new section should be added to the IPC, making ragging a punishable offence on the analogy of section 498A dealing with cruelty towards women (against dowry related incidents). We have already explained that ragging is an offence with a multiplicity of ingredients, each of which constitutes an offence punishable under the existing provisions of the Indian Penal Code. We further recommend that the Indian Evidence Act should also be suitably amended on the analogy of section 113A of that Act, to shift the burden of proof on those accused of ragging.

5.46. We recommend that a comprehensive definition should be included by way of *Explanation* in the proposed new section on ragging in the IPC, and all the punishable ingredients namely, abetment to ragging, criminal conspiracy to rag, unlawful assembly and rioting while ragging, public nuisance created during ragging, violation of decency and morals through ragging, injury to body, causing hurt or grievous hurt, wrongful restraint, wrongful confinement, use of criminal force, assault as well as sexual offences or even unnatural offences, extortion, criminal trespass, offences against property, criminal intimidation and attempts to commit any or all of the above mentioned offences against the victim should be incorporated thereto, prescribing appropriate punishments in respect of one or a group of offences.

5.47. The Committee believes that there cannot be a half way house in dealing with the menace of ragging. Mild and soft approach to ragging, even though required, has clearly not worked so far in curbing the menace. For example, punishments in the form of cancellation of admission, suspension from attending the classes, withholding/withdrawing scholarships, fellowship and other benefits, individual or collective fines, debarring from appearing in any test/examination and other evaluation process, withholding results, debarring from representing the institution in any national and international meet, tournament, youth festival, etc., suspension/expulsion from the hostel, rustication from the institution for periods varying from one or more semesters, expulsion from the institution and consequent debarring from admission to any other institution – all exist. The existing punishments can not be substitutes for the penal provisions of law, but only in addition to the punishments that must be handed out under the Indian Penal Code. We see no reason why enrolment in an institution or an academic programme should immunize perpetrators of heinous crimes which otherwise attract the penal provisions of law if committed by an adult citizen outside the academic precincts. Our message to the academic community is to ensure good governance which will respect human dignity by all concerned. It would indeed be sad if the penal provisions of law were to be used as a matter of routine to enforce deterrence in campuses.

5.48. Times have changed since the Hon'ble Supreme Court's caution of treating those indulging in ragging not as criminals and advising restraint in the use of the police force. While the intervention and presence of police in campuses is to be avoided normally, considering the alarming proportions the severity of ragging has grown to, we recommend that even as every possible measure to prevent ragging is taken on the lines recommended by us in the preceding paragraphs of this Chapter and such action is taken at every level – that of Schools, Institutions, Districts, Universities, States and finally at the national level – even as every possible strategy should be adopted to sensitize the public against the evils and ills of ragging through the use of the media and the civil society at each of the levels described by us; the time has come to treat every single incident of ragging, however isolated or "mild" or "positive" it may appear, with the heaviest hand possible. In support of our argument we could come across no judicial pronouncement better than the one in the matter of *Thiruvananthapuram Government Engineering College* v. *State of Kerala*, [WP (C) 656 of 1998; 2000 (2) KLT 11] in which Arijit Pasayat, CJ (as his Lordship then was) writing for a division bench of the High Court of Kerala held;

> "..*What was intended to be in good faith and provide untainted fun is now characterized as physical torture with a sadistic tendency and sexual perversions. There are few reported cases of loss of life also. One thing is clear that ragging, which was originally thought of to be a mere joke, has crossed bounds of decency and had entered the arena of physical and mental torture. It needs to be dealt with iron hands...*"

5.49. We recommend that the punishment to be meted out has to be exemplary and justifiably harsh to act as a deterrence against recurrence of such incidents. We therefore recommend that every single incident of ragging, where the victim or his parent/guardian or the Head of institution is not satisfied with the institutional arrangement for action a First Information Report must be filed compulsorily by the institutional authority with the local police authorities. We believe that the institutional authorities would become aware of such incidents through one of the many channels already identified by us – the Anti-Ragging squads, anti-ragging committees, mentoring cells, distress calls redirected by the Help Line, by NGOs, by the media and so on. Any failure or negligence or deliberate delay on the part of the institutional authority (comprising of the Head of Institution,/ the Warden etc.) to file an FIR with the local police, on the dissatisfaction of the victim with the institutional redress mechanism or *suo motu* by the Head of institution, should render the negligence culpable. Needless to add that every victim or his parent/ guardian of ragging can also file an FIR directly with the police, but failure on the part of the victim to do so should not justify the delay, or neglect or failure on the part of the institutional authorities.

5.50. We recommend that the Criminal Procedure Code should- be amended to ensure that cases involving ragging are tried on the fast-track so that there are no delays in dealing with such matters, keeping in mind the academic priorities of students who may be required to depose before the courts to assist the prosecution while the matter is sub-judice.

Annexure 2

Regulatory Bodies

(a) UGC Regulations on Curbing the Menace of Ragging in Higher Educational Institutions 2009

(under section 26(1)(g) of the University Grants Commission Act, 1956)

Preamble

In view of the directions of the Hon'ble Supreme Court in the matter of *University of Kerala* v. *Council of Principals of Colleges*, in SLP No. 24295 of 2006 dated 16.05.2007 and that dated 08.05.2009 in Civil Appeal number 887 of 2009, and in consideration of the determination of the Central Government and the University Grants Commission to prohibit, prevent and eliminate the scourge of ragging including any conduct by any student or students whether by words spoken or written or by an act which has the effect of teasing, treating or handling with rudeness a fresher or any other student, or indulging in rowdy or indisciplined activities by any student or students which causes or is likely to cause annoyance, hardship or psychological harm or to raise fear or apprehension thereof in any fresher or any other student or asking any student to do any act which such student will not in the ordinary course do and which has the effect of causing or generating a sense of shame, or torment or embarrassment so as to adversely affect the physique or psyche of such fresher or any other student, with or without an intent to derive a sadistic pleasure or showing off power, authority or superiority by a student over any fresher or any other student, in all higher education institutions in the country, and thereby, to provide for the healthy development, physically and psychologically, of all students, the University Grants Commission, in consultation with the Councils, brings forth this Regulation.

In exercise of the powers conferred by clause (g) of sub-section (1) of section 26 of the University Grants Commission Act, 1956, the University Grants Commission hereby makes the following Regulations, namely;:

1. Title, commencement and applicability.—(1.1) These regulations shall be called the "UGC Regulations on Curbing the Menace of Ragging in Higher Educational Institutions, 2009".

(1.2) They shall come into force from the date of their publication in the Official Gazette.

(1.3) They shall apply to all the institutions coming within the definition of an University under sub-section (f) of section (2) of the University Grants Commission Act, 1956, and to all institutions deemed to be a university under Section 3 of the University Grants Commission Act, 1956 to all other higher educational institutions, or elements of such universities or institutions, including its departments, constituent units and all the premises, whether being academic, residential, playgrounds, canteen, or other such premises of such universities, deemed universities and higher educational institutions, whether located within the campus or outside, and to all means of transportation of students, whether public or private, accessed by students for the pursuit of studies in such universities, deemed universities and higher educational institutions.

2. Objectives.—To prohibit any conduct by any student or students whether by words spoken or written or by an act which has the effect of teasing, treating or handling with rudeness a fresher or any other student, or indulging in rowdy or indisciplined activities by any student or students which causes or is likely to cause annoyance, hardship or psychological harm or to raise fear or apprehension thereof in any fresher or any other student or asking any student to do any act which such student will not in the ordinary course do and which has the effect of causing or generating a sense of shame, or torment or embarrassment so as to adversely affect the physique or psyche of such fresher or any other student, with or without an intent to derive a sadistic pleasure or showing off power, authority or superiority by a student over any fresher or any other student; and thereby, to eliminate ragging in all its forms from universities, deemed universities and other higher educational institutions in the country by prohibiting it under these Regulations, preventing its occurrence and punishing those who indulge in ragging as provided for in these Regulation and the appropriate law in force.

3. What constitutes Ragging.—Ragging constitutes one or more of any of the following acts:

(a) Any conduct by any student or students whether by words spoken or written or by an act which has the effect of teasing, treating or handling with rudeness a fresher or any other students;

(b) Indulging in rowdy or indisciplined activities by any student or students which causes or is likely to cause annoyance, hardship, physical or psychological harm or to raise fear or apprehension thereof in any fresher or any other student;

(c) Asking any student to do any which such student will not in the ordinary course do and which has the effect of causing or generating a sense of shame, or torment or embarrassment so as to adversely affect the physique or psyche of such fresher or any other student;

(d) Any act by a senior student that prevents, disrupts or disturbs the regular academic activity of any other student or a fresher;

(e) Exploiting the services of a fresher or any other student for completing the academic tasks assigned to an individual or a group of students;

(f) Any act of financial extortion or forceful expenditure burden put on a fresher or any other student by students;

(g) Any act of physical abuse including all variants of it: sexual abuse, homosexual assaults, stripping, forcing obscene and lewd acts, gestures, causing bodily harm or any other danger to health or person;

(h) Any act or abuse by spoken words, e-mails, post, public insults which would also include deriving perverted pleasure, vicarious or sadistic thrill from actively or passively participating in the discomfiture to fresher or any other student;

(i) Any act that affects the mental health and self – confidence of a fresher or any other student with or without an intent to derive a sadistic pleasure or showing off power, authority or superiority by a student over any fresher or any other student.

4. Definitions.—(1) In these regulations unless the context otherwise requires,

(a) "Act" means, the University Grants Commission Act, 1956 (3 of 1956);

(b) "Academic year" means the period from the commencement of admission of students in any course of study in the institution up to the completion of academic requirements for that particular year.

(c) "Anti-Ragging Helpline" means the Helpline established under clause (a) of Regulation 8.1 of these Regulations.

(d) "Commission" means the University Grants Commission;

(e) "Council" means a body so constituted by an Act of Parliament or an Act of any State Legislature for setting, or co-ordinating or maintaining standards in the relevant areas of higher education, such as the All India Council for Technical Education (AICTE), the Bar Council of India (BCI), The Dental Council of India (DCI), the Distance Education Council (DEC), the Indian Council of Agricultural Research (ICAR), the Indian Nursing Council (INC), the Medical Council of India (MCI), the National Council for Teacher Education (NCTE), the Pharmacy Council of India (PCI), etc., and the State Higher Education Councils.

(f) "District Level Anti-Ragging Committee" means the Committee, headed by the District Magistrate, constituted by the State Government, for the control and elimination of ragging in institutions within the jurisdiction of the district.

(g) "Head of the institutions" means the Vice-Chancellor in case of a university or a deemed to be university, the Principle or the Director or such other designation as the executive head of the institution or the college is referred.

(h) "Fresher" means a student who has been admitted to an institution and who is undergoing his/her first year of study in such institution.

(i) "Institution" means a higher educational institution including, but not limited to an university, a deemed university, a college, an institute, an institution of national importance set up by an Act of Parliament or a constituent unit of such institution, imparting higher education beyond of 12 years of schooling leading to, but not necessarily culminating in, a degree (graduate, postgraduate and/or higher level) and/or to a university diploma.

(j) "NAAC" means the National Academic and Accreditation Council established by the Commission under Section 12 (ccc) of the Act;

(k) "State Level Monitoring Cell" means the body constituted by the State Government for the control and elimination of ragging in institutions within the jurisdiction of the State, established under a State Law or on the advice of the Central Government, as the case may be.

(2) Words and expressions used and not defined herein but defined in the Act or in the General Clauses Act, 1897, shall have the meanings respectively assigned to them in the Act or in the General clauses Act, 1897, as the case may be.

5. Measures for prohibition of ragging at the institution level.—(a) No institution or any part of it thereof, including its elements, including, but not limited to, the departments, constituent units, colleges, centers of studies and all its premises, whether academic, residential, playgrounds, or canteen, whether located within the campus or outside, and in all means of transportation of students, whether public or private, accessed by students for the pursuit of studies in such institutions, shall permit or condone any reported incident of ragging in any form; and all institutions shall take all necessary and required measures, including but not limited to the provisions of these Regulations, to achieve the objective of eliminating ragging, within the institution or outside,

(b) All institutions shall take action in accordance with these Regulations against those found guilty of ragging and/or abetting ragging, actively or passively, or being part of a conspiracy to promote ragging.

6. Measures for prevention of ragging at the institution level.—(6.1) An institution shall take the following steps in regard to admission or registration of students; namely,

(a) Every public declaration of intent by any institution, in any electronic, audio-visual or print or any other media, for admission of students to any course of study shall expressly provide that ragging is totally prohibited in the institution and anyone found guilty of ragging and/or abetting, whether actively or passively, or being a part of a conspiracy to promote ragging, is liable to be punished in accordance with these Regulations as well as under the provisions of any penal law for the time being in force.

(b) The brochure of admission/instruction booklet or the prospectus, whether in print or electronic format, shall prominently print these Regulations in full.

Provided that the institution shall also draw attention to any law concerning ragging and its consequences, as many be applicable to the institution publishing such brochure of admission/instruction booklet or the prospectus.

Provided further that the telephone numbers of the Anti-Ragging Helpline and all the important functionaries in the institution, including but not limited to the Head of the institution, faculty members, members of the Anti-Ragging Committees and Anti-Ragging Squads, District and Sub-Divisional authorities, Wardens of hostels and other functionaries or authorities where relevant, shall be published in the brochure of admission/instruction booklet or the prospectus.

(c) Where an institution is affiliated to a University and publishes a brochure of admission/instruction booklet or a prospectus, the affiliating University shall ensure that the affiliated institution shall comply with the provisions of clause (a) and clause (b) of Regulation 6.1 of these Regulations.

(d) The application form for admission, enrolment or registration shall contain an affidavit, mandatorily in English and in Hindi and /or in one of the regional languages known to the applicant, as provided in the English language in Annexure I to these Regulations, to be filled up and signed by the applicant to the effect that he/she had read and understood the provisions of these Regulations as well as the provisions of any other law for the time being in force, and is aware of the prohibition of ragging and the punishments prescribed, both under penal laws as well as under these Regulations and also affirm to the effect that he/she has not been expelled and/or debarred by any institution and further aver that he/she would he/she would not indulge, actively or passively, in the act or abet the act of ragging and if found guilty of ragging and/or abetting ragging, is liable to be proceeded against under these Regulations or under any penal law or any other law for the time being in force and such action would include but is not limited to debarment or expulsion of such student.

(e) The application form for admission, enrolment or registration shall contain an affidavit, mandatorily in English and in Hindi and/or in one of the regional languages known to the parents/guardians of the applicant, as provided in the English language in Annexure I to these Regulations, to be filled up and signed by the parents/guardians of the applicant to the effect that he/she has read and understood the provisions of these Regulations as well as the provisions of any other law for the time being in force, and is aware of the prohibition of ragging and the punishments prescribed, both under penal laws as well as under these Regulations and also affirm to the effect that his/her ward has not been expelled and/or debarred by any institution and further aver that his/her ward would not indulge, actively or passively, in the act or abet the act of ragging and if found guilty of ragging and/or abetting ragging his/her ward is liable to be proceeded against under these Regulations or under any penal law or any other law for the time being in force and such action would include but is not limited to debarment or expulsion of his/her ward.

(f) The application for admission shall be accompanied by a document in the form of, or annexed to, the School Leaving Certificate/Transfer Certificated/ Migration Certificate/Character Certificate reporting on the inter – personal/ social behavioural pattern of the applicant, to be issued by the school or institution last attended by the applicant, so that the institution can thereafter keep watch on the applicant, if admitted, whose behavior has been commented in such document.

(g) A student seeking admission to a hostel forming part of the institution, or seeking to reside in any temporary premises not forming part of the institution, including a private commercially managed lodge or hostel, shall have to submit additional affidavits countersigned by his/her parents/ guardians in the from prescribed in Annexure I and Annexure II to these Regulations respectively along with his/her application.

(h) Before the commencement of the academic session in any institution, the Head of the Institution shall convene and address a meeting of various functionaries/agencies, such as Hostel Wardens, representatives of students parents/guardians, faculty, district administration including the police, to discuss the measures to be taken to prevent ragging in the institution and steps to be taken to identify those indulging in or abetting ragging and punish them.

(i) The institution shall, to make the community at large and the students in particular aware of the dehumanizing effect of ragging, and the approach of the institution towards those indulging in ragging, prominently display posters depicting the provisions of penal law applicable to incidents of ragging, and the provisions of these Regulations and also any other law for the time being in force, and the punishments thereof, shall be prominently displayed on Notice Boards of all departments, hostels and other buildings as well as at places, where students normally gather and at places, known to be vulnerable to occurrences of ragging incidents.

(j) The institution shall request the media to give adequate publicity to the law prohibiting ragging and the negative aspects of ragging and the institution's resolve to ban ragging and punish those found guilty without fear or favour.

(k) The institution shall identify, properly illuminate and keep a close watch on all locations known to be vulnerable to occurrences of ragging incidents.

(l) The institution shall tighten security in its premises, especially at vulnerable places and intense policing by Anti-Ragging Squad, referred to in these Regulations volunteers, if any, shall be resorted to at such points at odd hours during the first few months of the academic session.

(m) The institution shall utilize the vacation period before the start of the new academic year to launch a publicity campaign against ragging through posters, leaflets and such other means, as may be desirable or required, to promote the objectives of these Regulations.

(n) The faculties/departments/units of the institution shall have induction arrangements, including those which anticipate, identify and plan to meet any special need of any specific section of students, in place well in advance of the beginning of the academic year with an aim to promote the objectives of this Regulation.

(o) Every institution shall engage or seek the assistance of professional counsellors before the commencement of the academic session, to be available when required by the institution, for the purposes of offering counselling to freshers and to other students after the commencement of the academic year.

(p) The head of the institution shall provide information to the local police and local authorities, the details of every privately commercially managed hostels or lodges used for residential purposes by students enrolled in the institution and the head of the institution shall also ensure that the Anti-Ragging Squad shall ensure vigil in such locations to prevent the occurrences of ragging therein.

6.2 An institution shall, on admission or enrolment or registration of students, take the following steps, namely:

(a) Every fresh student admitted to institution shall be given a printed leaflet detailing to whom he/she has to turn to for help and guidance for various purposes including addresses and telephone number, so as to enable the student to contact the concerned person at any time, if and when required, of the Anti-Ragging Helpline referred to in these Regulations, Wardens, Head of the institution, all members of the Anti-Ragging Squads and Committees, relevant district and police authorities.

(b) The institution, through the leaflet specified in clause (a) of Regulation 6.2 of these Regulation shall explain to the freshers, the arrangements made for their induction and orientation which promote efficient and effective means of integrating them fully as students with those already admitted the institution in earlier years.

(c) The leaflet specified in clause (a) of Regulations 6.2 of these Regulations shall inform the fresher's about their rights as *bona fide* students of the institution and clearly instructing them that they should desist from doing anything, with or against their will, even if ordered to by the seniors students, and that any attempt of ragging shall be promptly reported to the Anti-ragging Squad or to the Warden or to the Head of the institution, as the case may be.

(d) The leaflet specified in clause (a) of Regulation 6.2 of these Regulations shall contain a calendar of events and activates laid down by institution to facilitate and complement familiarization of fresher's with the academic environments of the institution.

(e) The institution shall, on the arrival of senior students after the first week or after the second week, as the case may be, schedule orientation programmers as follows, namely; (I) joint sensitization programme and counselling of both freshers and senior students by a professional counsellor, referred to in clause (o) of Regulation 6.1 of these Regulations; (ii) joint orientation programme of freshers and seniors to be addressed by the Head of the institution and the anti-ragging committee; (iii) organization on a large scale of cultural, sports and other activities to provide a platform for the freshers and seniors to interact in the presence of faculty members; (iv) in the hostel, the warden should address all students; and may request two junior colleagues from the college faculty to assist the warden by becoming resident tutors for a temporary duration. (v) as far as possible faculty members should dine with the hostel residents in their respective hostels to instill a feeling of confidence among the fresher's.

(f) The institution shall set up appropriate Committees, including the course-in-charge, student advisor, Wardens and some senior students as its members, to actively monitor, promote and regulate healthy interaction between the freshers, junior students and senior students.

(g) Freshers or any other student(s), whether being victims, or witnesses, in any incident of ragging, shall be encouraged to report such occurrence, and the identity of such informants shall be protected and shall not be subject to any adverse consequence only for the reason for having reported such incidents.

(h) Each batch of freshers, on arrival at the institution, shall be divided into small groups and each such group shall be assigned to a member of the faculty, who shall interact individually with each member of the group every day for ascertaining the problems or difficulties, if any, faced by the fresher in the institution and shall extend necessary help to the fresher in overcoming the same.

(i) It shall be the responsibility of the member of the faculty assigned to the group of freshers, to co-ordinate with the Wardens of the hostels and to make surprise visits to the rooms in such hostels, where a member or members of the group are lodged; and such member of faculty shall maintain a diary of his/her interaction with the freshers under his/her charge.

(j) Fresher's shall be lodged, as far as many be, in a separate block, and where such facilities are not available, the institution shall ensure that access of seniors to accommodation allotted to fresher's is strictly monitored by wardens, security guards and other staff of the institution.

(k) A round the clock vigil against ragging in the hostel premises, in order to prevent ragging in the hostels after the classes are over, shall be ensured by the institution.

(l) It shall be the responsibility of the parents/guardians of freshers to promptly bring any instance of ragging to the notice of the Head of the Institution.

(m) Every student studying in the institution and his/her parents/guardians shall provide the specific affidavits required under clauses (d), (e) and (g) of Regulation 6.1 of these Regulations at the time of admission or registration, as the case may be, during each academic year.

(n) Every institution shall obtain the affidavit from every student as referred to above in clause (m) of Regulation 6.2 and maintain a proper record of the same and to ensure its safe upkeep thereof, including maintaining the copies of the affidavit in an electronic form, to be accessed easily when required either by the Commission or any of the Councils or by the institution or by the affiliating University or by any other person or organization authorized to do so.

(o) Every student at the time of his/her registration shall inform the institution about his/her place of residence while pursuing the course of study, and in case the student has not decided his/her place of residence or intends to change the same, the details of his place of residence shall be provided immediately on deciding the same; and specifically in regard to a private commercially managed lodge or hostel where he/she has taken up residence.

(p) The Head of the institution shall, on the basis of the information provided by the student under clause (o) of Regulation 6.2, apportion sectors to be assigned to members of the faculty, so that such member of faculty can maintain vigil and report any incident of ragging outside the campus or en route while commuting to the institution using any means of transportation of students, whether public or private.

(q) The Head of institution shall, at the end of each academic year, send a letter to the parents/guardians of the students who are completing their first year in the institution, informing them about these Regulations and any law for the time being in force prohibiting ragging and the punishment thereof as well as punishment prescribed under the penal laws, and appealing to them to impress upon their wards to desist from indulging in ragging on their return to the institution at the beginning of the academic session next.

6.3 Every institution shall constitute the following bodies; namely:

(a) Every institution shall constitute a Committee to be known as the Anti-Ragging Committee to be nominated and headed by the Head of the institution, and consisting of representatives of civil and police administration, local media, Non-Governmental Organizations involved in youth activities, representatives of faculty members, representatives of parents, representatives of students belonging to the freshers category as well as senior students, non-teaching staff; and shall have a diverse mix of membership in terms of levels as well as gender.

(b) It shall be the duty of the Anti-Ragging Committee to ensure compliance with the provisions of these Regulations as well as the provisions of any law for the time being in force concerning ragging; and also to monitor and oversee the performance of the Anti-Ragging Squad in prevention of ragging in the institution.

(c) Every institution shall also constitute a smaller body to be known as the Anti - Ragging Squad to be nominated by the Head of the Institution with such representation as may be considered necessary for maintaining vigil, oversight and patrolling functions and shall remain mobile, alert and active at all times.

Provided that the Anti-Ragging Squad shall have representation of various members of the campus community and shall have no outside representation.

(d) It shall be the duty of the Anti-Ragging Squad to be called upon to make surprise raids on hostels, and other places vulnerable to incidents of, and having the potential of, ragging and shall be empowered to inspect such places.

(e) It shall be the duty of the Anti-Ragging Squad to conduct an on the spot enquiry into any incident of ragging referred to it by the Head of the institution or any member of the faculty or any member of the staff or any student or any parent or guardian or any employee of a service provider or by any other person, as the case may be; and the enquiry report along with recommendations shall be submitted to the Anti-Ragging Committee for action under clause (a) of Regulation 9.1.

Provided that the Anti-Ragging Squad shall conduct such enquiry observing a fair and transparent procedure and the principles of natural justice and after giving adequate opportunity to the student or students accused of ragging and other witness to place before it the facts, documents and views concerning the incident of ragging, and considering such other relevant information as may be required.

(f) Every institution shall, at the end of each academic year, in order to promote the objectives of these Regulation, constitute a Mentoring cell consisting of students volunteering to be Mentors for fresher's, in the succeeding academic year; and there shall be as many levels or tiers of Mentor as the number of batches in the institution, at the rate of one Mentor for six fresher's and one Mentor of a higher level for six Mentors of the lower level.

(g) Every University shall constitute a body to be known as Monitoring cell on Ragging, which shall coordinate with the affiliated colleges and institutions under the domain of the University to achieve the objectives of these Regulations; and the Monitoring cell shall call for reports from the Heads of institutions in regard to the activities of the Anti-Ragging Committees, Anti-Ragging squads , and the Mentoring cells at the institutions, and it shall also keep itself abreast of the decisions of the District level Anti-Ragging Committee headed by the District Magistrate.

(h) The Monitoring cell shall also review the efforts made by institutions to publicize anti-ragging measures, soliciting of affidavits from parents/ guardians and from students, each academic year, to abstain from ragging activities or willingness to be penalized for violations; and shall function as the prime mover for initiating action on the part of the appropriate authorities of the University for amending the Statutes or Ordinances or Bye-laws to facilitate the implementation of anti-ragging measures at the level of the institution .

6.4 Every institution shall take the following other measures, namely;

(a) Each hostel or a place where groups of students reside, forming part of the institution, shall have a full-time Warden, to be appointed by the institution as per the eligibility criteria laid down for the post reflecting both the command and control aspects of maintaining discipline and preventing incidents of ragging within the hostel, as well as the softer skills of counselling and communicating with the youth outside the class-room situation; and who shall reside within the hostel, or at the very least, in the close vicinity thereof.

(b) The Warden shall be accessible at all hours and be available on telephone and other modes of communication, and for the purpose the Warden shall be provided with a mobile phone by the institution, the number of which shall be publicized among all students residing in the hostel.

(c) The institution shall review and suitably enhance the powers of Warden; and the security personnel posted in hostels shall be under the direct control of the Warden and their performance shall be assessed by them.

(d) The professional counsellors referred to under clause (o) of Regulation 6.1 of these Regulation shall, at the time of admission, counsel fresher's and/or any other student(s) desiring counselling , in order to prepare them for the life ahead, particularly in regard to the life in hostels and to the extent possible, also involve parents and teacher in the counselling sessions.

(e) The institution shall undertake measures for extensive publicity against ragging by means of audio-visual aids, counselling sessions, workshops, painting and design competitions among students and such other measures, as it may deem fit.

(f) In order to enable a student or any person to communicate with the Anti-Ragging Helpline, every institution shall permit unrestricted access to mobile phones and public phones in hostels and campuses, other than in class-rooms, seminar halls, library, and in such other places that the institution may deem it necessary to restrict the use of phones.

(g) The faculty of the institution and its non-teaching staff, which includes but is not limited to the administrative staff, contract employees, security guards and employees of service providers providing services within the institution, shall be sensitized towards the ills of ragging, its prevention and the consequences there of.

(h) The institution shall obtain an undertaking from every employee of the institution including all teaching and non-teaching members of staff, contract labour employed in the premises either for running canteen or as watch and ward staff or for cleaning or maintenance of the buildings/lawns and employees of service providers providing services within the institution, that he/she would report promptly any case of ragging which comes to his/her notice.

(i) The institution shall make a provision in the service rules of its employees for issuing certificates of appreciation to such members of the staff who report incidents of ragging, which will form part of their service record.

(j) The institution shall give necessary instructions to employees of the canteens and messing, whether that of the institution or that of a service provider providing this services, or their employers, as the case may be, to keep a strict vigil in the area of their work and to report the incidents of ragging to the Head of the institution or members of the Anti-Ragging Squad or members of the anti-Ragging Committee or the Wardens, as may be required.

(k) All Universities awarding a degree in education at any level shall be required to ensure that institutions imparting instruction in such courses or conducting training programme for teachers include inputs relating to anti-ragging and the appreciation of the relevant human rights, as well as inputs on topics regarding sensitization against corporal punishments and checking of bullying amongst students, so that every teacher is equipped to handle at least the rudiments of the counselling approach.

(l) Discreet random surveys shall be conducted amongst the fresher every fortnight during the first three months of the academic year to verify and cross-check whether the institution is indeed free of ragging or not and for the purpose the institution may design its own methodology of conducting such surveys.

(m) The institution shall cause to have an entry, apart from those relating to general conduct and behavior, made in the Migration/Transfer Certificate issued to the student while leaving the institution, as to whether the student has been punished for committing or abetting an act of ragging, as also whether the student has displayed persistent violent or aggressive behavior or any inclination to harm others, during his course of study in the institution.

(n) Notwithstanding anything contained in these Regulations with regard to obligations and responsibilities pertaining to the authorities or members of bodies prescribed above, it shall be the general collective responsibility of all levels and sections of authorities or functionaries including members of the faculty and employees of the institution, whether regular or temporary, and employees of service providers providing service within the institution, to prevent or to act promptly against the occurrence of ragging or any incident of ragging which comes to their notice.

(o) The Heads of institutions affiliated to a University or a constituent of the University, as the case may be, shall, during the first three months of an academic year, submit a weekly report on the status of compliance with Anti-Ragging measures under these Regulations, and a monthly report on such status thereafter, to the Vice-Chancellor of the University to which the institution is affiliated to or recognized by.

(p) The Vice-Chancellor of each University shall submit fortnightly reports of the University, including those of the Monitoring cell on Ragging in case of an affiliating university, to the State Level Monitoring cell.

7. Action to be taken by the Head of the institution.—On receipt of the recommendation of the Anti-Ragging squad or on receipt of any information concerning any reported incident of ragging, the Head of institution shall immediately determine if a case under the penal laws is made out and if so, either on his own or through a member of the Anti-Ragging Committee authorized by him in this behalf, proceed to file a First Information Report (FIR), within twenty four hours of receipt of such information or recommendation, with the police and local authorities, under the appropriate penal provisions relating to one or more of the following, namely;

i. Abetment to ragging;
ii. Criminal conspiracy to rag;
iii. Unlawful assembly and rioting while ragging;
iv. Public nuisance created during ragging;
v. Violation of decency and morals through ragging;
vi. Injury to body, causing hurt or grievous hurt;
vii. Wrongful Restraint;
viii. Wrongful confinement ;
ix. Use of criminal force;
x. Assault as well as sexual offences or unnatural offences;
xi. Extortion;
xii. Criminal trespass;
xiii. Offences against property;
xiv. Criminal intimidation;
xv. Attempts to commit any or all of the above mentioned offences against the victim(s);
xvi. Threat to commit any or all of the above mentioned offences against the victim(s);
xvii. Physical or psychological humiliation;
xviii. All other offences following from the definition of "Ragging".

Provided that the Head of the institution shall forthwith report the occurrence of the incident of ragging to the District Level Anti-Ragging Committee and the Nodal officer of the affiliating University, if the institution is an affiliated institution.

Provided further that the institution shall also continue with its own enquiry initiated under clause 9 of these Regulations and other measures without waiting for action on the part of the police/local authorities and such remedial action shall be initiated and completed immediately and in no case later than a period of seven days of the reported occurrence of the incident of ragging.

8. Duties and Responsibilities of the Commission and the Councils:.—(8.1) The Commission shall, with regard to providing facilitating communication of information regarding incidents of ragging in any institution, take the following steps, namely;

(a) The Commission shall establish, fund and operate, a toll-free Anti-Ragging Helpline, operational round the clock, which could be accessed by students in distress owing to ragging related incidents.

(b) Any distress message received at the Anti-Ragging Helpline shall be simultaneously relayed to the Head of the Institution, the Warden of the Hostels, the Nodal Officer of the affiliating University, if the incident reported has taken place in an institution affiliated to a University, the concerned District authorities and if so required, the District Magistrate, and the Superintendent of Police, and shall also be web enabled so as to be in the public domain simultaneously for the media and citizens to access it.

(c) The Head of the institution shall be obliged to act immediately in response to the information received from the Anti-Ragging Helpline as at sub-Clause (b) of this clause.

(d) The telephone numbers of the Anti-Ragging Helpline and all the important functionaries in every institution, Heads of institutions, faculty members, members of the anti-ragging committees and anti-ragging squads, district and sub-divisional authorities and State authorities, Wardens of hostels, and other functionaries or authorities where relevant, shall be widely disseminated for access or to seek help in emergencies.

(e) The Commission shall maintain an appropriate data base to be created out of affidavits affirmed by each student and his/her parents/guardians and stored electronically by the institution, either on its or through an agency to be designated by it; and such database shall also function as a record of ragging complaints received, and the status of the action taken thereon.

(f) The Commission shall make available the database to a non-governmental agency to be nominated by the Central Government, to build confidence in the public and also to provide information of non compliance with these Regulations to the Councils and to such bodies as may be authorized by the Commission or by the Central Government.

8.2 The Commission shall take the following regulatory steps, namely;

(a) The Commission shall make it mandatory for the institutions to incorporate in their prospectus, the directions of the Central Government or the State Level Monitoring Committee with regard to prohibition and consequences of ragging, and that non-compliance with these Regulations and directions so provided, shall be considered as lowering of academic standards by the institution, therefore making it liable for appropriate action.

(b) The Commission shall verify that the institutions strictly comply with the requirement of getting the affidavits from the students and their parents/guardians as envisaged under these Regulations.

(c) The Commission shall include a specific condition in the Utilization Certificate, in respect of any financial assistance or grants in-aid to any institution under any of the general or special schemes of the Commission, that the institution has complied with the anti-ragging measures.

(d) Any incident of ragging in an institution shall adversely affect its accreditation, ranking or grading by NAAC or by any other authorized accreditation agencies while assessing the institution for accreditation, ranking or grading purposes.

(e) The Commission may accord priority in financial grants-in-aid to those institutions, otherwise eligible to receive grants under section 12B of the Act, which report a blemishless record in terms of there being no reported incident of ragging.

(f) The Commission shall constitute an Inter-Council Committee, consisting of representatives of the various Councils, the Non-Governmental agency responsible for monitoring the database maintained by the Commission under clause (g) of Regulation 8.1 and such other bodies in higher education, to co-ordinate and monitor the anti-ragging measures in institutions across the country and to make recommendations from time to time; and shall meet at least once in six months each year.

(g) The Commission shall institute an Anti-Ragging Cell within the Commission as an institutional mechanism to provide secretarial support for collection of information and monitoring, and to coordinate with the State Level Monitoring Cell and University level Committees for effective implementation of anti-ragging measures, and the Cell shall also coordinate with the Non-Governmental agency responsible for monitoring the database maintained by the Commission appointed under clause (g) of Regulation 8.1.

9. Administrative action in the event of ragging.—(9.1) The institution shall punish a student found guilty of ragging after following the procedure and in the manner prescribed herein under:

(a) The Anti-Ragging Committee of the institution shall take an appropriated decision, in regard to punishment or otherwise, depending on the facts of each incident of ragging and nature and gravity of the incident of ragging established in the recommendations of the Anti-Ragging Squad.

(b) The Anti-Ragging Committee may, depending on the nature and gravity of the guilt established by the Anti-Ragging Squad, award, to those found guilty, one or more of the following punishments, namely;

i. Suspension from attending classes and academic privileges.

ii. Withholding/Withdrawing scholarship/fellowship and other benefits.

iii. Debarring from appearing in any test/examination or other evaluation process.

iv. Withholding results.

v. Debarring from representing the institution in any regional, national or international meet, tournament, youth festival, etc.

vi. Suspension/expulsion from the hostel.

vii. Cancellation of admission.

viii. Rustication from the institution for period ranging from one to four semesters.

ix. Expulsion from the institution and consequent debarring from admission to any other institution for a specified period.

Provided that where the persons committing or abetting the act of ragging are not identifies, the institution shall resort to collective punishment.

(c) An appeal against the order of punishment by the Anti-Ragging Committee shall lie,

i. in case of an order of an institution, affiliated to or constituent part, of a University, to the Vice-Chancellor of the University;

ii. in case of an order of a University, to its Chancellor.

iii. in case of an institution of national importance created by an Act of Parliament, to the Chairman or Chancellor of the institution, as the case may be.

9.2 Where an institution being constituent of, affiliated to or recognized by a University, fails to comply with any of the provisions of these Regulations or fails to curb ragging effectively, such University may take any one or more of the following actions, namely;

(i) Withdrawal of affiliation/recognition or other privileges conferred

(ii) Prohibiting such institution from presenting any student or student then undergoing any programme of study therein for the award of any degree/diploma of the university.

Provided that where an institution is prohibited from presenting its student or students, the Commission shall make suitable arrangements for the other students so as to ensure that such students are able to pursue their academic studies.

(iii) Withholding grants allocated to it by the university, if any

(iv) Withholding any grants channelized through the university the university to the institution.

(v) Any other appropriate penalty within the powers of the university.

9.3 Where in the opinion of the appointing authority, a lapse is attributable to any member of the faulty or staff of the institution, in the matter of reporting or taking prompt action to prevent an incident of ragging or who display an apathetic or insensitive attitude towards complaints of ragging, or who fail to take timely steps, whether required under these Regulations or otherwise, to prevent an incident or incidents of ragging, then such authority shall initiate departmental disciplinary action, in accordance with the prescribed procedure of the institution, against such member of the faulty or staff.

Provided that where such lapse is attributable to the Head of the institution, the authority designated to appoint such Head shall take such departmental disciplinary action; and such action shall be without prejudice to any action that may be taken under the penal laws for abetment of ragging for failure to take timely steps in the prevention of ragging or punishing any student found guilty of ragging.

9.4 The Commission shall, in respect of any institution that fails to take adequate steps to prevent ragging or fails to act in accordance with these Regulations or fails to punish perpetrators or incidents of ragging suitably, take one of more of the following measures, namely;

i. Withdrawal of declaration of fitness to receive grants under section 12B of the Act.

ii. Withholding any grant allocated.

iii. Declaring the institution ineligible for consideration for any assistance under any of the general or special assistance programmes of the Commission.

iv. Informing the general public, including potential candidates for admission, through a notice displayed prominently in the newspapers or other suitable media and posted on the website of the Commission, declaring that the institution does not possess the minimum academic standards.

v. Taking such other action within its powers as it may deem fit and impose such other penalties as may be provided in the Act for such duration of time as the institution complies with the provisions of these Regulations.

Provided that the action taken under this clause by the Commission against any institution shall be shared with all Councils.

Sd/-

(Dr. R. K. Chauhan)

Secretary

(b) All India Council for Technical Education

New Delhi-2009

Sub: Prevention and prohibition of Ragging in technical Institutions, Universities including Deemed to be Universities imparting technical education.

F.No.37-3/Legal/AICTE/2009 – In exercise of the powers conferred under Section 23 read with Section 10(b), (g), (p) and (q) of AICTE Act, 1987, the All India Council for Technical Education, hereby makes the following Regulations:-

1. Short title and commencement.—(i) These Regulations may be called the All India Council for Technical Education (Prevention and Prohibition of Ragging in Technical Institutions, Universities including Deemed to be Universities imparting technical education) Regulations 2009.

(ii) They shall come into force on the date of the notification.

2. Objectives.—In view of the directions of the Hon'ble Supreme Court in SLP No. 24295 of 2006 dated 16-05-2007 and in Civil Appeal number 887 of 2009, dated 08-05-2009 to prohibit, prevent and eliminate the scourge of ragging including any conduct by any student or students whether by words spoken or written or by an act which has the effect of teasing, treating or handling with rudeness a fresher or any other student, or indulging in rowdy or undisciplined activities by any student or students which causes or is likely to cause annoyance, hardship or psychological harm or to raise fear or apprehension thereof in any fresher or any other student or asking any student to do any act which such student will not in the ordinary course do and which has the effect of causing or generating a sense of shame, or torment or embarrassment so as to adversely affect the physique or psyche of such fresher or any other student, with or without an intent to derive a sadistic pleasure or showing off power, authority or superiority by a student over any fresher or any other student, in all higher education institutions in the country, and thereby, to provide for the healthy development, physically and psychologically, of all students, the All India Council for Technical Education, (AICTE) brings forth these Regulations.

3. Definitions.—(a) "Act" means the All India Council for Technical Education Act 1987 (52 of 1987);

(b) "Technical Institution" means an institution of Government, Government Aided and Private (self financing) conducting the courses/programmes in the field of technical education, training and research in Engineering, Technology including MCA, Architecture, Town Planning, Management, Pharmacy, Hotel Management & Catering Technology, Applied Arts & Crafts and such other programmes and areas as notified by the Council from time to time;

(c) 'University" means a University defined under clause (f) of section 2 of the University Grants Commission Act, 1956 and includes an institution deemed to be a University under section 3 of that Act.

(d) "Academic year" means the period from the commencement of admission of students in any course of study in the institution up to the completion of academic requirements for that particular year.

(e) "Head of the institution" means the Vice-Chancellor in case of a university or a deemed to be university, the Principal or the Director or such other designation as the executive head of the institution or the college is referred.

(f) "Fresher" means a student who has been admitted to an institution and who is undergoing his/her first year of study in such institution.

(g) Words and expressions used and not defined herein but defined in the Act or in the General Clauses Act, 1887, shall have the meanings respectively assigned to them in the Act or in the General Clauses Act, 1887, as the case may be. And

(h) All other words and expressions used herein and not defined but defined in the All India Council for Technical Education Act, 1987 (52 of 1987), shall have the meanings respectively assigned to them in the said Act;

4. What constitutes Ragging.—Ragging constitutes one or more of any of the following acts:

a. any conduct by any student or students whether by words spoken or written or by an act which has the effect of teasing, treating or handling with rudeness a fresher or any other student;

b. indulging in rowdy or undisciplined activities by any student or students which causes or is likely to cause annoyance, hardship, physical or psychological harm or to raise fear or apprehension thereof in any fresher or any other student;

c. asking any student to do any act which such student will not in the ordinary course do and which has the effect of causing or generating a sense of shame, or torment or embarrassment so as to adversely affect the physique or psyche of such fresher or any other student;

d. any act by a senior student that prevents, disrupts or disturbs the regular academic activity of any other student or a fresher;

e. exploiting the services of a fresher or any other student for completing the academic tasks assigned to an individual or a group of students.

f. any act of financial extortion or forceful expenditure burden put on a fresher or any other student by students;

g. any act of physical abuse including all variants of it: sexual abuse, homosexual assaults, stripping, forcing obscene and lewd acts, gestures, causing bodily harm or any other danger to health or person;

h. any act or abuse by spoken words, e-mails, posts, public insults which would also include deriving perverted pleasure, vicarious or sadistic thrill from actively or passively participating in the discomfiture to fresher or any other student;

i. any act that affects the mental health and self-confidence of a fresher or any other student with or without an intent to derive a sadistic pleasure or showing off power, authority or superiority by a student over any fresher or any other student.

5. Measures for prevention of ragging.—It shall be mandatory for every technical Institution, University, deemed to be University imparting technical education to take following measures for prevention of ragging at such institutions.

1. The advertisement issued for admission by a technical institution, University including Deemed to be University concerned and/or the admission authority/ affiliating University/State Government/UT/Central Government as the case may be, shall clearly mention that ragging is totally banned and anyone found guilty of ragging and/or abetting ragging is liable to be punished.
2. The 'Prospectus' and other admission related documents shall contain directions of the Supreme Court Affiliating University/admission Authority/ State Government/Central Government shall make it mandatory for the institutions under their jurisdiction to compulsorily incorporate such

information in their 'Prospectus' These Regulations shall be printed in the brochure of admission/instruction booklet for candidates.

3. The application form for admission/enrolment shall have a printed affidavit, preferably both in English and Hindi and/or in one of the regional languages. The affidavit should be filled up and signed by the candidate to the effect that he/she is aware of the law regarding prohibition of ragging as well as the punishments, and that he/she, if found guilty of the offence of ragging and/or abetting ragging, is liable to be punished appropriately.
4. The application form shall also contain a printed affidavit, preferably both in English and Hindi and/or in one of the regional languages and the affidavit should be signed by the parent/guardian of the applicant to the effect that he/she is also aware of the law in this regard and agrees to abide by the punishment meted out to his/her ward in case the latter is found guilty of ragging and/or abetting ragging.
5. The application for admission shall be accompanied by a document along with the School Leaving Certificate/Character Certificate which shall include a report on the behavioral patter of the applicant, so that the institution can thereafter keep intense watch upon the student who has a negative entry in this regard.
6. A student seeking admission to the hostel shall have to submit another affidavit along with his/her application for hostel accommodation that he/she is also aware of the law in this regard and agrees to abide by the punishments meted out if he/she is found guilty of ragging and/or abetting ragging.
7. Every technical institution, University including Deemed to be University imparting technical education shall maintain a proper record of the affidavits obtained to ensure its safe up keep thereof, including digital copies of the affidavits and such digital copy should be made available to the AICTE or to an Agency identified/nominated by AICTE.
8. The AICTE or an Agency identified/nominated for the purpose and affiliating Universities and Directorate of Technical Education of the concerned State Government/UT shall maintain an appropriate data base of the affidavits in the digital form obtained from every student at the time of admission to the technical institutions, Universities including Deemed to be Universities imparting technical education.
9. Each batch of freshers should be divided into small groups and each such group shall be assigned to a member of staff. Such staff member should interact individually with each member of the group on daily basis to ascertain the problems/difficulties, if any faced by the freshers in the Institution and extend necessary help.
10. Incase of freshers admitted to a Hostel it shall be the responsibility of the teacher in-charge of the group to co-ordinate with the warden of the Hostel and to make surprise visits to the rooms in the hostel where the members of the group are lodged. Freshers should be lodged in a separate hostel block wherever possible and where such facilities are not available, the college/ institution shall ensure that seniors' access to freshers' accommodation is strictly monitored by wardens, Security Guards and Staff.
11. Every institution should engage or seek the assistance of professional counselors at the time of admissions to counsel 'freshers' in order to prepare

them for the life ahead, particularly for adjusting to the life in hostels. At the commencement of the academic session the Head of the technical Institution, University including Deemed to be University imparting technical education shall convene and address a meeting of various functionaries/agencies, like Wardens, representatives of students, parents/guardians, faculty, district administration including police, to discuss the measures to be taken to prevent ragging and steps to be taken to identify the offenders and punish them suitably.

12. Every fresher admitted to the technical Institution, University including Deemed to be University imparting technical education shall be given a printed information booklet detailing when and whom he/she has to turn to for help and guidance for various purposes (including Wardens, Head of the institution, members of the anti–ragging committee, relevant district and police authorities), addresses and telephone numbers of such persons/ authorities, etc.
13. The technical institutions, University including Deemed to be University imparting technical education through the information booklet mentioned above shall explain to the new entrants the arrangements for their induction and orientation which promote efficient and effective means of integrating them fully as students.
14. The information booklet mentioned above shall also tell the freshers about their rights as bona fide students and clearly instructing them that they should desist from doing anything against their will even if ordered by the seniors, and that they have nothing to fear as the institution cares for them and shall not tolerate any atrocities against them.
15. The information booklet mentioned above shall contain a calendar of events and activities laid down by the institution to facilitate and complement familiarization of juniors with the academic environment of the institution.
16. To make the community at large and the students in particular aware of the dehumanizing effect of ragging, and the approach of the institution towards those indulging in ragging, big posters (preferably with different colors for the provisions of law, punishments, etc.) shall be prominently displayed on all Notice Boards of all departments, hostels and other buildings as well as at vulnerable places Some of such posters shall be of permanent nature in certain vulnerable places.
17. The technical Institution, University including Deemed to be University imparting technical education shall request the media to give adequate publicity to the law prohibiting ragging and the negative aspects of ragging and the institution resolve to ban ragging and punish those found guilty without fear or favor.
18. The technical Institution, University including Deemed to be University imparting technical education shall identify, properly illuminate and man all vulnerable locations.
19. The technical Institution, University including Deemed to be University imparting technical education shall tighten security in its premises, especially at the vulnerable places. If necessary, intense policing shall be resorted to at such points at odd hours during the early months of the academic session.
20. The technical Institution, University including Deemed to be University imparting technical education shall utilize the vacation period before the start

of the new academic year to launch wide publicity campaign against ragging through posters, information booklets, seminars, street plays, etc.

21. The faculties/departments/units of the technical Institution, University including Deemed to be University imparting technical education shall have induction arrangements (including those which anticipate, identify and plan to meet any special needs of any specific section of students) in place well in advance of the beginning of the academic year with a clear sense of the main aims and objectives of the induction process.

22. Mobile Phones and other communication devices may be permitted in residential areas including hostels to provide access to the students particularly freshers, to reach out for help from teachers, parents and Institution authorities.

6. Monitoring mechanism in technical institution, University including Deemed to be University imparting technical education—

(a) **Anti-ragging Committee**: Every institution University including Deemed to be University imparting technical education shall constitute a Committee to be known as the Anti-ragging Committee to be nominated and headed by the Head of the Institution, and consisting of representatives of civil and police administration, local media, Non-Governmental Organizations involved in youth activities, representatives of faculty members, representatives of parents, representatives of students belonging to the freshers' category as well as senior students, non-teaching staff; and shall have a diverse mix of membership in terms of level as well as gender.

(b) It shall be the duty of the Anti-Ragging Committee to ensure compliance with the provisions of these Regulations as well as the provisions of any law for the time being in force concerning ragging; and also to monitor and oversee the performance of the Anti-Ragging Squad in prevention of ragging in the institution.

(c) **Anti-Ragging Squad**: Every institution University including Deemed to be University imparting technical education shall also constitute a smaller body to be known as the Anti-Ragging Squad to be nominated by the Head of the Institution with such representation as may be considered necessary for maintaining vigil, oversight and patrolling functions and shall remain mobile, alert and active at all times. Provided that the Anti-Ragging Squad shall have representation of various members of the campus community and shall have no outside representation.

(d) It shall be the duty of the Anti-Ragging Squad to be called upon to make surprise raids on hostels, and other places vulnerable to incidents and having the potential for ragging and shall be empowered to inspect such places.

(e) It shall also be the duty of the Anti-Ragging Squad to conduct an on-the-spot enquiry into any incidents of ragging referred to it by the Head of the institution or any member of the faculty or any member of the staff or any student or any parent or guardian or any employee of a service provider or by any other person, as the case may be; and the enquiry report along with recommendations shall be submitted to the Anti-Ragging Committee for action. Provided that the Anti-Ragging Squad shall conduct such enquiry observing a fair and transparent procedure and the principles of natural justice and after giving adequate opportunity to the student or students accused of ragging and other witnesses to place before it the facts, documents and views concerning the incidents of ragging, and considerations such other relevant information as may be required.

(f) **Mentoring Cell**: Every institution shall, at the end of each academic year, in order to promote the objectives of these Regulations, constitute a Mentoring Cell consisting of students volunteering to be Mentors for freshers, in the succeeding academic year; and there shall be as many levels or tiers of Mentors as the number of batches in the institution, at the rate of one Mentor for six freshers and one Mentor of a higher level for six Mentors of the lower level.

(g) **Monitoring Cell on Ragging:**—The State Government/UT and the affiliating University shall set up a Monitoring Cell on Ragging to coordinate with the institutions to monitor the activities of the Anti-Ragging Committees, Squads , and Mentoring Cells, regarding compliance with the instructions on conducting orientation programmes, counseling sessions, etc., and regarding the incidents of ragging, the problem faced by wardens and other officials, etc. This Cell shall also review the efforts made by such institutions to publicize anti-ragging measures, cross-verify the receipt of affidavits from candidates/students and their parents/guardians every year, and shall be the prime mover for initiating action by the University authorities to suitably amend the Statutes or Ordinances or Bye-laws to facilitate the implementation of anti ragging measures at the level of the institution.

(h) The Monitoring Cell shall coördinate with institutions, universities including deemed to be universities imparting technical education to achieve the objectives of these Regulations; and the Monitoring Cell shall call for reports from the Heads of institutions in regard to the activities of the Anti-Ragging Committees, Anti-Ragging Squads, and the Mentoring Cells at the institutions, and it shall also keep itself abreast of the decisions of the Anti-Ragging Committees etc.

(i) The Monitoring Cell shall also review the efforts made by institutions to publicize anti-ragging measures, soliciting of affidavits from parents/guardians and from students, each academic year, to abstain from ragging activities or willingness to be penalized for violation; and shall function as the prime mover for initiating action for amending the Statues or Ordinances or Bye-laws to facilitate the implementation of anti-ragging measures at the level of the institution.

7. Action to be taken against the Principal or the Head of the Institution/Faculty Members/Non-Teaching staff of technical institution, Universities including Deemed to be Universities imparting technical education.—(1) The Head of the Institution along with other administrative authorities should take adequate measures for prevention of ragging. Any lapse on the part of these authorities shall make them liable for criminal action for negligence of duty. The technical Institution, University including Deemed to be University imparting technical education should incorporate a clause in their letter of appointment that the Director, Faculty and other administrative Heads should ensure all possible steps for prevention of ragging in the premises of the educational institutions, and that they are liable for action, in case of non-compliance.

(2) The Principal or Head of the Institution/Department shall obtain an affidavit from every employee of the Institution including teaching/non-teaching staff, contract labor employed in the premises either for running canteen or as watch and ward staff or for cleaning or maintenance of the building, lawns etc., that he/she would report promptly any case of ragging which comes to his/her notice. A provision shall be made in the service rules for issuing certificates of appreciation to such members of the staff who report ragging which will form part of their service records.

(3) Departmental enquiries shall be initiated, in addition to penal consequences against such heads of the Institution/Faculty members/non-teaching staff who display an apathetic or insensitive attitude towards complaints of ragging and would not take timely steps in the prevention of ragging and punishing those who rag.

(4) The Principal or the Head of the Institution/Faculty Members/Non-Teaching staff, if found negligent in taking necessary measures for ensuring safety of students and preventing the ragging would be declared unfit for holding any post in any technical institution, University including Deemed to be University imparting technical education.

8. Actions to be taken against students for indulging and abetting ragging in technical institutions Universities including Deemed to be University imparting technical education.—(1) The punishment to be meted out to the persons indulged in ragging has to be exemplary and justifiably harsh to act as a deterrent against recurrence of such incidents.

(2) Every single incident of ragging a First Information Report (FIR) must be filed without exception by the institutional authorities with the local police authorities.

(3) The Anti-Ragging Committee of the institution shall take an appropriate decision, with regard to punishment or otherwise, depending on the facts of each incident of ragging and nature and gravity of the incident of ragging.

(4) (a) Depending upon the nature and gravity of the offence as established the possible punishments for those found guilty of ragging at the institution level shall be any one or any combination of the following:-

(i) Cancellation of admission

(ii) Suspension from attending classes

(iii) Withholding/withdrawing scholarship/fellowship and other benefits

(iv) Debarring from appearing in any test/examination or other evaluation process

(v) Withholding results

(vi) Debarring from representing the institution in any regional, national or international meet, tournament, youth festival, etc.

(vii) Suspension/expulsion from the hostel

(viii) Rustication from the institution for period ranging from 1 to 4 semesters

(ix) Expulsion from the institution and consequent debarring from admission to any other institution.

(x) Collective punishment: when the persons committing or abetting the crime of ragging are not identified, the institution shall resort to collective punishment as a deterrent to ensure community pressure on the potential raggers.

(b) An appeal against the order of punishment by the Anti-Ragging Committee shall lie,

i. In case of an order of an institution, affiliated to or constituent part, of the University, to the Vice-Chancellor of the University;

ii. In case of an order of a University, to its Chancellor.

iii. In case of an institution of national importance created by an Act of Parliament, to the Chairman or Chancellor of the institution, as the case may be.

(5) The institutional authorities shall intimate the incidents of ragging occurred in their premises along with actions taken to the Council form time to time.

9. Action to be taken against the technical Institution, University including Deemed to be University imparting technical education which fail to take measures for prevention of ragging.—(1) Role of the concerned technical institutions, Universities including Deemed to be Universities imparting teehnical education shall be open to scrutiny for the purpose of finding out whether they have taken effective steps for preventing ragging and action taken against provision indulged and/or abetting ragging. The Council shall constitute Committees to inspect technical institutions, Universities including Deemed to be Universities imparting technical education to verify the status of anti ragging measures and to investigate specific instances of ragging and take appropriate action.

(2) The technical Institution, University including Deemed to be University imparting technical education should submit an affidavit along with its compliance report submitted to AICTE annually with details of measures taken for prevention of ragging in technical institutions. The Compliance Report should also contain the details of the instances of ragging and action taken against students, and others for indulging and abetting ragging.

(3) All Letters of Approval issued by AICTE such as extension of approval letters, letters issued for additional courses/increase in intake and letters issued for new technical institutions, release of grants, letters of approval issued to integrated campus, second shift etc., shall contain a specific clause of prevention of ragging.

(4) The AICTE shall, in respect of any institution that fails to take adequate steps to prevent ragging or fails to act in accordance with these Regulations or fails to punish perpetrators or incidents of ragging suitably, take one of more of the following measures, namely;

i. No admission/Withdrawal of approval granted under section 10(k) of AICTE Act.

ii. Withholding any grant allocated.

iii. Declaring the institution ineligible for consideration for any assistance under any of the general or special assistance programmes of the AICTE.

iv. Informing the general public, including potential candidates for admission, through a notice displayed prominently in the newspapers or other suitable media and posted on the website of the AICTE, declaring that the institution does not possess the minimum academic standards.

v. Taking such other action within its powers as it may deem fit and impose such other penalties as may be provided in the Act for such duration of time as the institution complies with the provisions of these Regulations.

(5) As regards the Universities including Deemed to be Universities imparting technical education the actions proposed to be taken such as stopping release of grants, withdrawal of approval/recognition will be sent to University Grants Commission (UGC), Ministry of Human Resource Development (MHRD), Government of India and the concerned State Government/UT. The UGC, MHRD Government of India, and the State Government/UT concerned shall initiate immediate action on the recommendations of the Council.

(10) Duties and Responsibilities of the All India Council for technical Education:—

(a) All India Council for technical Education, or the Central Government or the agency authorized for the purpose shall establish, fund and operate, a toll-free Anti-Ragging Helpline, operational round the clock, which could be accessed by students in distress owing to ragging related incidents.

(b) Any distress message received at the Anti-Ragging Helpline shall be simultaneously relayed to the Head of the Institution, the Warden of the Hostels, the Nodal Officer of the affiliating University, if the incident reported has taken place in an institution affiliated to a University, the concerned District authorities and if so required, the District Magistrate, and the Superintendent of Police, and shall also be web enabled so as to be in the public domain simultaneously for the media and citizens to access it.

(c) The Head of the institution shall be obliged to act immediately in response to the information received from the Anti-Ragging Helpline as at sub-clause (b) of this clause.

(d) The telephone numbers of the Anti-Ragging Helpline and all the important functionaries in every institution, Heads of institutions, faculty members, members of the anti-ragging committees and anti-ragging squads, district and sub-divisional authorities and State authorities, Wardens of hostels, and other functionaries or authorities where relevant, shall be widely disseminated for access or to seek help in emergencies.

(e) The All India Council for technical Education, the Central Government or the agency authorized for the purpose shall maintain an appropriate data base to be created out of affidavits, affirmed by each student and his/her parents/guardians and stored electronically by the institution; and such database shall also function as a record of ragging complaints received, and the status of the action taken thereon.

(f) The All India Council for technical Education, the Central Government or the agency authorized for the purpose shall make available the database to a non-governmental agency to be nominated by the Central Government, to build confidence in the public and also to provide information of non compliance with these Regulations to the Councils and to such bodies as may be authorized by the All India Council for technical Education/Central Government.

11. The All India Council for technical Education shall take the following regulatory steps, namely.—(a) The All India Council for technical Education shall make it mandatory for the institutions to incorporate in their prospectus, the directions of the Central Government or the State Level Monitoring Committee with regard to prohibition and consequences of ragging, and that non-compliance with these Regulations and directions so provided, shall be considered as lowering of academic standards by the institution, therefore making it liable for appropriate action.

(b) The All India Council for technical Education shall verify that the institutions strictly comply with the requirement of getting the affidavits from the students and their parents/guardians as envisaged under these Regulations.

(c) The All India Council for technical Education shall include a specific condition in the Utilization Certificate, in respect of any financial assistance or grants-in-aid to any institution under any of the general or special schemes of the All India Council for technical Education, that the institution has complied with the anti-ragging measures.

(d) Any incident of ragging in an institution shall adversely affect its accreditation, ranking or grading by National Board of Accreditation or by any other authorised accreditation agencies while assessing the institution for accreditation, ranking or grading purposes.

(e) The All India Council for technical Education shall constitute an Inter-Council Committee, consisting of representatives of the various Councils, the Non-Governmental agency responsible for monitoring the database maintained by the All India Council for technical Education/Central Government and such other bodies in higher education, to coordinate and monitor the anti-ragging measures in institutions across the country and to make recommendations from time to time; and shall meet at least once in six months each year.

(f) The All India Council for technical Education shall institute an Anti-Ragging Cell within the AICTE as an institutional mechanism to provide secretarial support for collection of information and monitoring, and to coordinate with the State Level Monitoring Cells and University Level Committees for effective implementation of anti-ragging measures, and the Cell shall also coordinate with the Non-Governmental agency responsible for monitoring the database maintained by the All India Council for Technical Education/Central Government.

(Member Secretary)

(c) Medical Council of India

New Delhi, the 3rd August, 2009 No. MCI-34(1)/2009-Med./25453, *In exercise of the powers conferred by Section 33 of the Indian Medical Council Act, 1956 (102 of 1956) the Medical Council of India with the previous sanction of the Central Government hereby makes the following Regulations, namely:—*

1. Short title, commencement and applicability.—(i) These Regulations may be called the Medical Council of India (Prevention and Prohibition of Ragging in Medical Colleges/Institutions) Regulations, 2009.

(ii) They shall come into force on the date of their publication in the Official Gazette.

2. Objective.—To root out ragging in all its forms from medical colleges/institutions in the country by prohibiting it by law, preventing its occurrence by following the provisions of these Regulations and punishing those who indulge in ragging as provided for in these Regulations and the appropriate law in force.

3. Definitions:- For the purposes of these Regulations.—(3.1) "Medical College" means an institution, whether known as such or by any other name, which provides for a programme, beyond 12 years of schooling, for obtaining recognized MBBS qualification from a university and which, in accordance with the rules and regulations of such university, is recognized as competent to provide for such programmes of study and present students undergoing such programmes of study for the examination for the award of recognized MBBS/PG Degree/Diploma qualifications.

(3.2) "Head of the institution" means the Dean/Principal/Director of the concerned medical college/institution.

(3.3) Ragging" includes the following:

Any conduct whether by words spoken or written or by an act which has the effect of harassing, teasing, treating or handling with rudeness any other student, indulging in rowdy or undisciplined activities which causes or is likely to cause annoyance, hardship or psychological harm or to raise fear or apprehension thereof in a fresher or a junior student or asking the students to do any act or perform something which such student will not in the ordinary course and which has the effect of causing or generating a sense of shame or embarrassment so as to adversely affect the physique or psyche of a fresher or a junior student.

(3.4) MCI means MCI constituted in terms of Section 3 of Indian Medical Council Act, 1956.

(3.5) "University" means a university established or incorporated by or under a Central Act, a Provincial Act or a State Act, an institution deemed to be university under Section 3 of the UGC Act, 1956, or an institution specially empowered by an Act of Parliament to confer or grant degrees.

4. Punishable ingredients of Ragging:—

- Abetment to ragging;
- Criminal conspiracy to rag;
- Unlawful assembly and rioting while ragging;
- Public nuisance created during ragging;
- Violation of decency and morals through ragging;
- Injury to body, causing hurt or grievous hurt;

- Wrongful restraint;
- Wrongful confinement;
- Use of criminal force;
- Assault as well as sexual offences or even unnatural offences;
- Extortion;
- Criminal trespass;
- Offences against property;
- Criminal intimidation;
- Attempts to commit any or all of the above mentioned offences against the victim(s);
- Physical or psychological humiliation.
- All other offences following from the definition of "Ragging".

5. Measures for prohibition of ragging.—

5.1 The Medical College/Institution/University shall strictly observe the provisions of the Act of the Central Government and the State Governments, if any, or if enacted and/or for the time being in force, considering ragging as a cognizable offence under the law at par with rape and other atrocities against women and ill-treatment of persons belonging to the SC/ST and prohibiting ragging in all its forms in all institutions.

5.2. Ragging in all its forms shall be totally banned in the entire Medical College/ Institution/University including its departments, constituent units, all its premises (academic, residential, sports, canteen, etc) whether located within the campus or outside and in all means of transportation of students whether public or private.

5.3. The Medical College/Institution/University shall take strict action against those found guilty of ragging and/or of abetting ragging.

6. Measures for prevention of ragging at the institution level:-

6.1. Before admissions:—

6.1.1. The advertisement for admissions shall clearly mention that ragging is totally banned/prohibited in the Medical College/Institution and anyone found guilty of ragging and/or abetting ragging is liable to be punished appropriately.

6.1.2. The brochure of admission/instruction booklet for candidates shall print in block letters these Regulations in full (including Annexures).

6.1.3. The 'Prospectus' and other admission related documents shall incorporate all directions of the Hon'ble Supreme Court and /or the Central or State Governments as applicable, so that the candidates and their parents/ guardians are sensitized in respect of the prohibition and consequences of ragging.

6.1.4. A Brochure or booklet/leaflet shall be distributed to each student at the beginning of each academic session for obtaining undertaking not to indulge or abet ragging and shall contain the blueprint of prevention and methods of redress.

The application form for admission/ enrolment shall have a printed undertaking, preferably both in English/Hindi and in one of the regional languages known to the institution and the applicant (English version given in Annexure I, Part I), to be filled up and signed by the candidate to the effect that he/she is aware of the law regarding prohibition of ragging as well as the punishments, and to the effect that he/she has not been expelled and/or debarred from admission by any institution and that he/she, if found guilty of the offence of ragging and/or abetting ragging, is liable to be punished appropriately.

6.1.5. The application form shall also contain a printed undertaking, preferably both in English/Hindi and in one of the regional languages known to the institution and the parent/guardian (English version given in Annexure I, Part II), to be signed by the parent/guardian of the applicant to the effect that he/she is also aware of the law in this regard and agrees to abide by the punishment meted out to his/her ward in case the latter is found guilty of ragging and/or abetting ragging.

A database shall be created out of affidavits affirmed by each student and his/her parents/guardians stored electronically, and shall contain the details of each student. The database shall also function as a record of ragging complaints received.

6.1.6. The application for admission shall be accompanied by a document in the form of the School Leaving Certificate/transfer certificate/migration certificate/ Character Certificate which shall include a report on the behavioral pattern of the applicant, so that the institution can thereafter keep intense watch upon a student who has a negative entry in this regard.

6.1.7. A student seeking admission to the hostel shall have to submit additional undertaking in the form of Annexure I (both Parts) along with his/ her application for hostel accommodation.

6.1.8. At the commencement of the academic session the Head of the Institution shall convene and address a meeting of various functionaries/agencies, like Wardens, representatives of students, parents/ guardians, faculty, district administration including police, to discuss the measures to be taken to prevent ragging in the Institution and steps to be taken to identify the offenders and punish them suitably.

6.1.9. To make the community at large and the students in particular aware of the dehumanizing effect of ragging, and the approach of the institution towards those indulging in ragging, big posters (preferably multicolored with different colours for the provisions of law, punishments, etc.) shall be prominently displayed on all Notice Boards of all departments, hostels and other buildings as well as at vulnerable places. Some of such posters shall be of permanent nature in certain vulnerable places.

6.1.10. Apart from placing posters mentioned in sub-clause 6.1.9 above at strategic places, the Medical College/Institution shall undertake measures for extensive publicity against ragging by means of audio-visual aids, by holding counseling sessions, workshops, painting and design competitions among students and other methods as it deems fit.

6.1.11. The Medical College/Institution/University shall request the media to give adequate publicity to the law prohibiting ragging and the negative aspects of ragging and the institution's resolve to ban ragging and punish those found guilty without fear or favour.

6.1.12. The Medical College/Institution/University shall identify, properly illuminate and man all vulnerable locations.

6.1.13. The Medical College/Institution/University shall tighten security in its premises, especially at the vulnerable places. If necessary, intense policing shall be resorted to at such points at odd hours during the early months of the academic session.

6.1.14. The Medical College/Institution/University shall utilize the vacation period before the start of the new academic year to launch wide publicity campaign against ragging through posters, leaflets, seminars, street plays, etc.

6.1.15. The faculties/departments/units of the Medical College/Institution/ University shall have induction arrangements (including those which anticipate, identify and plan to meet any special needs of any specific section of students) in place well in advance of the beginning of the academic year with a clear sense of the main aims and objectives of the induction process.

The Principal or Head of the Institution/Department shall obtain an undertaking from every employee of the institution including teaching and non-teaching members of staff, contract labour employed in the premises either for running canteen or as watch and ward staff or for cleaning or maintenance of the buildings/lawns etc., that he/she would report promptly any case of ragging which comes to his/her notice. A provision shall be made in the service rules for issuing certificates of appreciation to such members of the staff who report ragging which will form port of their service record.

6.2. On admission:—

6.2.1 Every fresher admitted to the Medical College/Institution/University shall be given a printed leaflet detailing when and to whom he/she has to turn to for help and guidance for various purposes (including Wardens, Head of the institution, members of the anti-ragging committees, relevant district and police authorities), addresses and telephone numbers of such persons/ authorities, etc., so that the fresher need not look up to the seniors for help in such matters and get indebted to them and start doing things, right or wrong, at their behest. Such a step will reduce the freshers' dependence on their seniors.

Every institution should engage or seek the assistance of professional counselors at the time of admissions to counsel 'freshers' in order to prepare them for the life ahead, particularly for adjusting to the life in hostels.

6.2.2 The Medical College/Institution/University through the leaflet mentioned above shall explain to the new entrants the arrangements for their induction and orientation which promote efficient and effective means of integrating them fully as students.

6.2.3 The leaflet mentioned above shall also inform the freshers about their rights as *bona fide* students of the institution and clearly instructing them that they should desist from doing anything against their will even if ordered by the seniors, and that they have nothing to fear as the institution cares for them and shall not tolerate any atrocities against them.

6.2.4 The leaflet mentioned above shall contain a calendar of events and activities laid down by the institution to facilitate and complement familiarization of freshers with the academic environment of the institution.

6.2.5 The Medical College/Institution/University shall also organize joint sensitization programmes of 'freshers' and seniors.

On the arrival of senior students after the first week or after the second week as the case may be, further orientation programmes must be scheduled as follows (i) joint sensitization programme and counselling of both 'freshers' and senior by a Professional counsellor; (ii) joint orientation programme of 'freshers' and seniors to be addressed by the principal/Head of the institution, and the anti-ragging committee ; (iii) organization on a large scale of cultural, sports and other activities to provide a platform for the 'freshers' and seniors to interact in the presence of faculty members ; (iv) in the hostel, the warden should address all students; may request two junior colleagues from the college faculty to assist the warden by becoming resident tutors for a temporary duration.

6.2.1 Freshers shall be encouraged to report incidents of ragging, either as victims, or even as witnesses.

6.3. At the end of the academic year:—

6.3.1 At the end of every academic year the Dean/Principal/Director shall send a letter to the parents/guardians of the students who are completing the first year informing them about the law regarding ragging and the punishments, and appealing to them to impress upon their wards to desist from indulging in ragging when they come back at the beginning of the next academic session.

6.3.2 At the end of every academic year the Medical College/Institution/University shall form a 'Mentoring Cell' consisting of Mentors for the succeeding academic year. There shall be as many levels or tiers of Mentors as the number of batches in the institution, at the rate of 1 Mentor for 6 freshers and 1 Mentor of a higher level for 6 Mentors of the lower level.

Each batch of freshers should be divided into small groups and each such group shall be assigned to a member of the staff. Such staff member should interact individually with, each member of the group on a daily basis for ascertaining the problems/difficulties if any faced by the fresher in the institution and extending necessary help.

In the case of freshers admitted to a hostel it shall be the responsibility of the teacher in-charge of the group to coordinate with the warden of the hostel and to make surprise visits to the rooms in the hostel where the members of the group are lodged.

6.4. Setting up of Committees and their functions:—

6.5.1 The Anti-Ragging Committee:-Every institution shall have an Anti-Ragging Committee and an Anti -Ragging Squad. The Anti-Ragging Committee shall be headed by the Head of the institution and shall consist of representatives of civil and police administration, local media, Non-Governmental Organizations involved in youth activities, faculty members, parents, students belonging to the freshers' category as well as seniors and non-teaching staff. It shall monitor the Anti Ragging activities in the institution, consider the recommendations of the Anti-Ragging Squad and take appropriate decisions, including spelling out suitable punishments to those found guilty.

6.5.2 The Anti-Ragging Squad:-The Anti-Ragging Squad shall be nominated by the Head of the institution with such representation as considered necessary and shall exclusively consist of members belonging to the various sections of the campus community. The Squad shall have vigil, oversight and patrolling functions. It shall be kept mobile, alert and active at all times and shall be empowered to inspect places of potential ragging and make surprise raids on hostels and other hot spots. The Squad shall investigate incidents of ragging and make recommendations to the Anti-Ragging Committee and shall work under the overall guidance of the Anti-Ragging Committee.

All matters of discipline within teaching institutions must be resolved within the campus except those impinging on law and order or breach of peace or public tranquility, all of which should be dealt with under the penal laws of the land.

University Monitoring Cell – At the level of the University, we recommend that there should be a Monitoring Cell on Ragging, which should co-ordinate with the affiliated colleges and institutions under its domain. The Cell should call for reports from the Heads of institutions in regard to the activities of the Anti-Ragging Committee, Anti-Ragging Squads, Monitoring Cells at the level of the institution, the compliance with instructions on conducting orientation programmes, counseling sessions, the incidents of ragging, the problems faced by wardens or other officials. It should also keep itself abreast of the decisions of the District level Anti-Ragging Committee. This Monitoring Cell should also review the efforts made by institutions o publicize anti-ragging measures, soliciting of undertaking from parents and students each year to abstain from ragging activities or willingness to be penalized for violations; and should function as the prime mover for initiating action on the part of the appropriate authorities of the university for amending the Statutes or Ordinances or Bye-laws to facilitate the implementation of anti-ragging measures at the level of the institution.

6.5. Other measures.—

6.5.1 The Annexures mentioned in 6.1.4, 6.1.5 and 6.1.7 of these Regulations shall be furnished at the beginning of each academic year by every student, that is, by freshers as well as seniors.

6.5.2 The Medical College/Institution/University shall arrange for regular and periodic psychological counseling and orientation for students (for freshers separately, as well as jointly with seniors) by professional counsellors during the first three months of the new academic year. This shall be done at the institution and department/course levels. Parents and teachers shall also be involved in such sessions.

6.5.3 Full-time warden shall be appointed as per the eligibility criteria laid down for the post reflecting both the command and control aspects of maintaining discipline, as well as the softer skills of counseling and communicating with the youth outside the class-room situations. Wardens shall be accessible at all hours and shall be provided with mobile phones and the details of their telephone number must be widely publicized. Similarly, the telephone numbers of the other important functionaries - Heads of institutions, faculty members, members of the anti-ragging committees, district and sub-divisional authorities and state authorities where relevant, should also be widely disseminated for the needy to get in touch or seek help in emergencies. The institution shall review and suitably enhance the powers and perquisites of Wardens and authorities involved in curbing the menace of ragging.

Further the institutions shall provide necessary incentives for the post of full-time warden, so as to attract suitable candidates.

6.5.4 Freshers shall be lodged in a separate hostel block, wherever possible, and where such facilities are not available, the college/institution shall ensure that seniors' access to freshers' accommodation is strictly monitored by wardens, security guards and college staff.

As ragging takes place mostly in the hostels after the classes are over in the college, a round the clock vigil against ragging in the hostel premises shall be provided. It is seen, that college canteens and hostel messes are also places where ragging often takes place. The employers/employees of the canteens/mess shall be given necessary instructions to keep strict vigil and to report the incidents of ragging to the college authorities if any.

The security personnel posted in hostels shall be under the direct control of the Wardens and assessed by them.

6.5.5 Private commercially managed lodges and hostels shall be registered with the local police authorities, and this shall be done necessarily on the recommendation of the Head of the institution. Local police, local administration and the institutional authorities shall ensure vigil on incidents that may come within the definition of ragging and shall be responsible for action in the event of ragging in such premises, just as they would be for incidents within the campus. Managements of such private hostels shall be responsible for action in the event of ragging in such premises, just as they would be for incidents within campuses.

6.5.6 Besides registering private hostels as stated above, the towns or cities where educational institutions are located should be apportioned as sectors among faculty members, as is being done by some institutions, so that they could maintain vigil and report any incidents of ragging outside campuses and en route while 'freshers' commute.

6.5.7 The Head of the institution shall take immediate action on receipt of the recommendations of the Ant-Ragging Squad. He/She shall also take action *suo motu* if the circumstances so warrant.

6.5.8 Freshers who do not report the incidents of ragging either as victims or as witnesses shall also be punished suitably.

6.5.9 Anonymous random surveys shall be conducted across the 1st year batch of students (freshers) every fortnight during the first three months of the academic year to verify and cross-check whether the campus is indeed free of ragging or not. The institution may design its own methodology of conducting such surveys.

6.5.10 The burden of proof shall lie on the perpetrator of ragging and not on the victim.

6.5.11 The institution shall file an FIR with the police/local authorities whenever a case of ragging is reported, but continue with its own enquiry and other measures without waiting for action on the part of the police/ local authorities. Remedial action shall be initiated and completed within the one week of the incident itself.

6.5.12 The Migration/Transfer Certificate issued to the student by the Medical College/Institution /University shall have an entry, apart from those relating to general conduct and behaviour, whether the student has been punished for the offence of committing or abetting ragging, or not, as also whether the student has displayed persistent violent or aggressive behaviour or any inclination to harm others.

6.5.13 Preventing or acting against ragging shall be the collective responsibility of all levels and sections of authorities or functionaries in the Medical College/ Institution/University, including faculty, and not merely that of the specific body/committee constituted for prevention of ragging.

6.5.14 As such the college canteens and hostel messes are also places where ragging often takes place, hence the employers/employees of the canteens/mess shall be given necessary instructions to keep strict vigil and to report the incidents of ragging to the college authorities, if any.

Further access to mobile phones and public phones shall be unrestricted in hostels and campuses, except in class-rooms, seminar halls, library etc., where jammers shall be installed to restrict the use of mobile phones.

6.6 Measures for encouraging healthy interaction between freshers and seniors:—

6.6.1 The Medical College/Institution/University shall set up appropriate committees including the course-in-charge, student advisor, Warden and some senior students to actively monitor, promote and regulate healthy interaction between the freshers and senior students.

6.6.2 Freshers' welcome parties shall be organized in each department by the senior students and the faculty together soon after admissions, preferably within the first two weeks of the beginning of the academic session, for proper introduction to one another and where the talents of the freshers are brought out properly in the presence of the faculty, thus helping them to shed their inferiority complex, if any, and remove their inhibitions.

6.6.3 The Medical College/Institution/University shall enhance the student-faculty interaction by involving the students in all matters of the institution, except those relating to the actual processes of evaluation and of faculty appointments, so that the students shall feel that they are responsible partners in managing the affairs of the institution and consequently the credit due to the institution for good work/ performance is due to them as well.

7. Regulatory Measures.—The inspecting/visiting Committees of MCI shall cross verify that the medical college/institution has strictly complied with the anti-ragging measures and has a blemishless record in terms of there being no incident of ragging during the impending period (*i.e.*, from earlier inspection) or otherwise.

8. Awardable Punishments.—

8.1 **At the Medical College/Institution level:**

Depending upon the nature and gravity of the offence as established by the Anti-Ragging Committee of the institution, the possible punishments for those found guilty of ragging at the institution level shall be any one or any combination of the following:

8.1.1 Suspension from attending classes and academic privileges.

8.1.2 Withholding/withdrawing scholarship/fellowship and other benefits

8.1.3 Debarring from appearing in any test/examination or other evaluation Process.

8.1.4 Withholding results

8.1.5 Debarring from representing the institution in any regional, national or international meet, tournament, youth festival, etc.

8.1.6 Suspension/expulsion from the hostel

8.1.7 Cancellation of admission.

8.1.8 Rustication from the institution for period ranging from 1 to 4 semesters

8.1.9 Expulsion from the institution and consequent debarring from admission to any other institution for a specific period.

8.1.10 Fine of Rs. 25,000 and Rs. 1 lakh.

8.1.11 Collective punishment: When the persons committing or abetting the crime of ragging are not identified, the institution shall resort to collective punishment.

8.2 Penal consequences for the heads of the institutions/administration of the institution who do not take timely steps in the prevention of ragging and punishing those who rag.—The authorities of the institution particularly the Head of the institution, shall be responsible to ensure that no incident of ragging takes place in the institution. In case any incident of ragging takes place, the Head shall take prompt and appropriate action against the person(s) whose dereliction of duty lead to the incident. The authority designated to appoint the Head shall, in its turn, take prompt and appropriate action against the Head.

In addition to penal consequences, departmental enquiries be initiated against such heads institutions/members of the administration/faculty members/non-teaching staff, who display an apathetic or insensitive attitude towards complaints of ragging.

8.3. At the MCI level

8.3.1 Impose an exemplary fine of Rs. 1 lakh for each incident of ragging payable by erring medical college/institution to such authority as may be designated by the appropriate Government, as the case may be.

8.3.2 Declare the erring Medical College/Institution/University as not having the minimum academic standards and warning the potential candidates for admission at such institution through public notice and posing on the MCI website.

8.3.3 Declare the erring Medical College/Institution/University to be ineligible for preferring any application under section 10A of the Indian Medical Council Act, 1956 for a minimum period of one year, extendable by such quantum by the Council as would be commensurate with the wrong.

(Lt. Col. (Retd.) Dr. A.R.N. Setalvad)

SECRETARY

Annexure 3

State Legislations

(a) The Tripura Educational Institutions (Prevention of Ragging) Act, 1990

(Tripura Act No. 12 of 1990)

An Act to prevent and eradicate the menace of ragging from the Educational Institutes situated in the State of Tripura.

Be it enacted by The Tripura Legislative Assembly in the Forty first Year of the Republic of India as follows:

1. Short title, extent and commencement.—(1) This Act may be called the Tripura Educational Institution (Prevention of Ragging) Act, 1990.

(2) It extends to the whole of Tripura. (3) It shall come into force at once.

2. Application of the Act.—This Act shall apply to all the Educational Institutions situated in the State of Tripura whether or not they are Government or private Institutions.

3. Definition.—In this Act, unless the context otherwise requires, Ragging will mean the following kind of offence:

Whoever, being a student in any Educational Institution, causes a fellow student to suffer physically or mentally by way of assault, intimidation, insult, tease, torment or any other form of torture commits ragging.

4. Punishment.—Whoever commits ragging shall be punished with imprisonment of either description for a term which may extend to four years or with fine or with both.

5. Procedure.—The offences of ragging shall be cognizable and non-bailable.

6. Establishment of courts.—The State Government may establish one or more special courts exclusively for trial of the cases under this Act and such courts may be presided over by a Judicial Magistrate or a special Judicial Magistrate appointed under section 13 of the Criminal procedure Code.

7. Disqualification for remaining as a student.—Whoever, being a student in any Educational Institution, has been convicted under section 5, shall cease to be a student of that Institution and he shall be deemed to have been expelled from the Institution with effect from the date of his conviction.

8. Eviction from hostel.—During any investigation or trial of offence under this Act an accused, who has been living in any hostel of the Institution, shall be entitled to continue his stay in that hostel.

9. On a prayer made in this behalf by the Investigating Officer the Special Court shall issue a direction to evict the accused from the hostel if he does not leave the hostel voluntarily at the commencement of the investigation or trial.

(b) Tamil Nadu Prohibition of Ragging Act, 1997

An Act to prohibit ragging in educational institutions in the State of Tamil Nadu

Be it enacted by the Legislative Assembly of the State of Tamil Nadu in the Forty-eighth Year of the Republic of India, as follows—

1. Short title, extent and commencement.—(1) This Act may be called the Tamil Nadu Prohibition of Ragging Act, 1997.

(2) It extends to the whole of the State of Tamil Nadu.

(3) It shall be deemed to have come into force on the 19th day of December 1996.

2. Definition.—In this Act unless the context otherwise requires, "ragging" means display of noisy, disorderly conduct doing any act which causes or is likely to cause physical or psychological harm or raise apprehension or fear or shame or embarrassment to a student in any educational institution and includes, -

(a) teasing, abusing of, playing practical jokes on, or causing hurt to such student; or

(b) asking the student to do any act or perform something which such student will not in the ordinary course willingly do.

3. Prohibition of ragging.—Ragging within or without any educational institution is prohibited.

4. Penalty for ragging.—Whoever directly or indirectly commits, participates in, abets or propagates " ragging " within or without any educational institution, shall be punished with imprisonment for a term which may extend to two years and shall also be liable to a fine which may extend to ten thousand rupees.

5. Dismissal of student.—Any student convicted of an offence under section 4 shall also be dismissed from the educational institution and such student shall not be admitted in any other educational institution.

6. Suspension of student.—(1) Without prejudice to the foregoing provisions, whenever any student complaints of ragging to the head of an educational institution, or to any other person responsible for the management of the educational institution, such head of the educational institution or person responsible for the management of the educational institution shall inquire into the same immediately and if found true shall suspend the student, who has committed the offence, from the educational institution.

(2) The decision of the head of the educational institution or the person responsible for the management of the educational institution that any student has indulged in ragging under sub-section (1) shall be final.

7. Deemed abetment.—If the head of the educational institution or the person responsible for the management of the educational institution fails or neglects to take action in the manner specified in sub -section (1) of section 6 when a complaint of ragging is made, such person shall be deemed to have abetted the offence of ragging and shall be punished as provided for in section 4.

8. Power to make Rules.—(1) The State Government may make Rules for carrying out all or any of the purposes of this Act.

(2) All Rules made under this Act shall be published in the Tamil Nadu Government Gazette and unless, they are expressed to come into force on a particular day, shall come into force on the day on which they are so published.

(3) Every rule made under this Act shall, as soon as possible after it is made, be placed on the table of the Legislative Assembly and in before the expiry of the session in which it is so placed or the next session, the Assembly makes any modification in any such rule, or the Assembly decides that the Rule should not be made, the Rule shall thereafter have effect only in such modified form or be of no effect, as the case may be, so, however, that any such modification or annulment shall be without pre-judice to the validity of anything previously done under that Rule.

9. Repeal and saving.—(1) The Tamil Nadu Prohibition of Ragging Ordinance, 1990 is hereby repealed.

(2) Notwithstanding such repeal, anything done or any action taken under the Ordinance shall be deemed to have been done or taken under this Act.

(By order of the Governor)
A.K. RAJAN,
Secretary to Government, Law Department

(c) Andhra Pradesh Prohibition of Ragging Act, 1997

An Act to prohibit ragging in educational institutions in the state of Andhra Pradesh.

BE it enacted by the Legislative Assembly of the State of Andhra Pradesh in the Forty-eighth Year of the Republic of India, as follows:—

1. Short title and commencement.—This Act may be called the Andhra Pradesh Prohibition of Ragging Act, 1997.

(1) It extends to the whole of the State of Andhra Pradesh.

(2) It shall be deemed to have come into force with effect from 4th July, 1997.

2. Definition.—In this Act, unless the context otherwise requires -

(a) 'act' includes words either spoken or written or signs or sounds or gestures or visible representations;-

(b) 'Educational Institution' means and includes a college, or other institution by whatever name called, carrying on the activity or imparting education therein (either exclusively or among other activities); and includes an orphanage or boarding home or hostel or a tutorial institution or any other premises attached thereto;

(c) 'government' means the State Government of Andhra Pradesh;

(d) 'notification' means the notification published in the Andhra Pradesh Gazette and the word 'notified' shall be construed accordingly;

(e) 'ragging' means doing an act which causes or is likely to cause insult or annoyance of fear or apprehension or threat or intimidation or outrage of modesty or injury to a student;

(f) 'student' means a person who is admitted to an educational institution and whose name is lawfully borne on the attendance register thereof;

(g) All words and expressions used but not defined in this Act shall have the meanings assigned to them under the Andhra Pradesh Education Act, 1982 or the Indian Penal Code, 1860 respectively.

3.—Ragging within or outside any educational institution is prohibited.

4.—Whoever, with the intention of causing ragging or with the knowledge that he is likely by such act to cause ragging, commits or abets ragging and thereby -

(i) teases or embarrasses or humiliates a student shall be punished with imprisonment for a term which may extend to six months or with fine which may extend to one thousand rupees or with both; or

(ii) assaults or uses criminal force to or criminally intimidates, a student shall be punished with imprisonment for a term which may extend to one year or with fine which may extend to two thousand rupees or with both; or

(iii) wrongfully restrains or wrongfully confines or causes hurt to a student shall be punished with imprisonment for a term which may extend to two years or with fine which may extend to five thousand rupees or with both; or

(iv) causes grievous hurt to or kidnaps or abducts or rapes or commits unnatural offence with a student shall be punished with imprisonment for a term which may extend to five years and with fine which may extend to ten thousand rupees; or

(v) causes death or abets suicide shall be punished with imprisonment for life or with imprisonment for a term which may extend to ten years and with a fine which may extend to fifty thousand rupees.

5.—(1) A student convicted of an offence under Section 4 and punished with imprisonment for a term shall be dismissed from the educational institution.

(2) A student convicted of an offence under Section 4 and punished with imprisonment for a term of more than six months shall not be admitted in any other educational institution.

6.—(1) Without prejudice to the foregoing provisions, whenever any student complains of ragging to the Head or Manager of an educational institution, such Head or Manager shall inquire into or cause an inquiry to be made into the same forthwith and if the complaint is *prima facie* found true, shall suspend the student or students complained against for such period as may be deemed necessary.

(2) The decision of the Head or Manager of the educational institution under sub-section (1) shall be final.

7.—(1) If the Head or the Manager of an educational institution fails or neglects to take action in the manner specified in sub-section (1) of Section 6, such person shall be deemed to have abetted the offence and shall be punished with the punishment provided for the offence.

(2) If a student commits suicide due to or in consequence of ragging, the person who commits such ragging shall be deemed to have abetted such suicide.

8.—The provisions of this Act shall be in addition to and not derogatory of any law for the time being in force.

9.—(1) The Government may by notification, make Rules for carrying out all or any of the purposes of this Act.

(2) Every rule made under this Act shall immediately after it is made, be laid before the Legislative Assembly of the State, if it is in session and if it is not in session, in the session immediately following for a total period of fourteen days which may be comprised in one session or in two successive sessions, and if, before the expiration of the session in which it is so laid or the session immediately following the Legislative Assembly agrees in making any modification in the rule or in the annulment of the rule, the rule shall, from the date on which the modification or annulment is notified, have effect only in such modified form or shall stand annulled as the case may be so, however, that any such modification or annulment shall be without prejudice to the validity of anything previously done under that rule.

10.—The Andhra Pradesh Prohibition of Ragging Ordinance, 1997 is hereby repealed.

(d) The Kerala Prohibition of Ragging Act, 1998

(Act 10 of 1998)

An Act to Prohibit ragging in educational institutions in the State of Kerala.

Preamble.—WHEREAS it is expedient to prohibit ragging in educational institutions in the State of Kerala.

Be it enacted in the Forty-Ninth Year of the Republic of India .as follows:-

1. Short title, extent and Commencement.—(1) This Act may be called the Kerala Prohibition of Ragging Act, 1998.

(2) It extends the whole of the State of Kerala.

(3) It shall be deemed to have come into force on the 23rd day of October, 1997.

2. Definition.—In this Act, unless the context otherwise required,—

(a) 'head of the educational institution' means the Principal or the Head master or the person responsible for the management of that educational institution;

(b) 'Ragging' means doing of any act, by disorderly conduct, to a student of an educational institution, which causes or is likely to cause physical or psychological harm or raising apprehension or fear or shame or embarrassment to that student and includes—

(i) teasing, abusing or paying practical jokes on, or causing hurt to, such student; or

(ii) asking a student to do any act or perform something which such student will not, in the ordinary course willingly, do.

3. Prohibition of ragging.—Ragging within or without any educational institution is prohibited.

4. Penalty for ragging.—Who ever commits, participates in, abets or propagates ragging within, or without, any educational institution shall, on conviction, be punished with imprisonment for a term which may extent to two years and shall al so be liable to a fine which may extend to ten thousand rupees.

5. Dismissal of student.—Any student convicted of an offence under section 4 shall be dismissed from the educational institution and such student shall not be admitted in any other educational institution for a period of three years from the date of order of such dismissal.

6. Suspension of student.—(1) Whenever any student or, as the case may be, the parents or guardian, or a teacher of an educational institution complaints, in writing, of ragging to the head of the educational institution, the head of that educational institution shall, without prejudice to the fore going provisions, within seven days of the receipt of the complaint, enquire into the matter mentioned in the complaint and if, *prima facie*, it is found true, suspend the student who is accused of the offence, and shall, immediately, forward the complaint to the police station having jurisdiction over the are a in which the educational institution is situate, for further action.

(2) Where, on enquiry by the head of the educational institution, it is proved that there is no substance *prima facie* in the complaint received under sub-section (1), he shall intimate the fact, in writing, to the complainant.

7. Deemed abetment.—If the head of the educational institution fails or neglects to take action in the manner specified in section 6 when a complaint of ragging is made, such person shall be deemed to have abetted the offence of ragging and shall, on conviction, be punished as provided for in section 4.

8. Power to make rules.—(1) The Government may, by notification in the Gazette, make Rules for carrying out all or any of the purposes of this Act.

(2) Every rule made under this Act shall be laid, as soon as may be after it is made, before the Legislative Assembly, while it is in session for a total period of four teen days, which may be comprised in one session or in two successive sessions, and if before the expiry of the session in which it is so laid, or the session immediately following, the Legislative Assembly makes any modification in the rule or decides that the rule should not be made, the rule shall, there after, have effect only in such modified form or be of no effect, as the case may be, so, however that any such modification or annulment shall be without prejudice to the validity of any thing previously done under that rule.

9. Repeal and saving.—(1)The Kerala prohibition of Ragging Ordinance, 1998 (2 of 1998) is hereby repealed.

(2) Notwithstanding such repeal, anything done or deemed to have been done or any action taken or deemed to have been taken under the said Ordinance shall be deemed to have been done or taken under this Act.

(e) Maharashtra Prohibition of Ragging Act, 1999

An Act to prohibit ragging in educational institutions in the State of Maharashtra.

WHEREAS it is expedient to enact a special law to prohibit ragging in educational institutions in the State of Maharashtra; It is hereby enacted in the Fiftieth Year of the Republic of India as follows:-

Statement of Object

For Statement of Objects and Reasons, see Maharashtra Government Gazette, Part V-A. Extraordinary, dated the 7th April, 1999, p. 169.

1. Short title and commencement.—(1) This Act may be called the Maharashtra Prohibition of Ragging Act, 1999.

(2) It shall come into force on such date as the State Government may, by notification in the Official Gazette, appoint.

2 Definitions.—In this Act, unless the context otherwise requires,-

(a) "educational institution" means and includes a collage, or other institution by whatever name called, carrying on the activity or imparting education therein (either exclusively or among other activities); and includes on orphanage or a boarding home or hostel or a tutorial institution or any other premises attached thereto;

(b) "head of the educational institution" means the Vice-Chancellor of the University, Dean of Medical Faculty, director of the Institution or the Principal, Headmaster or the person responsible for the management of the educational institution;

(c) "ragging" means display of disorderly conduct, doing of any act which causes or is likely to cause physical or psychological harm or raise apprehension or fear or shame or embarrassment to a student in any educational institution and includes -

(i) teasing, abusing, threatening or playing practical jokes on, or causing hurt to, such student; or

(ii) asking a student to do any act or perform something which such student will not, in the ordinary course, willingly, do.

3. Prohibition of ragging.—Ragging within or outside of any educational institution is prohibited.

4. Penalty for ragging.—Whoever directly or indirectly commits, participates in, abets or propagates ragging within or outside any educational institution shall, on conviction, be punished with imprisonment for a term which may extend to two years and shall also be liable to a fine which may extend to ten thousand rupees.

5. Dismissal of student.—Any student convicted of an offence under section 4 shall be dismissed from the educational institution and such student shall not be admitted in any other educational institution for a period of five years from the date of order of such dismissal.

6 Suspension of student.—(1) Whenever any student or, as the case may be, the parent or guardian, or a teacher of an educational institution complains, in writing, of ragging to the head of the educational institution, the head of that educational institution shall, without prejudice to the foregoing provisions, within seven days of the receipt of the complaint, enquire into the matter mentioned in the complaint and if, *prima facie*, it is found true, suspend the student who is accused of the offence, and shall, immediately forward the complaint to the Police Station having jurisdiction over the area in which the educational institution is situated, for further action.

(2) Where, on enquiry by the head of the educational institution, it is proved that there is no substance, *prima facie*, in the complaint received under sub-section (1), he shall intimate the fact, in writing, to the complainant.

(3) The decision of the head for the educational institution that the student has indulged in ragging under sub-section (1), shall be final.

7. Demand abetment.—If the head of the educational institution fails or neglects to take action in the manner specified in section 6 when a complaint or ragging is made, such person shall be deemed to have abetted the offence of ragging and shall, on conviction, be punished as provided for in section 4.

8. Power to make Rules.—(1) The State Government may, by notification in the Official Gazette, make rules for carrying out all or any of the purposes of this Act.

(2) Every Rule made under this Act shall be laid, as soon as may be, after it is made, before each House of the State Legislature, while it is in session for a total period of thirty days, which may be comprised in one session or in two or more successive sessions, and if, before the expiry of the session in which it is so laid or the session immediately following, both Houses agree in making any modification in the Rules or both Houses agree that the Rule should not be made, and notify such decision in the Official Gazette, the Rule shall, from the date of publication of such notification, have effect only in such modified form or be of no effect, as the case may be; so however, that any such modification or annulment shall be without prejudice to the validity of anything previously done or omitted to be done under that Rule.

(f) The West Bengal Prohibition of Ragging in Educational Institutions Act, 2000

(West Bengal Act XIII of 2000)

An Act to prohibit ragging in educational institutions in West Bengal.

WHEREAS it is expedient to prohibit ragging in educational institutions in West Bengal;

It is enacted in the Fifty-first year of the Republic of India by the Legislature of West Bengal, as follows:—

1. Short title, extent and commencement.—(1) This Act may be called the West Bengal Prohibition of Ragging in Educational Institutions, 2000.

(2) It extends to the whole of West Bengal.

(3) It shall come into force on such date as the State Government may by notification may appoint.

2. Definitions.—In this Act, unless the Context otherwise requires:

(1) "educational institution" means any educational institution by whatever name called, whether or not maintained and managed by the State Government recognised or deemed to have been recognised under any law for the time being in force or, affiliated to a University as defined in the University Grants Commission Act, 1956 (3 of 1956)

(2) "notification" means a notification published in the Official Gazette. (3) "prescribed" means prescribed by the Rules made under this Act.

(4) "ragging" means the doing of any act which causes, or is likely to cause any physical, psychological or physiological harm or apprehension or shame or embarrassment to a student, and includes–

(a) teasing or abusing of playing Practical joke on, or causing hurt to any student; or

(b) asking any student to do any act, or perform any thing, which he would not, in the ordinary course, be willing to do or perform.

(5) "student" means a student who has been pursuing his study in an educational institution.

3. Prohibition of Ragging.—(1) Ragging within an educational institution is hereby prohibited.

(2) No person shall participate in, abet, or propagate, ragging in any educational institution.

Explanation.—For the purpose of this Section, educational institution shall include— the premises or the campus of the educational institution, or the hall, that is to say, the unit of residence of students maintained by the educational institution, if any, or the hostel, that is to say, the unit for the residence of students, if any, not maintained by the educational institution but recognised under any law for the time being in force.

4. Penalty for Ragging.—Whoever contravenes the provisions of section 3 shall be punished with imprisonment of either description for a term which may extend to two years or with fine which may extend to five thousand rupees or both.

5. Dismissal of student on conviction and bay to admission and re-admission.—If any student is convicted of an act punishable under section 4, he shall be dismissed from the educational institution in which he has been prosecuting his studies for the time being, and shall not be re-admitted to that educational institution.

6. Expulsion of student.—Without prejudice to the foregoing provisions of this Act where a student complains of ragging by any other student to the head of the educational Institution or to any other person responsible for the management of the educational institution, such head of the educational institution shall forthwith inquire into the complaint and if, on such inquiry the complaint is found to be true, he shall expel the student, who has committed the offence, from the educational institution.

7. Constitution of Committee.—Notwithstanding anything contained in section 5 and 6, any student dismissed under section 5 or expelled under section 6 may appeal in the prescribed manner to the Committee to be constituted by the State Government in the manner prescribed, and the decision of the Committee on such appeal shall be final.

8. Failure or negligence to comply with the provisions of section 6.—(1) If the head of the educational institution or the person responsible to the management of the educational institution fails or neglects to comply with the provisions of section 6, a complaint of such failure may be made to the Committee constituted under section 7, by the student who complains of ragging under section 6 or by his guardian.

Explanation:—"Guardian" shall mean a person having the care of the student or any other person who has been declared to be the guardian of the student in the record, if any, maintained by the educational institution.

(2) On receipt of the complaint under sub-section (1), the Committee shall hold such inquiry as it my deem fit and shall make its recommendations to the such managing committee or the governing body of the educational institution or such authority, as the Committee considers appropriate and, the managing committee or the governing body as the case may be, shall take action in accordance with the recommendations as aforesaid.

9. Act to have overriding effect.—The provisions of this Act shall have effect notwithstanding anything inconsistent in any other law for the time being in force.

10. Power to make Rules.—(1) The State Government may by notification make Rules for carrying out the purposes of this Act.

(2) All Rules made under this Act shall, unless some later date is appointed in the State Government, come into force on the date of publication in the Official Gazette.

(g) Chhattisgarh Shaikshanik Sansthaon Me Pratarna Ka Pratishedh Adhiniyam, 2001

An Act to prevent ragging in educational institutions in the State and for matters connected therewith and incidental there to.

Be it enacted by the Chhattisgarh Legislature in the Fifty-second Year of the Republic of India as follows:—

1. Short title, extent and commencement.—(1) This Act may be called the Chhattisgarh Shaikshanik Sansthaon Me Pratarna Ka Pratishedh Adhiniyam, 2001.

(2) It extends to whole of Chhattisgarh.

(3) It shall come into force on such date as the State Government, may by notification, appoint.

2. Definitions.—In this Act, unless the context otherwise requires-

(a) "ragging" means causing, inducing compelling or forcing a student, whether by way of a practical joke or otherwise, to do any act which detracts from human dignity or violates his person or exposes him to ridicule or forbear from doing any unlawful act, by intimidating, wrongfully restraining, wrongfully confining, or injuring him or by using criminal force to him or by holding out to him any threat or such intimidation, wrongful restraint, wrongful confinement, injury or the use of criminal force.

(b) "educational institution" means any Government or non-Government educational institution of the State.

3. Prohibition of ragging.—No student or an educational institution shall either directly or indirectly commit or take part in ragging.

4. Punishment.—Any person who contravenes the provisions of section 3 or attempts to commit or abets the act of ragging or takes part either directly or indirectly in ragging shall be punished with either of the description for imprisonment which may extend upto five years or with fine which may extend to five thousand rupees or with both.

5. Offence to be cognizable, non-bailable and non-compoundable.—Every offence under this Act shall be cognizable, non-bailable and non-compoundable.

6. Trial of offence.—(1) Every offence punishable under this Act shall be tried by a judicial Magistrate of first class.

(2) The provisions of the Code of Criminal Procedure, 1973 (No. 2 of 1974) shall apply to investigation, inquiry and trial of the offences under this Act.

7. Disqualification for remaining as student.—(1) Pending investigation or trial of an offence under this Act, the head of the educational institution shall have the power to suspend a student accused of an offence under this Act and debar him from entry into premises of the educational institution and the hostel.

(2) A student of an educational institution who has been convicted under section 4 shall be liable to rustication from the educational institution.

(3) A student who has been rusticated or any other person who has been convicted under this Act shall not be admitted to another educational institution within the jurisdiction of the State for a period of three years.

(h) The Goa Prohibition of Ragging Act, 2008

An Act to prohibit ragging in educational institutions in the State of Goa.

Be it enacted by the Legislative Assembly of Goa in the Fifty-ninth Year of the Republic of India as follows:—

1. Short title, extent and commencement.—(1) This Act may be called the Goa Prohibition of Ragging Act, 2008.

(2) It shall extend to whole of the State of Goa.

(3) It shall come into force on such date as the Government may, by notification in the Official Gazette appoint.

2. Definitions.—In this Act, unless the context otherwise requires—

(a) "educational institution" means and includes a College, having Degree classes and/or Higher Secondary Classes and/or Post Graduates Classes, Junior College, Polytechnic or other institution by whatever name called, carrying on the activity of imparting education therein, either exclusively or among other activities, and includes an orphanage or a boarding home or hostel or a tutorial institution or any other premises attached thereto;

(b) "fresher" means a fresh or new student admitted to an educational institution and includes Junior students;

(c) "Government" means the Government of Goa;

(d) "head of the educational institution" means the Vice-Chancellor of the University, Dean of Medical Faculty, Director of the Institution or the Principal, Headmaster or the person responsible for the management of the educational institutions;

(e) "ragging" means any disorderly conduct, whether by words spoken or written or by an act which has the effect of teasing, treating or handling with rudeness any other student indulging in rowdy or indisciplined activities which causes or is likely to cause annoyance, hardship or psychological harm or to raise fear or apprehension thereof in a fresher or a Junior student or asking the student to do any act or perform something which such student will not do in the ordinary course and which has the effect of causing or generating a sense of shame or embarrassment or adversely affect the physique or psyche of a fresher or a Junior student;

(f) "senior" means a student studying in higher classes as compared to other students in an educational institution;

(g) "student" means a person who is admitted to an educational institution and whose name is lawfully borne on the attendance register thereof.

3. Anti-ragging movement.—It shall be the duty of every educational institution to prevent or deter the commission of ragging and shall initiate anti-ragging movement by taking all steps required. Without prejudice to the aforesaid;

(i) the prospectus, the form for admission and/or any other literature issued to the aspirants for admission shall clearly mention that ragging is banned in the institution and anyone indulging in ragging is likely to be punished;

(ii) the application form for admission/enrolment shall have a printed undertaking to be filled up and signed by the student to the effect that he/she is aware of the institution's approach towards ragging and the punishments to which he/she shall be liable if found guilty of ragging. A similar undertaking shall be obtained from the parent/guardian of the student;

(iii) the educational institution shall display on the notice board, the name and addresses and the contact numbers of the persons, to whom the freshers in the institution should approach for help and guidance for various purposes keeping in view needs of freshers in the institution at the time of admission so that the fresher need not look up to the seniors for help in such matters and feel indebted to or obliged by them;

(iv) Head of the educational institution or a person high in authority shall address meetings of Professors, Lecturers, Instructors, Teachers, parents and students collectively or in groups and create confidence by apprising them of their rights as well as obligations to fight against ragging, insisting on freshers to report to the head of educational institution and/or proctorial committee, any instance of ragging and to generate confidence in their mind and that any instance of ragging to which they are subjected to or which comes in their knowledge shall be promptly dealt with, while protecting the complainant from any harassment by the perpetrators of ragging;

(v) at the commencement of the academic session, the educational institution should constitute a Proctorial Committee consisting of Senior Faculty members and hostel authorities like Wardens and a few responsible senior students:—

(a) to keep a continuous watch and vigil over ragging so as to prevent its occurrence and recurrence;

(b) to promptly deal with the incidents of ragging brought to its notice and summarily punish the guilty, either by itself or by putting forth its finding// recommendations/suggestions before the authority competent to take decision;

(vi) all vulnerable locations shall be identified and especially watched;

(vii) the local community and the students in particular shall be made aware of the dehumanizing effect of ragging inherent in its perversity. Posters, notice boards and signboards etc., wherever necessary, may be used for the purpose;

(viii) migration certificate issued by the educational institution should have an entry apart from that of general conduct and behaviour whether the student had indulged in ragging and in particular was punished for ragging.

1[(ix) Every educational institution shall engage or seek the assistance of professional counsellors, at the time of admission, to counsel freshers in order to prepare them for the life ahead, particularly for adjusting the life in hostels;

(x) On the arrival of seniors after the first/second week, of academic session, further orientation programmes shall be scheduled, as follows:—

(a) joint sensitization programme and counselling of both freshers and seniors' by professional counsellors;

(b) joint orientation programme of freshers and seniors to be addressed by the head of the educational institution and the Anti-Ragging Committee;

(c) organization on a large scale of cultural sports and other activities to provide a platform for freshers and seniors to interact in the presence of faculty members;

(d) in the hostel, the warden shall address all students; and he may request two junior colleagues from the college faculty to assist him by becoming resident tutors for a temporary duration;

(e) as far as possible faculty members should dine with the hostel residents in their respective hostels to instill a feeling of confidence among the freshers.

(xi) the private commercially managed lodges or hostels outside campus shall, on the recommendation of concerned head of educational institution, be registered with the local police authorities. No such lodge or hostel shall be started without the permission of the concerned head of the educational institution. The local police, local administration and institutional authorities shall ensure vigil on any incident of ragging. The management of such private lodge or hostel shall be responsible for reporting cases of ragging in such premises. Non-reporting of such cases shall entitle the head of the educational institution to cancel the permission issued.

(xii) the educational institution shall ensure that each hostel has a full time warden who resides within the hostel, or at least in close vicinity thereof. The warden shall be accessible at all hours and also on telephone and other modes of communication. The warden shall be issued mobile phone by the institution and the number of such phone shall be given wide publicity.

(xiii) the head of the educational institution shall obtain an undertaking from every employee of the institution including teaching and non-teaching members of staff, contract labourers employed in the premises either for running a canteen or as watch and ward or for cleaning or maintenance of the buildings/lawns, etc., that he/she shall report promptly any case of ragging which comes to his/her notice. Certificates of appreciation shall be issued to such members of the staff who report ragging, which shall form part of their service record.

3A.—Monitoring cell, anti-ragging committee, etc.—(1) Every educational institution shall have an Anti-Ragging Committee and an Anti-Ragging Squad. The Anti- Ragging Committee at the level of the institution shall consist of representatives of civil and police administration, local media, Non-Government Organizations involved in youth activities, representatives of faculty members, representatives of parents, representatives of freshers, seniors and non-teaching staff. Such committee shall be headed by the head of the educational institution.

(2) There shall be Anti–Ragging Squad, a body with vigil, oversight and patrolling functions, to be nominated by the head of the educational institution with such representatives as considered necessary to keep it mobile, alert and active at all time. The Squad may be called upon to make surprise raids on hostels and other hot spots and shall be empowered to inspect places of potential ragging. The Squad shall work under the overall guidance of Anti-Ragging Committee. The Squad shall not have any outside representation and shall consist of members belonging to the various sections of the campus community. There shall be diverse mix of membership in terms of levels as well as gender in both the Anti-Ragging Squad and the Anti-Ragging Committee.

(3) There shall be a District Level Anti-Ragging Committee in each district headed by the District Magistrate, consisting of heads of educational institutions, Superintendent of Police, representatives of the local media, District level Non-Governmental Organizations actively associated in youth development programmes and of all students organizations, as members. The Additional District Magistrate shall be a Member Secretary of the District Level Anti-Ragging Committee.

The District level Anti-Ragging Committee shall hold preparatory meetings during the summer vacation to take stock of the state of preparedness of each institution and their compliance with the policies, directions and guidelines in regard to curbing the menace of ragging.

(4) There shall be a Monitoring Cell in the Goa University which shall co-ordinate with the affiliated colleges and institutions under its domain. The cell shall call for reports from the heads of the educational institutions in regard to the activities of the Anti-Ragging Committee, Anti-Ragging Squads, Monitoring Cells at the level of the institutions, the compliance with instructions on conducting orientation programmes, counselling sessions, the incidents of ragging, the problems faced by wardens or other officials. It shall also keep itself abreast of the decisions of the District level Anti-Ragging Committee. This Monitoring Cell shall also review the efforts made by institutions to publicize anti-ragging measures, soliciting of undertakings from parents and students for each academic year to abstain from ragging activities or willingness to be penalized for violations; and shall function as the prime mover for initiating action on the part of the appropriate authorities of the Goa University for amending its statutes or ordinances or bye-laws to facilitate the implementation of anti-ragging measures at the level of the institutions.

(5) At the State level, there shall be a Monitoring Cell at the level of the Chancellor of the Goa University who may also co-ordinate with the Central Government institutions located in the State of Goa.

The monitoring Cell in the Goa University and District Level Anti-Ragging Committees shall send to the State Level Monitoring Cell, status reports periodically and at such frequencies that it may lay down].

4. Prohibition of ragging.—Ragging within or outside of any educational institution is prohibited and no person shall commit, abet, propagate or participate in ragging within or outside of any educational institution.

5. Authority to impose penalties.—(1) Whenever any student or, as the case may be, the parent or guardian, or Professor or Lecturer or a teacher of an educational institution complains in writing, of ragging to the Head of the educational institution, the Head of that educational institution shall, within seven days of the receipt of the complaint, inquire into the complaint and if, *prima facie,* any complaint is found true, should resort to disciplinary action at his/her level. When ragging becomes unmanageable or amounts to a cognizable offence, the same may be reported to the police.

(2) Where, on an inquiry by the Head of the educational institution, it is proved that there is no substance in the complaint received under sub-section (1), he, shall intimate the fact, in writing, to the complainant.

(3) The decision of the Head of the educational institution that the student has indulged in ragging under sub-section (1) shall be final.

(4) If, the Head of the educational institution fails or neglects to take action in the manner specified hereinabove in sub-section (1) when a complaint of ragging is made, such person shall be deemed to have abetted the offence of ragging and shall be made personally accountable and liable for disciplinary proceedings before the authority competent to conduct such proceedings.

6. Punishment.—(1) Whoever, directly or indirectly, commits, participates in, abets or propagates, ragging, within or outside any educational institution, shall, on conviction, be dealt with by the Head of the educational institution by resorting to disciplinary action.

(2) If the individuals committing or abetting ragging are not identified, collective punishment should be resorted to so as to act as a deterrent punishment and to ensure collective pressure on the potential raggers.

(3) Any student so convicted shall further be removed from the roll of the educational institution and such students shall not be admitted in any other educational institution in the State of Goa for a period of three years from the date of such conviction.

(4) The punishment may also take the shape of:

(i) Withholding scholarships or other benefits;

(ii) Debarring from representation in events;

(iii) Withholding results; and

(iv) Suspension or expulsion from College or hostel or mess, and the like.

7. Provision of this Act to be in addition to any other law for the time being in force.—Nothing in this Act shall be deemed to affect the operation of any other law and the provisions of this Act shall be in addition to and not in derogation of such other law.

8. Power to remove difficulties.— If any difficulty arises in giving effect to the provisions of this Act, the Government may, by Order, not inconsistent with the provisions of this Act, remove the difficulty:

Provided that no such order shall be made after the expiry of a period of two years from the commencement of this Act.

(i) The Himachal Pradesh Educational Institutions (Prohibition of Ragging) Act, 2009

(Act No. 12 of 2009)

An Act to provide for prevention of the evil practice of ragging in educational institutions in the State of Himachal Pradesh and for matters connected there with or incident al thereto.

Be it enacted by the Legislative Assembly of Himachal Pradesh in the Sixtieth Year of the Republic of India as follows:—

1. Short title and commencement.—(1) This Act may be called the Himachal Pradesh Educational Institutions (Prohibition of Ragging) Act, 2009.

(2) It shall be deemed to have come into force on 25th day of March, 2009.

2. Definitions.—In this Act, unless the context otherwise requires,—

(a) "educational institution" means any University, any College affiliated to or maintained by the University, any school imparting secondary education, any school, Polytechnic or institution imparting technical education and includes such other institutions as may be notified by the State Government in the Official Gazette;

(b) "Officer-in-Charge" means and includes person appointed as the Principal of College, Head of Hostel, Dean of Faculty, Head of Teaching Department or the institution, the authority of the College, Warden or Manager (by what ever name called) of Hostel or canteen, the Student Welfare Officer or the Librarian of the College and University Library, Principal, Headmaster, Warden, Manager or teacher of the educational institution; and

(c) "ragging" means any act, conduct or practice by which dominant power of senior students, former students or outsiders, is brought to bear on students freshly enrolled or students who are in any way considered junior by other students and includes individual or collective acts or practices which—

(i) involve physical or psychological assault or threat or use of force or wrongful confinement or restraint; or

(ii) violate the status, dignity and honour of such students; or

(iii) expose students to ridicule and contempt and affect their self-esteem; or

(iv) entail verb a lab use and aggression, indecent gestures and obscene behaviour.

3. Prohibition of ragging.—(1) No person shall practise ragging in any form, within or outside the premises of an educational institution.

(2) Any person who contravenes the provisions of sub-section (1), shall, on conviction, be punished with imprisonment for a term which may extend to three years or with fine which may extend to fifty thousand rupees or with both.

4. Duties of certain persons to check and report incidents of ragging.—(1) Notwithstanding anything contained in any law for the time being in force or in any contract, every person who is the Officer-in-Charge of the educational institution or who is in the service or pay of or remunerated by the educational institution to do any work assigned to him in connection with the maintenance of discipline therein, shall be bound to take immediate action on the occurrence of any incident of ragging and to make report to the Vice-Chancellor or to any other officer authorised by him, in case of the University, or the Head of the educational institution, in case of the institution other than the University, the identity of those who have engaged in ragging and the nature of the incident.

(2) Every single incident of ragging where the victim or his parents or guardian or the Head of educational institution is not satisfied with the institutional arrangement for action, a First Information Report shall be lodged with out exception by the institutional authorities with the local police authorities.

(3) Any failure on the part of the institutional authority or negligence or deliberate delay in lodging the First Information Report with the local police, shall be construed to bean act of culpable negligence on the part of the institutional authority.

(4) If any victim or his parent or guardian intends to lodge First Information Report directly with the police that shall not absolve the institutional authority from the requirement of lodging the First Information Report.

(5) Any person who contravenes the provisions of sub-section (1) or sub-section (2) or sub-section (3), shall, on conviction, be punished with imprisonment for a term which may extend to one year or with fine which may extend to ten thousand rupees, or with both.

5. Abetment of offences under section 3.—Whoever being a Head of educational institution or an officer, directly or primarily in-charge of supervision for the proper maintenance of discipline in the educational institution, knowingly omits to check and report or connives or abets the commission of the offence under section 3, shall, on conviction, be punished with imprisonment for a term which may extend to two years or with fine which may extend to twenty five thousand rupees, or with both.

6. Offences to be cognizable, non-bailable and compoundable.—Every offence under this Act shall be cognizable, non-bailable and compoundable with the permission of the court.

7. Expulsion of student.—(1) Any student convicted of an offence under this Act shall be expelled from the educational institution.

(2) Student expelled under sub-section (1) or expelled otherwise on account of ragging shall not be admitted in any other educational institution for a period of three years from the date of order of such expulsion.

8. Suspension of student.—(1) When ever any student or, as the case may be, the parents or guardian or a teacher of an educational institution or an Officer-in-Charge makes a complaint, in writing, of ragging to the head of the educational institution, the head of that educational institution shall, without prejudice to the fore going provisions, within twenty four hours of the receipt of the complaint, enquire in to it and, if, *prima facie*, it is found true, suspend the student found guilty.

(2) Where, on enquiry by the head of the educational institution, it is proved that *prima facie* there is no substance in the complaint received under sub-section (1), he shall intimate the fact, in writing, to the complainant.

9. Power of the State Government to give directions.—The State Government may, in public interest, by order in writing for reasons to be recorded therein, give to the educational institutions general instructions to be followed by such institutions and such instructions may, notwithstanding anything contained in the Himachal Pradesh University Act, 1970 (17 of 1970) and the Himachal Pradesh Universities of Agriculture, Horticulture and Forestry Act, 1986 (4 of 1987), the Jaypee University of Information Technology Act, 2002 (14 of 2002), the Chitkara University (Establishment and Regulation) Act, 2008 (2 of 2009) the Eternal University (Establishment and Regulation) Act, 2008 (3 of 2009), any University established by Law in the State in private and public sector, the Himachal Pradesh Board of School Education Act, 1968 (14 of 1968), the Himachal Pradesh Board of Technical Education Act, 1986 (14 of 1986), the Societies Registration Act, 1860 (21 of 1860) and the Himachal Pradesh Societies Registration Act, 2006 (25 of 2006), include directions to make or amend any ordinances, statutes, regulations, rules, bye-laws relating to the prohibition of and the punishment for ragging, in such form and with in such period as may be specified in such order.

10. Provisions not to be derogatory to certain laws.—The provisions of this Act shall be in addition to and not in derogation of the Indian Penal Code, 1860 (45 of 1860), the Code of Criminal Procedure, 1973 (2 of 1974), and the statues framed under the Himachal Pradesh University Act, 1970 (17 of 1970), the Himachal Pradesh Universities of Agriculture, Horticulture and Forestry Act, 1986 (4 of 1987), the Jaypee University of Information Technology Act, 2002 (14 of 2002), the Chitkara University (Establishment and Regulation) Act, 2008 (2 of 2009), the Eternal University (Establishment and Regulation) Act, 2008 (3 of 2009), any University established by Law in the State in private and public sector, the Himachal Pradesh Board of School Education Act, 1968 (14 of 1968), the Himachal Pradesh Board of Technical Education Act, 1986 (14 of 1986), the Societies Registration Act, 1860 (21 of 1860) and the Himachal Pradesh Societies Registration Act, 2006 (25 of 2006).

11. Power to make Rules.—The State Government may, by notification published in the Official Gazette, make rules for carrying out the purposes of this Act.

12. Laying of Rules and orders.—Every order issued under section 9 and Rules made under section 11 shall be laid, as soon as may be after it is issued or made, before the Legislative Assembly while it is in session for a total period of not less than ten days which may be comprised in one session or in two or more successive sessions, and if be fore the expiry of the session in which it is so laid or the sessions afore said, the Assembly makes any modification in the rule, or as the case may be, in the order, or decides that the rule or the order, as the case may be, should not be issued or made, the rule or as the case may be, the order, shall, thereafter, have effect only in such modified form or be of no effect, as the case may be, so, however, that any such modification or annulment shall be without prejudice to the validity of any thing previously done under that rule or as the case may be, under that order.

13. Repeal of Ordinance No. 1 of 2009 and savings.—(1) The Himachal Pradesh Educational Institutions (Prohibitions of Ragging) Ordinance, 2009 is hereby repealed.

(2) Notwithstanding such repeal any action taken or anything done under the Ordinance so repealed shall be deemed to have been done or taken under the corresponding provisions of this Act.

(j) The Jammu and Kashmir Prohibition of Ragging Act, 2011

(Act No. VI of 2011)

[*9th April, 2011*]

An Act to prohibit ragging in educational institutions in the State of Jammu and Kashmir.

Be it enacted by the Jammu and Kashmir State Legislature in Sixty-second Year of Republic of India as follows :—

1. Short title and commencement.—(1) This Act may be called the Jammu and Kashmir Prohibition of Ragging Act, 2011.

(2) It shall come into force on the date of publication in the Government Gazette.

2. Definitions.—In this Act, unless the context otherwise requires,—

(a) "Act" means the Jammu and Kashmir Prohibition of Ragging Act, 2011;

(b) "educational institution" means and includes a University, College and any other institution, by whatever name called, whether a private or Government educational institution, carrying on the activity of imparting higher education therein, either exclusively or among other activities, and includes a polytechnic, an orphanage, a boarding home, a hostel, a tutorial institution and the premises attached thereto ;

(c) "fresher" means a fresh or new student admitted to an educational institution and includes junior students ;

(d) "Government" means the Government of Jammu and Kashmir ;

(e) "head of the educational institution" includes the Registrar of the University, Dean of a Faculty in the University, Dean of Medical Faculty, Director of the Institution or Principal, Headmaster, Manager or any other person responsible for the management of any educational institution ;

(f) "ragging" means any disorderly conduct, whether by words spoken or written, or by an act which has the effect of teasing, treating or handling with rudeness any other student, indulging in rowdy or undisciplined activities which causes or is likely to cause annoyance, hardship or psychological harm or to raise fear or apprehension thereof in a fresher or a junior student, or asking the student to do any act or perform something which such student will not do in the ordinary course and which has the effect of causing or generating a sense of shame or embarrassment or adverse affect on the physique or psyche of a fresher, or a junior student ;

(g) "student" means a person who is admitted to an educational institution and whose name is lawfully borne on the attendance register thereof ; and

(h) "State" means the State of Jammu and Kashmir.

3. Prohibition of ragging.—From the date of commencement of the Act, ragging within or outside any educational institution in the State shall be prohibited and no person shall commit, abet, propagate or participate in ragging within or outside any educational institution.

4. Penalty for ragging.—(1) Whosoever, directly or indirectly, commits or participates in or abets or propagates ragging within or, outside any educational institution shall, on conviction, be punished with imprisonment for a term which may extend to two years or with fine which may extend to ten thousand rupees or with both.

(2) If the particular person committing or abetting ragging is not identified, every person participating in, or present at, such ragging activity shall be liable to punishment under the Act and collective punishment shall be resorted to so as to act as a deterrent punishment and to ensure collective pressure on the potential raggers.

5. Procedure for making a complaint.—(1) Whenever any student or, as the case may be, the parents or guardian or a teacher of an educational institution complains, in writing, of ragging to the head of an educational institution, the head of that educational institution shall, within seven days of receipt of complaint, inquire into the matter mentioned in the complaint and if *prima facie* the complaint is found true, he shall immediately forward the complaint to the police station having jurisdiction over the area in which such educational institution is situated for registering a case under the Act.

(2) Where on an inquiry by the head of the educational institution, it is found that there is a no substance in the complaint received under sub-section (1), he shall intimate the fact in writing to the complainant.

6. Deemed abetment.—(1) If the head of any educational institution fails or neglects to take action in the manner specified in sub-section (1) of section 5 when a complaint of ragging is made, he shall be deemed to have abetted the offence of ragging and shall, on conviction, be punished as provided for in section 4.

(2) No Court shall take cognizance of an offence under sub-section (1) without a complaint in writing made by the District Magistrate concerned.

7. Removal from rolls of educational institution.—Any student convicted of an offence under section 4 shall be removed from the rolls of the educational institution and shall not be admitted in any educational institution in the State for a period of three years from the date of such removal.

8. Suspension of the student.—(1) Without prejudice to the foregoing provision, whenever a complaint is forwarded by the head of an educational institution to the police station under sub-section (1) of section 5, such student shall be suspended forthwith from the said institution and shall neither be allowed to enter the premises of the educational institution till the final outcome of the complaint under the Act nor shall be entitled to any of its facilities.

(2) Any student suspended under sub-section (1) shall be expelled from the boarding home, hostel and mess of the educational institution.

9. Prevention of ragging in educational institutions.—It shall be the duty of every educational institution to prevent ragging in such educational institution and for this purpose the educational institution shall, among other things, take the following steps:—

(i) the prospectus, the form for admission or any other literature issued to the aspirants for admission shall clearly mention that ragging is banned in the institution and anyone indulging in ragging is likely to be punished ;

(ii) the admission and enrolment form shall include a printed undertaking to be filled in and signed by the student to the effect that he/she is aware of the institution's approach towards ragging and the punishments to which he/she shall be liable if found, guilty of ragging ;

(iii) it shall display, on the notice board, the name, address and the contact number of the person or authority to whom a fresher should approach for help and guidance for various purposes ;

(iv) the head of the educational institution or a person higher in authority shall address meetings of professors, lecturers, instructors, teachers, parents or guardians and students, collectively or in groups, to create confidence by apprising them of their rights as well as obligations to fight against ragging, insisting on freshers to report to the head of educational institution or proctorial committee about instances of ragging and to generate confidence in their mind and to encourage them to report any instance of ragging to which they are subjected to or which comes in their knowledge ;

(v) at the commencement of the academic session, the educational institution should constitute a proctorial committee consisting of senior faculty members and hostel authorities like Wardens and a few responsible senior students to,—

(a) keep a continuous watch and vigil over ragging so as to prevent its occurrence and recurrence ; and

(b) promptly deal with the incidents of ragging brought to its notice and summarily punish the guilty, either by itself or by putting forth its finding/recommendations/suggestions before the authority competent to take action ;

(vi) all vulnerable locations shall be identified and especially watched ; (vii) the local community and the students in particular shall be made aware of the dehumanizing effect of ragging inherent in its perversity and posters, notice boards and signboards, wherever necessary, may be used for the purpose ; and

(viii) Migration certificate issued by the educational institution should have an entry apart from that of general conduct and behaviour as to whether the student has ever indulged in ragging and in particular was punished for such ragging.

10. Provision of the Act to be in addition to other laws.—Nothing in the Act shall be deemed to affect the operation of any other law for the time being in force in the State and the provisions of the Act shall be in addition to, and not in derogation of, such other laws.

11. Power to remove difficulties.—If any difficulty arises in giving effect to the provisions of the Act, the Government may, by order not inconsistent with the provisions of the Act, remove the difficulty

Provided that no such order shall be made after the expiry of a period of two years from the commencement of the Act.

12. Power to make Rules.—The Government may, by notification in the Government Gazette, make Rules to carry out the purposes of the Act.

Annexure 4

Bills

(a) Prevention of Ragging in Colleges and Institutions Bill, 2005

A Bill to provide for the prevention of ragging in colleges and institutions and for matters connected therewith. Be it enacted by Parliament in the Fifty-sixth Year of the Republic of India as follows:—

Statement of Object

The Bill intends to abolish the practice of ragging and/or harassment from all Colleges and Institutions, in an effort to clean up the social stigma that it causes. In no other country's education institutions ragging takes place except in India. The Bill intends to introduce stricter laws against ragging. The objective of the Bill is to make the campus areas free from any social injustice, mental, physical and/or sexual harassment that thousands of the students face each year during their first few months in college. The enactment of the Bill would see the decline and finally abolition of ragging on campus areas.

The Bill seeks to achieve the above objectives.

SANTOSH BAGRODIA

MEMORANDUM REGARDING DELEGATED LEGISLATION

Clause 8 of the Bill empowers the Central Government to make rules for carrying out the purposes of this Bill. The rules will relate to matters of details only.

The delegation of legislative power is of normal character.

1 Short title, extent and commencement.—(1) This Act may be called the Prevention of Ragging in Colleges and Institutions Act, 2005.

(2) It extends to the whole of India.

(3) It shall come into force at once.

2 Definitions.—In this Act unless the context otherwise requires,—

(a) "appropriate Government" means in the case of a State, the Government of that state and in other cases, the Central Government;

(b) "freshers" means those students who have taken admission in the first year of under-graduate level in any stream in any college or institution;

(c) "Institution" means a place or organization where facility for higher or professional education is provided whether private or Government;

(d) "prescribed" means prescribed by rules made under this Act;

(e) "ragging" means display of disorderly conduct, doing of any act which causes or is likely to cause physical or psychological harm or raise apprehension or fear or shame or embarrassment to a student in any college or institution;

(f) "seniors" means those students who are not in first Year of under-graduate or post-graduate level in any stream in any college or institution.

3 Clause 3.—(1) Notwithstanding anything contained in any other law for the time being in force the Central Government shall, as soon as may be, but within six months from the date of commencement of this Act, formulate such directives for a ban on ragging in all Colleges and Institutions functioning under Central Government as may be prescribed.

(2) The Central Government shall, issue similar directives to all State Governments for similar ban on ragging in all colleges and institutions in their respective jurisdiction.

(3) The ban under sub-section (1) shall also be extended to all colleges and institutions in all Union Territories.

4. Penalty.—(1) Whoever contravenes the provisions of section 3, shall be punished with rigorous imprisonment for three years and with a fine of rupee twenty-five thousand.

(2) The appropriate Government shall direct UGC or the funding agency of the college or the institution, as the case may be, to take such steps against the institution which fails to curb ragging as it may deem necessary.

5. Task Force.—(1) The appropriate Government shall, constitute a Task Force or a special unit under the respective local Police Department during the time of admission and the first quarter of academic session for active involvement in implementing the provision of this Act.

(2) After the first quarter the Task Force shall be used in the University Campus or College or Institution area in such manner as may be prescribed.

(3) In case the State Government fails to constitute such a Task Force or fails to lend support to the Task Force, the Central Government shall be empowered to intervene for constituting the Task Force for the State or States and grant it full rights under this Act.

(4) The appropriate Government shall extend its full support to the Task Force to enable it to perform its duties to the fullest to ensure that all Colleges and Institutions are rid of ragging and harassment of freshers.

(5) The Task Force shall comprise of both young policemen and women which shall be headed by a person not below the rank of a Police Inspector of the area in districts/towns/small cities for State level, and shall have the following duties;

(a) intimate the managements of all Colleges and Institutions in their campus areas of their objectives.

(b) ensure compliance of all Rules made under this Act.

(c) to move around in civil clothes and whenever required, in uniforms.

(d) ensure the safety of all staff and students (both freshers and seniors) in and around campus area.

(e) maintain strict secrecy and impartiality during exercises, operations and investigations.

(f) follow out number of surveillance exercises on campus areas.

(g) make surprise checks in any and all Colleges and Institutions to keep a check on ragging.

(h) make surprise checks in hostels.

(i) to be in constant touch with the staff and consult on various ragging incidences in their respective College or Institution.

(j) take inputs from various people including staff and freshers on any incident that comes to light.

(k) to give necessary support in terms of maintaining secrecy, moral, mental, medical, etc., to all students who have been victims of ragging.

(l) after thorough investigation, consider reports or complaints of parents of victims against any senior(s).

(m) to issue one formal warning after asserting the identity of any senior(s) either caught red handed or on a formal complaint by a junior or fresher against ragging.

(n) to intimate the management of that college about the warning of the student(s) on charges of ragging.

(o) after the warning if the same senior(s) indulge(s) in ragging or harassing, officers of the Task Force will make arrest and inform the college of the arrest.

6. Annual report on the functioning of Task Force.—(1) Every year all task forces shall present the facts and figures to their respective Commissioners of police on the number or ragging cases reported and details of actions taken against each case.

(2) The detail under sub-section (1) shall also be presented to the Ministry of Home Affairs and the Ministry of Human Resource Development of appropriate Government.

7. Overriding effect of the Act.—The provisions of this Act shall have effect notwithstanding anything inconsistent therewith contained in any enactment other than this Act, or any instrument having effect by virtue of any enactment other than this Act.

8. Power to make rules.—The Central Government may by notification in the Official Gazette, make rules for carrying out the purposes of this Act.

(b) The Prohibition and Eradication of Ragging Bill, 2011

AS INTRODUCED IN THE RAJYA SABHA

ON THE 19TH AUGUST, 2011

Bill No. XXVII of 2011

A Bill to prohibit and eradicate ragging in colleges and educational institutions and for matters connected therewith and incidental thereto.

Be it enacted by Parliament in the Sixty-second Year of the Republic of India as follows:—

1. (1) This Act may be called the Prohibition and Eradication of Ragging Act, 2011.

(2) It extends to the whole of India.

(3) It shall come into force on such date as the Central Government may, by notification in the Official Gazette, appoint and different dates may be appointed for different provisions of this Act and for different States, and any reference to commencement in any provision of this Act in relation to any State shall be construed as a reference to the commencement of that provision in that State.

2. In this Act unless the context otherwise requires,—

(a) "appropriate Government" means in the case of a State, the Government of that State and in other cases, the Central Government;

(b) "Committee" means the anti-ragging committee constituted under section 7; "helpline" means the anti-ragging helpline established under section 9 of this Act;

(c) "educational institution" means any college, institute, university whether established by the Government or by any citizen or body of citizens and whether in receipt of aid from Government or not, recognised by Central or State Government for the award of a certificate, diploma or a degree in any course of study, education or training;

(d) "freshers" means those students who have taken admission in the first year of under-graduate or post-graduate level in any stream in any college or educational institution;

(e) "head of the institution" means the Vice-Chancellor in case of a university or a deemed university and in case of any other institution or college, the Principal or the Director;

(f) "prescribed" means prescribed by rules made under this Act;

(g) "ragging" means display of disorderly conduct by a student as defined under section 4 of this Act;

(h) "seniors" means those students who are not in first year of under-graduate or post-graduate level in any stream in any college or educational institutions.

3. (1) The Act shall apply to all institutions coming within the definition of a University under sub-section (f) of section 2 of the University Grants Commission Act, 1956, and to all institutions deemed to be a university under section 3 of the University Grants Commission Act, 1956, to all other higher educational institutions, or elements of such universities or institutions, including its departments, constituent units and all the premises, whether being academic, residential, playgrounds, canteen, hostel or other such premises of such universities, deemed universities and higher educational institutions, whether located within the campus or outside, and to all means of transportation of students, whether public or private, accessed by students for the pursuit of studies in such universities, deemed universities and higher educational institutions.

(2) In addition to the educational institutions mentioned in sub-section (*1*), also applies to all vocational and professional institutions that admit students after twelve years of schooling.

4. The ragging shall constitute one or more of the following acts,—

(i) any conduct by any student or students whether by words spoken or written or by an act which has the effect of teasing, treating, torturing, or handling with rudeness a fresher or any other student;

(ii) indulging in rowdy or indisciplinary activities by an student or students which causes or is likely to cause annoyance, hardship, physical or psychological harm or to raise fear or apprehension thereof in any fresher or any other

(iii) asking any student to do any act which such student shall not in the ordinary course do and which has the effect of causing or generating a sense of shame, or torment or embarrassment so as to adversely affect they physique or psyche of such fresher or any other student;

(iv) any act by a student that prevents, disrupts or disturbs the regular academic activity of any other student or a fresher;

(v) exploiting the services of a fresher or any other student for completing the academic tasks assigned to an individual or a group of student;

(vi) any act of financial extortion or forceful expenditure burden put on a fresher or any other student by students;

(vii) any act of physical abuse including all variants of it; sexual abuse, homosexual assaults, stripping, forcing obscene and lewd acts, gestures, causing bodily harm or any other danger to health or person;

(viii) any act or abuse, by use of spoken words, telephone, short message service (SMS), e-mails, multi-media messaging service, post, public insults, pornographic material, photographs or video clips, etc., to derive perverted pleasure, vicarious or sadistic thrill from actively or passively participating in the discomfiture to fresher or any other student;

(ix) any act that affects the mental health and self-confidence of a fresher or any other student with or without an intent to derive a sadistic pleasure or showing off power, authority or superiority by a student over any fresher or any other student.

5. Notwithstanding anything contained in any other law, for the time being in force, in any trial under this Act, the burden of proof as to the innocence shall be on the accused.

6. (1) Notwithstanding anything contained in any other law for the time being in force the Central Government shall, as soon as may be, but within six months from the date of commencement of this Act, formulate such directives for prohibition of ragging in all colleges and educational institutions functioning under Central Government as may be prescribed.

(2) The Central Government shall, issue similar directives to all State Governments for prohibition of ragging in all colleges and educational institutions in their respective jurisdiction.

(3) The prohibition under sub-section (1) shall also be extended to all colleges and educational institutions in all Union Territories.

(4) Every public declaration of intent by any educational institution for admission of students to any course of study, brochure of admission or instruction booklet or the prospectus, in any electronic, audio-visual or print or any other media shall expressly provide that ragging is prohibited in the institution and anyone found guilty or ragging or abetting ragging whether actively or passively or being a part of conspiracy to promote ragging is liable to be punished in accordance with this Act.

7. (1) The appropriate Government shall ensure that an anti-ragging committee is constituted in every educational institution headed by the senior most faculty of the institution and consisting of representatives of civil and police administration including at least one female representative other representation from non-governmental organisation, parents, freshers and seniors.

(2) The appropriate Government shall extend its full support to the anti-ragging committee to enable it to perform its duties to the fullest to ensure that all colleges and educational institution are free from ragging and harassment of freshers.

(3) The anti-ragging committee shall perform the following functions:—

(a) to receive complaints on ragging and submit a report to the head of the institution;

(b) to take inputs from various people including staff and freshers on any incident of ragging;

(c) to conduct necessary awareness programme to enlighten the students regarding the effects of ragging;

(d) after conducting thorough investigation, action to be taken against the offenders as per the rules prescribed under this Act.

8. (1) Every educational institution shall have a anti-ragging squad.

(2) The anti-ragging squad shall function under the guidance of anti-ragging committee consisting of the representatives nominated by the head of the educational institution.

(3) The anti-ragging squad shall perform the following functions:—

(a) to make surprise checks in hostel and campus to keep a check on ragging;

(b) to report any incident of ragging to the committee;

(c) to be in constant touch with the staff and students and consult various incidence of ragging.

9. (1) The appropriate Government shall constitute an anti-ragging helpline, in the country round the clock, to register complaint from students, parents, friends or anybody who is a witness to the act of ragging.

(2) Every educational institution shall publish the telephone numbers of the helpline and other functionaries in the district in the brochure of admission or prospectus.

(3) The complaint shall be lodged through phone, fax, e-mail or SMS or anywhere in the country throughout the year round the clock.

(4) After registration of the complaint, necessary action shall be taken by the appropriate Government in such manner as may be prescribed.

10. (1) Any student convicted under this Act shall be debarred from continuing his studies in any educational institutions for a period of three years.

(2) Whoever contravenes the provisions of this Act shall be punished with fine which shall not be less than rupees twenty-five thousand but which may extend to rupees one lakh or with rigorous imprisonment for a term which may extend to three years or, with both.

(3) The appropriate Government shall direct University Grants Commission or the funding agency of the college or the educational institution, as the case may be, to take such steps against the head of the educational institution was fails to curb ragging as it may deem necessary.

11. The proceeding under this Act shall be tried by the Educational Tribunal or the High Court in the respective State as far as possible.

12. Save as provided under this Act, the provisions of the Code of Criminal Procedure 1973 shall be applicable to any trial under this Act.

13. The provisions of this Act shall be in addition to, and not in derogation of, any other law for the time being in force.

14. The Central Government may by notification in the Official Gazette, make rules for carrying out the purposes of this Act.

STATEMENT OF OBJECTS AND REASONS

Ragging is a serious problem. Besides the humanitarian and social aspects, which need no elaboration, it has also serious economic implications and has a bearing on the standards of education. It is a recognised form of Human Right violation. These are also instances whose students also suffered death due to forced ragging. There is a national outcry to prohibit ragging and all sections of the society demanded that the Government must take proactive steps to eradicate this menace. On the 8th May, 2009, the Hon'ble Supreme Court ordered the Union Government to implement a plan for prevention of ragging. Following this Judgment the (UGC) University Grants Commission and other regulatory authorities like All India Council for Technical Education (AICTE), Medical Council of India (MCI), Dental Council of India (DCI), etc. published a single set of regulations that would cover the entire nation and all educational institutions. The regulations of University Grants Commission (UGC) came into effect on June, 2009. This Bill combines the essential elements of UGC regulations and the order of the Hon'ble Supreme Court. Therefore, in a certain sense, the Bill simply formalises what exists as of today. All elements of the Bill are actually in place at present.

Hence, this Bill

DR. JANARDHAN WAGHMARE

FINANCIAL MEMORANDUM

Clause 9 of the Bill seeks to constitute an anti-ragging helpline by the appropriate Government to register complaint with regard to ragging. The Bill, if enacted, will involve expenditure from the Consolidated Fund of India. However, at this stage, it is not possible to quantify the exact amount of recurring and non-recurring expenditure likely to be involved.

MEMORANDUM REGARDING DELEGATED LEGISLATION

Clause 14 of the Bill empowers the Central Government to make rules for carrying out the purposes of this Bill. The rules will relate to matters of details only. The delegation of legislative power is of normal character.

RAJYA SABHA

(Dr. Janardhan Waghmare, M.P.)

(c) Prohibition of Ragging and Unfair Practices in Educational Institutions and Universities Bill, 2012

A BILL to provide for prohibition of ragging and unfair practices in educational institutions and universities and for matters connected therewith or incidental thereto.

Be it enacted by Parliament in the Sixty-third Year of the Republic of India as follows:—

Statement of Object

There has been mushrooming growth of higher educational institutions in recent years especially, the technical and medical educational institutions.

There have been allegations that these educational institutions are resorting to unfair practices such as charging of capitation fee, demanding donations, not issuing receipt in respect of payments made by or on behalf of students, low quality delivery of education services, false claims of quality education through misleading advertisement, etc. There is no law to check the malpractices in such educational institutions. A mechanism to provide for speedy resolution of matters relating to malpractices in higher educational institutions is required to be in place in order to provide relief to the victims of such malpractices. The Bill, therefore, seeks to provide, *inter alia,* for—

(1) banning of acts of ragging within or outside the educational institutions;

(2) prohibition of capitation fee and unfair practices by educational institutions; and

(3) constitution of redressal committee for early disposal of complaints.

Hence this Bill.

FINANCIAL MEMORANDUM

Clause 11 of the Bill provides for constitution of the Redressal Committees in every district of the country to enquire into malpractices by educational institutions. The State Governments will have to bear the expenditure in respect of educational institutions established under Act of Legislative Assembly from their respective Consolidated Funds. However, the Central Government shall have to bear the expenditure in respect of educational institutions established by or under an Act of Parliament as well as educational institutions in the Union Territories.

The Bill, therefore, if enacted, will involve expenditure from the Consolidated Fund of India. It is estimated that a sum of rupees three crore may be involved as recurring expenditure per annum.

A non-recurring expenditure of about rupees five crore is also likely to be involved.

MEMORANDUM REGARDING DELEGATED LEGISLATION

Clause 14 of the Bill gives power to the Central Government to make Rules for carrying out the purposes of the Bill. The Rules will relate to matters of detail only.

The delegation of legislative power is, therefore, of a normal character.

1. Short title, extent and commencement.—(1) This Act may be called the Prohibition of Ragging and Unfair Practices in Educational Institutions and Universities Act, 2012.

(2) It extends to the whole of India except the State of Jammu and Kashmir.

(3) It shall come into force on such date as the Central Government may, by notification in the Official Gazette, appoint.

2. Definitions.—In this Act, unless the context otherwise requires,-

(a) "appropriate Government' means in the case of a State, the Government of that State and in all other cases, the Central Government;

(b) "appropriate statutory authority' means any authority established under any law for the time being in force for co-ordinating or determining or maintaining the standards of education including technical and medical education and education in universities;

(c) "capitation fee' means any amount (by whatever name called),-

(i) demanded or charged or collected, directly or indirectly, for, or, on behalf of any institution, or paid by any person in consideration for admitting any person as student in such institution; and which is in excess of the fee payable towards tuition fee and other fees and other charges declared by any institution in its prospectus for admitting any person as student in such institution; or

(ii) paid or demanded or charged or collected, by way of donation, for, or, on behalf of any institution, or paid by any person in consideration for admitting any person as a student in such institution;

(d) 'educational institution' means a technical educational institution or medical educational institution or any such institution, whether registered under the Societies Registration Act, 1860 or not, and recognized as such, by the appropriate statutory authority or a university as defined in section 2 of the University Grants Commission Act, 1956 and includes an institution deemed to be a University under section 3 of that Act or under any other law for the time being in force;

(e) "prospectus" includes any publication, whether in print or displayed in internet or in any electronic device for public consumption, otherwise, issued for providing fair and transparent information, relating to an institution, to the general public (including to those seeking admission in such institution) by the management of such institution or any other authority or person authorised by such institution to do so;

(f) "ragging" means an act by a student or group of students inside or outside the educational institution which causes or is likely to cause physical or psychological harm or bring embarrassment to or creates fear in another student and includes acts of teasing, abusing, causing hurt or making one to do any act or perform something which he will not willingly do in the ordinary course.

(g) "prescribed" means prescribed by rules made under this Act; and

(h) "unfair practice" includes-

(i) charging of capitation fee;

(ii) charging of exorbitant fee;

(iii) lack of transparency in conducting entrance test;

(iv) recruiting teaching and office faculty with low salary;

(v) recruiting teachers without adequate qualification;

(vi) exploitation of teachers;

(vii) allowing students to take examination without adequate attendance;

(viii) malpractice in evaluation;

(ix) advertising falsely about infrastructure or institution with the intention to induce students to take admission;

(x) exorbitant charges for prospectus;

(xi) accepting any fee or charge without proper receipt;

(xii) admitting ineligible students;

(xiii) allowing students to copy;

(xiv) victimizing students, particularly those belonging to the Scheduled Castes, the Scheduled Tribes, the Other Backward Classes and the weaker sections of society;

(xv) withholding educational certificates to eligible students; and

(xvi) impounding of educational certificates or passports of teachers and office staff without valid reasons or compelling teachers to award pass marks to certain students.

3. **Prohibition of ragging.**—Ragging in educational institutions is hereby prohibited.

4. **Inquiry on ragging.**—(1) Any act of ragging brought to the notice of the head of the educational institution or any other person responsible for the management of the educational institution shall be inquired into expeditiously.

(2) Where after conclusion of enquiry, a student is found guilty of committing or participating in or abetting the act of ragging, he shall be expelled from the educational institution and shall not be admitted in any other educational institution.

(5) Where the findings of the inquiry report are disputed by the expelled student, the educational institution shall forward the enquiry report to the Redressal Committee constituted under section 11.

5. **Educational institutions not to accept fee and charges not mentioned in prospectus.**—(1) No educational institution shall, for admission in any course or programme of study, accept any payment, other than the fee and charges mentioned in its prospectus.

(2) Every educational institution shall issue a proper receipt of the fee and charges to the students admitted in the institution.

6. **Prohibition of capitation fee.**—(1) No educational institution shall, directly or indirectly, demand or charge or accept any capitation fee or donation, as a consideration for admission in a course or programme of study.

(2) No person shall, directly or indirectly, offer or pay any capitation fee or donation, either in cash or kind, for obtaining admission in a course or programme of study.

7. **Penalty for demanding or accepting capitation fee.**—Any educational institution, which violates the provisions of section 6, shall, without prejudice to proceedings for prosecution under any other law for the time being in force, be liable to a penalty which may extend to one lakh rupees.

8. **Mandatory publication of prospectus.**—Every educational institution shall, before the expiry of ninety days prior to the date of commencement of admission process to any of its course or programme of study, publish a prospectus containing all such minute details, as may be prescribed, regarding admission.

9. **Penalty for doing contrary to information in prospectus.**—Any educational institution, which does anything contrary to the information published by it in its prospectus or resort to any unfair practice, shall, without prejudice to any proceedings for prosecution any other law for the time being in force, be liable to a penalty which may extend to ten thousand rupees.

10. Complaint of unfair practice.—Any aggrieved person or any other person, on behalf of such aggrieved person, may make complaint of ragging or unfair practice or demand of capitation fee or donation, in such form and manner, as may be prescribed, to the Redressal Committee constituted under section 11.

11. Constitution of the Redressal Committee in every district.—(1) The appropriate Government shall constitute, in every district having any educational institution, a Committee to be known as the Redressal Committee.

(2) The Committee shall consist of—

(a) a Chairperson;

(b) two judicial members;

(c) two academic members; and

(d) two administrative members.

(3) The terms and conditions of service of the Chairperson and other members of the Committee shall be such as may be prescribed.

(4) The Committee shall have such number of officers and staff as may be required for its efficient functioning.

12. Functions of the Committee.—(1) The Committee shall—

(i) enquire into every case of ragging referred to it by the educational institutions within its territorial jurisdiction or received directly from any aggrieved person or any other person on behalf of such person;

(ii) enquire into every complaint of unfair practice or demand of capitation fee or donation by an educational institution within its territorial jurisdiction;

(iii) recommend punitive action against the erring educational institution; and

(iv) recommend compensation to the victims of ragging or unfair practices by the institution concerned;

(2) The Committee shall dispose of every complaint within a period of ninety days from the date of receipt of such complaint.

(3) The Committee shall afford an opportunity of being heard to every person or institution against whom a complaint is made.

(4) The Committee shall forward its report of enquiry into a complaint to the appropriate statutory authority, which shall recommend such action against the institution, as may be prescribed.

13. Act to have overriding effect.—The provisions of this Act shall have effect notwithstanding anything inconsistent therewith contained in any other law for the time being in force.

14. Power to make rules.—(1) The Central Government may, by notification in the Official Gazette, make rules for carrying out the purposes of this Act.

(2) Every rule made under this Act shall be laid, as soon as may be after it is made, before each House of Parliament, while it is in session, for a total period of thirty days which may be comprised in one session or in two or more successive sessions, and if, before the expiry of the session immediately following the session or the successive sessions aforesaid, both Houses agree in making any modification in the rule or both the Houses agree that the rule should not be made, the rule shall thereafter have effect only in such modified form or be of no effect, as the case may be; so, however, that any such modification or annulment shall be without prejudice to the validity of anything previously done under that rule.

Annexure 5

International Legislation

Sri Lanka Consolidated Acts

An act to eliminate ragging and other forms of violence, and cruel, inhuman and degrading treatment, from educational institutions

1. Short title.—This Act may be cited as the Prohibition of Ragging and Other Forms of Violence in Educational Institutions Act, No. 20 of 1998

2. Ragging.—(1) Any person who commits, or participates in; ragging, within or outside an educational institution, shall be guilty of an offence under this Act and shall on conviction after summary trial before a Magistrate be liable, to rigorous imprisonment for a term not exceeding two years and may also be ordered to pay compensation of an amount determined by court, to the person in respect of whom the offence was committed for the injuries caused to such person.

(2) A person who, whilst committing ragging causes sexual harassment or grievous hurt to any student or a member of the staff, of an educational institution shall be guilty of an offence under this Act and shall on conviction after summary trial before a Magistrate be liable to imprisonment for a term not exceeding ten years and may -also be ordered to pay compensation of an amount determined by court, to the person in respect of whom the offence was committed for the injuries caused to such person.

3. Criminal intimidation.—Any person who, within or outside an educational institution, threatens, verbally or in writing, to cause injury to the person, reputation or property of any student or a member of the staff, of all educational institution (in this section referred to as "the victim") or to the person, reputation or property of some other person in whom the victim is interested, with the intention of causing fear in the victim or of compelling the victim to do any act which the victim is not legally required to do, or to omit to do any act which the victim is entitled to do, shall be guilty of an offence under this Act and shall on conviction after summary trial before a Magistrate be liable to rigorous imprisonment for a term not exceeding five years.

4. Hostage taking.—Any person who does any act by which the personal liberty and the freedom of movement of any student or a member of the staff of an educational institution or other person within such educational institution or any premises under the management and control of such educational institution, is restrained without lawful justification and for the purpose of forcing such student, member of the staff or person to take a particular course of action, shall be guilty of an offence under this Act and shall on conviction after summary trial before a Magistrate, be liable to rigorous imprisonment for a term not exceeding seven years.

5. Wrongful restraint.—Any person who unlawfully obstructs any student or a member of the staff of an educational institution, in such a manner as to prevent such student or member of the staff from proceeding in any direction in which such student or member of the staff, has a right to proceed, shall be guilty of an offence under this Act and shall on conviction after summary trial before a Magistrate be liable to rigorous imprisonment for a term not exceeding seven years.

6. Unlawful confinement.—Any person who unlawfully restrains any student or a member of the staff of an educational institution in such a manner as to prevent such student or member of the staff from proceeding beyond certain circumscribing limits, shall be guilty of an offence under this Act and shall on conviction after summary trial before a Magistrate be liable to imprisonment for a term not exceeding seven years.

7. Forcible occupation and damage to property of an educational institution.—(1) Any person who, without lawful excuse, occupies, by force, any premises of, or under the management or control of, an educational institution shall be guilty of an offence under this Act, and shall on conviction after summary trial before a Magistrate be liable to imprisonment for a term not exceeding ten years or to a fine not exceeding ten thousand rupees or to both such imprisonment and fine.

(2) Any person who causes mischief in respect of any property of, or under the management or control of, an educational institution shall be guilty of an offence under this Act and shall on conviction after summary trial before a Magistrate he liable to imprisonment for a term to not exceeding twenty years and a fine of five thousand rupees or three times the amount of the loss or damage caused to such property, which ever amount is higher.

8. Orders of expulsion or dismissal.—Where a person is convicted of an offence under this Act, the court may, having regard to the gravity of the offence.

(a) in any case where the person convicted is a student of an educational institution, order that such person be expelled from such institution;

(b) in any case where the person convicted is a member of the staff of an educational institution, order that such person be dismissed from such educational institution.

9. Bail.—(1) A person suspected or accused of committing an offence under subsection (2) of section 2 or section 4 of this Act shall not be released on bail except by the judge of a High Court established by Article 154P of the Constitution. In exercising his discretion to grant bail such Judge shall have regard to the provisions of section 14 of the Bail Act, No. 30 of 1997.

(2) Where a person is convicted of an offence under subsection (2) of section 2 or section 4 of this Act, and an appeal is preferred against such conviction, the Court convicting such person may, taking into consideration the gravity of the offence and the antecedents of the person convicted, either release or refuse to release, such person on bail.

10. Certain Provisions of the Code of Criminal Procedure Act not to apply to persons convicted or found guilty of an offence under this Act.—Notwithstanding anything in the Code of Criminal Procedure Act, No. 15 of 1979.

(a) the provisions of section 303 of that Act shall not apply in the case of any person who is convicted,

(b) the provisions of section 306 of that Act shall not apply in the case of any person who pleads or is found guilty,

11. Offences under this Act deemed to be cognizable offences.—All offences under this Act shall be deemed to be cognizable Offences for the purposes of the application of the provisions of the Code of Criminal Procedure Act, No. 15 of 1979, notwithstanding anything contained in the First Schedule to that Act.

12. Certificate.—Where in any prosecution for an offence under this Act, a question arises whether any person is a student or a member of the staff of an educational institution or whether any premises or property is the property of, or is under the management and control of, an educational institution a certificate purporting to be under the hand of the head or other officer of such educational institution to the effect that the person named therein is a student or a member of the staff of such educational institution, or that the premises or property specified therein is the property of, or is under the management and control of, such educational institution, shall be admissible in evidence without proof of signature and shall be *prima facie* evidence of the facts stated therein.

13. Admissibility of statement in evidence.—(1) If in the course, of a trial for an offence under this Act, any witness shall on any material point contradict either expressly or by necessary implication a statement previously given by him in the course of any investigation into such offence, it shall be lawful for the Magistrate if, after due inquiry into the circumstances in which the statement was inside, he considers it safe and just"

(a) to act upon the statement given by the witness in the course of the investigation, if such statement is corroborated in material particulars by evidence from an independent source; and

(b) to have such witness at the conclusion of such trial, tried before such court upon a charge for intentionally giving false evidence in a stage of a judicial proceeding,

(2) At any trial under paragraph (b) of subsection (1) it shall be sufficient to prove that the accused made the contradictory statements alleged in the charge and it shall not by necessary to prove which of such statements is false.

14. Provisions of this Act to be in addition to and not in derogation of the provisions of the 14. Penal Code & c.—The provisions of this Act shall be in addition to and not in derogation of, the provisions of the Penal Code, the Convention Against Torture and Other Cruel, Inhuman or Degrading Treatment or Punishment Act, No. 22 of 1994 or any other law.

15. Priority for trials and appeals under this Act.—Every Court shall give priority to the trial of any person charged with any offence under this Act and to the bearing of any appeal from the conviction of any person for appeals under any such offence and any sentence imposed on such conviction.

17. Sinhala text to Prevail in case of inconsistency.—In this Act unless the context otherwise requires " "criminal force", "fear", "force", "grievous hurt", "hurt" and "mischief shall have the respective meanings assigned to them in the Penal Code; "educational institution" means—

(a) a Higher Educational Institution;

(b) any other Institution recognized under Chapter IV of the Universities Act, No, 16 of 1978;

(c) the Buddhist and Pali University established by the Buddhist and Pali University of Sri Lanka Act, No. 74 of 1981;

(d) the Buddha Sravaka Bhikku University, established by the Buddha Sravaka Bhikku University Act, No. 26 of 1996;

(e) any Institute registered under section 14 of the Tertiary and Vocational Education Act, No. 20 of 1990;

(f) any Advanced Technical Institute established under the Sri Lanka Institute- of Technical Education Act, No. 29 of 1995;

(g) a Pirivena registered under the Pirivena Education Act, No. 64 of 1979 and receiving grants from State funds and includes a Pirivena Training Institute established under that Act;

(h) the Sri Lanka Law College;

(i) the National Institute of Education established; by the National Institute of Education Act, No.

(j) the College of Education established by the: Colleges of Education Act, No. 30 of 1986, or a Training College;

(k) a Government school or an assisted school or an unaided school, within the meaning of the Education Ordinance (Chapter 185);

and includes any other institution established for the purpose of providing education, instruction or training; "head of an educational institution" means the Vice-Chancellor, Mahopadyaya, Director, President, Principal or any other person howsoever designated charged with the administration and management of the affairs of such educational institution; "Higher Educational institution" has the meaning assigned to it in the Universities Act, No. 16 of 1978; "ragging" means any act which causes or is likely to cause physical or psychological injury or mental pain or : fear to a student or a member of the staff of an educational institution; "student" means a student of an educational institution; "sexual harassment" means the use of criminal force, words or actions to cause sexual annoyance or harassment to a student or a member of the staff, of an educational institution.

Annexure 6

Affidavit

1. UGC

(a) Affidavit by the Student

I, (full name of student with admission/registration/enrolment number) S/o D/o Mr./Mrs./Ms. ...., having been admitted to (name of the institution), have received a copy of the UGC Regulations on Curbing the Menace of Ragging in Higher Educational Institutions, 2009, (hereinafter called the "Regulations") carefully read and fully understood the provisions contained in the said Regulations. (2) I have, in particular, perused clause 3 of the Regulations and am aware as to what constitutes ragging. (3) I have also, in particular, perused clause 7 and clause 9.1 of the Regulations and am fully aware of the penal and administrative action that is liable to be taken against me in case I am found guilty of or abetting ragging, actively or passively, or being part of a conspiracy to promote ragging. (4) I hereby solemnly aver and undertake that

(a) I will not indulge in any behaviour or act that may be constituted as ragging under clause 3 of the Regulations.

(b) I will not participate in or abet or propagate through any act of commission or omission that may be constituted as ragging under clause 3 of the Regulations.

(5) I hereby affirm that, if found guilty of ragging, I am liable for punishment according to clause 9.1 of the Regulations, without prejudice to any other criminal action that may be taken against me under any penal law or any law for the time being in force. 6) I hereby declare that I have not been expelled or debarred from admission in any institution in the country on account of being found guilty of, abetting or being part of a conspiracy to promote, ragging; and further affirm that, in case the declaration is found to be untrue, I am aware that my admission is liable to be cancelled.

Declared this ....day of...............month of..............year.

...............................Signature of deponent

Name.............................

VERIFICATION Verified that the contents of this affidavit are true to the best of my knowledge and no part of the affidavit is false and nothing has been concealed or misstated therein.

Verified at (place) on this the (day) of (month), (year).

Signature of deponent

Solemnly affirmed and signed in my presence on this the (day) of (month), (year) after reading the contents of this affidavit.

OATH COMMISSIONER

(b) Affidavit by Parent/Guardian

I, Mr./Mrs./Ms. ....(full name of parent/ guardian) father/mother/guardian of , (full name of student with admission/registration/ enrolment number), having been admitted to................ (name of the institution), have received a copy of the UGC Regulations on Curbing the Menace of Ragging in Higher Educational Institutions, 2009, (hereinafter called the "Regulations"), carefully read and fully understood the provisions contained in the said Regulations. 2) I have, in particular, perused clause 3 of the Regulations and am aware as to what constitutes ragging. 3) I have also, in particular, perused clause 7 and clause 9.1 of the Regulations and am fully aware of the penal and administrative action that is liable to be taken against my ward in case he/she is found guilty of or abetting ragging, actively or passively, or being part of a conspiracy to promote ragging. 4) I hereby solemnly aver and undertake that

(a) My ward will not indulge in any behaviour or act that may be constituted as ragging under clause 3 of the Regulations.

(b) My ward will not participate in or abet or propagate through any act of commission or omission that may be constituted as ragging under clause 3 of the Regulations.

(5) I hereby affirm that, if found guilty of ragging, my ward is liable for punishment according to clause 9.1 of the Regulations, without prejudice to any other criminal action that may be taken against my ward under any penal law or any law for the time being in force. 6) I hereby declare that my ward has not been expelled or debarred from admission in any institution in the country on account of being found guilty of, abetting or being part of a conspiracy to promote, ragging; and further affirm that, in case the declaration is found to be untrue, the admission of my ward is liable to be cancelled.

Declared this ....day of................. month of ....year.

..............................Signature of deponent

Name.............................

Address: Telephone/Mobile No.:

Verification

Verified that the contents of this affidavit are true to the best of my knowledge and no part of the affidavit is false and nothing has been concealed or misstated therein. Verified at (place) on this the (day) of (month), (year).

Signature of deponent

Solemnly affirmed and signed in my presence on this the (day) of (month), (year) after reading the contents of this affidavit.

OATH COMMISSIONER

2. MCI

(a) Undertaking by Candidate/Student

1. I, ... S/o. D/o. of Mr./Mrs./Ms. ...., have carefully read and fully understood the law prohibiting ragging and the directions of the Supreme Court and the Central/State Government in this regard. 2. I have received a copy of the MCI Regulations on Curbing the Menace of Ragging in Higher Educational Institutions, 2009. 3. I hereby undertake that- • I will not indulge in any behavior or act that may come under the definition of ragging, • I will not participate in or abet or propagate ragging in any form, • I will not hurt anyone physically or psychologically or cause any other harm. 4. I hereby agree that if found guilty of any aspect of ragging, I may be punished as per the provisions of the MCI Regulations mentioned above and/or as per the law in force. Signed this .... day of............................month of..........................year Signature Address: .... Name: (1) Witness: (2) Witness: 12

(b) Undertaking by Parent/Guardian

1. I, ...F/o. M/o. G/o.................................., have carefully read and fully understood the law prohibiting ragging and the directions of the Hon'ble Supreme Court and the Central/State Government in this regard as well as the MCI Regulations on Curbing the Menace of Ragging in Higher Educational Institutions, 2009. 2. I assure you that my son/daughter/ward will not indulge in any act of ragging. 3. I hereby agree that if he/she is found guilty of any aspect of ragging, he/she may be punished as per the provisions of the MCI Regulations mentioned above and/or as per the law in force. Signed this .... day of .... month of..................... Year Signature Address: .... Name: (1) Witness: (2) Witness:

3. AICTE

(a) Affidavit by the Student

I, (full name of student with admission/registration/enrolment number)

S/o..- D/o. Mr./Mrs./Ms...

(1) having been admitted to (name of the institution) have received a copy of the AICTE regulations on Curbing the menace of Ragging in Higher Educational Institutions, 2009, (hereinafter called the "Regulations") carefully read and fully understood the provisions contained in the said Regulations.

(2) I have, in particular, perused clause 3 of the Regulations and am aware as to what constitutes ragging.

(3) I have also, in particular, perused clause 7 and clause 9.1 of the Regulation and am fully aware of the penal and administrative action that is liable to be taken against me in case I am found guilty of or abetting ragging, actively or passively, or being part of a conspiracy to promote ragging.

(4) I hereby solemnly aver and undertake that

   (a) I will not indulge in any behavior or act that may be constituted as ragging under clause 3 of the Regulations.

   (b) I will not participate in or abet or propagate through any act of commission or omission that may be constituted as ragging under clause 3 of the Regulations.

(5) I hereby affirm that, if found guilty of ragging, I am liable for punishment according to clause 9.1 of the Regulations, without prejudice to any other criminal action that may be taken against me under any penal law or any law for the time being in force.

(6) I hereby declare that I have not been expelled or debarred from admission in any institution in the country on account of being found guilty of, abetting or being part of a conspiracy to promote, ragging; and further affirm that, in case the declaration is found to be untrue, I am aware that my admission is liable to be cancelled.

Declared this ....day of..................... month of ....year.....................

Signature of Deponent

Name

Verification

Verified that the contents of this affidavit are true to the best of my knowledge and no part of the affidavit is false and nothing has been concealed or misstated therein.

Verified at (place) on this the (day) of (month) (year)

....

Signature of deponent Solemnly affirmed and signed in my presence on this the (day) of month, (year) after reading the contents of this affidavit.

OATH COMMISSIONER

(b) Affidavit by Parent/Guardian

I,.. Mr./Mrs./Ms.

(full name of parent/guardian) father / mother/guardian of ....(full name of student with admission /registration/enrolment number),

(1) having been admitted to ____________ (name of the Institution), have received a copy of the AICTE regulations on Curbing the menace of Ragging in Higher Educational Institutions, 2009, (hereinafter called the "Regulations") carefully read and fully understood the provisions contained in the said Regulations.

(2) I have, in particular, perused clause 3 of the Regulations and am aware as to what constitutes ragging.

(3) I have also, in particular, perused clause 7 and clause 9.1 of the Regulations and am fully aware of the penal and administrative action that is liable to be taken against my ward in case he/she is found guilty or abetting ragging, actively or passively, or being part of a conspiracy to promote ragging.

(4) I hereby solemnly aver and undertake that

  (a) My ward will not indulge in any behavior or act that may be constituted as ragging under clause 3 of the Regulations.

  (b) My ward will not participate in or abet or propagate through any act of commission or omission that may be constituted as ragging under clause 3 of the Regulations.

(5) I hereby affirm that, if found guilty of ragging, my ward is liable for punishment according to clause 9.1 of the Regulations, without prejudice to any other criminal action that may be taken against my ward under any penal law or any law for the time being in force.

(6) I hereby declare that my ward has not been expelled or debarred from admission in any institution in the country on account of being found guilty of, abetting or being part of a conspiracy to promote, ragging; and further affirm that, in case the declaration is found to be untrue, I am aware that admission of my ward is liable to be cancelled.

Declared this ....day of .... month of ....year.....................

Signature of Deponent
Name:
Address:
Telephone/Mobile No:

Verification

Verified that the contents of this affidavit are true to the best of my knowledge and no part of the affidavit is false and nothing has been concealed or misstated therein.

Verified at __ (place) on this the________(day) of _ (month) and ________(year)

Signature of deponent

Solemnly affirmed and signed in my presence on this the (day) of month, (year) after reading the contents of this affidavit.

OATH COMMISSIONER

Bibliography

Anant Kumar Asthana, Eradication of Ragging: Realities and Recommendations a legal Perspective, CURE Report: CR2007/03-03, available at http://noragging.com/index.php/Research/Reports/Ragging-and-Human-Rights.html.

Arun Ferreira, Prison Diaries, available at http://www.openthemagazine.com/article/nation/prison-diaries.

Coalition to Uproot Ragging from Education (CURE), available at http://noragging.com/index.php/CURE/About/About-CURE.html.

Common Forms of Ragging, available athttp://www.no2ragging.org/raggingforms.html.

Diego Gambetta, Codes of The Underworld: How Criminals Communicate, 1st Edn., 2009.

Discrimination and Ragging, CURE REPORT CR 2006/02-25,available at http://www.noragging.com/analysis/CR2007_02_25_DiscriminationAndRagging.pdf.

Dr. Ch Venkateswarlu and N. Satyasri, Effects of Ragging on Human Dignity-A Critique, International Journal of Multidisciplinary Educational Research ISSN: 2277-7881, Volume1, Issue 4, Sept 2012.

Education in Ancient India, available at http://www.savehinduism.in/vichaar/article/464.html.

Eric D. Werker and Faisal Z. Ahmed, What Do Non-Governmental Organizations Do? available at http://www.hbs.edu/faculty/Publication%20Files/08-041.pdf.

G. Pramod Kumar, Ram Singh's death: Rape and ugly sexual violence in Indian jails, available at http://www.firstpost.com/india/ram-singhs-death-rape-and-ugly-sexual-violence-in-indian-jails-657071.html.

Gaurav Singhal, Head, RTI cell of Society against Violence in Education (SAVE), available athttp://www.no2ragging.org/morerti.html.

Gulshan Naveen, Ragging – The Red Alert, 1st ed. 2010.

Harsh Agarwal, Evolution of Ragging, CURE Report CR2005/07-27, available at http://noragging.com/index.php/Research/Ragging-The-Phenomenon/Evolution-of-Ragging.html.

Harsh Agarwal,, Paper on "Legal Awareness Programme on Anti-Ragging" available at http://www.humiliationstudies.org/documents/AgarwalPsychologyBehindRagging.pdf.

Harsh's on "Ragging" in Colleges in India, Research Report by Harsh Agarwal, available at http://www.humiliationstudies.org/documents/BrittonAgarwalConversationonRagging.pdf.

http://www.amanmovement.org.

http://www.no2ragging.org.

https://antiragging.in.

Jorge Srabstein, 'Deaths Linked to Bullying and Hazing', International Journal Adolescent and Medicine Health 2008;20:235-9.

K. Jaishankar and Debarati Halder, "Cyber bullying among school students in India", International perspectives on crime & justice, 1st Edn., 2009.

Lamb J, Pepler DJ and Craig W., Approach to bullying and victimization, Can Fam Physician 2009;55:356-60.

Madhavi Chopra, Ragging in Educational Institutes: A Human Rights Perspective available at http://www.legalserviceindia.com/articles/ragging.html.

Michael Yaziji and Jonathan Doh, NGOs and Corporations: Conflict and Collaboration, available at http://assets.cambridge.org/97805218/66842/excerpt/9780521866842_excerpt.pdf,.

Mohit Garg, What is Ragging?, available at http://noragging.com/index.php/Research/Ragging-The-Phenomenon/-What-is-Ragging.html.

Ms. Jayasree Sar, Ragging: Is it a Pathological or Casual Phenomenon of College Culture? An Exploratory Study, unpublished M.Sc. dissertation from Dept of Psychology, Univ. of Calcutta, 2006.

Naveen Agarwal, Tips for Overcoming Ragging Trauma, available at http://noragging.com/index.php/Research/Finding-a-CURE/Tips-for-Overcoming-Ragging-Trauma.html.

PUCL Bulletin, Jan. 2001, available at http://www.pucl.org/reports/WestBengal/2001/nhrc.htm.

Park K., Concept of Health and Diseases, In: Textbook of Preventive and Social Medicine, 19th Edn., Jabalpur, Banarsidas Bhanot Publishers, 2007.

R.K. Raghavan., Campus Menace, Frontline, Volume 26, Issue No. 16, Aug. 01-14, 2009.

Ragging in India, A Summary Report on Incidents, Social Perceptions and Psychological Perspectives, CURE REPORT: CR2007_05-16, May 16 2007, available at http://www.noragging.com/analysis/CR2007_05-16_RaggingInIndiaSummary.pdf.

Ragging in Indian Universities and Colleges, available athttp://www.noragging.com/CURE1.pdf.

Ragging:.March Against a Social Menace, available at http://www.gnit.ac.in/pdf/Anti-RaggingHandbook.pdf.

Rajesh Garg, Ragging: A Public Health Problem in India, Indian Journal of Medical Sciences, Vol. 63, Issue No. 6, June 2009.

Rajiv Ram, Common Myths about Ragging, available at http://noragging.com/index.php/Research/Reports/Common-Myths-about-Ragging.html.

Rajiv Ram, Ragging: A Vision for the Future, available at http://noragging.com/index.php/Research/Finding-a-CURE/-Ragging-A-Vision-for-the-future.html .

S. Banerjee, A. Sharma, S. Mathu, Some Points to Remember about Ragging, available at http://www.cse.iitd.ernet.in/~suban/ragging/note.pdf.

Sanjay A. Pai and Prabha S. Chandra, Ragging: Human Rights Abuse Tolerated by the Authorities, Indian Journal of Medical Ethics, Vol. VI, Issue No. 2, April-June 2009.

Soumya Dutta, Social Responsibility of Media and Indian Democracy, Global Media Journal – Indian Edition, Summer Issue, June 2011.

Sumit Malhotra, Ragging in Medical Colleges: Call for adopting a Zero Tolerance Policy, The National Medical Journal of India, Vol. 23, No. 2 of 2010.

The Menace of Ragging in Educational Institutions and Measures to Curb It, Report of the Raghavan Committee constituted by the Hon'ble Supreme Court of India.

V. Venkatesan, Campus Cruelty, frontline, Volume 26, Issue No. 07, Mar. 28-Apr. 10, 2009.

Varun Aggarwal and Mohit Garg, Parents, Teachers and Seniors, available at, http://noragging.com/index.php/Research/Finding-a-CURE/Parents-Teachers-and-Seniors.html.

Varun Aggarwal, Ragging Makes us Bold, available at http://noragging.com/index.php/Research/Articles/Ragging-Makes-Us-Bold.html.

Varun Aggarwal, Ragging: Why at All?, available at http://noragging.com/index.php/Research/Ragging-The-Phenomenon/-Ragging-Why-at-All.html.

Vedic and Post – Vedic Education, available at http://www.mu.ac.in/myweb_test/ma%20edu/History%20of%20Edu.pdf.

SUBJECT INDEX

•••